UHI
Millennium
Institute

Please return/renew this item by the last date shown

Tillibh/ath-chlaraidh seo ron cheann-latha mu dheireadh

Good Practice Series

Edited by Jacki Pritchard

This series explores topics of current concern to professionals working in social work, health care and the probation service. Contributors are drawn from a wide variety of settings, in both the voluntary and statutory sectors.

Good Practice in Risk Assessment and Risk Management 1

Edited by Hazel Kemshall and Jacki Pritchard

ISBN 1 85302 338 8

Good Practice Series 3

Good Practice in Child Protection

Manual for Professionals

Edited by Hilary Owen and Jacki Pritchard

ISBN 1 85302 205 5

Good Practice Series 1

Good Practice in Supervision

Statutory and Voluntary Organisations

Edited by Jacki Pritchard

ISBN 1 85302 279 9

Good Practice Series 2

Good Practice in Counselling People Who Have Been Abused

Edited by Zetta Bear

ISBN 1 85302 424 4

Good Practice Series 4

Good Practice in Working with Violence

Edited by Hazel Kemshall and Jacki Pritchard

ISBN 1 85302 641 7

Good Practice Series 6

Good Practice in Working with Victims of Violence

Edited by Hazel Kemshall and Jacki Pritchard

ISBN 1 85302 768 5

Good Practice Series 8

Good Practice with Vulnerable Adults

Edited by Jacki Pritchard

ISBN 1 85302 982 3

Good Practice Series 9

GOOD PRACTICE IN RISK ASSESSMENT AND RISK MANAGEMENT 2

PROTECTION, RIGHTS AND RESPONSIBILITIES

Edited by
Hazel Kemshall and Jacki Pritchard

Jessica Kingsley Publishers
London and New York

The right of the contributors to be identified as authors of this work has been asserted by them in accordance with the Copyright, Designs and Patients Act 1998

First published in the United Kingdom in 1997
by Jessica Kingsley Publishers Ltd
116 Pentonville Road
London N1 9JB, England
and
29 West 35th Street, 10th fl.
New York, NY 10001-2299, USA

www.jkp.com

Second impression 1999
Third impression 2002
Fourth impression 2003

Library of Congress Cataloging in Publication Data
A CIP catalog record for this book is available from the Library of Congress

British Library Cataloguing in Publication Data
A CIP catalogue record for this book is available from the British Library

ISBN 1 85302 441 4

Printed and Bound in Great Britain by
Athenaeum Press, Gateshead, Tyne and Wear

Dedication

To all those practitioners and managers **still** running the risk!

Contents

INTRODUCTION 9
Hazel Kemshall, University of Birmingham
Jacki Pritchard, Trainer and Consultant

1 IMPROVING JUDGEMENT AND APPRECIATING BIASES 15
WITHIN THE RISK ASSESSMENT PROCESS
Robert Strachan, Bradford Social Services
Chris Tallant, West Yorkshire Probation Service

2 TAKING THE RISK? ASSESSING LESBIAN AND GAY CARERS 27
Stephen Hicks, Department of Applied Community Studies,
Manchester Metropolitan University

3 MAKING FAMILY PLACEMENTS: WORKING WITH RISKS 40
AND BUILDING ON STRENGTHS
Anne van Meeuwen, Barnardos

4 RISK IN ADOPTION AND FOSTERING 52
Sheila Byrne, British Agencies for Adoption and Fostering

5 ONE OF THE HARDEST JOBS IN THE WORLD: ATTEMPTING 66
TO MANAGE RISK IN CHILDREN'S HOMES
Hilary Owen, Community Health Sheffield

6 VULNERABLE PEOPLE TAKING RISKS: OLDER PEOPLE 80
AND RESIDENTIAL CARE
Jacki Pritchard, Trainer and Consultant

7 PEOPLE WITH LEARNING DIFFICULTIES: 103
CITIZENSHIP, PERSONAL DEVELOPMENT
AND THE MANAGEMENT OF RISK
Bob Tindall, United Response

8 WE CAN TAKE IT: YOUNG PEOPLE AND DRUG USE 118
Peter Argall, The Basement Project, London
Ben Cowderoy, The Basement Project, London

9   ALCOHOL: THE EFFECTS AND RISKS FOR INDIVIDUALS   127
    Pamela Askham, independent trainer and counsellor

10 HOMELESSNESS AND MENTAL HEALTH: RISK ASSESSMENT   141
    Sue Lipscombe, The Joint Homelessness Team, Westminster, London

11 RISK, RESIDENTIAL SERVICES AND PEOPLE WITH MENTAL   159
    HEALTH NEEDS
    Tony Ryan, Turning Point and The University of Lancaster

12 COMMUNITY CARE HOMICIDE INQUIRIES AND   174
    RISK ASSESSMENT
    Michael Howlett, The Zito Trust

13 RISK AND PRISON SUICIDE   188
    Alison Liebling, The Institute of Criminology, University of
    Cambridge

14 TEENAGE SUICIDE AND SELF-HARM: 205
    ASSESSING AND MANAGING RISK
    Juliet Lyon, Trust for the Study of Adolescence

15 RISK AND PAROLE: ISSUES IN RISK ASSESSMENT   233
    FOR RELEASE
    Hazel Kemshall, Department of Social Policy and Social Work,
    University of Birmingham

16 RIGHTS VERSUS RISKS: ISSUES IN WORK WITH PRISONERS   255
    Brian Williams, Department of Applied Social Studies, University
    of Keele

17 RISK, DOMESTIC VIOLENCE AND PROBATION PRACTICE   267
    Katherine Beattie, West Midlands Probation Service

18 THROUGHCARE PRACTICE, RISK AND CONTACT
    WITH VICTIMS   288
    Peter Johnston, West Yorkshire Probation Service

19 RISK: THE ROLE AND RESPONSIBILITIES OF   301
    MIDDLE MANAGERS
    Christine Lawrie, Her Majesty's Inspectorate of Probation

    THE CONTRIBUTORS   312

    SUBJECT INDEX   315

    AUTHOR INDEX   322

Introduction

Hazel Kemshall and Jacki Pritchard

In 1994 we decided to address the complex issue of risk assessment and risk management, particularly the lack of an adequate knowledge base to inform assessment, and the gap between policy expectations and practical guidance for the implementation of risk policies. This resulted in *Good Practice in Risk Assessment and Risk Management 1* which brought together developments from both academic research and practice. Volume 1 addressed the practical implications of implementing current requirements in risk work across a range of settings and client groups. In particular the volume recognised the 'uncertainty' of risk decision making (Brearley 1982) and that staff were often at risk themselves as they implemented risk policies.

Whilst policy, practice and academic research have continued to progress in the interim, gaps remain. Risk work with particular client groups and in particular settings remain unaddressed, and also significant dilemmas which staff and managers face in their daily risk decision making. This second volume attempts to address these outstanding areas.

Risk is now a key concern and preoccupation for both staff and managers in social care organisations. As policies and practices develop some difficult issues are emerging, particularly in the areas of protection, rights and responsibilities. Whilst practitioners and managers may have faced dilemmas in these areas before, risk with its sharper focus upon accountability, public scrutiny, censure and blame in the event of negative outcomes and the spectre of litigation or loss of credibility, has brought these issues to the foreground of both management and practice. This second volume addresses these themes in addition to focusing upon particular settings, areas of practice and client groups. In some chapters the issues are explicitly explored (see Owen, Chapter 5; Ryan, Chapter 11; Williams, Chapter 16), in others the dilemmas are addressed more implicitly through the use of case studies or personal experience (see Tindall, Chapter 7; Argall and Cowderoy, Chapter 8; Askham, Chapter 9; Lipscombe, Chapter 10; Beattie, Chapter 17).

Child protection is one arena in which daily dilemmas over the nature and extent of protection are faced. The recent case of Rikki Neave (Cambridge Social Services) has again highlighted the difficult balance to be struck between protection of children, the rights of parents, and the wish by workers to support families through policies of normalisation (see Chapters 2, 3, and 4 on fostering and adoption).

Whilst risk assessment and risk management are now central to work in child protection, particularly since the Children Act 1989 (Department of Health 1991b), the right of other groups in society to be protected is now increasingly recognised. In the field of criminal justice the Criminal Justice Act 1991 (Wasik and Taylor 1991), and the recent white paper 'Protecting the Public – the Government's Strategy on Crime' (Home Office 1996b), establish the rights of the public and victims to be protected. This is supported by the *Victims Charter* (Home Office 1990, 1996a) which has placed a concern for victims in the foreground of the Probation Service's work, increasing the emphasis upon risk assessment and risk management (see Johnston, Chapter 18).

Community Care legislation (NHS and Community Care Act 1990) establishes a duty of care towards adults by both health authorities and local social services departments. This legislation has established a principle of protection within which the assessment of need, vulnerability and risk are essential. However, the legislative framework for work with vulnerable adults is yet to gain full expression and force in terms of agency policy and practice. In particular, the legislation itself is open to interpretation by policy makers. This has led to inconsistencies and variation in practice and levels of service delivery. In addition, when considering services to vulnerable adults the debate on whether good practice can only be achieved by following the child protection route remains unresolved (Stevenson 1996). Services continue to be subject to resource constraints, and this diminishes both the extent and quality of work on protection.

However, life without risk would be sterile (Luce-Dickinson 1981), and an individual's quality of life is often enhanced by risk-taking. However, risk-taking has to be balanced against exposing self, others or their property to unnecessary harms and dangers. The right to protection and the right to risk take have to be carefully considered, and many risk assessments will produce dilemmas for practitioners as they attempt to reconcile these two positions. Many dilemmas are related both to work setting and to client group. For example, probation officers are continually required to reconcile the rights of victims and public to be protected from further harm, with the risk-taking often involved in the rehabilitative process (see Kemshall and Williams for contrasting positions).

The transition from community care to residential care or institutional setting is often the point at which dilemmas between rights and protection occur. These can involve conflicts between rights of service users, informal carers and workers (see Pritchard, Chapter 6). It may also involve conflicts between members of the community (e.g. neighbours) and service users whose behaviour is perceived as increasingly problematic as community services diminish. This is particularly pertinent for highly stigmatised client groups such as the mentally ill (see Howlett, Chapter 12). Central to the resolution of such conflicts is the prioritisation of rights and the role of choice. For example, in probation work with offenders the prioritisation of victim and public rights is clearly expressed by both legislation and national standards

(Home Office 1995, Wasik and Taylor 1991). Whilst individual practitioners and managers may not always willingly accept such prioritisation, the objective of public protection now outweighs offender rights and needs (Home Office 1996b and 1996c, see Lawrie, Chapter 19). Probation policy and practice is increasingly targeted at risk reduction and this necessarily constrains the choices which managers and practitioners can make.

In other areas of social care, dilemmas can be more prevalent because either the legislative framework is weak or policy guidance is unclear. This can lead to a lack of criteria for resolving competing needs, for example between a dependent adult and her/his carer. A dependent adult may choose not to accept respite care, but the carer may be in desperate need of the break which such care could provide. Practitioners often find themselves in a situation where they have a clear understanding of the needs, vulnerabilities and risks of the dependent person and the carer, but prioritising these is a difficult decision. Whilst the Community Care legislation encourages an assessment of the needs of all parties, it offers no clear criteria for prioritising them. However, if such needs are not met, exposure to risk, for example of ill health or abuse, may increase. The practitioners' guide (Department of Health 1991a), acknowledges that:

> ...one of the most difficult tasks for the practitioner is to disentangle the range of needs and understand how they interact with one another and with the needs of the user's family and friends. (Section 3.3.6, p.53)

Agencies have interpreted this guidance as they see fit. This can leave both assessors and care managers defining their own criteria by which to resolve these dilemmas with subsequent inconsistencies in practice and potential for discriminatory service delivery. In this situation both the rights and choices of service users may not predominate, and protection can be compromised. Without clear criteria to inform professional judgements, practitioners may draw upon varying personal values, attitudes and beliefs in order to resolve their daily practice dilemmas (Kemshall 1995; see Strachan and Tallant, Chapter 1). This suggests that agency risk polices should be underpinned by a statement of values and principles to inform the actions and choices of practitioners. These may vary across settings or client groups, but should reflect statutory obligations and agency objectives. Community care legislation, for example, establishes the following values and rights:

- A commitment to ensure that all users and carers enjoy the same **rights of citizenship** as everyone else in the community, offering an equal access to service provision, irrespective of gender, race or disability.
- A respect for the **independence** of individuals and their rights to self-determination and to take risks, minimising any restraint upon that freedom of action.
- A regard for the **privacy** of the individual, intruding no more than necessary to achieve the agreed purpose and guaranteeing confidentiality.
- An understanding of the **dignity** and **individuality** of every user and carer.

- A quest, within the available resources, to maximise **individual choice** in the type of services on offer and the way in which those services are delivered.
- A responsibility to provide services in a way that promotes the realisation of an **individual's aspirations and abilities** in all aspects of daily life. (page 23, Department of Health 1991a)

Lawson (1996) has argued that principles and values play a crucial role in the risk decision making process. She argues that the basic principles are:

- equal opportunities
- user focus
- encouragement of independence
- self-determination
- confidentiality
- staff support. (Lawson 1996, pp.52–55)

The way in which these principles underpin a local authority social services policy on work with older persons is well explored, as is how these can be applied to practice decisions. However, the present volume illustrates the difficulty of transferring such principles to a range of settings and client groups. Encouraging the independence and self-determination of those who present risks to others (e.g. offenders) is highly contentious, or where risk-taking behaviours attract societal censure (e.g. drug misuse, see Argall and Cowderoy, Chapter 8). User focus can be blurred in situations where the user is compelled to be a user of a service (e.g. offenders) and where the worker is aware of persons at risk but for whom they may not have a direct statutory responsibility (e.g. in situations of domestic violence, see Beattie, Chapter 17).

Principles and values cannot operate in isolation from statutory responsibilities, societal expectations or indeed those of funders. Whilst practitioners carry out numerous responsibilities in their day-to-day work, these can be subsumed under three main headings:

- a duty of care to service users
- the requirement for some agencies to protect non-service users (e.g. the public or victims)
- an adequate and relevant standard of care.

In order to achieve these responsibilities an agency and its workers need to carry out a number of specific duties and tasks. For example, all three areas of responsibility require staff to undertake risk assessments that are comprehensive and equitable. They also require staff to provide risk management strategies which are relevant and where levels of intrusion are commensurate with levels of risk. Child protection is an obvious example of the requirement to match agency intrusion with presented needs and risk. The Cleveland Inquiry (1988) demonstrated the media and societal reaction to perceptions of over intrusion and violation of rights by workers. More recently the case of Rikki Neave demonstrated the penalties of lack of intrusion by an agency and the cost to individual social workers when protective measures fall short. Duty and standards of care may also be affected by perceptions of quality of life. The promotion of quality of life and risk reduction may not be compatible objectives. Service users may perceive that their quality of life can be enhanced by their risk-taking, whilst workers may perceive that such risk-taking is undesirable either because of the cost to others, to the service user or to staff. Indeed, workers may perceive that quality of life can only be preserved or enhanced through risk reduction (see Chapters 13 and 14 on suicide). Perceptions of quality of life, and indeed of levels of risk, may differ between worker and user, and are rooted in the value frame which each brings to the situation (see Strachan and Tallant, Chapter 1). This framing can result in inconsistencies in how workers interpret and carry out their duty of care.

Such perceptions also carry notions of worthiness and value within them, leading to discriminations against certain categories of people. This can express itself in terms of who should provide care (see Hicks, Chapter 2), and who should receive it. Intrinsic to such decisions are ideas of citizenship, for example who is considered to be a worthy citizen and who is entitled to full rights as a citizen (see Tindall, Chapter 7); and those who jeopardise such rights to citizenship because of their riskiness (e.g. prisoners), or because of their dependent status.

Empowerment can be considered as a central feature of citizenship and of social care service delivery (Stevenson 1994). It can be understood as the entitlement to take risks and to exercise choice, but also as an entitlement to protection from undesirable risks (Ross and Waterson 1996). Empowerment also raises difficult choices around autonomy and protection, where protection from undesirable risks may conflict with the pursuit and achievement of personal autonomy (see Tindall, Chapter 7). Risk management is almost exclusively portrayed as a strategy for diminishing threatening and undesirable hazards; rarely is it presented as a mechanism for enhancing empowerment and independence from services (Ryan 1996). Agencies and workers often avoid the contentious issues of empowerment and citizenship. However, as risk has the power to exclude persons from services as well as to include them; to stigmatise and diminish the rights of individuals as well as to protect them; and to provide intrusion as well as safety; every decision on risk has implications for empowerment and citizenship. Clarity about these implications and the consequences for users and workers should be at the root of good practice in risk work. The issues and dilemmas are many, and this volume does not claim to resolve them. As with volume 1, the material is meant to stimulate the reader to think through those dilemmas pertinent to their own situation. We anticipate that the debates will continue long after the book has been returned to the shelf.

REFERENCES

Brearley, C.P. (1982) *Risk and Social Work: Hazards and Helping*. London: Routledge and Kegan Paul.

Cleveland Inquiry (1988) *Report of the Inquiry into Child Sexual Abuse in Cleveland 1987*. London: HMSO.

Department of Health (1990) *NHS and Community Care Act 1990*. London: HMSO.

Department of Health (1991a) *Care Management and Assessment: Practitioners' Guide*. London: HMSO.

Department of Health (1991b) *The Children Act 1989 Guidance and Regulations.* London: HMSO.

Home Office (1990, 1996a) *The Victims Charter.* London: Home Office.

Home Office (1995) *National Standards for the Supervision of Offenders in the Community.* London: Home Office.

Home Office (1996b) *Protecting the Public – The Government's Strategy on Crime.* Cmnd. 3190. London: HMSO.

Home Office (1996c) *Three Year Plan for the Probation Service 1996–1999.* London: Home Office.

Kemshall, H. (1995) *Responses to Offender Risk: Probation Practice, Organisational Setting and the Society.* Risk Paper for the Economic and Social Research Council 'Risk in Organisational Settings' conference at the White House, Regents Park, London, 16th–17th May 1995.

Lawson, J. (1996) 'A framework of risk assessment and management for older People.' In H. Kemshall and J. Pritchard (eds) *Good Practice in Risk Assessment and Risk Management 1.* London: Jessica Kingsley Publishers.

Luce-Dickinson, J. (1981) 'Thoughts on "Risk".' *Maternal Health News 6,* 4.

Ross, L. and Waterson, J. (1996) 'Risk for whom? Social work and people with physical disabilities.' In H. Kemshall and J. Pritchard (eds) *Good Practice in Risk Assessment and Risk Management 1.* London: Jessica Kingsley Publishers.

Ryan, T. (1996) 'Risk management and people with mental health problems.' In H. Kemshall and J. Pritchard (eds) *Good Practice in Risk Assessment and Risk Management.* London: Jessica Kingsley Publishers.

Stevenson, O. (1994) 'Social work in the 1990s: empowerment – fact or fiction?' In R. Page and J. Baldock (eds) *Social Policy Review 6.* Canterbury: Social Policy Association.

Stevenson (1996) *Elder Protection in the Community: What Can we Learn From Child Protection?* London: Age Concern Institute of Gerontology King's College.

Wasik, M. and Taylor, R.D. (1991) *Blackstone's Guide to the Criminal Justice Act.* Oxford: Blackstone Press Ltd.

CHAPTER 1

Improving Judgement and Appreciating Biases Within the Risk Assessment Process

Robert Strachan and Chris Tallant

INTRODUCTION

During the course of their normal working day, social workers make decisions that have an impact on people's lives. Often they are operating with minimal information and are forced to make decisions within specific time frames. Many of the decisions they make involve dealing with significant risk and often have far reaching effects on the lives of individuals. It is therefore extremely important that the influences and biases that affect these decision processes are better understood.

Current training fails to take into account the individual psychological processes which social workers utilise when making judgements involving risk and uncertainty. One reason for this is that it is a very specialised area and is difficult to take a generic training perspective. In this chapter, whilst we will not seek to tell social workers how to make particular decisions in specific situations, we do feel that an appreciation and understanding of professional decision making processes and biases can provide practitioners with an invaluable insight into their own judgements and so provide them with the basis on which to make better decisions.

In this chapter we will provide practical guidelines for practitioners to examine their judgement of risk by close reference to social work case scenarios. These scenarios will be used not only to explore and illustrate those biases that affect individual judgement, but also to form the basis for acquiring a better appreciation of those decision making processes that individual workers are forced to rely upon when making decisions under conditions of risk and uncertainty. In particular, we will examine the notion of *framing* and associated psychological biases. We will then go on to explore specific methods that can support professionals in their judgement processes, by suggesting practical and systematic methods of improving decision making processes through the application of de-biasing strategies when making judgements in the context of risk and uncertainty.

When considering the current thinking about risk it is apparent that there is a need for practitioners to become aware of, and improve the capability of, the cognitive processes they go through when assessing risk. This is based on the belief that raising levels of awareness of the processes we go through when making decisions will enable a more accurate assessment to be made, thus enabling risk to be minimised and uncertainties reduced. In this chapter we will avoid becoming involved in philosophical discussions of the nature or definition of risk – other authors have adequately covered this area in detail (see Brearley 1982, Kemshall 1995). We would consider that the overall purpose of assessment and management is to seek to control and, if possible, to prevent the future occurrence of harmful behaviour to self or others.

We would perceive that the major difficulties for practitioners initially comes in the assessment of risk rather than in its management. After all, once a potentially dangerous and risky situation has developed, the task of addressing it and formulating strategies is relatively straightforward compared with the initial recognition of the risk factors prior to the assessment. Many traditional models of risk work on the premise that the best predictor of future behaviour is past behaviour. However, it is important to note that in real world social work situations workers are forced to carry out assessments with incomplete information, time restrictions in which to consider courses of action, and restricted resources and alternatives. The implication of this is that if a model of risk assessment is to be of real practical value to workers in the field, then it needs to take into account these factors and also allow for the general unpredictability and rapid changes present within most social work situations.

RISK ASSESSMENT AND FRAMING

If we accept the above, then how should we approach risk assessments? In answer to this there is a growing body of literature (Bazerman 1984, Kahneman and Tversky 1972, Thaller 1980) which shows that individuals treat risks differently depending on how they frame situations. The importance of the 'framing' concept to assessments is that even when making the most fundamental, everyday decisions, people are never able to consider all the relevant information because they can never have access to it (it is often only with the benefit of hindsight that specific information becomes 'relevant'). At a practical level, individuals deal with this by adopting mental frameworks which simplify and structure the information they encounter. Russo and Shoemaker (1992) argue that these structures, or 'decision frames', keep complexity within the dimensions which our minds can manage. They consider that people cannot make a decision without utilising the 'framing' concept. They describe the concept of framing as, 'structuring the question'. This means defining,

> what must be decided and determining in a preliminary way what criteria would cause you to prefer one option over another. In framing, good decision-makers think about the viewpoint from which they and others will look at the issue and decide which aspects they consider important and which they do not. Thus they simplify the world. (Russo and Shoemaker 1992, p.2)

There are, however, potential problems with this approach, particularly since, by using only one 'frame', the assessor can have only a partial view of the problem.

> This over simplification could also lead to manipulation by others so that poor or inappropriate decisions are made by the assessor. It cannot be emphasised enough that frames have enormous power and the way in which people initially frame a problem directly results in their final decision. (Tallant and Strachan 1995, p.204)

It is therefore important to consider situations from more than just one frame. For instance, when analysing a case, do not only consider a Freudian approach – take into account a cognitive behavioural one as well. However, it is the combination of this concept with another which we consider to be the cornerstone to improving professional judgement within risk assessment situations.

Over the past 20 years the notion has been developed that individuals internally frame the world in terms of 'gains' or 'losses' (Kahneman and Tversky 1972). The importance of this for social work practitioners is that when people consider themselves to be in 'the zone of gains' they are 'risk averse' but when they view themselves to be in 'the zone of losses' they are more likely to adopt 'risk seeking' behaviour.

An illustration of this would be if you were at the races and during the afternoon you back several winners with low odds. On the final race we would suggest that you would be more likely to back the favourite and therefore be considered to be risk averse (since you are framing the situation from a position of gain). Alternatively, if you had backed a series of losers throughout the race card you would be considerably more likely to take a risk and back the outsider in the last race in an attempt to recoup your money. The explanation for this would be that having lost consecutive bets you frame your position from the zone of losses and are therefore more likely to be risk seeking (betting and losing your shirt on the last race!). We would consider that these observations regarding risk seeking and risk avoiding behaviour have practical applications for risk assessment. The central factor of this model is that people view or 'frame' the world in terms of 'gains' or 'losses' relative to a moveable reference point.

Consider the following case scenario:

A woman, F, works as a prostitute. F is now 25 years old. She was put into care when she was 13 years old because her parents were 'unable to cope' with her behaviour. At 17 F had her first child – a baby girl. F said at the time that she could not bond with the child and gave her up for adoption. At 19 F became pregnant again and gave birth to another girl. This time she wanted to keep the child; however, it was forcibly taken from her when F 'went underground' after leaving her baby with an acquaintance. Two years later F emerged again with a 6-month-old boy. Measures were taken by social services to keep him with his mother, but again F's continuous chaotic lifestyle resulted in the child eventually being taken into care.

Recently social services have discovered that F is about to give birth to another child. She desperately wants to keep this child and agrees to co-operate with the authorities if she is allowed to do so. The authorities, based on F's previous history, are of the opinion that the risks attendant with this course of action would be unacceptable and the baby girl is removed at birth.

The authorities have access at this point to large amounts of information relevant to F's personal history focused around personality, character, and past behaviour. Potentially all the relevant information is present in order to make a good decision. The options at this stage ranged from allowing F to keep her baby, through allowing her to keep the child under close supervision, to taking the child into care. In terms of risk, the authorities chose the option which had least potential losses to the child, based on an interpretation of F's previous behaviour and attitude. The view was taken that she had had many chances to prove herself to be a responsible parent and had failed on all occasions. Therefore, there was nothing to indicate that things would be different this time around. The principal frame in this scenario was the safety and protection of the child and not the certain loss to the mother.

The case goes to court and the decision is taken by the Judge that F should be given 'one more chance'. She will be allowed to keep her daughter and, in accordance with her wishes, also have custody of her son (who is now 2 years old). However, the court also orders that F must comply with the following conditions: register with a GP; attend a local family centre 3 half days per week; permit regular visits from the health visitor and social worker; and keep social services informed of any baby sitters she uses (names, addresses etc.). This situation is to be reviewed by the court in 3 months time when a final decision relating to the custody of the children will be taken.

Unfortunately, within 3 weeks F fails to register the child with a GP, is not at home when the health visitor calls, refuses to attend the family centre regularly and is uncooperative and abusive to the social worker. Neighbours report seeing the little boy 'running wild' and unsupervised next to the nearby main road on regular occasions.

F and her children 'disappear'. When checked, the baby-sitters report not having seen the children or F for the last 3 days. The relevant authorities are alerted. One week later a woman contacts social services and asks when F will be collecting her children – they have been with her for the last 10 days and F has not been in contact. Two days later F is arrested and brought to court. The end result is similar to the previous episodes – the children are removed from F by a court order and are eventually fostered.

So how is the court's decision and F's behaviour explained? In the scenario the court framed the situation differently to social services. F was to be given a final chance to keep some of her children, although strict controls were imposed to minimise the risks involved. The court now viewed F as being placed within the 'zone of gains' and expected her to adopt behaviour that would be 'risk averse' (in order to keep her children with her).

Traditional risk assessment models would suggest that F acted irrationally. After all, she only had to comply with the basic conditions imposed by the court in order to obtain her expressed prime objective of keeping custody of her children. It had been spelt out to her in no uncertain terms what she had to do and the consequences if she failed to do it. Why did she not comply? Perhaps the concept of 'framing' can provide us with some insight into the evidently irrational behaviour on behalf of F.

A social worker's perspective might take the view that when the child was taken away from F she was put into the 'zone of losses'. She therefore took the risky choice of going back to court in order to regain custody of the child. This paid off for her in that she not only regained custody of her new born daughter, but also regained custody of her son. This would evidently move her into the 'zone of gains' which, according to the notion of framing, would suggest she would adopt behaviour that would be risk averse and she would therefore comply with the court conditions.

However, her behaviour was anything but risk averse and indeed she demonstrated, by her actions, a propensity actively to adopt courses of action which she knew must at the very least seriously compromise the chances of her keeping her children. It is apparent that her framing of the situation differed markedly from that of the authorities. Her behaviour suggests she adopted a risk seeking stance which in turn suggests she viewed or 'framed' herself to be firmly within the zone of losses. We would suggest that F's previous experience of dealing with social services and related agencies had caused her to frame her situation as being continuously within the zone of losses and never considered herself to be within a gain position. She may well have considered herself to have moved slightly towards a gain situation by regaining temporary custody of her children, but felt that in the long run this would not be the case and so behaved in a way that would at least allow her to spend some time with her two children and adopted correspondingly risky behaviour in order to achieve this.

This interpretation of F's frame may or may not be accurate. What is more important is that an attempt to appreciate F's potential framing of the situation by the social services might well have led to a different end conclusion. The crux of framing's relevance to risk assessment is to move people into the zone of gains where their decision making will be less risk seeking.

BIAS AND RISK WITHIN THE ASSESSMENT PROCESS

As previously noted, risk assessment scenarios within social work are typically characterised by significant amounts of uncertainty. Practitioners, armed with few resources, lack of relevant or complete information, and operating within restricted time frames, are often faced with situations which require them to assess potential risks presented both to and from those individuals with whom they are working,. In such situations, where assessments are to be carried out under conditions of high pressure, yet also quickly and accurately, it is perhaps surprising that tragedies within social work are not more commonplace.

Over the years, researchers (Kahneman and Tversky 1973) have attempted to identify the strategies employed by professionals which help make risky decision making manageable. One major conclusion is that individuals deal with complex, difficult, and risky situations by employing a limited number of pre-tried psychological routines known as *heuristics*. However, because these routines are simplified short-cuts to making decisions they can result in systematic decision biases and errors.

A number of these biases have been identified. However, we would consider that the biases most relevant to social work assessments are: **Representativeness, Availability,** and **Confirmation/Dis-Confirmation** (Thaller 1980).

The Representativeness Bias

The source of this bias stems from the way in which decision makers attempt to assess the risks in a given situation by judging how similar or 'representative' it is to previously encountered situations. Such short-hand assessment methods usually work well by allowing us to form quick assessments of situations by comparing them with previous sets of similar circumstances. One might, for example, reasonably choose livestock by assessing the degree to which offspring are similar or 'representative' to other animals that have grown up into prize adults. However, this can be problematic when the representativeness does not actually exist. Take the simple example of the roulette wheel which turns up six consecutive wins on the red. It feels compelling to place the next bet on black since it *feels right* that it is time for a black win (when we know logically that the roulette wheel has no memory of the previous six spins – each spin is a completely new and independent event with the same 50–50 chance of a black or a red win). In such situations our original model is itself wrong. Decision makers are often mistaken in their understanding of the basic statistical rules governing probability and mistakenly base their assessments of risk on patterns that 'feel right' and which appear to be representative.

Examples of this error are common in social work. For instance, our initial perception of the immediate dangers or risks presented by a known violent offender during an unplanned home visit are often assessed not in reference to that person's actual record of violent offending (or to the wider statistical occurrences of such behaviour), but by comparing that person's similarity to one's own stereotype of how we would expect a 'dangerous person' to look or act. Consider the 'isolated old man' who gives sweets to children. How much easier is it for us to picture such a person as being representative of the 'archetypal abuser' when we know from statistics that most children are abused by family members or friends of the family?

The representative bias is particularly powerful when we encounter and then compare an unusual or rare situation with a previous one which appears to share many of the same characteristics. In such circumstances, people are even more likely to fall prey to the representative bias by basing their judgements on the **law of small numbers**. These conditions are often perfect for the formation of stereotypical views such as, 'all drug pushers are black', 'most juvenile offenders are from single parent families', etc. More accurate assessments can be achieved by taking into account wider sample sizes and by questioning closely whether apparently representative situations are actual or perceived.

The Availability Bias

> The tendency to judge an event more probable the more easily it can be recalled or pictured mentally. (Kahneman and Tversky 1972)

An important aspect of this bias is that vividness can influence availability. Generally the availability heuristic serves us well. We know from our everyday experience that things we see frequently are easier to recall than things we see seldom. More frequency equals better memory. However, it can also lead to inaccuracies since factors other than frequency can produce better memory. For example, the headline '*300 die in air crash disaster*' might increase the 'availability' that air travel is dangerous (when statistically it is one of the safest forms of transport). The availability heuristic can have its greatest effects on judgement when the event is relatively rare.

Bazerman (1994) suggests that people often fall victim to the availability bias when assessing the likelihood of two events occurring together. He cites the example 'is cannabis use related to delinquency?' He suggests that in answering this question most people typically remember several delinquent cannabis users and assume an illusory correlation based upon the availability of this mental data. Thus if we know a lot of cannabis users who are delinquents, we assume that cannabis use is related to delinquency. He suggests that a more accurate and less biased method of approaching this question would be to recall to mind four groups of say; cannabis users who are delinquents, cannabis users who are not delinquents, delinquents who do not use cannabis, and non-delinquents who do not use cannabis. By using this process the resulting assessment would be far more accurate and could potentially caution against the assumption that cannabis use is directly related to delinquency (when it may or may not be).

The Confirmation Bias

Studies indicate how individuals, having made an initial assessment, have a tendency to search for evidence which backs up their original assumptions and ignore information which does not. In other words, 'individuals not only emphasise positive instances, they also tend to actively search for confirming instances to the extent that it is less likely for dis-confirming evidence to be found' (Eiser and van der Plight 1988, p.95–96). Therefore, the social worker visiting a house in order to investigate a report of abuse will be more prone to see signs which confirm the probability of abuse than to look for evidence which could contradict this. A recent example of this bias was the Cleveland

(Cleveland Inquiry 1988) child abuse investigations where evidence which confirmed signs of ritual abuse was actively sought. If the original assessments had fully considered dis-confirming information, different conclusions might have been reached.

The influence of heuristical biases upon professional assessments can be profound. Consider the following case scenario of an actual social work assessment:

> A 20-year-old Pakistani Muslim woman has overdosed on paracetamol and has been admitted to the Accident and Emergency ward of her local hospital. On recovery she is seen by the duty psychiatrist. During the course of taking a social history the woman tells the psychiatrist that she was born in this country, has been married for two years and has a nine-month-old baby. She states that she is very unhappy – 'because things are not right at home'. The psychiatrist then goes on to ask if her marriage was arranged and she replies that it was. The psychiatrist also learns that she is living with her in-laws in the same house and relationships between them are strained.
>
> (Patel and Strachan 1996)

On this occasion the duty psychiatrist made the assessment with two particular points in mind: the risk factor of a repeat of the overdose and if there was an intention to die. In the psychiatrist's view both factors were very low, therefore the need for further psychiatric involvement was not considered appropriate. The identified problems were seen as being due to the 'arranged marriage' and 'cultural conflict'. The woman was not referred elsewhere for counselling or therapy since she had many family members visiting who expressed concern and therefore she seemed to have a high level of family support. The assessment was picked up by the duty social worker who confirmed the psychiatrist's views that further support was not necessary.

The issues, however, were not resolved and the woman approached a female Asian mental health worker who took the case on board, visited the woman's home and interviewed all the family members. The original assessment was contradicted in that while it was confirmed that the marriage had been arranged it was in fact stable and both partners were happy with each other. The issues were actually around the fact that two families were living together in cramped conditions and the arrival of a new baby was putting further strain on the already tense situation. The relationship between mother and daughter-in-law brought other additional problems. During the course of the assessment it became clear that the mother-in-law had not resolved her own feelings about 'losing her son' and 'losing control' to another woman, and having someone else care for him. Therefore she would continually fall out with her daughter-in-law which caused a constant strain.

The Asian woman mental health social worker offered practical support on two levels. First, by offering counselling for members within the household and practical support with respect to having access to mother and toddler groups etc. Second, she sought to resolve the housing issues by exploring alternative living arrangements in order to maintain good relationships.

The final assessment made it clear that the issues associated with the woman's overdose were threefold – social, economic and personal. The factors identified by the psychiatrist and duty social worker (such as arranged marriage, being born in the UK etc.) were not considered to be of major significance. So why did both the psychiatrist and the duty social worker assess this case so differently from the specialist worker? If the scenario is analysed by way of a heuristical approach, a series of patterns emerge.

With regard to the representativeness heuristic, we recall that individuals have a tendency to generalise when assessing situations by looking for similarities of prior general 'facts' that appear to match or 'represent' factors within the present situation. In the processes of doing this misconceptions about randomness and actual representativeness can easily occur. In the case of the 20-year-old Pakistani woman, the psychiatrist was immediately aware of the representative fact that she was a married Asian woman who had been born in England. Having become sensitised to the stereotypical representative aspects of the case, the assessor then began to notice certain factors that were immediately 'available' during the course of the interview. Again, we must remember that the availability heuristic suggests that those factors that are vivid (such as a person's ethnicity) are more available to memory. Individuals therefore have a tendency to assume and judge that events or factors are more probable or likely the more easily they can be recalled or pictured mentally. In this case certain vivid factors appeared to present themselves to the assessor such as an Asian woman living within a 'typical' extended Asian family, who had been born in England. The availability heuristic additionally suggests that having identified certain 'noticeable' and 'significant' factors, causal links are then formed between two or more aspects which are, in such circumstances, often illusory (or have no actual 'cause and effect' relationship). In this case the original assessment appeared to establish causal links between:

Arranged marriage – forced situation causing unhappiness.

Born in England – conflict with elders who have different value bases.

Asian woman – oppressed

It should be noted that arranged marriages are not generally forced marriages, and the vast majority are successful. Highly representative cases of occasional 'forced' marriages, as graphically portrayed by the media, serve to reinforce and support the availability of such rare instances to individuals (i.e. '300 die in air crash' – the law of low numbers). An accurate knowledge of the true base rate data concerning such factors as arranged marriage success/failure rates serves to create a far more accurate picture (the law of high numbers). The same biases also apply to the other correlations, including 'born in England' automatically equalling conflict with parents and Asian women being assumed to be passive, subservient and oppressed.

Having established such illusory correlations, the assessor then began to actively search for evidence and data that confirmed them and ignored information that might contradict or dis-confirm these assumptions. Indeed, the subsequent assessment, as carried out by the Asian Mental Health Worker, supports the illusory nature of the original assessment and assumptions.

THE WAY FORWARD

De-Biasing

For most people growing up in this country, Black or White, negative stereotypical images are unconsciously received and absorbed on a day-to-day basis and are sustained through language, the media, professional values, political and legal system. Social workers, along with other professionals, are not exempt from this. One area where this is clearly evidenced is in the zone of professional assessments and judgement.

We have already seen how people often base their assessments on such cognitive short-hand methods as assuming that the probability of event A causes the event B by the degree to which A is representative of B. People often connect events A and B by assessing the degree of similarity or 'representativeness' between them. As previously noted, such methods often work well enough. However, because these routines constitute shorthand assessments they also have their flaws. One major factor that should affect probability judgements is that of the prior probability or the prior frequency of the occurrence or event. Taking into account the prior probability severely re-adjusts our view of the problem, as does failure to take into account base rates.

Try and avoid relying on anecdotal evidence. Attempt to obtain reliable base rate data. Be aware of one's own stereotyping and tendency to evaluate and assess by selecting outcomes that most closely match that stereotype. Statistical data is likely to have less impact than information that is presented in the form of a personal experience which could include concrete, vivid, emotion-arousing instances and which will therefore be more available (and therefore also more attractive) to your own judgmental processes. In addition, try to decrease your reliance on memory. The representativeness heuristic can seriously mislead judgement and instil a feeling of over-confidence at the sacrifice of facts which might not quite fit the preferred hypothesis. People actively select evidence which confirms the hypothesis under consideration. Familiar situations need to be recognised and ambiguous symptoms need to be attributed to common, as opposed to rare causes (more often than not). Force yourself to weigh up alternatives and try to look at a problem from a different angle or point of view. Similarly, be aware that factors such as familiarity, salience, and recency of an occurrence of an event affect the retrievability of information and enhance the potency of the availability heuristic.

Framing

It is important that risk assessment should not be undertaken in isolation from the client or service user. Assessors of risk should be working towards a model in which self-management of risk by the service user is paramount. In order to achieve this it is imperative that individuals are made aware of those factors which will potentially influence their future negative conduct. A useful way of beginning this process is by using the Neutral Reference Point (NRP)

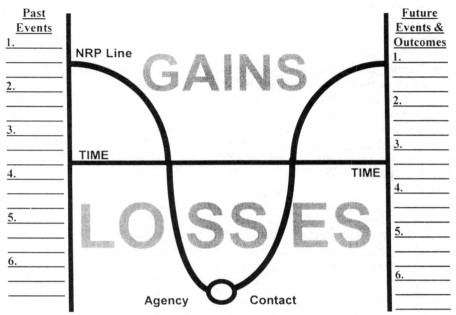

Figure 1.1.

Assessor in Figure 1.1 as a visual aide both for the client to understand how his/her behaviour has developed and as a vehicle for illustrating the way forward.

Using the NRP Assessor take the client back to a time when things were going well for them and they considered themselves to be in the zone of gains. Mark the position on the line and discuss what factors were positive for them at that time. Then take the client through the sequence of events which led to their involvement with your agency and note those down. Inevitably you will find that as their Neutral Reference Point moves down into the losses zone the way they respond to events, both behavioural and emotional, becomes riskier.

It is important to stress that losses loom larger than gains to people and that this affects the way we make decisions. Therefore people make riskier decisions in order either to prevent themselves going further down the curve into losses or in order to get themselves back into a gains situation. When they reach the stage where they had contact with your agency, or you became aware of issues with an existing service user, the relevant risk factors should have identified themselves. Then ask the client where they view themself to be on the graph at that present time. If they state that they are in the gains zone or on the border line check out why that is and clarify what steps they are taking either to maintain that position or move positively up the NRP line. Work through how they got there and make sure that their analysis fits with your own perception or framing of the situation. Then write down the trigger factors, both emotional and behavioural, which would lead to negative behaviour by a return to the zone of losses. The service user should keep a copy of the risk factors.

The importance of this in terms of risk assessment is that individuals can move from a gains to a loss situation very quickly and as workers we cannot always be there. Indeed, experience tells us that if things are not going well for service users they often fail to keep appointments or lessen agency contact. This could in fact be seen as a first indicator of a potentially risk laden situation. If there is a disparity between the service user's perceptions of where s/he is on the NRP line and your own, i.e. they perceive themselves to be within the zone of gains and you view them to be within the zone of losses (or visa versa), ensure that this addressed. First, it will give you an insight into their 'frame' on the world and second, it will provide you with the opportunity to re-evaluate their perceptions of their behaviour and the decisions they have taken in the past

REFERENCES

Bazerman, M.H. (1984) 'The relevance of Kahneman and Tversky's concept of framing to organization behaviour.' *Journal of Management 10*, 333–343.

Bazerman, M.H. (1994) *Judgement in Managerial Decision Making*. Chichester: Wiley.

Brearley, C.P. (1982) *Risk and Social Work: Hazards and Helping*. London: Routledge and Kegan Paul.

Eiser, J.R. and van der Plight, J. (1988) *Attitudes and Decisions*. London: Routledge.

The Cleveland Inquiry (1988) Report of the Inquiry into Child Sexual Abuse in Cleveland 1987. Presented to the Secretary of State for Social Services by the Right Honourable Lord Butler-Sloss DBE, Cm412. London: HMSO.

Kahneman, D. and Tversky, A. (1972) 'Subjective probability: a judgement of representativeness.' *Cognitive Psychology 3*, 430–454.

Kahneman, D. and Tversky, A. (1973) 'On the psychology of prediction.' *Psychological Review 80*, 237–251.

Kemshall, H. (1995) Responses to Offender Risk; Probation Practice, Organisational Setting and the Risk Society, Economic and Social Research Council. Risk in Organisational Settings Conference at the White House, Regents Park, 16th–17th May 1995.

Patel, K. and Strachan, R. (1996) 'Anti-racist practice or heuristics.' *Paper Submission, XXVI International Congress of Psychology Montreal, Quebec*, August, 1996.

Russo, J. Edward and Schoemaker, Paul J.H. (1992) *Confident Decision Making*. London: Piatkus.

Tallant, C. and Strachan, R. (1995) 'The importance of framing: a pragmatic approach to risk assessment.' *Probation Journal*, December, 1995, pp.202–207.

Tallant, C. and Strachan, R. (1996) *The NRP*. Unpublished.

Thaller, R. (1980) 'Toward a positive theory of consumer choice.' *Journal of Economic Behavior and Organization 1*, 39–80.

CHAPTER 2

Taking The Risk?
Assessing Lesbian and Gay Carers

Stephen Hicks

INTRODUCTION

This chapter is concerned with the notion of 'risk' as it relates to the fostering or adoption of children by lesbians and gay men. I focus mainly upon the issue of risk assessment, as my research is based upon the experiences of lesbian and gay carer applicants, all of whom have been through a process of formal scrutiny by social workers (Hicks 1993, 1996). There are two key questions that need to be addressed here, and they are: do lesbians and gay men *per se* pose a 'risk' to children? and why are those lesbians and gay men, who are successfully approved as foster or adoptive carers, still regarded as 'risky', to be used as a 'last resort'? (BBC 'Heart of the Matter' 1993, Community Care 1993, Hicks 1996).

I shall consider the issues of 'risk' in the field of lesbian and gay fostering and adoption in two related areas. First, I shall discuss what are perceived to be 'risks' to children posed by lesbian and gay parents of whatever 'variety' (that is, whether the children are by birth, or fostered or adopted, conceived by self-insemination, or whatever). Second, I want to look at the process of the formal social work assessment of all potential foster/adoptive carers, and to consider how this relates to lesbian and gay applicants. I report examples of discriminatory assessment practices in order to begin to suggest ways forward for social workers. Why should lesbian or gay carers be seen as 'second-class citizens', as one lesbian foster and adoptive mother pointed out to me? (Hicks 1993).

THE DEBATE ABOUT LESBIAN AND GAY FOSTERING AND ADOPTION

Cases of lesbian and gay fostering and adoption continue to excite much public and media interest, and the debate about lesbian and gay suitability has been taking place within social policy documents, most notably the guidance on the Children Act 1989 (DoH 1990, 1991) and the review of adoption law (DoH/Welsh Office 1992, DoH *et al.* 1993). Consultation on foster placement regulations sparked the debate by suggesting that '"equal rights" and "gay rights" policies have no place in fostering services' (DoH 1990, para.16). This sentence was removed from the final guidance (DoH 1991) but only after much lobbying of the Department of Health. The adoption law review (DoH/Welsh Office 1992) recommended no changes to the law regarding 'single' adopters and had the following to say:

> ...we do not propose any changes to the law relating to single applicants, including lesbians and gay men. There are examples of extremely successful adoptions, particularly of older children and children with disabilities, by single adopters. (DoH/Welsh Office 1992, p.50).

Following publication of this consultative document, the media focused largely on the 'lesbian and gay issue', one sentence of a lengthy report, and ministers went to great lengths to insist that most children need to grow up with a mother and a father, and that lesbians and gay men should be used only as a 'last resort' (BBC North West News 1993, Hicks 1996, Marchant 1992). The later publication of the adoption White Paper (DoH *et al*. 1993) saw a marked backtracking on both issues of race and 'family structures', in response to claims that practices of same-race placements and consideration of non-heterosexual couples had become nothing but 'political correctness'. In relation to 'family structures' in particular, the White Paper emphasised that married couples provide the best of homes for children (DoH *et al*. 1993, p.9).

Research on the fostering or adoption of children by lesbians and gay men is scarce, with published findings provided only by Skeates and Jabri (1988) in Britain, and Ricketts (1991; and Ricketts and Achtenberg, 1987, 1990) in the United States. Skeates and Jabri (1988) found that lesbians and gay men who 'came out' to the local authorities assessing them received less favourable responses (p.49) and that their applications took much longer to process than those of heterosexuals or people who did not disclose their sexuality (p.50). They also found that lesbian or gay applicants had to deal with a lack of knowledge about lesbian/gay issues, many feeling that they had to 'educate' their social worker (p.49). The study found many examples of discriminatory practices in the assessment of lesbians and gay men, and that for those who were black or disabled the process was doubly difficult (p.28).

These, and other examples of discriminatory practice, were confirmed by my own earlier research (Hicks 1993), which I discuss later. In particular, such examples point to the fact that many regard lesbians and gay men as a 'risk' to children, or that they are too 'risky' to assess, or that local authorities are not prepared to 'take the risk' in placing children within their care. If they are willing to do so, then such children are likely to be 'hard to place' and/or disabled (Hicks 1993, 1996, Skeates and Jabri 1988, p.28).

Social work has been slow to respond positively to this debate. Whilst there are isolated examples of local authorities both prepared to work with lesbian and gay carers, and to develop good anti-discriminatory practice, for the most part lesbians and gay men are rejected *a priori* or face particularly discriminatory practices in assessment. Indeed arguments about 'the best interests of the child' have been used to mask what is, in fact, anti-lesbian and anti-gay practice (Reece 1995).

NOTIONS OF 'RISK' IN RELATION TO LESBIAN AND GAY FOSTERING OR ADOPTION

'Risks' to Children

Objections to the care of children by lesbians and gay men are most frequently based upon suggestions of 'risk'. The usual arguments are that such children are likely to be 'at risk' of sexual abuse, impaired social development and relations with peers, distorted psychological and gender role development, and dysfunctional sexuality. These are 'strong' arguments, particularly when they have young children at their centre, and they run something like this...

Children living with gay men or lesbians will automatically become gay by force of example (see, for example, the case *Re P* in Rights of Women Lesbian Custody Group (1984, p.127)). 'Corruption theory' (Berry 1987) suggests that children living with lesbians, but more especially so with gay men, will be sexually molested and 'initiated into' the ways of gay sex (see Ferris 1977). Such children will also have distorted gender role models, and will not understand the difference between a 'man' and a 'woman', or more usually a 'daddy' and a 'mummy'. Finally, these children will suffer undue stigma because they live with lesbians or gay men. The argument here is usually that their peer relations will be impaired and that they will be mercilessly teased at school.

These arguments are a 'pop psychology' amalgam of psychoanalytic, social learning and cognitive developmental theories (see Golombok and Tasker 1994), and are sometimes referred to as the 'myths' about lesbian or gay carers (Skeates and Jabri 1988, Ricketts 1991). 'Myths', however, suggests some kind of passive construction of ideas, as though they simply float around in the air to be used as necessary. My argument is that these ideas are, rather, *actively constructed versions* of lesbians and gay men, and that social work practice contributes to such construction. Therefore I believe that it is important to address these arguments seriously, because as I have noted, their proponents place the notion of very tangible 'risks' to children at their centre. I want to ask two questions about such perceived 'risks' here; first, whether they are actually concerned with the well-being of children, that is their need for good foster or adoptive care, and second whether research evidence supports these assumptions.

My first argument is that such 'risk'-based objections are, in fact, very little to do with the development of children, and are far more about the anxiety to maintain compulsory heterosexuality, traditional gender roles and male power. They have very little to do with the care of children by lesbians and gay men. In fact, these objections betray the desire to ensure – or indeed enforce – that children must all grow up to be heterosexual, proper 'men' and 'women' who know their place within the family. Feminist arguments about the oppression of women due to traditional gender roles, heterosexual relations and the power of men within the 'family' are key here (Abbott and Wallace 1992, Barrett and McIntosh 1991, Hester, Kelly and Radford 1996, Maynard and Purvis 1995, Richardson 1996, Wilkinson and Kitzinger 1993). 'Risk'-based arguments about the care of such children are often rather about anxieties to maintain compulsory heterosexuality and traditional gender roles into adulthood (Pollack 1987, Rich 1980, Sedgwick 1991).

Responding to notions of 'risk' by asserting that most of the children of lesbians and gay men grow up to be heterosexual, with typical gender and social role development, can sometimes be in danger of reinforcing the supposed 'naturalness' of heterosexuality and traditional gender identities. Nevertheless, research knowledge does show this to be the case and I shall go on to present some of these findings, but only in order to counter notions of lesbian and gay parents as a 'risk'.

Whilst there are no outcome studies of children placed with lesbian or gay carers as yet, there are research studies which consider the children of lesbians and gay men, and indeed they are actually too many to detail here. Excellent summaries of the existing research are provided by Golombok and Tasker (1994), Green and Bozett (1991), Patterson (1992) or Saffron (1996).

The research of Golombok and Tasker is of major importance as it is based upon a longitudinal study of 25 children growing up in lesbian families, and a control group of 21 children of heterosexual single mothers (Golombok, Spencer and Rutter 1983, Golombok and Tasker 1996, Tasker and Golombok 1991, 1995). Tasker and Golombok (1995) argue that their study results '…are also of relevance to children who are fostered or adopted by lesbian mothers' (1995, p.214). In the earlier study (Golombok et al. 1983), the children of lesbians, then aged on average nine and a half years, showed typical psychosocial and gender role development, and conventional preferences in toys, activities and friendships.

The follow-up studies (Golombok and Tasker 1996, Tasker and Golombok 1995) were conducted with the same subjects, now young adults aged on average twenty-three and a half years. Were they more likely to have 'become' lesbian or gay? Golombok and Tasker (1996) report that:

> …those who had grown up in a lesbian family were more likely to consider the possibility of having lesbian or gay relationships, and to actually do so. However, the commonly held assumption that children brought up by lesbian mothers will themselves grow up to be lesbian or gay is not supported by the findings of the study; the majority of children who grew up in lesbian families identified as heterosexual in adulthood. (p.8).

Did they have poor psychosocial development? The follow-up studies found that the young adults who had been brought up in a lesbian household described their relationship with their mother's female partner significantly more positively than those raised by a heterosexual mother with a male partner (Tasker and Golombok 1995, p.209). They were more likely to recall having been teased about being gay or lesbian themselves, but 'no more likely to remember general teasing or bullying by their peers than were those from heterosexual single-parent homes' (p.210). The study also found no significant difference in tests of anxiety or depression levels for those who had been raised by lesbian or heterosexual mothers (p.211). Indeed, overall the studies found:

> Those raised by lesbian mothers continued to [function well] in adulthood and experienced no long-term detrimental effects arising from their early upbringing. (p.211)

Studies of the children of gay fathers are less common, but of the work that has been done, the research of Bozett (1981, 1985, 1987a, 1987b, 1990), Barret and Robinson (1990) and Bailey *et al.* (1995) has considered the effects of fathers' sexuality upon children. The research of Bozett (1981, 1985, 1987a, 1987b, 1990) has been mainly concerned with the identity of the gay father, but he notes what is an absolutely key point here, which is that no research has yet found sexuality to be directly related to nurturing ability (Bozett 1985, p.343). He also notes that gay fathers made strenuous efforts to shield their children from social stigma, and that most of the children grew up to be heterosexual (Bozett 1987a, pp.45–7).

Barret and Robinson (1990) report that most of the children of gay fathers in their research sample were heterosexual (p.40), and that, while some did report teasing, it was not a major issue for such children (p.41). They found no evidence of the sexual abuse or molestation of children by gay fathers (p.42), and the children were all well adjusted (p.80).

Bailey *et al.* (1995) have been conducting the most extensive research, to date, concerning gay fathers and their children. In their reported findings so far, Bailey *et al.* (1995) found that, of the sons of gay fathers whose sexual orientation they could rate with confidence, nine per cent were nonheterosexual and ninety-one per cent heterosexual (p.126). They therefore conclude that 'sexual orientation was not positively correlated with the amount of time that sons lived with their [gay] fathers' (Bailey *et al.* 1995, p.128).

'Risks' in Foster/Adoptive Care

Given that the perceived 'risks' posed to children and young people by lesbians and gay men *per se* are not supported by the research evidence, what then are the implications of this for social workers attempting to assess lesbian or gay carer applicants?

With regard to children and young people being placed for fostering or adoption, the situation of 'risk' is in one sense reversed. Those children usually come to the attentions of social workers because they already carry such risks with them. They may have been abused in different ways, they may have been rejected or neglected, their emotional and psychological development is impaired, they usually have fairly poor relationships with peers, and indeed some display sexualised acting-out behaviour. Certainly anecdotal evidence from my own involvement in lesbian and gay foster and adoptive carers networks suggests that most of the children placed do have such histories in one form or another. These are 'damaged' children who require carers who will be able to meet their needs and cope with sometimes very demanding problems. The task for social work practitioners, then, is to assess for potential carers who, first, do not themselves pose such risks to children, and second, will be able to provide good child care which is responsive to the personal problems that such children bring.

The process of the formal assessment of all prospective carers, usually based upon 'Form F' (BAAF 1991), is at least therefore partly about trying to identify, and reject, adults who do pose a risk to children placed within their care. This is right and proper, and I have no argument with all prospective carers, whatever their sexuality, being assessed in this way. The kinds of risks that a social worker is looking for in doing such an assessment are detailed below:

- Emotionally/physically/sexually abusive.
- Neglectful of child care.
- Poor child care/parenting skills.
- No knowledge of children's needs/development.
- Lack of space/time to give a child.
- Child used to replace/fulfil adult needs.
- Chaotic lifestyle, unreliable.
- Unstable/damaging relationships.
- Socially isolated/lack of support/using child for friendship.
- Lack of awareness of oppression – racist, sexist, homophobic, disablist views.
- Rigid gender roles.
- Overly-routined/rigid lifestyle.
- Unrealistic expectations of a child.
- Overly disciplinarian.
- Inability to share information with a child about its origins, or maintain contact arrangements with birth family.

Figure 2.1 Possible risks presented by adult carer applicants

However, for lesbian and gay applicants, this process of assessment far too easily weighs against them. For some, they are rejected *a priori* on the basis of sexuality and are not given the chance to be assessed (Hicks 1993, 1996, Whitehouse 1985). For others, the assessment itself becomes focused on their sexuality alone, to the exclusion of all else. This is also dangerous social work practice, as carer assessments ought to be based upon the risks detailed in Figure 2.1; that is, whether the person can provide good-enough child care. I am not arguing that lesbians' and gay men's sexuality should be ignored in assessment – far from it – but first and foremost the assessment ought to be about adequate child care. A 'risky' carer is someone who cannot provide a child with adequate care and they ought to be rejected, but this cannot be based upon sexuality and there is no evidence to suggest that it should be (Golombok and Tasker 1994).

I now want to present some of the findings of my earlier research (Hicks 1993), as I believe that this has much to tell us about how lesbians and gay men are assessed. I have elsewhere (Hicks 1996) detailed some experiences reported by lesbians and gay men who have been through the process of social work assessment, so I will summarise the research findings that relate to this here.

Lesbian and gay applicants report that carer preparation groups, if these were offered at all, rarely responded to their particular needs. During the assessment itself, many of the perceived 'risks' to children discussed earlier came up. Around the issue of gender roles in particular, social workers seemed to be concerned to ensure that lesbian and gay applicants would be able to provide *traditional* masculine and feminine 'models'. Gay men reported suspicions about why they wanted to care for boys, which they felt may have been to do with assumptions that they would sexually abuse (Hicks 1993, p.43).

Lesbian and gay applicants were frequently left to bring up the issue of sexuality themselves in the assessment. Some social workers chose to ignore this and actively avoided talking about the carers' sexuality. Some lesbians and gay men felt that social workers 'played down' their sexuality, later representing them as 'the foster parent and her friend', particularly to birth parents. Jo and Louise told me:

> We believe that the Local Authority were able to sweep the issue of our being lesbians under the carpet. (Hicks 1993, p.35)

The 'matching' of the child, for whom Jo and Louise now provide shared/respite care, was done in the name of one of them only, and allowed the child's social worker to represent them to birth parents as 'Jo, the foster carer, and her friend who shares her house' (p.35).

Many applicants felt that they had to educate heterosexual social workers about lesbian or gay issues. For some, in contrast, the assessment became focused upon their sexuality to the exclusion of all else. One lesbian applicant reported:

> I felt cheated…I wanted to talk about child care, and I wanted to prove to them that I could be a good parent, that I had experience of kids, that I knew about child development… All they wanted to do was talk about me being a lesbian… (Interview notes, Hicks 1993)

I have provided these examples because I wanted to illustrate the experiences of lesbian and gay applicants, many of whom feel their assessments either focus exclusively on their sexuality, or at the opposite extreme, ignore it. Of course, this is not the experience of all lesbian and gay applicants, nor is it the practice of all social workers. However, I do believe that the examples of good practice that I have come across, wherein the social worker conducts a balanced assessment focusing both upon child care issues and sexuality, are in a small minority. How, then, can social workers assess lesbians and gay men in a way which, first, does not start from the premiss that they are *per se* a risk to children, second, acknowledges and discusses their sexuality as a part of the whole assessment, and finally, deals with the issue of weeding out any adult who would pose a risk to children in terms of the issues detailed in Figure 2.1?

The work of Brown (1991, 1992) is helpful here as she focuses upon the kinds of knowledge, values and skills social workers will need in assessing lesbians and gay men (Brown 1991, p.14). She suggests that social workers ought to familiarise themselves with the research knowledge discussed earlier, if they are to be able to answer the question 'are lesbians and gay men able to parent?'. Brown notes that existing research proves that it 'would be wrong to exclude a potential group of carers on the grounds of their sexual orientation' (p.15). In relation to values, she proposes that social workers need to abandon both negative and positive stereotyping in relation to lesbians and gay men, and to focus on sexuality as a part of the whole (Brown 1991). I would also suggest that, if social workers have not examined their own values in relation to lesbians and gay men, then they need to do so (and see Logan *et al.* 1996, for helpful exercises). A social worker who does not feel able to work with the possibility that lesbians and gay men can provide child care ought not to do such an assessment.

Brown argues that social workers will draw upon a range of skills in carrying out assessments, many of which will be common to all such pieces of work. As I have also argued (Hicks 1996), she suggests that there are specific areas, to do with sexuality, that should be covered with lesbian and gay applicants (Brown 1991, p.16). Some of these, I suggest, will include how the carers propose to cope with any teasing of a child if it occurs; who will tell the child about the carers' sexuality and when; how the carers will handle working with schools; and how they will work with birth parents, especially in shared care schemes (and see also Martin 1993 here). Lesbian and gay applicants usually appreciate being able to talk about such issues and it is not discriminatory for a social worker to do so in my view:

> I don't think the social worker handled the issues to do with our sexuality well...she wanted to be so non-discriminating that she just treated us like she would a heterosexual couple...and on one level that was good because she focused on child care, but we also needed to talk about the specifics of being lesbian adopters, and there are many issues we all needed to think through... (Interview notes)

The question that I want to ask, then, is this: does focusing on the perceived 'risks' that lesbians and gay men supposedly pose to children – risk of sexual abuse, impaired psychosocial development, development of atypical gender role or sexuality – help social workers in conducting good assessments of lesbian and gay carer applicants? My answer of course is no. This kind of focus is inherently discriminatory, based upon Brown's negative stereotypes (1991, p.15). Is there any evidence that assessments have focused on these issues? In reports from lesbian and gay carers, I did find evidence of suspicions that gay men wanted to abuse young boys (Hicks 1993, p.29), concerns that lesbians and gay men would not be able to provide access to opposite-gender role models and 'traditional' sex-roles (p.29), and evidence of greater or special scrutiny of lesbian or gay cases (p.37).

Focusing on these kinds of 'risks' can exclude – and indeed has done – the very real need to focus on wider issues of good-enough child care, carers who are at ease with their own sexuality and have well-defined notions of sexual boundaries, and the ability to provide children with a stable and loving home environment.

'TAKING THE RISK'?

For social work practitioners, I am suggesting that the assessment of lesbian and gay potential carers is a prime site for developing anti-discriminatory practice. This would involve a combination of the assessment of good child care skills and the specific issues facing lesbian and gay carers, as a part of a whole, rather than focussing on sexuality alone (negative stereotype) or avoiding it altogether (positive stereotype).

A model of approaches to the assessment of lesbians and gay men is shown at Figure 2.2. At the far left is the disqualification *a priori* of all lesbian or gay applicants on the basis of sexuality alone, and this I have suggested often rests upon notions of supposed 'risks' posed to children. The next point on the continuum – 'just sexuality' – is the kind of assessment that focuses on sexuality to the exclusion of all else. Again, I have suggested that this is poor, even 'risky', practice as it does not look at issues of child care skills. The middle point – 'just see how it goes' – is an approach whereby the social worker goes in to assess lesbian or gay carers without thinking through issues of sexuality in advance. This approach is unhelpful as it puts the onus on lesbian or gay applicants to raise all issues of sexuality, and it does not allow the social worker to discuss these in a skilled and confident manner. The next point is moving towards a better assessment practice, which manages to combine both the issues of sexuality and child care as a part of the whole picture. The social worker here will have looked at research knowledge, examined their own skills and values, and have thought through issues of sexuality in advance. The final point on the right represents anti-oppressive responses, and I would suggest that these also take account of the particular needs of lesbian or gay applicants during the process of recruitment and assessment: How are lesbians and gay men recruited? What initial responses are made to them? Are forms designed for heterosexuals? What account of their needs is taken in training/preparation groups?

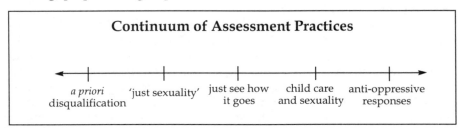

Figure 2.2

Some pointers for social workers to think through in preparing for assessments of lesbians or gay men might be:

- What steps does your agency, or do you as a worker, take to meet the needs of black carers being assessed? Are there any parallel considerations here for lesbian or gay applicants?
- What skills, knowledge and values (Brown 1991) do you have in relation to lesbians and gay men as the carers of children? What do you need in order to carry out such an assessment?

- There are specific areas that lesbian and gay applicants will appreciate talking about during the assessment – their own sexuality, the history of their coming out and relationships, how they will handle anti-gay teasing with a child, how they will tell a child about their sexuality and when, how they will work with the child's school or with birth parents. It is my view that social workers ought to talk about these issues with lesbian and gay applicants and that it is not 'discriminatory' to do so.
- What training have you, as a social worker, had on lesbian and gay issues? If you have not had any, then think about ways to raise this at work.

In this chapter, I have highlighted the ways in which notions of lesbians and gay men as risks to children distort and prevent adequate assessment of the parenting skills of such carers. There are, however, as many examples of potential discrimination post-assessment, in going to approval panel or in having children placed within their care, faced by lesbians and gay men, which I do not have the space to go into here.

Evidence from existing research has found no links between sexuality and the ability to nurture children (Bozett 1985, p.343). It is for this reason that I suggest social work 'takes the risk' of accepting lesbian or gay applicants as the potential carers of children. However, there should in fact be no issues of 'risk' here: any lesbian or gay man who has been properly assessed to be capable of meeting the needs of children can do just that, and a social worker who has assessed them can feel confident in presenting their case based upon sound child care principles (Brown 1991). I have proposed that social workers engaged in such assessments move to a balanced approach which combines the issues of sexuality with all of those others involved in the scrutiny of applicants (Figure 2.1), but I have also suggested that many lesbians and gay men currently experience such assessments as discriminatory on the basis of their sexuality (Hicks 1993, 1996).

What is more disheartening is the *a priori* rejection of lesbian and gay applicants, or indeed their positioning as the point of 'last resort' (Hicks 1996). As I have noted, there is no evidence to suggest that sexuality ought to rule out the care of children, and the exclusion of whole groups of potential carers for this reason alone can only suggest a social work practice that is based upon oppressive values. Nevertheless many lesbians and gay men remain committed to challenging such values, either from within social work or from without, and still others continue to demonstrate by their day-to-day care of children that lesbian and gay fostering and adoption is indeed possible.

REFERENCES

Abbott, P. and Wallace, C. (1992) *The Family and the New Right*. London: Pluto Press.

BAAF (British Agencies for Adoption and Fostering) (1991) *Form F: Information on Prospective Substitute Parent(s)*. London: BAAF.

Bailey, J.M., Bobrow, D., Wolfe, M. and Mikach, S. (1995) 'Sexual orientation of adult sons of gay fathers.' In *Developmental Psychology 31*, 1, pp.124–129.

Barret, R.L. and Robinson, B.E. (1990) *Gay Fathers*. Lexington, MA: Lexington Books.

Barrett, M. and McIntosh, M. (1991) *The Anti-Social Family*. London: Verso; second edn., orig. 1982.

BBC 'Heart of the Matter' (1993) 'Fostering Prejudice?' 14/2/93, BBC 1.

BBC North West (1993) News, 11/2/93.

Berry, P. (1987) 'Life as a gay worker...' In *Community Care*, 25/6/87 (suppt.;pp.vi–vii).

Bozett, F.W. (1981) 'Gay fathers: evolution of the gay-father identity.' In *American Journal of Orthopsychiatry 51*, 3, pp.552–559.

Bozett, F.W. (1985) 'Gay men as fathers.' In S.M.H. Hanson and F.W. Bozett (eds) *Dimensions of Fatherhood*. Beverly Hills: Sage.

Bozett, F.W. (1987a) 'Children of gay fathers.' In F.W. Bozett (ed) *Gay and Lesbian Parents*. New York: Praeger.

Bozett, F.W. (1987b) 'Gay fathers.' In F.W. Bozett (ed) *Gay and Lesbian Parents*. New York: Praeger.

Bozett, F.W. (1990) 'Fathers who are gay.' In R.J. Kus (ed) *Keys to Caring: Assisting your Gay and Lesbian Clients*. Boston: Alyson.

Brown, H.C. (1991) 'Competent child-focused practice: working with lesbian and gay carers.' In *Adoption and Fostering 15*, 2, pp.11–17.

Brown, H.C. (1992) 'Gender, sex and sexuality in the assessment of prospective carers.' In *Adoption and Fostering 16*, 2, pp.30–34.

Community Care (1993) 'Gay couples approved in Hampshire's foster policy.' In *Community Care 951*, 28/1/93, p.2.

Department of Health (1990) *Foster Placement (Guidance and Regulations) Consultation Paper No. 16*. London: HMSO.

Department of Health (1991) *The Children Act 1989: Guidance and Regulations: Volume 3: Family Placements*. London: HMSO.

Department of Health/Welsh Office (1992) *Review of Adoption Law: Report to Ministers of an Interdepartmental Working Group: A Consultation Document*. London: HMSO.

Department of Health/Welsh Office/Home Office/Lord Chancellor's Department (1993) *Adoption: The Future*. London: HMSO.

Ferris, D. (1977) *Homosexuality and the Social Services: The Report of an N.C.C.L. Survey of Local Authority Social Services Committees*. London: National Council for Civil Liberties.

Golombok, S., Spencer, A. and Rutter, M. (1983) 'Children in lesbian and single-parent households: psychosexual and psychiatric appraisal.' *Journal of Child Psychology and Psychiatry 24*, 4, pp.551–572.

Golombok, S. and Tasker, F. (1994) 'Children in lesbian and gay families: theories and evidence.' In *Annual Review of Sex Research 4*, pp.73–100.

Golombok, S. and Tasker, F. (1996) 'Do parents influence the sexual orientation of their children? Findings from a longitudinal study of lesbian families.' In *Developmental Psychology 32*, 1, pp.3–11.

Green, G.D. and Bozett, F.W. (1991) 'Lesbian mothers and gay fathers.' In J.C. Gonsiorek and J.D. Weinrich (eds) *Homosexuality: Research Implications for Public Policy*. London: Sage.

Hester, M., Kelly, L. and Radford, J. (eds) (1996) *Women, Violence and Male Power: Feminist Activism, Research and Practice*. Buckingham: Open University Press.

Hicks, S. (1993) *The Experiences of Lesbians and Gay Men in Fostering and Adoption: A Study of the Impact of the Process of Assessment Upon Prospective Carers*. Victoria University of Manchester: unpublished M.A. thesis.

Hicks, S. (1996) 'The "last resort"?: lesbian and gay experiences of the social work assessment process in fostering and adoption.' In *Practice 8*, 2, pp.15–24.

Logan, J., Kershaw, S., Karban, K., Mills, S., Trotter, J. and Sinclair, M. (1996) *Confronting Prejudice: Lesbian and Gay Issues in Social Work Education*. Aldershot: Arena.

Marchant, C. (1992) 'Adoption shake-up avoids blanket ban.' In *Community Care*, 22/10/92, p.1.

Martin, A. (1993) *The Lesbian and Gay Parenting Handbook: Creating and Raising Our Families*. New York: HarperCollins.

Maynard, M. and Purvis, J. (eds) (1995) *(Hetero)sexual Politics*. London: Taylor and Francis.

Patterson, C.J. (1992) 'Children of lesbian and gay parents.' In *Child Development 63*, pp.1025–1042.

Patterson, C.J. (1994) 'Children of the lesbian baby boom: behavioural adjustment, self-concepts, and sex-role identity.' In B. Greene and G.M. Herek (eds) *Lesbian and Gay Psychology: Theory, Research and Clinical Applications*. Newbury Park: Sage.

Patterson, C.J. (1995) 'Families of the lesbian baby boom: division of labor and children's adjustment.' In *Developmental Psychology 31*, 1, pp.115–123.

Pollack, S. (1987) 'Lesbian mothers: a lesbian-feminist perspective on research.' In S. Pollack and J. Vaughn (eds) *Politics of the Heart: A Lesbian Parenting Anthology*. Ithaca: Firebrand Books.

Reece, H. (1995) 'Subverting stigmatization: homosexuality and the welfare of the child.' Conference paper at 'Legal Queeries', University of Lancaster, Sept. 1995.

Rich, A. (1980) 'Compulsory heterosexuality and lesbian existence.' In *Signs 5*, pp.631–660.

Richardson, D. (ed) (1996) *Theorising Heterosexuality: Telling it Straight*. Buckingham: Open University Press.

Ricketts, W. (1991) *Lesbians and Gay Men as Foster Parents*. Portland, Maine: University of Southern Maine, National Child Welfare Resource Center for Management and Administration.

Ricketts, W. and Achtenberg, R. (1987) 'The adoptive and foster gay and lesbian parent.' In F.W. Bozett (ed) *Gay and Lesbian Parents*. New York: Praeger.

Ricketts, W. and Achtenberg, R. (1990) 'Adoption and foster parenting for lesbians and gay men: creating new traditions in family.' In *Marriage and Family Review*, 14:3/4, pp.83–118.

Rights of Women Lesbian Custody Group (1986) *Lesbian Mothers' Legal Handbook*. London: The Women's Press.

Saffron, L. (1996) *'What About the Children?': Sons and Daughters of Lesbian and Gay Parents Talk About Their Lives*. London: Cassell.

Sedgwick, E.K. (1991) 'How to bring your kids up gay.' In *Social Text 29*, pp.18–27.

Skeates, J. and Jabri, D. (eds) (1988) *Fostering and Adoption by Lesbians and Gay Men*. London: London Strategic Policy Unit.

Tasker, F.L. and Golombok, S. (1991) 'Children raised by lesbian mothers: the empirical evidence.' In *Family Law 21*, pp.184–187.

Tasker, F. and Golombok, S. (1995) 'Adults raised as children in lesbian families.' In *American Journal of Orthopsychiatry 65*, 2, pp.203–215.

Whitehouse, A. (1985) 'They said because we were gay they could not take the risk.' In *Community Care*, 30/5/85, pp.20–22.

Wilkinson, S. and Kitzinger, C. (eds) (1993) *Heterosexuality: A 'Feminism and Psychology' Reader*. London: Sage.

ACKNOWLEDGEMENTS

I would like to thank all those social work practitioners, educators and students who attended the event 'Lesbian and Gay Fostering – Practical Issues for Social Workers' at Manchester Town Hall on 26 November 1996, for their feedback on some of the issues contained in this chapter. I am also grateful to the members of the Positive Parenting Campaign in Manchester – Liz Bennett, Paul Fairweather, Maggie Murdoch and Maggie Walker – for organizing the event, and for inviting me.

CHAPTER 3

Making Family Placements
Working With Risk and Building on Strengths

Anne van Meeuwen

INTRODUCTION

Placing a child in the care of strangers, with the hope that positive relationships will develop and that the child will be able to thrive, inevitably involves an element of risk. When we add to the equation the impact of that child's previous experience of family life, which may well have included abuse, neglect, ambivalent or disorganised attachments, the level of risk is clearly increased. However, the concepts of risk assessment and risk management are rarely explicitly articulated in our research and practice literature on adoption and foster care. Practitioners in this field know that they are taking risks and they equally know that not to do so would be to deny many children who are temporarily or permanently separated from their birth families, the opportunity for close, supportive relationships.

This chapter aims to explore how the concepts of risk assessment and risk management can provide a helpful framework for analysing the process of making and supporting placements in foster care and adoption. It does not attempt to look more broadly at care planning and the assessment of risks in determining whether children can safely remain with or be returned to the care of their birth families. That area of work would require a separate chapter of its own. However the quality of work with birth families and the quality of planning for looked after children must have a significant impact on the outcomes of family placement.

A foster or adoptive placement clearly has an impact on the lives of a number of people; the carers themselves, their birth children and other family members, the child's birth parent and other relatives. However, the focus of this chapter will be on the child at the centre of the process and on the risks that placement in another family can entail for them. So what are the risks? Traditionally much of the research literature in this field has looked at the risk of disruption, of the placement not lasting as long as it was needed (Barth and Berry 1988, Berridge and Cleaver 1987, O'Hara and Haggan 1988). Various studies have identified rates of disruption ranging from 7 per cent of adoptive placements of infants (Lambert and Streather 1980) to 53 per cent of foster care placements of adolescents (Rowe, Hundleby and Garnett 1989). Whilst the impact of disruption on the child will vary according to the nature of the placement and the circumstances of the move, the potentially negative consequences for the child's sense of security, self-esteem and ability to form trusting relationships with adults are clearly to be avoided.

In recent years more attention has been focused on the risk of abuse in adoption and foster care. Concerns have arisen about the likelihood of agencies being targeted by those who seek opportunities to abuse children and about abuse occurring when carers are extremely stressed by the demands of looking after children with sexualised or very challenging behaviour. To date these concerns have not generated the volume of research devoted to disruption but they have resulted in practice development around the assessment of 'safe carers' and an emphasis on encouraging 'safe caring' within the placement (National Foster Care Association 1994). These developments have been primarily concerned with the risk of sexual abuse by carers, although evidence from child protection investigations within birth families would suggest that physical abuse and neglect are likely to be at least if not more prevalent.

In seeking to minimise the risks of disruption and abuse, our approach could be described as one of harm prevention. However, in seeking to intervene significantly in the lives of children, we must surely hope that the service we provide has positive benefits. The risk of placing children in an environment which does not actively promote their health, development and ability to form satisfying relationships must be an integral part of any risk assessment and risk management strategy. This emphasis on considering the quality of parenting received by children and the relationship between intervention and outcomes has been the cornerstone of the Department of Health initiative 'Looking After Children' (Ward 1995). A final area of risk that must be considered, particularly for those children for whom a return home is unlikely, is what happens if we do nothing. Vera Fahlberg writes:

> Child care workers are repeatedly asked to make major life decisions on behalf of children whom they do not know well. They must achieve a delicate balance: on the one hand, they must never minimise the life-long impact of the decisions they make; on the other, they must not allow themselves to become paralysed by fear of making a wrong decision. (Fahlberg 1994, p.225)

Any placement for a child will involve weighing up potential gains and losses and, for some children, the complexity of their needs may suggest the level of risk is considerable. However the equation will not be complete unless it also includes the potential implications of leaving that child to drift in a situation where their future is uncertain and unplanned.

An essential element of assessing and managing risk is enabling the voice of the child to be heard. Our judgements must be informed by what children have to say, individually and collectively, about how they perceive the risks to them and what would help them to feel protected. We need to find ways of enabling them to communicate these messages.

This chapter will consider how practitioners assess and manage risk through the process of recruiting foster carers and adopters, identifying children's needs, linking a child with a family and supporting and monitoring the placement. It will examine the knowledge base from which decisions are made and explore whether resources are being appropriately distributed between the various stages of the process in order to minimise risk and enhance positive outcomes for children.

WHAT IS OUR KNOWLEDGE BASE?

In order to use the information we collect on children and carers and make judgements on the risks that may be involved, we need to be able to place it within a context. The theoretical models we use, our knowledge of relevant research findings, our own and colleagues' practice experience, the requirements of legislation, guidance and agency policy, all come together to provide a framework within which we make predictions, test them out and monitor their validity in practice. Our judgements are not value-free as personal beliefs about such issues as the importance of racial identity or the significance of sibling relationships can clearly influence how information is weighed and conclusions reached. However, by examining what evidence we have for our judgements and relating it to a body of knowledge, we can, one hopes, minimise the impact of subjectivity.

Theoretical Models

CHILD DEVELOPMENT

A knowledge of child development is central to child placement work. Workers need to be able to distinguish between behaviours which are normal for children at certain ages and those which indicate unmet developmental needs. They need to be able to identify whether children are 'stuck' at an earlier developmental stage and what input might be required to enable them to move forward. Direct work with children and the process of moving a child from one family to another needs to be informed by a knowledge of how children process information and attempt to make sense of what has or is happening to them at different developmental stages.

ATTACHMENT

Awareness of the considerable difficulty some children experience in forming relationships within adoptive families has led to renewed interest in the relevance of attachment theory. Fahlberg (1994) has written extensively on ways of encouraging attachment between children and carers. An assessment of the child's attachments within the birth family has implications for their capacity to make new attachments and for determining their needs in relation to future family contact. The work of Stern on the relevance of early attachment history to future parenting has also been applied by some agencies in the assessment of carers (Kaniuk 1992).

SEPARATION AND LOSS

Separation and loss are central themes in the lives of children in foster and adoptive care. An understanding of how these processes impact upon the child and may affect their ability to form relationships is an essential element in the worker's knowledge base. Loss may also be a key issue for carers, for example in relation to infertility.

IDENTITY

The issue of identity is of major significance for children separated from their birth families. Policy and practice in areas such as maintaining family links, access to life-history information and meeting children's racial and cultural needs should clearly be informed by an understanding of how children develop a concept of who they are and a sense of self-esteem.

FAMILY SYSTEMS THEORY

The assessment of potential carers involves evaluating how the family operates as a unit, as well as the strengths and limitations of the individuals within it. Barnardo's family placement project in Edinburgh has developed its practice in assessment and post-placement support by drawing on systemic family therapy, to consider the processes by which families reach decisions, negotiate change, accommodate a new family member (MacFadyen 1994, unpublished).

During the assessment, systemic interviews with the whole family focus on areas such as motivation, the potential impact on existing family members, parenting, family roles and managing stress. Techniques such as circular questioning enable the dynamics of family functioning to be more clearly observed than with traditional assessment practice.

SOCIAL AND COGNITIVE THEORY

Barth and Berry have drawn on social learning and cognitive theories to develop a model which relates the particular stresses which are faced by older children being placed for adoption, the individual adopter and the adoptive family, the tasks they have to accomplish and the coping resources which may be available to them (Barth and Berry 1988). In this model the relationship between the impact of the child joining the family and the availability of strategies to reduce stress can determine whether the conflicts that inevitably arise can be diffused or will accumulate. The model could also apply to foster care.

Research Findings

A Department of Health publication on patterns and outcomes states:

> Research can never produce an exact answer about the degree of risk of a particular placement for an individual child because the interplay of the factors which determine success or failure will be unique in each case. However research findings do offer a framework for informed decisions because they can provide information about general patterns of outcome. When research demonstrates that certain factors tend to be associated with the desired outcome – or the reverse – practitioners can take steps to maximise the positive factors and minimise risk by providing counterbalances to the negative ones. (Department of Health 1991, p.65)

An example of drawing on research findings to inform practice is demonstrated in Table 3.1 which is based on Barth and Berry's study of older child adoptions (Barth and Berry 1988).

Table 3.1 – Risk in Adopting Older Children	
Risk Factors	*Protective Factors*
• Lack of information for adopters about child's emotional and behavioural problems. • Mis-match between adopters' expectations and reality of child. • Lack of availability of family support. • Lengthy prior stay in foster care. • High expectations/rigidity of adopters. • Changes in social worker. • Child's inability to reciprocate • Other adopted children in home.	• Preparation involving experienced adopters. • Preparation for specific child – meeting carers, reading file. • Preparation of child. • Post-placement support. • Availability of appropriate input from other agencies.

The Department of Health publication quoted above identifies a number of other factors which various studies have linked with unsuccessful placement and a higher than average risk of disruption:

- significantly higher rate of disruption with increasing age at placement
- previous experience of disruption
- other children in family close in age to placed child
- child ambivalent or opposed to placement
- severe behaviour problems
- child is cut off from all that is familiar – birth family, siblings, school and neighbourhood.

Practice Experience

Thoburn and Sellick have recently examined what research findings are available on effectiveness in family placement work, and identified a number of gaps in our knowledge base (Thoburn and Sellick 1996). For example, concerns about the risk of abuse in foster care have led to increasingly lengthy and detailed assessment processes for prospective carers but we do not know from research whether these result in better outcomes for children. In the absence of research evidence, we rely on the practice experience that we and our colleagues have accumulated. Such experience clearly has its place. My own experience of work with foster carers from the early 1970s to the 1990s has led me to believe that more thorough assessment and preparation and ongoing training and support has resulted in current carers being better equipped to meet the complex needs of many of the children in placement. However, we must proceed with caution if we are to ensure that our judgements are not skewed by individual experiences which may have been particularly positive or negative but which will not necessarily be replicated.

THE PLACEMENT PROCESS – STAGES IN RISK ASSESSMENT AND RISK MANAGEMENT

Prediction – Recruitment and Assessment of Carers

Recruitment and assessment involve making predictions about the capacity of each applicant to undertake the tasks of foster care or adoption. Where the demands of the task far exceed the resources possessed by the applicant, we can reasonably assume that the risks of disruption, abuse or failure to deliver good outcomes for children are likely to be higher. Clearly all applicants will have particular strengths and limitations and the assessment process can enable us to identify where additional input by the agency, for example developing skills in managing challenging behaviour, may help to minimise risk. To make predictions, we need to be clear what the task involves and what experience, knowledge, understanding and skills someone would need in order to perform it effectively. Traditionally these have not always been made explicit in family placement practice and some applicants have been left feeling that they have to 'second-guess' what the agency expected of them. More recently there has been interest in drawing up 'job specifications' for carers. The Assessment section of the National Foster Care Association series 'Making it Work' contains lists of tasks and competencies for foster care. The competency list includes the following:

- an ability to work within a written agreement, including the undertaking of specific tasks
- an ability to keep clear recorded information
- an ability to contribute to the department's planning for the child/young person
- an ability to listen and communicate with children as appropriate to their age and understanding. (National Foster Care Association 1993)

The introduction of a National Vocational Qualification in Foster Care in June 1996 is a further development in the application of a competency-based approach. Table 3.2 illustrates some of tasks identified within my own agency as part of a job specification for adoptive parents.

Table 3.2 – Tasks for Adopters

- To enable a child to develop a sense of pride in their heritage and where relevant, to practice their religion and maintain their language.
- To recognise how the child's past experiences have affected them and to build on this understanding in order to promote attachment and enable the child to relate positively to others and learn socially acceptable behaviour.
- To recognise the importance of safe caring and to be prepared to modify their household 'rules' to help a child feel safe.
- To value the child's history and to recognise the significance of people from the past.
- To encourage positive contact with significant people from the past in line with the child's needs at the particular point in time.
- To create opportunities for sharing life-history information with the child in a way that acknowledges difficulties, without judgement, and recognises positives.
- To recognise their needs for support and to use what is available from both their informal networks and the agency.

(Taken from Adoption Practice Resource Pack – Barnardo's)

Having defined the tasks and the criteria on which our assessment will be made, we need to collect the evidence on which our predictions will be based. One criticism that is sometimes appropriately levelled at assessment reports is that they provide a considerable amount of very detailed information about applicants, particularly in relation to their childhood experiences, without any real evaluation of the information or a clear indication of how it relates to the final judgement that the applicant should be approved as a carer. Having explicit criteria will, one hopes, encourage a focus on that information which can provide evidence that criteria have or have not been met. For example, an applicant's flexibility may be partly judged on the way in which s/he has been able to negotiate and accommodate change within his/her relationships with partners, birth children or parents. An evidence-based approach should help to guard against the racial and cultural bias that may be a feature of more subjective judgements.

The task of risk assessment is not solely undertaken by the agency. Applicants themselves are making predictions about the possible impact of foster care or adoption on themselves and their family and on their own ability to meet the demands. In order to make an effective judgement about the potential gains and the risks involved in taking on this new role, they need to be fully informed about what will be expected of them. Thorough preparation of applicants must include honest information about the needs of children requiring placement and the demands this can place upon the family. The risks should be openly acknowledged and applicants need to know what support they can expect from the agency to help manage and minimise these risks. One of the predictions the applicant will make is which children they could effectively care for. Barth and Berry comment on the risk involved in not hearing this and attempting to 'stretch' families to take the children the agency most needs to place (Barth and Berry 1988). Self-assessment is an integral part of the process but the final responsibility for assessing whether the level of risk is acceptable must remain with the agency, in order to protect the welfare of children.

Although the assessment stage is primarily about prediction, it also sets the scene for the subsequent management of risk. The extent to which an effective partnership can be formed between the applicant and the agency influences whether difficulties that arise at the placement stage can be acknowledged and agency support used. In relation to safe caring, Fry (1996) has written of assessment and preparation providing a framework within which to explore the role of male members of the household and their involvement in the direct care of children. She suggests that this can set the pattern for including male carers in subsequent agency involvement such as reviews and enable male carers to understand how their vulnerability under stress could lead to the possibility of abuse. Group preparation of applicants can offer not only information about the task and a better understanding of children's needs but also the opportunity to forge links with other carers whose support may be a protective factor at the placement stage.

Finally, the use of Panels to consider applications can ensure that responsibility for risk taking is shared and can, it is to be hoped, provide a forum for the link between the evidence and the workers' predictions to be validated or, if appropriate, challenged.

Cost/Benefit Analysis – Linking the Child With a Carer

The next two sections of this chapter apply primarily to planned placements. When children are placed or moved in an emergency, there is unlikely to be the time available to undertake any detailed analysis of the pros and cons (i.e., the risks) of a particular placement. There may well be a limited or no choice of carer and little information available on the child's needs. If, however, the placement is planned, any assessment of the risks involved should be based on a detailed understanding of the child and their particular needs. The Department of Health's (1995) *Looking After Children: Assessment and Action Records* offers a systematic format for recording how the child is progressing in the various areas of their life and for identifying where particular difficulties or concerns exist and what action is needed to address them. The Record can therefore provide the basis for drawing up a full profile of the child's needs. The assessment of the child's needs also involves making predictions. For example, an early history of attachment difficulties may increase the risk of disruption because the child may be unable to reciprocate, whereas a relationship with a sibling may be a protective factor because it adds to the child's coping resources. If it is known what the particular issues are for the child, it is possible to try to identify what resources the carer will need in order to address them, both in terms of their own experience and skills and in input from the agency. A linking format that makes this explicit by recording the child's needs and the carer's resources in adjoining columns can be helpful in assessing whether the benefits outweigh the costs and in determining the level of risk.

As with assessment, this process of cost/benefit analysis also needs to be undertaken by the potential carer(s). In order to do this, they must have full and accurate information about the child. As stated earlier, research has indicated that the failure of the agency to provide adequate information about a child's emotional and behavioural problems is a significant risk for disruption. Clearly agencies can only provide what they know and carers need to be prepared for further information, such as a disclosure of abuse, to emerge after placement; but presenting an over-optimistic picture of the child may secure a placement in the short-term, at a subsequently high cost. Children also need an opportunity to express and explore their wishes and feelings about a future placement and this process needs to be facilitated by information on what options may be available for them.

Initial Testing Out of Predictions – Introductions

The introductory period provides an opportunity to begin to test out the predictions that have been made about the carer(s) and the child and the suitability of the link between them. However, whilst some links will not proceed beyond this stage, possibly because of an unpredictable failure of 'chemistry' between the individuals involved, the real test will only come in the placement itself. Introductions do play a valuable role in minimising the trauma of the move for the child and do enable concerns to be raised at an early stage before the final commitment to placement has to be made. All parties, including the child's current carer(s), need opportunities to reflect on (and feedback on) how the introductions are progressing. Their concerns may have implications for the level of risk the placement poses and whether it should still proceed, or may indicate that further agency input will be required in order to manage the risks.

Risk Management – Post Placement Services

Agencies clearly have a statutory responsibility to monitor and review placements in order to safeguard and promote the welfare of the child. When concerns arise about the standard or appropriateness of the care provided, the lack of progress made by the child or the level of conflict between carer(s) and child, an assessment may be needed of whether the risks to the child of remaining in the placement outweigh any potential benefits and the risks of a move. In some cases action may be required to ensure the child's safety and, in others, a planned disruption may be the least detrimental alternative available. Carers themselves may reach a point where the costs to them and their family of continuing with the placement may outweigh any possible benefits. However, the primary focus of this section is to consider how enhancing protective factors can enable risk to be effectively managed. Writing about keeping children safe in foster care, Boushel (1994) suggests a framework for strengthening children's protective environment. She identifies four important factors:

- how children are valued
- how women and children are valued
- the social inter-connectedness of child and carer
- the existence and quality of statutory and professional safety nets.

The framework enables strengths and weaknesses to be identified and the impact of discrimination, disadvantage and cultural diversity to be acknowledged. Strengthening the environment is addressed through specific strategies, for example to help children to deal with bullying or to promote a positive racial identity, to develop the skills and confidence of female carers, to develop support networks for children and carers. Smith has written of the importance of providing specific skills training to foster carers in areas such as recognising indicators of abuse, responding to disclosures and helping children recover from the impact of abuse. The aim is to enable carers to become effective protectors of children (Smith 1996).

In their study of adoption disruption, Barth and Berry identify a number of interventions which they consider would minimise risk:

- support groups, buddy systems and helplines for adopters
- intensive preservation programmes for placements at risk
- availability of respite care
- availability of adoption allowances
- informed therapists who can offer advice on behaviour management
- voluntary reviews of placement to consider need for continuing agency support, particularly in adolescence
- support in negotiations with school system. (Barth and Berry 1988)

In relation to foster care, Fry (1996) suggests that support should include information, clarifying tasks, respite, therapy and help with managing endings. Reviews for both children and carers provide a valuable opportunity to identify those areas where additional agency input, providing further training for carers or resources to enable children to pursue leisure interests or develop particular talents, can build on the protective elements in the placement.

One issue that has not yet been mentioned is contact with the birth family. Research indicates that positive contact can be a protective factor for children (Fratter *et al.* 1991) although conflict over contact would clearly contribute to the level of risk. Contact arrangements need to be clear and child-centred, with support available to address any difficulties that arise.

The aim of all these interventions is to enhance the coping resources that are available to the child and the carer(s). If these resources can adequately match the demands and stresses of the placement, the level of risk will, one hopes, be minimised and positive outcomes are more likely to result.

CONCLUSION

All stages in the placement process require an investment in agency time and resources. We need to ensure that these are employed in the most effective manner and, where possible, try to determine what relationship exists between the level and type of intervention and the outcomes for children. This is not a straightforward task as a number of different factors will impact on children's lives. One of the themes throughout this chapter has been the need for assessments of risk to be based on informed judgements. Our knowledge of what interventions are effective may be incomplete but we can ensure that we use what we have, in terms of theory, research findings and practice experience. Our judgements also should be clearly related to the evidence that is available to us. Without adequate information who can determine whether the level of risk will be within acceptable limits? Carers need to be able to make informed judgements about whether the task is right for them and whether a particular child is right for their family. Children also need the opportunity to express their views about their placements and we need to be more effective in listening to them.

There is a danger that a focus on risk can lead to a pre-occupation with the potential negative consequences of a decision. The recent emphasis on recruiting 'safe carers' could result in the development of more and more time-consuming and sophisticated assessments of applicants in the hope that we will eventually be able to 'spot the abuser'. Research evidence on sexual offending suggests that whilst there is useful knowledge to be shared about the strategies offenders use to target and groom children, there is no Holy Grail waiting to be discovered which will enable us to predict with certainty who poses a risk to children. Similarly, the research on disruption provides only a limited number of variables which are carer-related. I am not suggesting we abandon assessment, although the criteria on which judgements are made could be more explicit. However, I would suggest that we give more attention to the management of risk within placements and specifically to enhancing protective factors, to building on strengths and to enabling children and their carers develop the resources they need to make the placement a positive experience.

REFERENCES

Barth, R. and Berry, M. (1988) *Adoption and Disruption Rates, Risks and Responses*. New York: Aldine de Gruyter.

Boushel, M. (1994) 'Keeping safe: strengthening the protective environment of children in foster care.' *Adoption and Fostering 18*, 1, 33–39.

Berridge, D. and Cleaver, H. (1987) *Foster Home Breakdown*. Oxford: Blackwell.

Department of Health (1991) *Patterns and Outcomes in Child Placement*. London: HMSO.

Department of Health (1995) *Looking After Children: Assessment and Action Records*. London: HMSO.

Fahlberg, V. (1994) *A Child's Journey Through Placement*. London: British Agencies for Adoption and Fostering.

Fratter, J., Rowe, J., Sapsford, D. and Thoburn, J. (1991) *Permanent Family Placement: A Decade of Experience*. London: British Agencies for Adoption and Fostering.

Fry, E. (1996) 'Supporting carers to ensure safe caring.' In D. Batty and D. Cullen (eds) *Child Protection: The Therapeutic Option*. London: British Agencies for Adoption and Fostering.

Kanuik, J. (1992) 'The use of relationship in the preparation and support of adopters.' *Adoption and Fostering 16*, 2, 47–52.

Lambert, L. and Streather, J. (1980) *Children in Changing Families*. London: MacMillan.

MacFadyen, S. (1994) *Systemic Assessments*. Barnardo's – unpublished.

National Foster Care Association (1993) *The Foster Care Service – Making it Work*. London: National Foster Care Association.

National Foster Care Association (1994) *Safe Caring*. London: National Foster Care Association.

O'Hara, J. and Hoggan, P. (1988). 'Permanent substitute care in Lothian placement outcomes.' *Adoption and Fostering 12*, 3, 35–38.

Rowe, J., Hundleby, M. and Garnett, L. (1989) *Child Care Now – A Survey of Placement Patterns*. London: British Agencies for Adoption and Fostering.

Smith, G. (1996) 'Reassessing protectiveness.' In D. Batty and D. Cullen (eds) *Child Protection: The Therapeutic Option*. London: British Agencies for Adoption and Fostering.

Thoburn, J. and Sellick, C. (1996) *What Works in Family Placement*. Barkingside: Barnardo's.

Ward, H. (ed) (1995) *Looking After Children: Research into Practice*. London: HMSO.

CHAPTER 4

Risk in Adoption and Fostering

Sheila Byrne

Our early attachments are the cornerstone of our capacity to make and sustain human relationships. When they are interrupted so too are the vital developmental processes that define our perception of self and others. Separating children from their family of origin brings with it risks, tensions and consequent life tasks with far-reaching implications. For separation implies loss and its impact is characterised by a multitude of emotions which may be shared by both child and adult alike, and will almost inevitably resurface from time to time throughout life. Within child care risk is a term commonly associated with physical, sexual or emotional abuse. This chapter approaches the subject from a far broader perspective and is founded on the premise that the concept of risk permeates every aspect of child placement practice and touches all who are involved. The focus will be on those children who are unable to return home and for whom permanent alternative care is necessary whether by fostering or adoption. Using the major stages of the placement process as a framework, it will attempt to draw out selected key areas of risk, acknowledging that many others are omitted, and comment on practice implications in the light of current placement trends. However, the majority of foster care is brief by nature and it therefore seems important to begin by addressing risk factors associated with short-term care and establishing principles which should underpin all services for children whether temporary or permanent.

PLANNING – SHORT-TERM CARE

When a child is separated from their family a situation of crisis exists. Intensive work needs to take place to help the child to make sense of what is happening, to acknowledge their fears and confusions about their situation and to engage the adults in working together towards prompt restoration. We know that the vast majority of looked after children will return home within six months (Department of Health 1993) yet there is another small but significant group for whom short-term arrangements prove to be anything but temporary. It would be foolhardy to suggest that the concept of drift identified by Rowe and Lambert (1973) in their seminal study *Children Who Wait* is no longer valid in current child care. Its more extreme manifestations may be less apparent, but recent inspections of fostering (Department of

Health 1996a) and adoption services (Department of Health 1996b) highlight the critical lack of fostering resources resulting in lack of placement choice combined with inadequate assessment of individual needs and a significant number of children experiencing too many placement moves and unacceptable delays in achieving permanence. There are no grounds for complacency.

Shared ongoing assessment and clear planning are essential tools in re-establishing children with their family of origin. A cohesive child-centred approach will ensure that children's needs and family strengths are identified, agency services activated and agreed tasks undertaken in order to assist restoration. At this crucial stage a major risk for the child is that his or her needs can often be overlooked in the midst of adult issues and concerns. In the case of family groups, individual needs can sometimes be submerged and a shared identity is assigned to siblings which ignores the likelihood of each child having quite different roles, attachments and emotional needs (Wedge and Mantle 1991). Parents are at considerable risk of feeling displaced, powerless and inadequate and skilled work is required to engage them constructively and positively in maintaining attachments, identifying difficulties and working towards resolution. Social work practice, though better at involving extended family members, still tends to focus on parental involvement and change rather than enlisting the potential shared strengths of the wider family network. Ultimately, permanently placing children outside their birth family cannot be morally justified unless a genuine commitment is made to high quality preventive services which aim for reunification. Families have a right to open and honest discussion of the issues, knowledge of services they can expect, a mutual exploration of anticipated change, written agreements and ongoing involvement in the process of decision making. It would be naïve to suggest that given appropriate social work help, every child could return home. Plans need to be effective within the child's timescale and to acknowledge that a small minority of children, despite all efforts, will not be able or safe enough to return.

There are particular risks for black children of African/Caribbean/Asian descent in short-term care. Every child will struggle with the uncertainty and confusion of separation but many such children are temporarily cared for by white carers (including private foster carers) and are therefore separated not only from their family and friends but also from their community and culture. Somehow the commitment to meeting racial, cultural, religious and linguistic needs which is generally prioritised in permanent placements is seen as less important in temporary care. Yet the impact for the black child can be considerable, compounding their loss and isolation and having potential repercussions for further moves. There is an urgent need to ensure a broad range of resources to meet the needs of all children and to recognise that when the only possible resource is a trans-racial placement, supplementary plans need to be made in order to meet important racial, cultural and religious needs.

Family Group Conferences

Working openly and creatively with families demands of agencies a philosophical stance which translates into policy and practice. Family group conferences are a particularly interesting example of innovative work between social services departments and families and a number of agencies are currently testing its usefulness. Its premise is that families themselves are the key to solving problems relating to their children and that their capacity to share issues and find acceptable solutions should be maximised.

Indicators so far have been positive, if realistically cautious. The National Research Project (Marsh and Crowe 1997) aims to evaluate six agency projects. Interim findings (Hughes 1996) highlight the importance of appropriate training and preparation for social workers together with adequate commitment of resources and the value of independent co-ordinators. A closer look at the underlying philosophy (see Ryburn and Atherton 1996) reveals the degree to which long-established values and attitudes are challenged by this approach. It is not a panacea for all child care problems and more evaluative work is needed on outcomes. However, its potential for partnership and empowerment when combined with informed assessment and genuine respect for the wishes and feelings of individual children may have much to teach us.

Concurrent Planning

Another creative approach to work with separated children is Katz's work on concurrent planning which challenges the traditional British practice of sequential planning. Katz (1996) questions how effective this is for children and their families and demonstrates how a US agency has developed a method of early assessment and identification with a goal of working towards reunification while simultaneously developing an alternative permanent placement plan. The aim is to work openly and honestly with parents using written agreements, clear alternatives and time-focused reviews. Meanwhile, the child is placed in a racially and culturally appropriate permanent foster home where, if reunification is not successful, they can stay and move on towards adoption. A fuller appraisal of Katz's ideas will be necessary for the reader but the approach confronts much of our entrenched thinking about the use of fostering resources. Katz's conviction that temporary care is not a positive option for children and that the anxiety and uncertainty inherent in the process is more appropriately contained by the adults rather than the child is hard to dispute.

The principles of concurrent planning may prove especially useful for that small group of children for whom the possibility of returning home seems most unlikely. Appropriate identification requires a detailed knowledge of the child's needs, family strengths and an honest capacity to face the concerns realistically and not to ignore the evidence in terms of prognosis. Katz's worksheets may prove helpful for practitioners in terms of assessing and defining risk. Change is always possible but evidence should be tangible and children's lives cannot be determined by wishful thinking or over-optimism in the face of blatant and long-standing concerns. Most children will appropriately return to their families but a small minority need protection from the risk of drift, continuing upheaval, interrupted attachments and abuse by the very system which purports to protect them.

PREPARATION FOR PERMANENCE

Working with the Child

Once the decision has been made for permanent out of family care, preparation is necessary to ensure that a positive transition can be effected. Whatever the nature of their experience, every separated child will know at some level the devastation of not being able to live with his or her family. This risk to the emotional life of the child should not be underestimated nor should the importance of planned preparatory work to help him or her to begin to work on their inner turmoil. Preparatory work is not solely about life story books or photograph albums, it is a process of engaging with the child and helping them to answer fundamental questions about who they are, why they are not at home and what is happening to them. This takes time, commitment, sensitivity and the capacity to communicate with the child using a variety of mediums.

Children may take with them into a permanent placement a mass of unexpressed confusion and unanswered questions and this in turn puts the new placement at risk as carers strive to build an attachment, but where the child is too busy investing emotional energy in unfinished business. There are certain groups of children especially at risk. Young, particularly pre-verbal, children are often deemed not to understand when their language or cognitive ability is limited and similar assumptions are often made concerning children with learning disabilities. This often says more about the anxiety of professionals in communicating with such children than about the children themselves. Direct work with children is both ongoing and dynamic and the child will continue to work with their personal material throughout their development. Obviously concepts need to be conveyed in age appropriate ways but the important thing is that the worker or carer takes the risk of facing the child's pain and loss and, in doing so, contains it for the child. This, in turn, gives the child a sense of hope and optimism that the possibly traumatic events of their lives are manageable. If we fail to support children in beginning to face their reality in whatever limited way they are able, we risk prolonging their fear, guilt and hopelessness and do them and their families a disservice. Some children may be blocked and too fearful to face the past. Defence mechanisms are vital aspects of our emotional lives and demand a healthy respect (see Harper 1996). Preparatory work is not about forcing children to relive painful memories, it is making available to children channels whereby they can begin to share something of their bewilderment and pain about their fragmented lives. They may choose not to use the channels and that is their right, but to deny them the possibility adds to their burden and risks further alienation.

Working with the Birth Family

Ideally, the child's parents and family will be the best resources to draw on for information about the past. Only they will have the detailed knowledge of the child's experience that will be so useful in later years and their contribution can make the difference between a stark set of facts and a history which is alive and personal. Sometimes it is not possible to engage relatives in this task, but more commonly, insufficient effort is made to actively involve family members in helping children to move on. This work is rarely easy and is sometimes conflictual. For a parent to acknowledge that they are not able to care for their child is immensely painful and distressing, particularly when that decision is made against their wishes. Like the child, adults too need to grieve for the family life that might have been. Sensitive work can acknowledge the pain of parents, which may be displayed in a variety of different ways, and help them to move towards a more proactive and healing involvement. This area of practice is one of the most important in diminishing risk for all involved in permanent placement yet it is often under-valued. In infant adoptions it is commonplace for adopters to meet with birth parents prior to placement and experience shows how positive this is for those concerned. Yet for older children when the climate is likely to be more adversarial and/or the child's circumstances especially complex, efforts to involve relatives are often lacking. Time and skill needs to be available at this crucial time to support family members who in turn may help the child to make the best use of a permanent placement. If anger, resentment and separate agendas perpetuate, this will hold back both the child and the adults from moving forward with their lives.

Birth relatives will value and respond to practitioners who can genuinely support them through the placement process. Most will want to express their wishes and feelings about their child's new family, be involved in the choice of resource, prepare something for the child about their past and share preparatory work with the child which reflects their shared experience. Many would welcome the opportunity, where appropriate, to attend panel to express their views and to meet new carers in order to pass on information, diminish the element of fantasy, feel reassured about their child's future life and negotiate mutually agreeable contact arrangements. Skilled work can often diminish the potential for conflict and avoid antagonistic positions which are always unhelpful. This is not achieved without a considerable commitment on the part of the social worker and sometimes an independent worker may be the best person to offer acceptable support. To work effectively with birth families implies letting go of the judgemental attitudes that can exist within placement work and that result in punitive and exclusive practice which is not in the interests of either the child or the adults concerned. This is not to imply that every relative will necessarily be able to participate positively in this way but there should at least be the opportunity to do so. Bearing in mind previous comments regarding the value of family group conferences, there may be lessons to learn in terms of a model which enables concerned adults to meet together at an early stage with an independent co-ordinator in order to clarify aspects of preparation, information giving and, where appropriate, contact. However, care needs to be taken that this does not become an adult-focused exercise. The carefully ascertained wishes, feelings and interests of the child should always be the central focus of the discussion and mediation skills may prove a valuable professional resource to utilise in potentially conflictual situations.

Working with Carers

Many children who require permanent alternative families bring with them painful and difficult histories which have considerable impact upon their development. Trauma and abuse can leave deep scars and result in a fragmented emotional response. Highly dysfunctional family relationships may result in well established but unhealthy behaviour patterns that are resistant to change and far from easy to manage. Parenting such children is therefore a major undertaking. The preparation process aims to enable applicants to weigh up the risks entailed and come to a decision about whether or not to proceed. Similarly, the social worker, on behalf of the agency, is assessing the likely risks from a professional perspective and ultimately whether or not to recommend the acceptance of the application. This raises questions concerning the effectiveness of preparation in terms of achieving these ends and minimising the level of risk for both child and new family.

Looking to evaluative research for help in this area proves disappointing as it is noticeable by its absence. Consumer accounts of the process indicate that while there are aspects which are clearly valued by applicants, we also know that others experience preparation as daunting (Thoburn, Murdoch and O'Brien 1986). Thus their response will often reflect what they perceive to be the expectations of the agency, knowing that to meet these expectations will enable them to achieve their desired objective of a placement. This is not a good basis from which to explore risk and agencies struggle to reconcile their legal responsibility with empowering applicants and enabling an honest exploration of the issues. Current practice relies heavily on a fixed combination of group work and home studies and can be hampered by a marked power imbalance, individual value bases and eurocentric attitudes. Some agencies (see Douglas 1996) are incorporating valuable assessment tools such as those drawn from Fahlberg (1994) and applying the learning from systemic assessment to preparatory work with carers. One radical but important question seems to be whether or not social workers are really the best people to facilitate the personal reflection and self evaluation that seems such an essential part of the task. This may require a fundamental change of role and attitude which challenges social workers to redefine their skills and contribution in this vital area and, perhaps, to genuinely recognise the potential for co-working with experienced carers. To what degree professionals themselves can take these risks remains to be seen.

Risk is implicit in every aspect of preparation as carers and family members try to make sense of the needs that a child may bring and how they might deal with the impact. Research is not always consistent about successful outcome but some risk factors do emerge, notably where there is a child in the family close in age to the child to be placed. Yet even this widely accepted danger zone needs to be viewed with caution. Current inter-country adoption research (Beckett and Groothues 1997) indicates that close in age placements can be very successful where families are childless or have grown up children and points to the importance of assessing individual needs in specific situations. A wide variety of individuals and couples have demonstrated successful parenting and an open attitude towards potential resources combined with child-focused assessment is important. Other characteristics associated with positive outcomes include good support networks and child-focused adults who enjoy challenges. There is, however, an urgent need for more research evidence to inform practitioners about the relationship between recruitment, preparation and successful outcome. More recent knowledge and practice experience has drawn attention to three particular areas of risk in permanency which are receiving increasing attention.

Attachment

A central issue in placement outcomes is the degree to which the child can build healthy and positive attachments within his or her new family. Very few children in public care will be unattached – most will manifest a range of dysfunctional attachment behaviours described within the insecure/disorganised range (Howe 1995). Their inner working models can be well entrenched and the professional has a key role in minimising associated risk. Their capacity to share a sound understanding of the child's attachment history and behaviours can enable carers to make sense of what is happening and why and support them in devising strategies that will encourage healthier patterns of relating. A number of the children currently needing permanent placement will have had such neglectful/abusive early experience that their capacity to modify their behaviour may be quite limited, indeed a small minority will find it impossible to tolerate living in a family because of the emotional demands it makes of them. Carers will need help and ongoing support in order to persevere with and best manage challenging behaviours. Research suggests (Howe 1996) that for some it is not until their children reach early adulthood that they begin to see the fruits of their commitment.

Work on inter-generational attachment (Main and Goldwyn 1984) has interesting implications for placement work. It suggests that it is not so much the quality of past experience that determines future parenting outcome but the ability of the adult to reflect accurately and openly on the reality of their own early relationships. Poor early experience may result in a degree of emotional vulnerability, but alongside considerable insight, resilience and determination. Alternatively, it may indicate a variety of risk factors such as denial, dismissiveness and/or high levels of anger regarding early adverse experience that may make the possibility of healthy attachment less realistic. This may be relevant both for work with birth families as well as with permanent carers and current work is underway (Coram's Research Unit, ongoing) which looks at the relationship between the attachment history of adopters and that of the child placed with them.

Openness

As more and more separated children are continuing to maintain contacts with significant others the concept of openness has become central, particularly within adoption. Fratter (1996) found that both adopted children and their placements can benefit from ongoing links with important attachment figures, while Hughes (1995) reports mixed views on direct contact from birth parents. Placements can be jeopardised when automatic assumptions are made concerning the benefits of direct contact. Each child's situation is unique and their individual interests should be the determining factor in ascertaining contact needs. Experience suggests that successful outcomes are associated with an absence of conflict between the adults concerned and where clarity exists around roles and responsibilities. There can be a danger of applicants paying lip service to contact needs and agreeing to minimal arrangements simply to achieve a placement. Yet contact is never static; just as we change, grow and develop throughout life so too do our relationships and contacts. What may be appropriate now may be very different in five, ten, fifteen years time. Applicants need to acknowledge this and to recognise that openness is not only about accepting life story books or exchanging annual letters; rather it is an underlying attitude that respects the individual history of each child and that this history, however distressing, remains an intrinsic part of the child. Whatever the child's age, one of the most important tasks for the carer will be to help them to integrate their past with their present in order to build a healthy, whole future. This will involve helping the child and exploring their individual story, sometimes with direct or indirect contact. The attitudes of new carers will be critical in facilitating this process and supporting the child in their ongoing journey. The ongoing psychological aspects of adoption, which are now more clearly understood, must inform practice in this area.

Safe Caring

The increasing numbers of sexually abused children requiring placement has raised awareness of both the complex needs of these children and the potential ramifications for carers. Agencies are now far more alert to the importance of recruiting protective families and developing assessment programmes that allow salient issues to be thoroughly explored. Communication, power, openness, values, attitudes, family boundaries, support networks and discussion of sexual issues are all topics that will play a part in assessing for safe caring. Sexualised behaviours can impact dramatically within a family and, as well as the need to safeguard vulnerable children, it is essential to inform and assist carers to protect themselves and their families (National Foster Care Association 1994). Providing a healing and safe environment for an abused child is far from easy and will often require additional support services. While sexual abuse has received most attention in terms of agency practice, it is important to remember the ways in which emotionally hurt children can powerfully act out their inner conflicts and the implications of this for daily management. The best prepared carers can be taken aback by the depth of their reaction to confused, angry manipulative behaviour. The risks for both adult and child are immense and cannot be underestimated. It is salutary to note the rise in number of child protection investigations and complaints procedures relating to permanent placements. Minimising risk implies ensuring that the internal strengths exist within the family but also that external supports are in place and available when needed. Carers cannot be expected to care for our most vulnerable children and young people without a range of appropriately skilled support services to help them.

LINKING

Linking can be a stressful time for all involved. The level of emotional investment is high and carers may often find it difficult to really hear and absorb detailed information about the child. It is therefore especially important that adequate time is built in for carers and workers to reflect together on the child's history and needs in order that informed decisions can be made about proceeding. Creative and varied ways of conveying information need to be employed. These should not rely solely on verbal discussion of written material but also utilise visual aids such as flow charts to show the impact of change in the lives of children and ensure that carers have the opportunity to meet as many key people in the child's life as possible. The rapport between the adults can make all the difference to a successful outcome. It is particularly useful for new carers to meet birth family members and begin to create a realistic picture of the child and their story for themselves. These meetings can often be a useful means of dispelling hidden agendas and set the tone for working co-operatively in the future, particularly if contact is planned. Clarity is necessary about the needs of the child and the strengths and vulnerabilities of the resource. Compromise is often necessary but it is important to acknowledge it in order to build in appropriate compensatory action or support systems.

INTRODUCTIONS

Once introductions begin they often take on a life of their own. It is important that all involved are prepared and supported throughout the process as each will have their own feelings and responses to work through. Risks at this time often centre on hasty decision making that may be premature. This is a time of great significance and such potentially life-changing decisions need to be made thoughtfully and with due consideration. The purpose of introductions is to allow the child and the new family quality time together where they can begin to test out the possibility of building mutual relationships. This time needs to be planned, facilitated and reviewed in the light of identified needs.

Introductions, by their very nature, will always contain a large element of falseness but, despite the limitations, the professional task is to reflect with the child and family as they begin to know each other and test out the possibility of a shared commitment. Honesty is important yet difficult. Much is invested in making the introductions successful and disruption experience shows us that carers and workers can sometimes feel unease but feel unable to say so. Hopes and fears are part of every new relationship but unless they are shared they cannot be worked with. They may be resolved in the passage of time – alternatively they can simmer or even fester and serve to undermine the placement at a later stage.

One further risk needs to be mentioned. Often children who have experienced considerable trauma or deprivation will move into short-term care and make marked progress in many areas of their development. There is a real danger of social workers focusing on this encouraging and positive aspect and minimising the impact of the child's history and early life. Progress in temporary care can be deceptive and when children move into permanent families a very different picture can emerge. The stakes are far higher for all concerned and permanent relationships are implicitly characterised by different expectations and commitments. When emotional demands are made of the child, earlier hurts can be reactivated. We know enough about the impact of emotional deprivation to know that many children can only begin to face their pain when they feel safe enough to do so. Professionals need to be wary of colluding with over-optimistic perceptions in the face of disturbing past experience. This places both carers and child at risk when commitments to permanence are made without a full understanding of the long-term implications of early deprivation.

PLACEMENT

There can sometimes be a temptation to relax once a placement is made, yet this is the time when a vital phase of work begins. In time, relationships begin to be forged, real selves emerge, commitments are tested and old hurts emerge. Carers and child need to be heard and supported as they struggle to build vital connections once the early adjustment phase has passed. A variety of supports may be needed in order to maintain their placements and ideally these should be discussed prior to placement. It is not helpful to wait until crises occur before enlisting outside help. Perhaps the best and most inexpensive support comes from other carers, especially those who are experienced and can offer invaluable encouragement and a depth of understanding which is impossible for most professionals. Such support networks should be built in to every agency's approach but so too should a commitment to adequate financial help, respite care (and not only for children with disabilities), ongoing skills training and access to specialist therapeutic provision when necessary. Table 4.1 (Douglas 1996) attempts to outline the level of risk/complexity associated with children of different ages and experience combined with carers' qualities and support required. We should not expect families to care for our most vulnerable children without the appropriate help to do so.

DISRUPTION

Disruption will always be part of child placement and this is one of the hardest risks for those involved to contemplate. Research can present a confusing picture as individual studies have used varied definitions and considered different types of placement. However, there are some generally agreed factors which certainly increase risk – of which age is the most important. Generally, the placement of very young children is felt to be very successful with approximately three per cent disrupting (Fratter et al. 1991). However, disruption rates rise considerably for the older child. In their summary of research into permanent placement (both fostering and adoption), Sellick and Thoburn (1996) conclude that one in ten of those placed at five, one in five of those placed at seven/eight and almost fifty per cent of eleven/twelve-year-olds will disrupt. Other risk factors are behavioural and emotional difficulties, a history of abuse and/or neglect and being placed apart from siblings (Fratter et al. 1991). When we consider the small group of children currently needing

Table 4.1

	Low risk/complexity	Medium risk/complexity	High risk/complexity
Child factors	Good enough early parenting. Not too extreme behaviour. Evidence of capacity to form good attachments and grow and develop. Child under 10	Poor early parenting. Significant behaviour problems. More limited capacity to form attachments and modify behaviour. Child under 10	Very poor early parenting. Severe behavioural problems. Persistence of these problems over time, despite sensitive caring. Lack of attachment. Child 10+ on placement
Basis of placement	Adoption	Fostering/adoption	Fostering/residential treatment
Essential qualities required by families	Relevant experience/evidence of understanding child's needs. Ability to use support. Acceptance of difference in foster/adoptive parenting. Safe caring.	As low risk plus: flexibility and ability and willingness to adjust expectations of the child. Ability to find satisfaction in small increments of improvement.	As before plus perseverance, commitment, sense of humour and tolerance of child's rejection. Ability to delay gratification.
Support package required	Adoption allowance. Access to social work support as needed. Appropriate specialist help. Access to support group. Access to ongoing training, e.g. behavioural management techniques. Active involvement from adoption agency may not be required for long periods of time. Support reactivated at key transitions, e.g. adolescence. Reunion with birth parents.	As low risk plus: specific specialist help, e.g. in education. Respite care. Therapy. Mediation re: openness.	Carers as key elements of support in package of care that may involve respite, therapy and residential treatment.

permanent placements it is clear that the risk factors for the majority are considerable. Minimising that risk implies careful attention to the assessment, planning and good practice issues previously outlined, but disruption will never be eliminated and children, carers and indeed workers need to be aware of its implications. Experience shows how devastating an impact disruption can have on the lives of those concerned. Yet, as with other painful life events, it can also help us to learn about ourselves and more especially about the needs of the child. Many children and carers go on to make successful placements following a disruption but the pain and guilt that permeate when placements end unexpectedly do need to be sensitively worked with and are well documented (Fitzgerald 1990, Smith 1994).

POST PLACEMENT

There is a substantial body of evidence (see Brodzinskey and Schechter 1990) concerning the long-term psychological impact of adoption and this is reinforced by the shared experience of birth parents and adoptees as reported in many studies. Some of this will relate to exclusive adoption where children were completely severed from their birth family and subsequently struggled with profound identity issues compounded by lack of information and the previously closed and secretive nature of adoption. In today's more open climate many children, though not all, will maintain some contacts with family members and hopefully this will help them to gradually absorb the circumstances of their story. For others, contact has proved so distressing, undermining or simply unsafe that it has had to be terminated. Even when contact is in the interests of the child it is not always easy and needs to worked at in common with most other relationships. Contact needs may well change over time according to the wishes, feelings and life circumstances of those involved. Re-negotiation may be necessary in order to respond to different needs and situations and sometimes professionals will be needed in order to help those involved agree the best way forward.

Whether fostered or adopted, carers and children will need access to supportive services. Their availability is an important sign to the family that agencies recognise that separation, and particularly adoption, can impact across the life cycle and that responsive services are at hand. Foster carers will hopefully be actively engaged with the agency in regularly reviewing the placement and the needs of those involved. Sadly, adopters or carers with residence orders can sometimes feel isolated and abandoned as they strive to identify resources that can help them with difficulties. Placements are often at risk in the long term because the developmental progress of the child brings new challenges at different times for both child and family. Cognitive and emotional development enable a deeper exploration of the reasons for separation which may evoke painful memories and feelings. Adolescence is a turbulent period for most young people but for separated youngsters it is a time when many earlier conflicts resurface and control, autonomy and identify can become major battlegrounds. The value of skilled child placement consultation and/or supportive peer networks, respite care and therapeutic provision cannot be underestimated.

Even in adulthood the pain of separation recurs – especially at life's major points such as marriage, childbirth, divorce, death of a parent, mid-life. At such times personal review is common and for adoptees this can often lead to a need for additional information and for some a wish to trace birth relatives. Self-help groups can be vital supports to the different parties involved in adoption at this potentially stressful time. The grief and loss of birth family members is frequently underestimated and attempts to gain appropriate information about separated relatives are sometimes met with a less than helpful professional response. Similarly, for adults fostered as children and subsequently seeking more information about their history, gaining access to records can be a daunting task. Record keeping requirements are not as stringent as in adoption and consequently vital information can either be missing or destroyed. This points to the necessity for detailed history taking at an early stage and for the safe and confidential collating of records. Separated adults lose enough – their right to factual information about their history should be a priority, for without it their sense of self is threatened.

CONCLUSION

Separating a child from his or her family of origin is a hazardous undertaking. Most will return promptly, but for a small minority alternative family care will provide them with their best chance of security and stability. Ensuring positive outcomes is not easy and there is much to learn. There is however a growing body of research and practice experience to help practitioners in weighing the risks which are so prevalent in this area of work. Child placement is about welcoming, joining and healing. It is also about losing, grieving and missing an intrinsic part of oneself. Such a juxtaposition will always present risks and challenges and require a skilled professional response which acknowledges the multiplicity of needs involved while maintaining a clear focus on the interests of the child.

REFERENCES

Beckett, C. and Groothues, C. (1997) Forthcoming article in Adoption & Fostering.

Brodzinsky, D. and Schechter, M. (eds) (1990) The Psychology of Adoption. Oxford: Oxford University Press.

Department of Health (1993) Children Act Report. London: HMSO.

Department of Health (1996a) Inspection of Local Authority Fostering 1995–6 National Summary Report. London: HMSO.

Department of Health (1996b) For Children's Sake: An SSI Inspection of Local Authority Adoption Services. London: HMSO.

Douglas, C. (1996) 'A model of assessment and matching.' In R. Philips and E. McWilliam (eds) After Adoption. London: BAAF.

Fahlberg, V. (1994) A Child's Journey through Placement. London: BAAF.

Fitzgerald, J. (1990) Understanding Disruption. London: BAAF.

Fratter, J. (1996) Adoption with Contact. London: BAAF.

Fratter, J., Rowe, J., Sapsford, D. and Thoburn, J. (1991) *Permanent Family Placement: a Decade of Experience.* London: BAAF.

Harper, J. (1996) 'Recapturing the past: alternative methods of life story work in adoption and fostering.' *Adoption and Fostering 20*, 3, 21–28.

Howe, D. (1995) *Attachment Theory for Social Work Practice.* Basingstoke: Macmillan.

Howe, D. (1996) *Adopters on Adoption.* London: BAAF.

Hughes, B. (1995) 'Openness and contact in adoption – a child centred perspective.' *Adoption and Fostering 25*, 6, 729–747.

Hughes, G. (1996) 'Implications for agency practice.' In K. Morris and J. Tunnard (eds) *Messages from UK Practice and Research.* London: Family Rights Group.

Katz, L. (1996) 'Permanency action through concurrent planning.' *Adoption and Fostering 20*, 2, 8–13 (Training materials developed by Linda Katz are available from Manchester Adoption Society, 47 Bury New Road, Sedgley Park, Manchester M25 9JY. Tel. 0161 773 0973).

Main, M. and Goldwyn, R. (1984) 'Predicting rejection of her infant from the mother's representation of her own experience: implications for the abused-abusing intergenerational cycle.' *Child Abuse and Neglect 8*, 203–217.

Marsh, P. and Crowe, G. (1997) FRG National Research Project Report on Family group Conferences – forthcoming.

National Foster Care Association (1994) *Safe Caring.* London: NFCA.

Rowe, J. and Lambert, L. (1973) *Children Who Wait.* London: ABAA.

Ryburn, M. and Atherton, C. (1996) 'Family group conferences: partnership in practice.' *Adoption and Fostering 20*, 1, 16–23.

Sellick, C. and Thoburn, J. (1996) *What Works in Family Placement?* Ilford: Barnardos.

Smith, S. (1994) *Learning from Disruption – Making Better Placements.* London: BAAF.

Thoburn, J., Murdoch, A. and O'Brien, A (1986) *Permanence in Child Care.* Oxford: Basil Blackwell.

Wedge, P. and Mantle, G. (1991) *Sibling Groups in Social Work.* Aldershot: Avebury.

CHAPTER 5

One of the Hardest Jobs in the World
Attempting to Manage Risk in Children's Homes

Hilary Owen

INTRODUCTION

The 1990s have seen the public expression of an unprecedented amount of concern about children living in children's homes. It is becoming difficult to keep track of the numbers of inquiries set up to investigate abuse of children in residential care: Staffordshire, Sheffield, Leicester, Northumberland, Islington, Clwyd, Cheshire and Kirklees have all come to the attention of the media. Hundreds of children have been abused in a setting which is meant to keep them safer and healthier than they were at home. Unfortunately, it is also becoming difficult to keep track of the numbers of Department of Health reports produced in an attempt to allay public concern and prevent abuse in the future: the Wagner report (1987), the Utting report (1991), the Howe report (1992), the Warner report (1992). The newspapers in the summer of 1996 have been full of articles about abuse being investigated in children's homes in Merseyside and Cardiff (see, for example, *The Guardian* 12/6/96, 7/9/96, 18/9/96). The government, in response to these most recent concerns, has even commissioned another report: in June of 1996 Sir William Utting was asked by the Secretary of State for Health, Stephen Dorrell, to 'review the safeguards against harm to children in residential care' introduced following the Children Act (1989) and 'assess whether they are the most effective that can realistically be designed'. Mr Dorrell admitted that 'it has become clear...that the scale of abuse and of abuse risks was higher than generally appreciated' (Dorrell: PQ 3731/1995/1996).

Some would say that the government's failure to appreciate the scale of the problem was less innocent than they care to admit. For example, Allan Levy QC, who chaired the 'Pindown' inquiry in 1990–1991, said in a recent article in *The Independent*:

> Scandal after scandal has surfaced since the pioneering 'pindown' inquiry in Staffordshire five years ago. Recommendations have been made, committees and support groups set up, and much said by politicians... The Government in particular must provide a practical lead in dealing with a national problem requiring oversight, co-ordina-

tion and action. The findings and recommendations of numerous inquiries have gone largely unheeded. (22/4/96)

The fact is that children living in children's homes are still extremely vulnerable to many different dangers, not just abuse by members of staff. In considering the many risks, it is easy to feel that there may be some homes which are very dangerous places indeed and these should not be allowed to continue. Such places may well exist, but the government is unlikely to be able to identify them because of its failure to monitor practice in residential childcare. The Warner report was particularly important because it reported the findings of the first and only 'comprehensive national survey of the characteristics, staffing and employment practices in local authority and independent sector children's homes' (Department of Health 1992). In *The Guardian* on 19/6/96, Norman Warner wrote:

> Our report...made 83 recommendations... If fully implemented, these recommendations would have made children's homes safer and better places to live. But the government does not know how much has changed since 1992 because there has never been any systematic follow-up.

In the intervening four years, the only action the government has taken is, first, to set up a temporary 'Residential Support Force' (now disbanded) to assist local authorities in implementing the recommended changes and, second, to write to local authorities asking for information about the changes they have made.

In this chapter, I shall describe potential risks in children's homes and how they can affect children if they are realised. I shall include information about children's emotional responses to their experiences in homes from the literature and also from my own discussions with children and young people as a social services Child Protection Co-ordinator.

Whilst the government has not ensured that the recommendations of reports have been implemented, even where these relate directly and specifically to action only the government itself can take (see, in particular, the Warner report), those recommendations themselves, coming in report after report, have been consistent, detailed and practical. I shall describe how senior managers could reduce risk to many children in their care significantly, if only they had the proper resources and commitment to develop their services and train their staff in accordance with these recommendations. The failure so far of government and local authorities to ensure that this is achieved rightly causes immense concern. However, individual residential care staff, those in charge of homes and professionals from different agencies who may contribute to the welfare, health and education of the residents, can still improve their own professional performance by ensuring that they take likely risks seriously and understand fully the impact their practice has on children. I shall detail how this can be done. It is important to recognise, however, that safety in children's homes will only be achieved when the government, local authorities and care staff all work together in a co-ordinated and committed way.

THE RISKS

It is possible, from inquiry reports and from the media, to identify very clearly the kinds of harm to which children in homes may be at risk. My own experience in administering Sheffield Area Child Protection Committee's inquiry 1992 into the employment of a paedophile in its children's homes (Poupard and Jordan 1993) assists this identification. I suggest the following classification:

1. Not receiving appropriate emotional support.

2. Sexual abuse by paedophiles who are staff members.

3. Physical abuse by staff.

4. Abuse by other residents.

5. Sexual abuse by paedophiles who gain access to the residents of children's homes as 'friends'.

6. Being lured into prostitution.

7. Not receiving a proper education.

8. Not receiving appropriate health care.

9. Losing touch with family.

Some of these kinds of harm may well be more likely to occur than others, but it is difficult to judge relative likelihood because of the lack of relevant research and data collection. One could guess, for example, that the risk of losing contact with family members may be greater than the risk of being sexually abused by a staff member, but there is no evidence to support this. In addition, one could guess that certain kinds of harm listed may be more serious than others, depending upon the circumstances and the particular children affected.

Whilst it may seem a particularly negative and disheartening exercise to list the risks in this way, it is essential that those with responsibility for children's homes at all levels are fully aware of them. It is quite possible for one resident to experience several of these types of harm in the course of their time in residential care; there are many young people who have experienced all of them.

Before going on to address each of these risks, how they can affect children and how they can be reduced, it is important to recognise that there are several characteristics of the workforce in children's homes which impede progress generally. These are all detailed in the Warner Report (Department of Health 1992). First, '…80 per cent of care staff and 40 per cent of heads of homes in local authority homes have no social work or other relevant qualification' (p.114) – it is not possible to discover whether this situation has improved in the last four years. Second, '…there are difficulties in recruiting staff because of the unattractive image of the work' (p.25) – it means that local authorities sometimes use 'agency' staff to cover vacancies and absences. This has its own risks: 'About 15 per cent of local authorities made no background checks for agency staff' (p.36). Third, '…local authority care staff had longer working weeks than their equivalents in other types of work' (p.28) – some employers have addressed this issue but, again, it is impossible to know how many and to what extent. Fourth, care staff in children's homes receive poor supervision: 'Many employing authorities report that the bulk of supervision in children's homes is "informal". By this we can only assume that they mean it is un-planned, ad hoc and irregular.' (p.95).

REDUCING THE RISKS

Not Receiving Proper Emotional Support

This particular risk, I would argue, needs to be considered first because the effects of many of the other types of harm can be amplified by it. The Department of Health, in its recent publication *Child Protection: Messages from Research* (1995), introduces the idea of some children experiencing a 'low warmth, high criticism' environment at home with their families, and this exacerbating the effects of abuse and making it harder for the children to recover from it (p.19). I would argue that this concept can be very useful in looking at the quality of care offered in children's homes. The 'Pindown' regime described in Allan Levy and Barbara Kahan's report (1991) could be seen as a particularly extreme version of it. They report a description of a meeting about a child's progress in one of Staffordshire's children's homes: '...nothing positive was said about the child, all the bad things...he had been naughty but every single thing he had done badly was brought up in totally derogatory terms...' (p.97). They further state (and one wonders with how much anxiety):

> It has been suggested 'that "Pindown" by any other name probably exists the length and breadth of the country and is probably more prevalent than anyone would officially care to admit.' We received no such admissions in evidence. The practice of Pindown has ceased in Staffordshire. If it exists under any other name elsewhere it should, in our view, be summarily terminated. (p.169)

Certainly, it has been my own experience that elements of Pindown have existed in other parts of the country: practices like keeping children in their pyjamas, or in their slippers, for extended periods, sometimes days on end, so they cannot abscond have been quite common ones, as has making children have a bath or a shower on entering or returning to the children's home.

Following the Pindown report, the Department of Health published with the Children Act (1989) its volume of detailed guidance and regulations relating to residential care (Department of Health 1991). It is in many ways a direct attempt to ensure that any elements of Pindown which do exist nation-ally are eradicated.

Given that many residents of children's homes have been abused in some way, in some cases immediately prior to admission, if we apply the idea of the low warmth, high criticism environment making it more difficult for a child to recover from abuse, we can see how important it is that a children's home provides good emotional support to its residents. In addition, The Department of Health (1991) guidance indicates that: 'Many children in homes need to experience care which compensates for the loss of attention and security they would otherwise receive through the direct care of their parents.' (p.16).

The advice to residential care staff and their managers which this document contains regarding how to make children feel valued and cared for is excellent as a starting point for creating the 'high warmth, low criticism' environment necessary for recovery from trauma. There is an emphasis on ensuring that the way a children's home is managed allows residents to exercise individual choice and to benefit from opportunities. Staff are to be encouraged to promote a child's integrity. Simple things like the way a child is taken shopping for personal belongings, or the extent of their involvement in planning meals, can add or detract from their feelings of self-worth. A particularly helpful piece of general advice is given in the guidance:

> Where it is not possible for the child's own parents to fulfill the role of interested and supportive parents the care staff should assume the role. They should observe the child carefully so that they have a sound understanding of his strengths and also those areas in which he has difficulties. They should recognise and applaud a young person's achievements and encourage him to take pride in his successes. Similarly, when a young person encounters disappointments staff need to provide sympathetic support and encouragement to persevere. (p.22)

Sexual Abuse by Staff who are Paedophiles

Sexual abuse by a staff member in a children's home will undoubtedly have many of the effects upon a child which we have come to associate with every kind of sexual abuse: fear, low self-esteem, self-disgust, possible self-mutilation, running away, thoughts of suicide, post-traumatic stress disorder, clinical depression, anxiety and the possibility of becoming an abuser. One can imagine the desperation a child might experience having been abused at home if s/he is then brought to a children's unit which can provide only low warmth and high criticism, rather than simple kindness. However, there are some characteristics unique to sexual abuse by a staff member in this setting. Staff and managers need to be aware of them at all times so that any abuse being perpetrated by a member of staff can be recognised quickly and harm limited. First, paedophiles who are senior members of staff can manipulate work rotas and sleeping-in duties to ensure that they have access alone to the children they favour. In a recent newspaper article an abusive residential care worker described his 'modus operandi':

> I manipulated the staff doing every sleep-in… The staff thought nothing of seeing me around the school at night… A lot of the staff there were women; it's their second job and they treat it as a very happy holiday. Come twenty-to-ten, it's getting to knocking off time at night. I used to say, 'Don't worry, I'll sort that for you. I'm on sleep-in anyway…' I was manipulating everybody really – the school rules, the staff and obviously the victims. (Dean, *The Guardian* 6/11/96)

The paedophile may well choose his victims carefully by ensuring, possibly by reading the children's files, that they are extremely vulnerable – perhaps because of previous abuse, learning difficulties, communication difficulties or because they are unsure about their own sexuality. They will be both compliant and unable to raise the alarm. Any of these vulnerabilities can damage a child's credibility with police officers, Crown Prosecution Service solicitors and courts. The children themselves will feel completely trapped and powerless. They may feel unable to talk to other staff or their field social worker, if they have one, because they have had experience of information about themselves being shared. Children who do not attend school regularly, or who have education provided on the premises, may well have no other trusted adult to talk to. A paedophile may well have targeted a child because this is the case. If the paedophile has manipulated the situation so that he is the child's residential keyworker with the responsibility to ensure all the child's needs are met, he can control the child's access to medical treatment. If a child plucks up the courage to talk to someone in authority about abuse, the risks to his/her safety multiply if s/he is not believed and is returned to the 'care' of the abuser. In these circumstances, absconding may well be the only option the child sees to escape the abuse. A child who has also been abused at home is then placed at high risk; where does s/he go for refuge?

There are many things which can be done to lessen significantly the risk of sexual abuse by staff members. Employers can ensure that they check the criminal records of all staff members on being appointed. They can also check the Department of Health's own Consultancy Service, which holds details of individuals who have been dismissed for misdemeanours and unprofessional conduct whilst working with children. The Department of Health can issue, as recommended by the Warner Report, guidance to employers about the circumstances in which individuals should be referred to the Service; there have been many instances over the years of employers allowing individuals to resign as an alternative to facing disciplinary procedures. These people have simply gone on to seek work of a similar nature in other areas. Employers should adopt the policy of not destroying any records of disciplinary proceedings relating to children's workers. Employers must ensure that where they use agency staff to cover shortages, their records have been checked – rather than simply assuming the agency will have done so. The police do not have the time to attend to all the record checks requested of them, and have to be selective about the organisations they respond to, so it may well be that negotiations have to take place between local authorities and police forces to ensure requests for checks are responded to within a practicable timescale. Employers can exercise rigour in the way they recruit care staff: a full employment history can be requested from applicants and checked.

Employers can ensure that residential care staff receive training in recognising the symptoms of child abuse and in how to refer suspicions appropriately for investigation by field social work staff and police officers. Some employers have made it a disciplinary offence knowingly not to 'blow the whistle' on abusive staff members. They should certainly develop procedures through their local Area Child Protection Committee to ensure that all agencies will co-operate well in the referral and investigation of this sort of abuse.

As required by the Department of Health (1991) guidance, a telephone should be provided for residents to use in private so that they have the means at hand to request assistance from outside the children's home (p.13).

Employers can implement a policy that avoids the situation where a sole member of staff is on duty. Managers can make sure that staff rotas are adhered to and that no one person dominates decision making about them. They can also make sure that children are referred appropriately for medical treatment or therapy.

As indicated earlier, absconding is a very realistic option for a child who feels trapped by an abuser. Many young adults, describing their past experiences in care, have described the horror they felt when their absconding was simply assumed by care workers and field social workers to be part of their delinquent behaviour, often without question, and they were returned to the care of the person abusing them. Tragically, they often mention the lack of a kind and committed person to approach for help; adults they do remember as being kind have often only demonstrated common decency towards them and one decent act has been amplified in the young person's memory. Residential care staff should never assume that a child is delinquent and incorrigible but should instead consider that there may be a good reason for their behaviour and remain alive to the possibility that the child needs help. Obviously, if a care worker shows consistent kindness to a child, the child will be much more likely to seek help from them when in distress – simply making a good relationship with a child and behaving honourably towards them reduces the risk of sexual abuse by other staff members.

Physical Abuse by Staff

The risk of physical abuse by staff in children's homes is, I believe, one of the most difficult risks to manage – perhaps because it has a variety of causes, as opposed to sexual abuse. In a home for disabled children, many of whom are highly dependent upon staff for all their physical needs, it is almost impossible to manage.

The sorts of situations in which physical abuse typically takes place are: first, where a member of staff uses force, overtly or covertly, as a matter of routine, to elicit obedience from children; second, where a sex abuser uses force to ensure compliance and secrecy; third, where a staff member who is not normally violent ceases, for whatever reason, to be able to cope with the work and loses control of their behaviour when a child is being particularly demanding; and fourth, where a child is justifiably being restrained because they are causing danger to themselves or to others, or are damaging property, and the restraint is too severe. Unfortunately, there are occasions when 'restraint' is used as an excuse for overt abuse. Where disabled children are concerned, 'opportunities' to abuse are multiplied many times: some children need mechanical restraint as a matter of course to avoid, for example, falling out of a chair and many need to be 'handled' to a high degree by staff because they cannot feed themselves dress themselves, go to the toilet themselves or move around a room by themselves to participate in activities. Many disabled children are unable to communicate well, or use language, and therefore cannot complain if they are abused in any way.

It is possible to alleviate the risk of physical abuse by creating clear procedures and good management structures, and providing training for staff and sufficient high quality supervision of staff. This obviously involves committing resources to staff development, something which employers have not been able to do very well in recent years. Every establishment should be clear about what sort of physical contact is appropriate between staff and residents and what is not, and should have a policy on what restraint is and when it can be used. Staff should be given the opportunity to receive training on restraint. Parents and children should be told what the policy is before the child is placed. As a basis, the Department of Health (1991) guidance on residential care has a helpful section on 'prohibited measures' which includes:

Corporal punishment
The use of corporal punishment is not permitted in residential child care establishments. The term 'corporal punishment' should be taken to cover any intentional application of force as punishment including slapping, throwing of missiles and rough handling. It would also include punching or pushing in the heat of the moment in response to violence from young people. It does not prevent a person taking neces- sary physical action, where any other course of action would be likely to fail, to avert an immediate danger of personal injury to the child or another person, or to avoid immediate danger to property. The use of 'holding' which is a commonly used, and often helpful, containing experience for a distressed child is not excluded. (p.17)

With regular good supervision, managers should be in a position to pick up on particular stresses which staff members are experiencing and which are having a detrimental effect on their relationships with residents and putting them at risk. Problems can be addressed at an early stage to avoid crises. Unfortunately, it is possible that some care workers are still obliged to work longer hours than other social work staff, as the Warner report found in 1992, although some employers have acted to remedy this situation.

Disabled children often have particular and highly individual care rou- tines. A high level of communication should be achieved between staff looking after a child and his/her parents so that difficulties can be dealt with in a clear, consistent way which is supported by all the adults involved with the child's care. For example, a child who uses a specially adapted chair may need to be put into that chair in a particular way to avoid discomfort. The child may, on occasion, protest about being in the chair and staff can agree with parents what is to be done when that happens. In this way, if the child sustains bruising whilst at the children's home, it will be possible at least to clarify whether the child was handled appropriately or not.

Disabled children often regularly spend different parts of the week in different places because of school and respite care arrangements. If a child is physically abused it is almost impossible, therefore, to be certain about where the abuse took place. Different establishments are not above arguing about this during the formal investigation process. Many establishments use natural opportunities in the child's routine to carry out and record 'body checks', whilst bathing, for example, which assists in the investigative process, but it is obviously inappropriate for these to occur outside the child's normal care routine.

Where s/he has some communication skills, it is always an excellent idea to involve his/her communication therapist in decisions about whether or not to interview a disabled child who has been abused and then in the interview process itself. Unfortunately, this is not yet common practice.

Abuse by Other Residents

Of all the risks to a child in a home, this one is highly likely to be realised. The Warner report found that in local authority children's homes about one-third of residents had been sexually abused at some point in their lives (p.19). A number of these will go on to become abusers themselves. In addition, some youngsters will be living in children's homes because they are already abusers. This poses incredible difficulties for a local authority trying to plan its residential accommodation for children strategically. If they try to ensure that children who have already been sexually abused are not placed at further risk of abuse, compounding the trauma, this implies that those youngsters who are already confirmed abusers need to be placed away from them in a different unit. This can sometimes mean that other abusers in that unit are then themselves at incredibly high risk of abuse. One abuser can assault all the other residents of a children's home and exert pressure to try and ensure no one discloses what is happening.

It is difficult to manage this level of risk. However, it is possible to go some way towards doing so. Staff should be trained in working with young abusers, where necessary, and in recognising the signs and symptoms of sexual abuse so that further abuse can be prevented. They should have access to specialist support from psychological, psychotherapeutic and psychiatric services, both in terms of professional consultation in relation to the whole group of residents and in terms of obtaining treatment services for individual abusers and victims. Access to specialist health services should be greatly assisted in the future by the requirement placed on local authorities to produce multi-agency service plans for children, and there are moves to use the networks created by area child protection committees to achieve this.

Unfortunately, it is still the case that where care workers bring to the attention of field social workers an incident of suspected abuse of a resident by a resident, low priority is attached to investigating it and children and staff can be in a state of uncertainty and confusion about what should happen for too long. Obviously it is helpful if prompt strategy meetings can be convened under local child protection procedures, to decide on short-term action like where the alleged perpetrator and victim need to be placed whilst the investigation proceeds and how the victim is to be protected until proper plans can be made for the future.

Whilst physical abuse by other residents obviously occurs from time to time, it does not, in my experience, seem to occur as often as sexual abuse. Indeed, there is little specific reference to it in the literature. Obviously, it can be dealt with through normal child protection procedures. The Department of Health guidance (1991) indicates that:

a clear distinction will need to be made between, on the one hand, behaviour which amounts to serious physical assault, intimidation and sexual assault which requires external child protection intervention and possibly criminal investigation and, on the other hand, normal childhood behaviour or sexual exploration which should be dealt with by care staff. (p.33)

A more common risk is of bullying. The guidance indicates that managers should provide training and guidance so that staff know what sort of behaviour is not to be tolerated. Good staff-resident relationships and a good level of monitoring of residents' well-being will mean that some bullying is prevented. Where it does take place, it can be detected quickly. Managers should ensure that strategies are in place for staff to use to prevent further bullying occurring.

Sexual Abuse by Paedophiles who Gain Access to the Residents of Children's Homes as 'Friends'

Occasionally, residential care staff will pick up partial information from young people about adults who have befriended them and whose homes they visit, often staying overnight. It is very easy for paedophiles in the community to target young residents by intercepting them going to and from the home and offering a variety of bribes, like cigarettes or an evening watching videos, drinking beer or eating pizza, to lure them to their homes. The young people may be particularly vulnerable because of the lack of consistent care they have received from anyone and often simply respond to the interest shown in them. They are persuaded to take part in sexual activity either because of the desire to maintain the friendship and the treats or by the offering of small sums of money. It is important, in circumstances where staff suspect young people are seeing adults outside the home who are not family members or family friends, that they share any information between themselves and with other professionals involved with the young people so that a fuller picture of what is going on can be pieced together. If young people are returning to the home with money or gifts, then suspicions may be raised. Once an adult has been identified, then the police can be asked to check their criminal record. If the adult already has a conviction for child abuse, or any of the young people indicate that possibly abusive activities have occurred, then an investigation under Section 47 of the Children Act 1989 can be planned by police, field social workers and residential care staff in an attempt to assess and treat any harm already done and reduce future risk to the young people.

Being Lured into Prostitution

The recently published report on the sexual exploitation of children, *Splintered Lives* (Kelly *et al.* 1995) reports estimates of 80% of rent boys and 50% of young women working as prostitutes in London as having been in local authority care (p.61). Additionally, there are reports of children currently in children's units being drawn into prostitution by local pimps who pretend 'romantic' relationships with the girls (p.61). This, again, can be a difficult risk to address, particularly in the context of police failure to take action on pimps generally and the very justifiable fear that the pimps will ensure by violent means that no one will give evidence against them at the end of the day.

The police can certainly improve the situation by putting more of their resources into attempting to collect independent evidence about pimping activities in their areas themselves rather than having to rely on the evidence of the young people and prostitutes. Local authorities can improve the situation by ensuring that they do not locate children's units in areas known for prostitution. Care staff, as above, can share information about their concerns with fieldwork staff and with the police, so that at the very least, if it is going to be possible to take action, it can be done without delay.

Area child protection committees should develop specific procedures relating to prostitution where children and young people are concerned, which define it firmly as child sexual abuse, and should bring pressure to bear on agencies to co-operate in tackling it. Care staff can be proactive in terms of attempting to reduce other risks which often accompany prostitution, like drug addiction (often a method used by pimps to control prostitutes) and infection with HIV and other sexually transmitted diseases. Educating those young people suspected of being involved to appreciate the risks fully is helpful and there are often specialist services available to assist in this.

Not Receiving a Proper Education

It is a source of great bitterness to many of the young adults who lived in children's homes in the past that their education opportunities were reduced by being there and that their futures have been blighted by the consequent lack of qualifications achieved. I have certainly been approached by individuals who have said 'I don't care so much about the dreadful things that happened to me whilst I was in the homes, I just want some financial compensation so that I can afford to take some exams.' Whilst care staff have a big role in ensuring they have close liaison with teaching staff to ensure that residents are fully supported in school work they are undertaking and activities they are given an opportunity to participate in, it has become evident that Education Authorities are not putting a great deal of commitment into their duty to ensure that children in homes receive education appropriate to their needs. The authors of the Warner report stated 'We have visited homes where children are receiving little or no education because no places could be found for them in local schools.' (p.144). A very recent study from the Who Cares? Trust indicated that up to 75% of children in local authority care leave school with no formal qualifications and that only between 12% and 19% go on to further education, compared with 68% of the general population (Who Cares? 1996).

There are many special difficulties which residents may face, like the disruption to education caused by being moved from placement to placement, low self-esteem getting in the way of proper achievement, poor concentration and difficult behaviours. The Warner report recommended nothing less than local audits of educational needs of children in homes – to be carried out by social services departments and education authorities, a sort of 'starting from scratch' – so that services can be tailored to needs. Again, local authorities have a good opportunity to carry this out as part of their annual planning for children's services.

Not Receiving Appropriate Health Care

It is undoubtedly true to say that a stay in a children's home should provide an excellent opportunity to ensure that a child whose health may well have been neglected at home can be properly assessed and treated. Dental care and eye care can be assured. However, as the Department of Health (1991) guidance on residential care puts it: 'Regrettably there is sometimes a poverty of expectation about the standard of health children in homes should enjoy.' (p.20)

This 'poverty of expectation' extends from routine physical health care, normally received from a GP, to specialist treatment. The situation is exacerbated by changes of placement. Care staff must have close communication with children's parents to ensure they are aware of any specific health problems a child has and to try and ensure continuity of care. Field social workers need to pass on information about the child's health whenever a change of placement is made. GPs who are asked to carry out routine medicals on children whom they do not know who are entering children's homes need to be much more proactive about the sort of care they offer. They need to follow up problems and ensure treatment is provided, rather than simply carrying out a cursory interview or examination and making recommendations. Some local authorities have been reduced to sending a computer print-out of all the children they are responsible for who have been in care for longer than a few months to a nominated Clinical Medical Officer (school doctor) so that they can be certain that at least some medical care has been offered to them.

Just as children in homes have specific education needs, so too they often have specific specialist health care needs relating to their emotional or behavioural difficulties. The Warner report indicates that local authorities and NHS services should co-operate to carry out an audit of health care needs of residents of children's homes to ensure a close match between services provided and services needed.

Losing Touch with Family

One of the main difficulties with a situation where local authorities cannot afford many children's homes, catering for different needs, is that so-called specialist facilities tend to be a long way from a child's home town. One has to remain sceptical about the nature of specialist facilities following the Warner report, which indicated that:

> Respondents to our survey were asked to indicate whether therapeutic methods and techniques were used in their homes. We received a relatively small number of replies...of this small number...a fifth have no access to external professional support. Although the evidence is not conclusive, we are left with an uncomfortable sense that there are homes attempting to practise therapeutic techniques without the necessary skills and competence. (p.144)

However, distance from home and family has always been a problem for some children and often results in absconding. In the past, contact with family members has sometimes been used as a 'privilege' or 'treat' to be withdrawn for poor behaviour. This is now expressly prohibited, along with deprivation of food or sleep (rather like a prison rule book), by the Department of Health guidance on residential care.

The Children Act 1989 and its associated guidance places great emphasis upon the responsibility of social services departments to ensure that in all circumstances where children are living away from home, good quality contact is maintained between children and all relevant family members (not just parents) where this is consistent with the child's welfare. In the vast majority of cases, it will be. The Children Act 1989 is also clear that parents should be enabled to continue to be involved in decision-making about their child's life. I believe field social workers very rarely appreciate the isolation experienced by children living away from home and the motivation to help them keep in touch with relatives diminishes with the distance the social worker has to travel in order to visit or to escort relatives. It is very easy for a field social worker to feel that a child in a home is 'safe' and therefore other 'riskier' cases take priority in a busy caseload. As we have seen, however, the potential risk to children in homes is overwhelming. Social work managers need to ensure that sufficient priority is attached to maintaining a good level of contact with such children. Field social workers themselves need to be proactive about enabling family members to keep in close contact. Residential care staff can assist by encouraging and facilitating frequent telephone and letter contact. They can ensure that when relatives do visit, they are made to feel as comfortable as possible.

LEARNING FROM THE RECENT PAST: A DEBT WE OWE

Before the Children Act 1989, and its clear messages that the child's interests are paramount and that a child's parents must be enabled to retain active responsibility for him/her as long as this is consistent with his/her welfare, children's homes could be grim and lonely places for their residents. Britain has many young citizens who were badly damaged by their experiences in them during the 1970s and 1980s. We now know so much about what went on because they themselves have had the courage to come forward and tell us. As professionals we need to have a clear idea of the sorts of things that happened to them so we can ensure children in homes today have a much better experience. Two young people in particular stand out in my mind and my commitment to reducing the risks in children's homes is greatly strengthened when I remind myself of them. One is the girl, J., who was kept in pindown in Staffordshire during 1984, who 'At times was on a strict regime, the staff refusing to talk to her. She tended to shout out in her sleep and had bad nights.' (Levy and Kahan 1991, p.44). She attempted, though distressed, to maintain her sanity and integrity by reading. The staff log book, remarkable, as excerpted throughout the pindown report, for its incredibly poor spelling and grammar, records astonishment at the fact that she had read 'a *whole* book' (p.44) and then taken two more. She then asked for schoolwork.

The care worker records in the log book that he 'put J. on domestic science. Cleaning kitchen!!' (p.45). The second young person is a woman I spoke to last year who, having been sexually abused by her father, had run away from home in the 1970s at the age of fifteen to London, only to be raped by a pimp. She was picked up by the police for prostitution and returned home to her abusive father. She again ran away. On being picked up again by the police, she was placed in a local authority secure unit. There she was locked in solitary confinement in a room with a bed and a bucket in it. She was denied sanitary protection and had to go to the toilet in the bucket.

Sir William Utting (1991) has the knowledge and experience to make an excellent job of reviewing the safeguards against harm to children in residential care. However, it is difficult to see, particularly following the Warner report, quite what new recommendations can be made. The government had more than enough information about what needs to be done to reduce risks in children's homes before it commissioned Sir William's report. What it lacked was simply the commitment to undertake such a large, complex and expensive piece of work. Sir William's review was commissioned in response to revelations about large-scale sexual abuse of children by staff. However, as we have seen, this is only one of a number of risks, all potentially very damaging. In many ways, Stephen Dorrell is simply buying time by commissioning this review. At the end of the day, the government either improves the lot of residents of children's homes or it does not. The government should be judged by the standards it enshrined in its own Children Act. They are good ones.

REFERENCES

Dean, M. 'A cruel abuse of trust', *The Guardian*, 6 November 1996.

Department of Health (1991) *The Children Act 1989 Guidance and Regulations Vol. 4 – Residential Care*. London: HMSO.

Department of Health (1992) *The Warner Report: Choosing with Care*. London: HMSO.

Department of Health (1995) *Child Protection: Messages from Research*. London: HMSO.

Dorrell, S. Written answer to parliamentary question, PQ 3731/1995/96.

Howe, Lady (1992) *The Quality of Care*. London: HMSO.

Kelly, E., Wingfield, R., Burton, S. and Regan, L. (1995) *Splintered Lives*. Ilford: Barnardo's.

Levy, A. and Kahan, B. (1991) *The Pindown Experience and the Protection of Children*. Stafford: Staffordshire County Council.

Levy, A. Our Dereliction of Duty, *The Independent*, 22 April 1996.

Poupard, S. and Jordan, M. (1993) *A review of Malcolm Thompson's employment by Sheffield City Council 1977–1990*. Sheffield: Area Child Protection Committee.

Utting, W. (1991) *Children in the Public Care*. London: HMSO.

Wagner, Lady (1987) *Residential Care – A Positive Choice*. London: HMSO.

Warner, N. (1992) *Homes fit for Children*. London: HMSO.

Who Cares? (1996) *Who Cares about Education?* London: Who Cares? Trust.

CHAPTER 6

Vulnerable People Taking Risks
Older People and Residential Care

Jacki Pritchard

Every human being takes risks throughout their life and this pattern does not change in the later stages of adulthood. However, people who are involved with the life of an older person (family members, friends, professionals, volunteers) sometimes seem to assume that risks should not be taken and become 'over protective' towards the older person. This chapter will consider the risks which may face an older person who is living in residential care, whether it is a local authority home or a home in the private sector, and discuss ways of managing risk.

DEFINING RISK

For years social workers have used the term 'at risk' but rarely has there been clear definitions or criteria to explain what they mean by this term. The term 'vulnerable' has become more commonplace in recent years due to the increased interest in the concept of 'vulnerable adults'. Many social services departments and health authorities have produced multidisciplinary guidelines for dealing with vulnerable adults who may be at risk of abuse. The Oxford English Dictionary defines vulnerable as: 'that may be hurt, wounded or injured; unprotected, exposed to danger, attack, or criticism.'

A vulnerable adult is defined in many ways by different organisations; some examples are:

> An adult (18 years or over) who, by reason of frailty associated with ageing, physical or sensory illness or disability, mental illness or learning disabilities (mental handicap) is deemed to be at risk if there has been some significant and avoidable lack of care or ill treatment either through commission or omission by him/her self or others.

> (Gloucestershire County Council 1991)

Discrete groups who are most often believed to be in need of protection:

(a) the elderly and very frail

(b) those who suffer from mental illness including dementia

(c) those who have a sensory or physical disability

(d) those who have a learning disability

(e) those who suffer from severe physical illness.

(Association of Directors of Social Services 1991)

A person is vulnerable if by reason of old age, infirmity or disability (including mental disorder within the meaning of the Mental Health Act 1983) he is unable to take care of himself or to protect himself from others. (Law Commission 1993)

...a 'vulnerable person' should mean any person of 16 or over who (1) is or may be in need of community care services by reason of mental or other disability, age or illness and who (2) is or may be unable to take care of himself or herself, or unable to protect himself or herself against significant harm or serious exploitation (Law Commission 1996)

The increased awareness regarding vulnerable adults will implicitly impact on risk taking and risk assessment. If an older person is considered to be 'vulnerable', risk taking may be actively discouraged because it is felt the older person needs to be protected from danger(s). In any risk assessment the older person's wishes and rights must be taken into consideration and not be minimised because other people are being 'over protective' and feel the need to 'rescue' the older person. The concept of vulnerability is important and must be taken into consideration throughout any risk assessment.

We all take risks to achieve something we want and in many situations we experience various emotions whilst taking the risk – enjoyment, excitement, fear, anxiety. If we achieve what we want, we then experience a great sense of achievement and fulfilment and we may get approval and respect from others. Risks are sometimes taken in order to develop skills and knowledge. This is particularly important for an older person. Many ageist assumptions are made about this stage of life – people often forget that older adulthood *is* a period of development. Older people need to develop skills to manage the changes (which could be many) in their life. However, it must be remembered that risk taking can sometimes involve losses as well as gains.

Throughout our lives we take both major and minor risks and this is the same for an older person living in residential care. No matter what the level of risk is, residential workers must assess and implement a management scheme. This is both to ensure a good quality of life for the resident and to ensure good practice by residential workers.

It is important that we define clearly what is meant by 'risk'. Brearley's work is still extremely relevant and useful for today's practitioners and before proceeding to discuss risk and residents, it will be useful to consider some key points of his work. Risk can be defined as:

1. Hazard, danger, peril.

2. Harm, loss, reduction, damage, diminution.

3. Probability, possibility, likelihood, chance, uncertainty.

(Brearley 1982b, p.7)

The basic definitions of risk are as follows:

1. 'Risk' refers to the relative variation in possible loss outcomes

2. 'Probability' refers to the relative likelihood of outcomes

3. 'Uncertainty' refers to the subjective responses of the person who is exposed to risk. (Brearley 1982b, p.26)

Brearley's main argument is:

> There are two broad elements to understanding risk. The first of these is the estimation or measurement of risk and the second is the evaluation of the risk. Risk estimation includes two dimensions. One factor involves an estimation of the probability that an outcome will occur: this includes such concepts as possibility and likelihood. The second dimension involves the recognition that in any one situation a number of possible outcomes may occur, each of which has a relative probability: this can then be referred to as the words that are used – need, risk, safety, protection – in relation to older people

> (Brearley 1982a, pp.3–4)

Brearley introduced the ideas of *hazards* and *dangers*, which will be fundamental to the discussion of the good practice issues which will follow when considering older people living in residential care:

> *Hazard* refers to any factor – an action, event, lack or deficiency, or other entity – which introduces the possibility or increases the probability of an undesirable outcome

> *Danger* refers to a feared outcome of a hazard which is either expected to be a loss outcome or is associated with loss in the expectation of the observer (Brearley 1982a, p.4)

So, it is now important to consider the hazards, dangers and risks an older person may experience (i) when deciding to come into residential care and (ii) whilst being resident in a residential setting (either as a permanent resident or as a respite service user). In order to facilitate this process, Exercise 6.1 can be used to get workers to think about the general concept of risk and how this has affected their own lives. Exercises 6.2 and 6.3 will lead them on to transfer their thoughts to risk and older people.

Exercise 6.1: Risk Taking in Your Own Life

OBJECTIVE

To make participants think about the risks they have taken through their own lives

PARTICIPANTS

Stage 1 to be undertaken by individuals

Stage 2 to be undertaken in groups of four

Stage 3 feedback in large group

EQUIPMENT

Pen and paper

Flipchart paper and pens

TIME

Stage 1 – 15 minutes

Stage 2 – 60 minutes

Stage 3 – 10 minutes

TASK

Stage 1:
Each participant is asked to think about a risk they have taken in:

> (a) childhood
> (b) adolescence
> (c) adulthood

Then write brief notes on Handout 6.1

Stage 2:
Each participant has 15 minutes to talk about the three risks s/he has taken.

Someone in the group will write down the type of risks taken by each person on the flipchart sheet.

Stage 3:
Flipcharts will be put up on the wall and read by participants. Discussion to follow.

Handout for Exercise 6.1

RISK 1 (Childhood)	RISK 2 (Adolescence)	RISK 3 (Adulthood)

1. What risk did you take?

2. Why and how was it a risk to you?

3. Was it a risk to anyone else? If yes, who?

4. Did anyone try to dissuade you from taking the risk? (If yes, how and why did they do this? Did you listen to them? Did you consider what they said?)

5. Did you regret taking the risk or was it worthwhile? What were the outcomes?

Exercise 6.2: Hazards and Dangers

OBJECTIVE

To think about hazards and dangers which could occur in a resident's life

PARTICIPANTS

To be done in small groups (ideally 4–5)

EQUIPMENT

Flipchart paper and pens

TIME

10 minutes for task

20 minutes feedback

TASK

Groups are asked to brainstorm about what hazards and dangers an older person may face when they are living in residential care

NOTE

This exercise can be repeated by using specific examples from Table 6.1 (p.91). Participants are asked to consider each risk situation and to list the specific hazards and dangers which the resident may face if s/he takes the risk.

Exercise 6.3: Risks

OBJECTIVE

To think about common risks which may occur in a resident's life

PARTICIPANTS

To be done in small groups (ideally 4–5)

EQUIPMENT

Flipchart paper and pens

TIME

10 minutes for task

20 minutes feedback

TASK

Groups are asked to brainstorm about what common risks an older person may face when they are living in residential care. Participants are asked to think about particular problems which may have occurred in their own unit or work with older people.

TAKING A RISK BEFORE COMING INTO RESIDENTIAL CARE

An older person may believe that even considering whether to come into residential care is a risk in itself. S/he may see this proposed change in their life as incorporating many losses – freedom, independence, individuality, privacy, friends, family, familiar surroundings and the memories which go in hand with a locality, house, possessions, etc. Some common fears are:

- I won't be able to do what I want when I want
- I won't like it
- I might not like the staff or other people there
- they might not let me out
- can I take my furniture with me?
- what if I change my mind and want to come home?
- I might get like them (referring to confused people)
- they'll never visit me once I'm in there (referring to family)
- they won't have the kind of food I like – like chicken, rice and peas on Sunday (an Afro-Caribbean man).

In 1989 the Social Services Inspectorate produced *Homes are for Living In*, which was a model for evaluating quality of care provided and quality of life experienced in residential care homes for older people (Department of Health 1989). This is an extremely useful document as it provides forms and *aides-mémoire* for each of the basic six values which staff need to regularly evaluate in their home:

- **Privacy** – the right of individuals to be left alone or undisturbed and free from intrusion or public attention into their affairs.
- **Dignity** – recognition of the intrinsic value of people regardless of circumstances by respecting their uniqueness and their personal needs; treating with respect.
- **Independence** – opportunities to act and think without reference to another person, including a willingness to incur a degree of calculated risk.
- **Choice** – opportunity to select independently from a range of options.
- **Rights** – the maintenance of all entitlements associated with citizenship.
- **Fulfilment** – the realisation of personal aspirations and abilities in all aspects of daily life.

If these values are in place, most of the feared hazards and dangers mentioned above will be avoided. These values should underpin any risk assessment in a residential home. The Social Services Inspectorate have also produced *Guidance on Standards for Residential Homes for People with a Physical Disability* (Department of Health 1990a) which 'offers a statement of fundamental aspects of good practice'. It states at the outset that 'A standard is a means of evaluating. Standards are criteria for judging. Standards themselves stand up to scrutiny and should be explicit and precise as possible because they must be subject to measurement' (p.2). Other useful guidance is *Guidance on Standards for Residential Homes for Elderly People* (Department of Health 1990b) and

Inspecting for Quality, Standards for the Residential Care of Elderly People with Mental Illness (Department of Health 1993).

It is useful for residential workers to look at guidance relating to people with physical disability, learning disability and mental health problems. I feel that older people are sometimes just considered to be 'elderly' and specific disabilities problems are not given enough attention. This seems particularly true of older people with a learning disability who may have received very few services in the past and their disability has virtually been ignored. Workers need to learn more about different forms of disability and develop skills to work with them. This is crucial to fundamental good practice if these residents are to take risks in the future. The same is true of older people who have mental health problems. Staff may have limited knowledge about mental health problems and make judgements about certain conditions. This is not helpful to the risk assessment process.

In addition to the fear of what may actually happen to them in the residential home, older people also run the risk that they will lose certain people or relationships – hence the fear of being 'abandoned to care':

Case Examples

Mary was 86 years old and severely disabled. She was scared of continuing to live in the same neighbourhood, because she had been burgled three times. She wanted to go into residential care and a full needs assessment was completed. Everyone supported Mary in her decision to go into care except her son and daughter. They threatened Mary that if she went into care they would never visit her. They did not want her to go into care because Mary's savings would be used up and her house would be sold, which they considered to be their inheritance.

Frank had lived in the same flat for twenty years, which was next door to his best friend, William, whom he had known since he was five years old. William was housebound due to having suffered several strokes. Frank was considering his own need for residential care but felt he did not want to leave William who he used to talk to every day.

So, an older person may envisage many hazards and dangers even before coming into a residential unit. It is crucial that when carrying out a full needs assessment the assessor should make an assessment of the risk as seen from the older person's point of view. Useful questions may be:

- What are the older person's fears about residential care?
- Are there real dangers and hazards to the older person?
- How likely are they to occur?
- Can anything be done to prevent these dangers and hazards occurring?

Some of these fears may seem very trivial to an outsider, but to the older person they are extremely important. Coming into residential care is a major change in an older person's life – it can be compared to the stresses of getting married, divorced or moving house. There is the risk of losing material as well as personal things like relationships. Work must be done with the older person to assess the real risks pertinent to that person and whether the potential losses will outweigh the benefits of residential care.

RISKS IN RESIDENTIAL CARE

But what are the real risks in a residential home? As in life generally, there can be many different types and level of risk. Residents may risk or be at risk of:

- abuse (physical, emotional, financial, neglect, sexual)
- injury
- falling
- getting lost
- disorientation
- isolation
- immobility
- ill health (physical or mental)
- death.

RISK POLICY AND PROCEDURES

In order to manage risk, every home should have a risk policy and risk assessment procedures. Some homes may be part of an agency which already has a policy in place. Staff should have training on this and become familiar with procedures (this is discussed further below). It is very important that if a resident wants to take risks then s/he should receive support in considering this. This is where risk assessment comes in.

Any risk policy should have aims, objectives and criteria which are written clearly (and not in jargon) and which are meaningful and useful to both workers and service users. Every worker within an agency needs to be clear about their role in risk assessment and risk management. Workers tend to welcome a specific framework to work within, so they know exactly what they are meant to be assessing rather than working with woolly generalised aims of a policy which means nothing to them. This is vital for residential workers who may undervalue themselves. They literally 'live' with residents for prolonged periods of time and can make good assessments. This is important both for permanent residents and also for people who come in for respite care. Residential workers can contribute to risk assessment for these people living in the community.

Residential workers are often frightened about what may happen to a resident if s/he is allowed to take a risk. It is very realistic to worry about what relatives would say if a resident came to some harm. It is crucial, therefore, that a proper risk assessment is carried out with the resident, family members, other appropriate people (friends, advocates) and workers involved (residential staff, social worker, GP, district nurse, community psychiatric nurse). Unfortunately, we are living in a time when workers have to cover their backs so that they are not scapegoated if something does go wrong. *All* agencies should have a risk policy and assessment procedures in place in order to protect workers as well as the service users.

A framework for working with risk should include guidance about:

- assessment
- case meeting
- plan of action (incorporated in a care plan)
- recording (process, decisions and outcomes)
- review.

Where a residential home does have policies in place, they should be explained to potential residents and their families before admission to residential care. Families need to be aware that homes cannot guarantee complete safety and they also need to know what workers can and cannot do.

RISK ASSESSMENT

Principles underpinning the assessment and management of risk have been discussed in depth elsewhere (Lawson 1996), but it is useful to revisit them when considering risk assessment in residential care:

- equal opportunities
- user focus
- encouraging independence
- self-determination
- confidentiality
- staff support.

It is absolutely crucial to the whole dilemma of managing risk for workers to remember that older people have rights (Norman 1980). When assessing risk in a residential unit, it is vital that the assessment should focus on the resident and what s/he wants to achieve. Some typical examples are shown in Table 6.1.

Workers must encourage self-determination and empower the resident in any way possible. They must resist the temptation to impose their own values and judgements on the older person. Workers in the home need to work *with* the resident to assess the level of risk. The starting point is to talk to the resident, who may not even regard what s/he wants to do (or is currently doing) as a problem and cannot see 'what all the fuss is about'. Again it is crucial to avoid the use of jargon. Residential staff and other professionals involved in assessment may be used to jargon like 'assessment', 'risk', 'need', 'criteria' because they use it every day, but what does it mean to the resident?

Table 6.1: Examples of Risk Taking

Mary wants to walk to the corner shop every morning to buy her own newspaper.

Fred wants to get in and out of the bath on his own without the help of a care assistant

Gerty suffers from severe asthma attacks, which she has frequently – especially when she tries to exert herself. She wants to go on the day trip to Blackpool, which involves a three-hour coach ride there and back.

Bert is terminally ill. Doctors say he has about six months to live. He feels well at the moment. He wants to go on the residents' holiday to Spain next month.

George is very much overweight. He has suffered one heart attack already. He refuses to diet and eats lots of sweet things, chocolate and fatty foods which he really likes.

David has always smoked sixty cigarettes a day and says he is not going to change his habit of a lifetime just because the hospital says his lungs are damaged.

Madge is unsteady on her feet but insists on baking in the kitchen and likes to make herself hot drinks in the middle of the night.

Eric likes to have a wet shave every morning and to do it himself. Every day he cuts himself.

Laura wants to smoke in bed.

Timothy wants to die in the home, not in hospital. The GP thinks he needs hospital care because the home is short-staffed and will not be able to cope.

It is important not to frighten the resident and cause more anxiety. The discussion needs to focus on:

- what the resident wants to do/achieve
- why it is important to him/her
- how it can be achieved (what support can be offered without undermining the resident)
- how it affects the resident (good and bad things – do not always focus on the negatives, i.e. talk about dangers, hazards, include *positive* outcomes, i.e. benefits)
- are other people going to be affected? (maybe the resident has not even thought about this).

This is just the starting point. The initial discussion may be undertaken by a keyworker or other members of staff with whom the resident has a good relationship. This is important because maybe the resident is a little bit frightened about what they want to do and they will only confide in someone about this if they trust that person. It is after this initial discussion that the worker may recognise that a risk assessment needs to be undertaken and the reasons for this must be explained to the resident. No one likes to be told they are going to be 'assessed' and in ordinary life we are not usually assessed by someone else when we want to do something!

It is at this stage that other people may be brought in – family, friends, advocates, professionals – *but* the boundaries of confidentiality must be discussed with the resident in the first place. S/he needs to understand what will happen in the assessment process and that honesty, openness and maybe the sharing of information is helpful and important to everyone involved.

As was said previously, the assessment needs to involve all the key people, that is people who are important to the risk taking process. The assessment should not be rushed through. Time needs to be spent talking with the resident and the other key people. The resident should be given ample time to think and contemplate the risk s/he wishes to take. The assessment should be done at the resident's pace *not* to suit the needs or pressures of the workers in the home. Workers need to think about how they are going to assess the level of risk. Brearley (1982b) said that risk is a relative term based on probability and that there are two key questions which need to be answered: *What are the possible outcomes accessible in the state of the current knowledge?* and *What is the probability that each of the possible outcomes will occur?* (p.13).

During the assessment the worker must focus on *how* probability and likelihood are going to be measured and discuss this with the resident. I think it is useful for residential staff to brainstorm a list of very simple and general questions which they need to ask themselves, for example:

- What is the risk?
- What does it mean to the resident?
- Who else does it affect?
- How can the resident be supported in taking the risk?
- Who will be involved in the decision making process?
- How often will the action/care plan be reviewed?

Case Study

THE RISK: MARY WANTS TO WALK TO THE CORNER SHOP EVERY MORNING TO BUY HER OWN NEWSPAPER.

Specific Questions:

Why does Mary want to go to the shop by herself?

Is she capable of going alone?

What are her difficulties?

How far is the shop?

How long would it take her?

What are the hazards and dangers?

Does it affect anyone else?

How could some of these difficulties be overcome?

Mary was 77 years old and had previously lived next door to a newsagent's shop. She had always gone to the corner shop for her paper everyday at 7.00 a.m. When in residential care she wanted to maintain her independence by continuing to go to the nearest shop for a paper and was adamant that she did not want the paper delivered to the home. Mary suffered from severe arthritis and walked with a stick. Staff were concerned that the nearest shop would be too far for Mary to walk every morning and they felt she may fall or collapse.

A risk assessment was carried out. Staff explained their concerns to Mary, who agreed to walk with a care assistant to see just how far the shop was and how long it would take her. Whilst making the journey Mary did realise that it was further than she thought and she became very breathless during the walk. A meeting took place with Mary and her son. Mary said that she realised now what the workers had been concerned about but she still wanted to try and not give up completely. It was agreed that Mary would make the journey twice a week with a care assistant to see how things went over a month and then review the situation.

Workers need to plan how they are going to set about getting the answers to these questions, that is what tools/instruments are they going to use to measure probability and likelihood? Another list of more specific questions needs to be asked in regard to the risk. To illustrate this an example will be taken as a case study from Table 6.1 above.

DECISION MAKING AND CASE MEETINGS

After an assessment has been carried out, a case meeting needs to take place in order for decisions to made. Guttmans' model for decision making (Guttman 1978) is helpful to the process of risk assessment and consequent risk management:

- awareness of a need or problem
- engages the individual in seeking a solution
- a selection is made and decision taken about whether or nor to act
- the action is evaluated.

Counsel and Care (1993) have stated that 'decisions about risks are a balance between the right to choice and the resident's competence. The role of the home's staff is to seek ways to enhance competence, or to compensate for it, or to offer extra support in order to make it possible for the resident to undertake an activity with an acceptable degree of risk' (p.5)

The case meeting is a stage of the assessment process which is often missed out. It is essential to formalise the decision making process. Residential staff have frequently told me that decisions have been made about a resident but they have no idea who actually made the decision or when it was made. Decision making must:

- involve the resident
- involve other relevant people who have been involved in the assessment process
- be written down and recorded (signatures and dates included)
- reviewed (as circumstances can change for better or worse).

Decisions should never be made behind the resident's back. S/he needs to know the views and feelings of workers and other key people. Much useful discussion can come out of such a meeting:

> I never realised that the staff were so worried about me and really I hadn't thought about some of the things that could happen to me. They certainly made me think a bit more.

> I suppose I had the idea that Mum would be totally safe in here. I never knew that there were rules and regulations. I wanted them to tie Mum in bed at night like I used to do. At that meeting they explained to me why they couldn't and Mum spoke up too. I never realised she hated being tied in. She'd never said at home. She's says a lot more to me now and that's good, isn't it?

The case meeting can also ease the burden on residential workers to a certain degree, in particular keyworkers who may feel 'totally responsible' for a resident. The case meeting is a forum where everyone is part of the decision making process – any decisions are made jointly. The meeting should include information giving and sharing before decisions are made. Other professionals (GPs, community psychiatric nurses, physiotherapists) may be able to offer advice or make suggestions which will help the risk taking process. These people can facilitate the decision making process and must be encouraged to attend the meeting. If they do not see it as a priority, the importance must be explained to them!

Although many people do not like formal meetings, they are important in case anything does go wrong in the future – for example a resident has an accident or comes to some harm. This is why accurate recording is also crucial to the process. Everyone who is part of the meeting should sign the written record and action/care plan. This helps to avoid apportioning blame on any one person in the future.

It is crucial that during the case meeting everyone discusses the hazards and dangers, but also that the likelihood of these things occurring is measured as accurately as possible. In the example above, Mary herself was able to say that she thought it was 'very likely' that she would collapse if she went on her own to the shop because she knew she would try to rush there and back. With a care assistant present, she would be reminded to slow down and takes rests on the benches along the way. The 'trial run' had been very valuable as part of the assessment process. Mary was able to assess the probability herself. So it is crucial that assessments are not just done on paper. Ways of measuring risk need to be thought out during the assessment process.

REVIEW

It has been said already that risk decisions need to be reviewed. Risk management is about managing decisions which have been taken and reviewing them. Sometimes decisions have to be modified, but to do this it is essential that decisions are reviewed regularly. This is because circumstances do change and not always for the worse. It should never be assumed that a resident's situation is going to become worse. In Mary's case she actually became stronger because of the regular exercise she had walking to the shop twice a week and by taking exercise classes which were put on once a week in the home. Six months later Mary went to the shop four times a week (still with a care assistant).

RESIDENTS WHO HAVE SPECIFIC PROBLEMS

So far discussion has focused on the structure and process of risk taking. The assumption has been made that the resident is able to contribute to, and participate in, the assessment process, but this is not always the case. Attention now needs to turn to specific problems and issues. In particular, consideration needs to be given to those residents who cannot make informed decisions, who have difficulty in communicating, who have specific problems and are deemed 'at risk', but also to the issues of restraint and support of residential staff.

There are some residents who are not able to make informed decisions and others who have specific problems which make it difficult to communicate and carry out a risk assessment (for example a resident suffering with dementia or who has a severe learning disability). It is still important that workers think about the values which should exist for these residents and work towards a positive risk assessment and management scheme. Some residents may be seen as a 'nuisance' but, as Gibson (1991) says, 'the troublesome individual is worthy of help in his/her own right'. Risk assessment with these individuals may take more time and effort but workers do have a 'duty to care'.

It was said at the outset that social workers have used the term 'at risk' for many years and residential workers also use the term for many residents. Residents who may be regarded as 'at risk' are those who:

- suffer from a dementia
- wander
- self neglect
- are violent to themselves or others (workers or residents).

If staff are concerned about the behaviours of these residents then a risk assessment must be undertaken for their own safety and also to protect other residents and workers. Workers should make themselves more aware of methods of communicating with people who are demented, aggressive, visually impaired or whatever. It is not possible to consider these methods here but various techniques can and should be used.

Workers need to be made aware of the value and benefits of different methods through training and supervision. Many useful publications are available regarding different work – for example reminiscence work and life story books undertaken with dementia sufferers, care plans for people who wander, dealing with challenging and aggressive behaviour (Bornat 1994, Gibson 1989 and 1991, Murphy 1994, Allan 1994, Armstrong and Reymbaut 1996 and Holden and Chapman 1994). Utilisation of these methods will help workers with managing the resident and also with assessing risk and involving the resident in the assessment process.

Where a resident cannot make informed decisions for whatever reason, residential staff should consider whether an advocate would be helpful as well as talking to other key people such as family members (to ascertain more about the resident's past, views, wishes and lifestyle) and professionals (for advice and suggestions).

A common problem which exists in residential care is residents who wander, and that leads to the whole debate about physical restraint. Staff worry constantly about residents who wander about who they see as being 'at risk'. Anxiety is increased because very often workers know that they do not have enough staff working on each shift and 'we haven't got eyes in the back of our heads. Anything could happen on other floors'. Someone who wanders frequently needs to be watched and accompanied when appropriate. If workers feel that a resident is 'at risk' because s/he wanders, a proper risk assessment should be undertaken as soon as possible. Resorting to restricting residents' movements by tying them to a chair, putting a tray across their chair so they cannot get up, locking them in a room or administering medication are not the answers.

A risk assessment needs to first consider why the resident is wandering. Allan (1994) says that 'wandering is not just one simple behaviour. Characteristics can include disorientation, aimlessness, purpose, agitation, being lost and being at risk... For the purpose of understanding an individual's behaviour, it is crucial to think about what aspects of wandering are relevant to that person, as this will lead to different practical problems and therefore different avenues for managing the behaviour' (p.16). She goes on to consider why people with dementia may wander:

- continuation of lifestyle
- neurological damage
- anxiety
- boredom
- physiological/psychiatric factors
- loss of navigational skills
- faulty goal-directed behaviour
- need for exercise
- form of communication
- medication
- expression of preference

(for full discussion see Allan 1994, pp.116–18)

Various interventions can help the resident who wanders take risks and again workers need to familiarise themselves with alternative methods in order to assess and manage risk. Allan discusses her work on a project carried out in a psychiatric day hospital which 'attempted to manage problems with wandering creatively', but many other useful works are available (Radar 1985, Radar, Doan and Schwab 1985).

Restraint is a key issue which often arises in residential care. More often than not, one can understand why relatives might ask staff to do certain things like restraining a resident – they think they are doing their best to keep the older person safe from harm. What relatives do not understand is that legally workers cannot physically restrain someone (for full discussion relating to risk and the law see Carson 1996). The Social Services Inspectorate has given guidance regarding restraint:

> In general terms many potential risks can be avoided by adequate observation of users by staff or by staff diverting users' attention to some other activity. Where this seems insufficient advice from other professionals such as a specialist in psychiatry or community psychiatric nurse maybe appropriate and helpful... There may be some cases where these methods do not work and where restraint has to be contemplated. The need to consider the use of physical restraint should be rare... It should only be contemplated when an emergency situation

arises and when there is perceived to be an immediate danger or unacceptable consequence to the user or others if this action is not taken.

(Department of Health 1993, pp.15–16)

Risk assessment has to include work about making safety judgements, that is measuring the risk and deciding the acceptability and inevitability of risk.

It is important to understand what we mean by restraint and to think in broad terms. The various forms of restraint were classified by Counsel and Care (1992) under six headings:

1.   Individual physical restraint on movement.

2.   Physical restraints to circulation within and beyond building.

3.   Drugs.

4.   Supervision and observation.

5.   Institutional, professional and cultural factors.

6.   Financial matters.

Some people argue that there may be circumstances where some forms of restraint are necessary, but workers need to think very carefully about this and some managers may find it useful to develop a restraint policy for their home. Workers really need to be taken through a process whereby they think about what is restraint and what are the alternatives. To do this it is a useful exercise to ask specific questions about the use of restraint:

- Are there any circumstances when some form of restraint may be necessary/acceptable?
- Are there any types of restraint which are acceptable?
- What are the hazards and dangers of these types of restraints? (and to whom?)
- What are the benefits of these types of restraints? (and to whom?)
- Are there alternative options to restraint?

Bad practices do exist where there has been a lack of training. A real concern is where workers have 'done care for years' without training and what was acceptable ten years ago might not be acceptable now. However, they continue to practice with little supervision and then they train new workers (perhaps very young workers aged 16 or 17 years) who learn by 'watching and doing'.

In these situations bad practice continues and is never challenged. For example, a common problem is regarding medication and the resident's refusal to take it. A new member of staff or untrained worker may put forward the argument that it is alright to hide medication in a resident's food because 'it is for their own good'. Or perhaps workers believe that a resident is likely to fall out of bed, so they put up cot sides. Bad practices must be confronted and this can only be done through training and regular and close supervision.

SUPPORT AND TRAINING FOR WORKERS

Much has been said about supporting the resident in making choices and decisions in risk taking, but workers need support too. We must give some attention to the feelings and wishes of workers. They are there to do a job, but that job often affects them very deeply. Sometimes they feel they are not doing enough for residents who may be at risk.

Even though they are involved in assessment and the aftermath (management of risk), workers may feel very vulnerable and at risk themselves. It is common to feel that 'we are not doing enough'. It is a natural instinct to feel protective towards a resident who appears vulnerable, but residents are adults and we should *never* resort to infantilisation and treat them as children.

It was said earlier that all agencies should have a risk policy in place. Where this happens this gives a framework for supporting workers. However, the policy will only be effective if workers receive appropriate training. It is not good enough just to produce a policy and implement it. Workers needs to understand the policy and what is expected of them. Consequently, training on risk assessment and risk management is imperative on induction courses for new workers and also for established staff who may have been doing the job for years but may not have had much training. Time needs to be spent exploring the whole concept of risk, not just going through policy and guidelines. Training needs to help workers address specific issues:

- why it is acceptable for older people to take risks
- the underpinning values to evaluate good practice
- the fact that accidents do happen
- the concept of self-determination
- how to empower residents in the decision making process
- how to effectively measure 'likelihood' and 'probability'
- the process of assessment
- how to record accurately and write care plans.

Staff need the opportunity to talk about their feeling in supervision, but, as was mentioned earlier, they also need to be protected. This is why the recording of risk decisions is of paramount importance. It is a joint decision making process and no one worker should ever take full responsibility for making a decision. This is why recording of decisions is so important. The decisions then have to be managed. Problems may occur in managing the risk and plans may need to be reviewed more regularly. On the other hand, sometimes situations improve, that is the outcomes are better than anticipated. If things are going well it is important to report that back to everyone who was involved in the decision making process.

In the interim, workers must be offered the opportunity to talk about their own feelings. This should be done through regular supervision sessions with the manager of the home, but workers can also gain support from colleagues and other professionals who are involved in the risk taking process. A worker should be able to express how they are feeling about the decisions which been have taken and the management process. When expressing their feelings they should be offered emotional support and not criticised for being 'too soft' or 'unprofessional'. Extra support should be offered when there are 'bad out-comes' – for example when an accident happens. A worker may feel they are to blame because the resident was allowed to take a risk. It does not help either if family members apportion blame to workers, so again it is crucial that workers get support from management (and also protection – perhaps from verbal abuse) and that they also support each other.

Finally, it is important to say that workers may feel vulnerable because they believe that the agency they work for is putting residents at risk because of lack of resources – the main one being the lack of staff. Workers may want to do certain work with residents but they just do not have the time. Many workers feel that all they do is 'basic care'. A common complaint is that residents are 'at risk' because there are not enough workers to watch them all the time. Workers feel extremely vulnerable when they know they cannot walk with Mrs X when she wants to wander about the home because Mr Y needs toiletting now and there is no one else to do it!

Workers may also feel vulnerable when a particular resident is challenging or violent towards them. The worker may be vulnerable when s/he finds him/herself isolated on a floor and is attacked by a resident. It may take time for another worker, who is on another floor, to respond to the alarm. We talk about dealing with challenging behaviour and obviously we should try to do this, but sometimes a resident has been placed in a home inappropriately or his/her condition deteriorates. In these circumstances another full needs assessment (including risk assessment) should be undertaken and the resident will have to be moved if it is felt necessary. Workers often feel 'guilty' about this because 'it is moving them away from their home'. During the full needs assessment the assessor must assess the degree of risk to the resident, other residents and the workers. Risk taking affects everyone in the home.

CONCLUSION

This chapter has argued that risk is a very important issue for older people who live permanently in residential care and also for those older people who have respite care. Although risk taking is an integral part of daily life, there may be situations where a resident's situation needs to be formally assessed for their own safety and for the safety of others, namely other residents and residential workers. To conclude, the following summary is a list of points for good practice:

- To work successfully and meaningfully with risk in a residential setting, a proper policy (which includes the underpinning principles and values of good practice) and guidance on procedures must be in place.
- A resident must be included in the assessment process (this involves spending time talking to the resident and respecting their views, choices and rights).
- Confidentiality must be adhered to.
- Other key people must be included in the assessment process.

- Tools and instruments must be developed to assess likelihood and probability.
- Formal case meetings must be convened to facilitate decision making.
- The assessment process must be recorded and decisions must be reviewed regularly.
- Residential homes must develop their own policies on issues such as restraint.
- Staff must receive training on risk and also regular support and supervision.

REFERENCES

Allan, K. (1994) *Wandering*. Stirling: Dementia Services Development Centre.

Armstrong, L. and Reymbaut, E. (1996) *Getting the Message Across: an Introduction to Interpersonal Communication for Staff Working with People Who Have Dementia*. Stirling: Dementia Services Development Centre.

Association of Directors of Social Services (1991) *Adults at Risk*. Stockport: ADSS.

Bornat, J. (1994) *Reminiscence Reviewed*. Buckingham: Open University Press.

Brearley, C.P. (1982a) *Risk and Ageing*. London: Routledge and Kegan Paul.

Brearley, C.P. (1982b) *Risk in Social Work*. London: Routledge and Kegan Paul.

Carson, D. (1996) 'Risking legal repercussions.' In H. Kemshall and J. Pritchard (eds) *Good Practice in Risk Assessment and Risk Management 1*. London: Jessica Kingsley Publishers.

Counsel and Care (1993) *The Right to Take Risks*. London: Counsel and Care.

Counsel and Care (1992) *What if They Hurt Themselves*. London: Counsel and Care.

Department of Health (1989) *Homes are for Living in*. London: HMSO.

Department of Health (1990a) *Guidance on Standards for Residential Homes for People with a Physical Disability*. London: HMSO.

Department of Health (1990b) *Guidance on Standards for Residential Homes for Elderly People*. London: HMSO.

Department of Health (1993) *Standards for the Residential Care of Elderly People with Mental Disorders*. London: HMSO.

Gibson, F. (1989) *Using Reminiscence: a Training Pack*. London: Help the Aged.

Gibson, F. (1991) *The Lost Ones: Recovering the Past to Help Their Present*. Stirling: Dementia Services Development Centre.

Gloucestershire Social Services Department (1991) *Adults at Risk: Procedural Guidelines for Professionals*. Gloucester: Gloucestershire County Council.

Guttman, D. (1978) 'Life events and decision-making by adults.' *The Gerontologist* 18, 5, 462–467.

Holden, U. and Chapman, A. (1994) *Wait a Minute: a Practice Guide on Challenging Behaviour and Aggression for Staff Working with Individuals Who Have Dementia*. Stirling: Dementia Services Development Centre.

Law Commission (1993) *Mentally Incapacitated and Other Vulnerable Adults*. Consultation paper 129. London: HMSO.

Law Commission (1996) *Mental Incapacity*. Consultation Paper 231. London HMSO.

Lawson, J. (1996) 'A framework for risk assessment and management for older people.' In H. Kemshall and J. Pritchard (eds) *Good Practice in Risk Assessment and Risk Management*. London: Jessica Kingsley Publishers.

Murphy, C.J. (1994) *It Started with a Shell: Life Story Work and People with Dementia*. Stirling: Dementia Services Development Centre.

Norman, A.J. (1980) *Rights and Risk*. London: Centre for Policy on Ageing.

Radar, J. (1985) 'A comprehensive staff approach to problem wandering.' *The Gerontologist 27*, 756–760.

Radar, J., Doan, J. and Schwab, M. (1985) 'How to decrease wandering, a form of agenda behaviour.' *Geriatric Nursing 6*, 196–199.

CHAPTER 7

People with Learning Difficulties
Citizenship, Personal Development and the Management of Risk

Bob Tindall

Supporting people who have learning difficulties can present particular challenges in terms of risk management. The challenge is predominantly to agencies which provide support, rather than a reflection of the abilities of people with learning difficulties themselves to negotiate risk and learn from it. The purpose of this chapter is therefore to examine what effective risk management should actually consist of in supporting people with learning difficulties.

The influence of social role valorisation (normalisation) on services for people with learning difficulties since the mid 1970s has heightened the consciousness of their rights as citizens amongst people who are paid to support them. However, a great deal still needs to be done to match the rhetoric with the reality. Genuine empowerment is littered with obstacles which need to be negotiated in order that people with learning difficulties can – without hindrance – gain confidence from success and learn from failure. Why should this be the case?

The perceived vulnerability of people with learning difficulties can in itself trigger a complex range of public responses where risk taking is concerned. Public perceptions vary, and range from seeing people with learning difficulties as objects of pity to seeing them as a potential threat (Wolfensberger 1975). This ambivalence carries with it an emphasis either on protection and security for the individual who is perceived as being vulnerable, or on the need to minimise exposure to risk on grounds of public safety. This can create difficulties for agencies which are funded by public money but have a firm commitment to empowering the people they support. They may not only wish to act in accordance with the wishes of the people they support – and to assist them in taking risks in ways which will maximise the possibility of a positive outcome – but will be required to demonstrate that they have paid due regard to public concerns about the possibility of harm occurring to people who may not necessarily appreciate the possible outcome of the actions they wish to take.

Negative outcomes from taking risks create the possibility of the 'hindsight effect' (Carson 1994) based on the negative stereotypes referred to earlier. In such circumstances, we need to consider how the rights and expectations of common citizenship can be extended for people with learning difficulties when they are being supported by organisations funded by public money. This means that individuals or organisations supported by public money need to define clearly the values which will underpin their approach to assisting people with learning difficulties to understand and negotiate risk, and to define the processes by which this will be achieved and sustained.

HIGH QUALITY RISK MANAGEMENT

There are a number of factors which characterise a high quality approach to risk management in supporting people with learning difficulties, and which can be defined as follows:

- All efforts to manage risk should have the wishes and needs of the individual person with learning difficulties as the primary consideration.
- People with learning difficulties should, wherever possible, actively participate in the process of risk assessment, and the process should be designed to make it easy for them to do so.
- The agreed plan of action for reducing risk should respect the rights of the individual person with learning difficulties as a citizen.
- The risk assessment process should clearly define the factors which indicate that risk is present.
- Potential benefits and potential harms should be clearly highlighted. To ensure that risk assessments allow for a positive view of risk taking, benefits should be identified as the first stage of the process, followed by a consideration of potential harms. This assists in developing a positive view of risk taking, with a clear focus on its possibilities for the personal development of individual people with learning difficulties, rather than fostering a more prohibitive culture.
- Actions agreed should be recorded as simply as possible, so that they can be understood by not only the people who were present, but by other people who were not present, but need to know what was agreed.
- Plans should be reviewed, and the point of review identified.
- Action plans that require the involvement of professional staff should be carried out by people who have been adequately trained and are well supported.
- Organisations which manage risk should have management staff who are committed to developing and sustaining a positive risk-taking culture.
- Adequate debriefing and reparation should follow any risk which has a negative outcome.

- Organisations should build into their risk management process the capacity to gather information on the outcomes of risk assessments, and to disseminate examples of good practice across staff teams as part of a wider quality assurance process.
- Risk management processes should not create inflexible or bureaucratic duties or tasks but should be integrated with other planning processes necessary in supporting people with learning difficulties.

CITIZENSHIP, OBLIGATIONS AND SAFEGUARDS

As indicated earlier, social role valorisation has had a significant effect on the thinking of people providing paid services to people with learning difficulties. However, there are nevertheless considerable tensions endemic in assisting people using 'culturally valued means in order to establish and/or maintain personal behaviours, experiences and characteristics that are culturally normative or valued' (Wolfensberger 1977).

First, services often find it difficult – or even very difficult – to offer their support in ways which are totally effective for the individual receiving them, and this can result in individuals challenging the service they receive in a variety of ways, not least by acting in ways which offer the possibility of self harm, or harm to others. In these circumstances, individuals will not be taking part in a reflective process which will establish hazards to be negotiated in order to achieve a greater degree of autonomy and personal satisfaction, but will be presenting hazards to others, some of which will require a prompt, or even immediate response.

Second, paid staff have to negotiate a number of differing pressures in assisting people with learning difficulties to encounter and overcome potential hazards. In addition to the ambivalence of public opinion previously mentioned, they should respond sensitively to the possible fears of people close to the individual for whom an element of risk taking is planned, such as family members. They may also, depending on the culture of the organisation for which they work – and the value placed upon positive and creative risk management – fear to make a mistake which might not only damage the individual they are trying to support, but have an adverse effect on their career, or even their livelihood.

To resolve these difficulties, organisations must develop processes of risk management which not only maximise the possibility of individual people achieving degrees of autonomy which are respected and valued by the public at large, but address the real conflicts, pressures and anxieties that can be experienced in the process, providing a framework of support for staff members.

The process of risk assessment is essentially one that should consider the requirements of individuals, rather than groups. The huge diversity of circumstances in which risk can occur and the equally diverse abilities of individuals with learning difficulties to recognise and negotiate potential hazards allows for no other option; to apply risk assessments to groups would inevitably lead to courses of action which would be overly restrictive for some, and leave others without sufficient protection. There is therefore a clear and necessary link between planning with individuals (whatever title this is given – individual planning, reviews, personal futures planning etc.) and high quality risk assessment.

Individual planning – at its best – assists individual people to assert, or perhaps decide after a process of exploration, what it is that they want and what support they will need to ensure that they get it. It allows for the possibility that groups of paid staff may need to work together towards particular outcomes – and this has often been interpreted by them as meaning that they all have to get together with the individual on a large group basis to help him/her decide on his/her specific requirements. In reality, working out what is required and deciding whom it would be necessary to involve can be done by the individual with only one other person.

WORKING OUT WHAT IS REQUIRED

Taking risks should be worth the effort. This suggests that the basis of embarking on a course of action which involves risk should be because:

- the risk involved – however great – is necessary because the desired outcome is of particular importance to the individual
- a lot of benefit can be derived from a relatively small risk, even though the outcome is not of prime importance to the individual.

The first task in effective risk assessment is therefore to establish a close relationship between the individual with learning difficulties and the person who is going to help him/her establish what s/he wants, and which people need to be involved to help achieve it. It requires a determination – whatever communication difficulties exist – to establish what the individual feels to be important, and to recognise any elements of risk inherent in any gap that exists between aspirations and current abilities. This implies a detailed, painstaking process – but it should be recognised that individuals may already be giving very clear indications of what it is that they want, but in ways that present difficulties and challenges to others. Equally, by such behaviour, they may be indicating distress without the root cause being immediately apparent. The greater the degree of insight that the assessor has into the underlying causes of challenging behaviour, the more effective any action taken to reduce risk should be, as it is likely to address underlying causes, rather than attempt to 'contain' the behaviour. The assessor also carries the responsibility of communicating what the individual wants to other people who may help contribute suggestions as to how risk might be minimised.

Because of the nature of their difficulties, responsibility for communicating information about people with learning difficulties to others may occur more frequently than with other groups. This responsibility carries with it a particularly strong emphasis on confidentiality, as people with learning difficulties are particularly vulnerable in such circumstances. It may be necessary to come to a simple agreement with individuals about what they want others to know about themselves and what they do not.

WORKING TO A PLAN OR RESPONDING TO DILEMMAS: MINIMISING RISK

Once individuals have considered – usually with support – what it is that they want to achieve, the risk assessment can begin to explore the gap between aspirations and current abilities. Equally, as indicated above, the assessment may need to concern itself with dilemmas presented by an individual's current behaviour, rather than a carefully arrived-at summary of personal priorities.

The following factors apply at this stage:

1. Determining whether the risk is being deliberately embarked on in order to further develop the skills of the individual, or whether the individual has already made a choice to take particular risks, leaving others to consider the potential outcomes.

2. Being clear about when to intervene and when not to intervene.

3. Considering not only risks presented by the actions or proposed actions of individuals, but risks presented by the environment in which the individual acts.

4. Considering who should be involved in the process of risk assessment.

The above factors require further consideration.

PLANNED RISKS AND REACTIVE ASSESSMENTS

The aim of a successful risk management process should be to maximise opportunities for people with learning difficulties to take risks which are carefully assessed and planned in order that they can maintain a good quality of life, develop new skills or try previously untried experiences. By implication, this means that it should also minimise the occurrence of unanticipated, negative events which present risk. The difference is essentially between a **positive** and **creative** process, and a **reactive** process. The difference can be illustrated by the following:

CASE EXAMPLE 1

Susan has a boyfriend, Ian, who lives three miles away. They like to go to a particular pub on Wednesday nights, but Ian does not finish his work until 9pm. and it would be time consuming for him to travel to Susan in order to accompany her there.

However, Susan has epilepsy, and is not totally sure of what to do in traffic, which makes crossing roads potentially hazardous. She is keen to meet Ian from work, so she works out with people who support her a plan of action which will help her cross roads safely and use buses. Her GP is consulted about the possibility of her having an epileptic seizure on the journey, and he checks her medication. After a period of time with close support, she now travels to see Ian alone and safely.

CASE EXAMPLE 2

Tom lives in his own flat, receiving support from others with daily living tasks. Over a period of time, Tom begins to reject help, often throwing objects at people when they call. He is reported to have run out of his flat into busy traffic on a number of occasions, without regard for his own safety. People get together to consider why Tom's behaviour has changed, and what should be done to make things safer. Tom refuses to join them.

In considering the two examples, it is clear that people supporting both individuals are in very different circumstances. Working with Susan is a clear process, in which she can communicate what it is that she wants in ways that others can easily understand, and exposure to risk can be controlled, by both her and the people who support her. Working with Tom is a different matter. His behaviour indicates a high level of discontent and anxiety, and because of the risks he is taking, this anxiety will be felt by the people who support him. The meaning of his behaviour may not be clear, and this lack of ability to understand him may cause insecurity and low morale. In such circumstances, a degree of panic may set in, and Tom may be subject to coercive measures before the meaning of his behaviour is understood.

Yet it is possible to follow broadly the same process of risk assessment (based on the work of David Carson) with both individuals, as paralleled below:

CASE EXAMPLE 1 – Susan	CASE EXAMPLE 2 – Tom
• What does Susan want to do?	• What is Tom doing? What is he telling us he wants by doing this?
• What will be the benefits to Susan in doing what she wants to do?	• Are there any positive things about the way in which Tom is behaving?
• Who – or what – might be harmed/damaged if Susan does what she wants to do?	• Who – or what – might be harmed/damaged if Tom continues to act in this way?
• How can plans be made so that Susan gets the maximum benefit from what she wants to do?	• How can Tom be helped to develop the positive aspects of his behaviour?
• How can any potential harm or damage arising from the actions that Susan wants to take be minimised?	• How can the possibility of harm or damage arising from Tom's current actions be minimised?
• What has been decided?	• What has been decided?
• When will the risk assessment be reviewed?	• When will the risk assessment be reviewed?

As illustrated above, working with Susan is a positive and creative process, in which steady progression is made towards a personal goal, even if there may be a need, during the process, to adjust pace. Tom, however, obliges people to respond to him, and this is essentially a reactive process; minimising the possibility of harm may well be the uppermost consideration, and the time that people have to respond may be limited – because immediate action may be required.

The risk assessment process illustrated above refers to the subject of the assessment in the third person. However, particularly where risk is being embarked upon to further the personal development of the individual, (positive and creative risk), this process should be customised to allow for the line of enquiry throughout the process to be directed, wherever possible by the person who is the subject of the assessment. In practical terms, this means changing from the third to the first person, and assisting the individual to work through the process.

INTERVENTION AND NON-INTERVENTION

People with learning difficulties often experience others intervening on their behalf, although they are not always clear why intervention is necessary and, on some occasions, may neither desire nor request intervention. Clarity over the grounds for intervention is therefore important, as the process of risk management is to support people's rights rather than obscure them.

There are three different sets of circumstances in which intervention, involving an assessment of risk, might be required.

1. The example of Susan illustrates **intervention by consent**. People paid to support Susan help her work out the quickest and safest method of achieving what she wants to achieve, and assist her to do so.

2. The example of Tom illustrates the pressures which can lead to **intervention without consent in order to prevent harm**. Action to prevent harm may be required immediately. In such circumstances, the person perceiving the immediate danger follows a logical sequence of thought not dissimilar to that of the risk assessment process outlined earlier, but has to do so in an instant.

3. On occasions, individual people with learning difficulties may cause others significant concern in circumstances in which the perceived potential harm is not immediate. Examples of this might be worries that a sexual relationship is exploitative, or that a relationship is financially exploitative. What may be required is **evidence to justify intervention.**

Examples similar to (2) and (3) above can occur in a diverse range of circumstances, and organisations providing support to people with learning difficulties should respond to them in the context of their understanding of their duty of care, and their policies addressing the prevention and detection of abuse. Broadly, intervention should be justifiable if what is happening is:

- illegal
- is life threatening, or involves potential harm to the individual or others **and** the individual is not fully aware of the consequences of his/her actions.

However, if the individual **does** understand the potential consequences, the **level** of intervention may need to be considered with particular care. Such consideration requires the evidence of, or the need to develop, a policy or guidelines on the circumstances in which restraint or physical intervention of any kind should be exercised, with due regard to the law and to the requirement to take reasonable action to prevent harm occurring.

There may also be a very limited range of circumstances in which a risk assessment should be carried out without the involvement of the individual who is the focus of the assessment. Such circumstances would be characterised by a need to consult in order to check out whether others have information which may legitimise concerns. An example of this would be circumstances in which exploitation is suspected but insufficient evidence is available, and others need to be consulted (strictly on a need to know basis). In these circumstances, the responsibility rests with those who coordinate the assessment to be very specific about the grounds upon which the individual is being excluded.

ENVIRONMENT

The process of risk assessment described previously is not complete without consideration of the environment in which people with learning difficulties find themselves. In some instances, this will constitute the settings in which organisations provide services, creating a particular obligation for them to provide a safe environment, including legal obligations (e.g. Health and Safety at Work Act 1974, Control of Substances Hazardous to Health Regulations 1988, Food Safety Act 1990). Wolfensberger and Thomas (1983) describe the need for service settings to be arranged in a way which will not expose people to undue hazard, nor overprotect them. As with all other aspects of risk assessment, the degree of hazard present will vary in accordance with the ability of individual people to comprehend the potential for harm and take action to avoid being harmed.

Accommodation and Support Services

Settings which provide accommodation and support require scrutiny on a regular basis to ensure that undue hazards are not present, and measures taken to prevent hazard should be achieved by means which avoid institutional features. Aspects of the setting that should be considered are:

SPECIFIC

FIRE — Flammability of household items, availability of fire prevention equipment and (where appropriate) regularity of servicing. Alongside this should be considered the availability of training in fire prevention and evacuation in the event of an emergency.

CHEMICALS — The storage of hazardous chemicals in a safe place, and their use in the proximity of people who find it difficult to discriminate between harmful and non-harmful substances.

ELECTRICITY & ELECTRICAL EQUIPMENT — Safety of supply (e.g. wiring and fuses) safety of electrical points and electrical equipment.

GAS — Safety of supply and of equipment.

WATER — Assessment as to whether temperature needs to be automatically controlled, or whether people likely to use it are aware of potential hazards. Bathing itself is a significant source of hazard for some people (e.g. people who have regular epileptic seizures) but action to reduce hazard should be addressed via a risk assessment with the individual concerned, rather than via an assessment of the setting, unless the bathing area itself is unsafe.

HYGIENE PRACTICES — Safety practices relating to the control of infection, dealing with spillages (including bodily fluids) disposing of waste, etc. plus practices relating to food hygiene, particularly the requirements of the Food Safety Act 1990.

LIFTING — The setting can present particular hazards in terms of lifting both people and objects, due to design features or the lack of appropriate equipment. Manual handling assessments required by the Manual Handling Operatives Regulations 1992 and levels of staff training are both relevant features of the assessment.

Effective risk assessments related to lifting people should pay regard to a number of factors:

- the circumstances in which lifting is required
- the extent to which the individual may understand what is to happen and the need to explain in terms which will maximise the possibility of understanding

- the individual's attitude to being lifted, particularly if s/he is likely to become fearful or angry
- the extent to which active cooperation can be exercised by the person to be lifted
- weight of the person to be lifted
- knowledge of what equipment can be used and how to use it
- type of lift required and the number of people needed to carry it out.

DRUGS

The procedures used for distributing medication should be considered, to ensure accuracy of dosage. Assessment of risk in relation to individual people with learning difficulties taking their own medication should be the subject of individual risk assessments, rather those relating to the setting.

NON-SPECIFIC HAZARDS

These should be reviewed regularly, and can cover anything from frayed carpet to singed lampshades.

EXTERNAL HAZARDS

A number of external features could constitute potential hazards, e.g. garden ponds, ramshackle outhouses, lawnmowers, external steps, nearby main roads.

HOLIDAYS

A change in service setting itself can be a source of risk. This is particularly the case for some people with learning difficulties who may be confident in a familiar environment but find that a change of setting is in itself a disabilitating factor. Identifying potential hazards as soon as possible following arrival is important, as is building in specific safeguards, such as emergency telephone contact numbers, and basic medical information in case there is a need – particularly abroad – to use medical services.

VEHICLES

Whilst not strictly an item related to the setting in which an individual receives support, adequate checks on the safety of vehicles is an essential component of risk management. In large scale support services which use minibuses which can accommodate 9–16 passengers, Schedule 7 of the Road Vehicles (Construction and Use) Regulations 1986 applies, along with Regulations 26 to 28 of the Minibus (Conditions of Fitness, Equipment and Use) Regulations 1977.

Some people with learning difficulties may not be aware of the hazard created by distracting the attention of the driver of a moving vehicle, and wherever possible unpredictability in behaviour should be planned for with particular reference to seating and support arrangements, as part of the risk assessment process.

There are many aspects of the assessment of risk as it relates to environmental factors which reflect those which are considered when working with individuals in relation to an assessment of risk. Broadly, the process in relation to environmental factors can be described as follows:

- identification of the hazard
- consideration of **who** or **what** might be harmed
- examinination of whether or not the risk is adequately controlled
- consideration of further action to control the risk, if necessary
- decision on a date or review.

Domiciliary Services

All aspects of risk assessment as applied to accommodation and support services can be applied to circumstances in which people with learning difficulties live independently with support given on a sessional basis. The process of enquiry as to the potential existence of hazard can be collated into a checklist, such as that above, which the tenant can go through with support from his/her sessional support worker. Effective risk management also requires a clear process for gaining access to emergency support and a plan, created in conjunction with the tenant, of what will happen if there were to be a major crisis, for example loss of accommodation due to sudden damage.

Day Services

Many of the hazards to be found in accommodation and support services may also be found in buildings in which day services are provided, with the addition – in cases of day centre or sheltered workshop provision – of potentially hazardous machinery. Supported employment services have the additional consideration of the challenges presented by an 'ordinary' (i.e. non-segregated) employment settings, though the individualised nature of systematic instruction would usually accommodate these.

Community Settings

All specific services should provide the opportunity for people with learning difficulties to spend as much time as possible in community settings, rather than those designed for the specific purpose of congregating people with disabilities in large or small numbers. The potential hazards presented by community settings are varied, but are best addressed by assessing them on an individual basis, guided by what it is that the individual wishes to achieve. Adequate support given to individuals in community settings assists in identifying potential hazards whilst assistance is at hand, so that actions taken to reduce risk can be informed by observation of specific difficulties at close quarters.

RECORDING AND AMENDING ASSESSMENTS

This can be achieved either through specific recording of a risk assessment in the general documentation that exists for the individual for whom paid support services are provided, or via a specific risk assessment form itself. Whatever method is used, it should assist the process of assessment by guiding those involved through the logical process of:

- considering the action to be taken (or the action that an individual has already decided to take which is presenting a degree of risk)
- examining the potential benefits
- examining the potential harms
- identifying ways of maximising benefits
- identifying ways of minimising harm
- agreeing on a course of action (which does not preclude deciding not to proceed due to the level of potential harm)
- agreeing who is to be involved
- agreeing a time to review.

Records of risk assessments are essential, particularly when people with learning difficulties are supported by more than one person, a staff team, for example. People with learning difficulties themselves may have difficulties in recalling the detail of what was decided, or may have significant problems in communicating it to others. Staff teams may have these difficulties too. Recording should therefore consist of logging the detail of every stage of the process as succinctly, and as simply, as possible. Presentation of the main points in symbol form, or on tape, may well assist the high proportion of people with learning difficulties who have problems with literacy. The more accessible the record is, the more it is likely to be used as a working document, particularly by people who may only provide support on an occasional basis, such as relief staff. A basic standard would be that the record should be clear to everyone, whether they know the person who is the subject of the assessment or not. A common error in recording risk assessments is assuming that the reader is very familiar with the person in question, or overlooking stages of the assessment process. For example:

> Andrea likes to walk in the garden on fine days. An occupational therapy assessment is necessary as further advice is needed on the layout of the garden.

This record assumes that everyone knows that the descent from Andrea's house to her garden is known to be often slippery and has several steps, and that Andrea has difficulties perceiving the distance between objects, making walking – and negotiating steps in particular – hazardous. The record also leaps from identifying what Andrea wants to identifying action necessary to reduce risk, without considering potential benefits and hazards in any detail.

Doing so requires monitoring of the actions planned in the assessment and a willingness to communicate openly with people with learning difficulties in circumstances where they appear to be having difficulties with what has been proposed, should they themselves not recognise that the scale or nature of these difficulties.

There are several considerations when changing the scale or pace of action, which are:

What outcome was the action aimed to achieve?
Does X still wish to achieve the same outcome?

NO	YES
Discontinue current action, review what outcome is now required and create new plan	Modify the action to the minimum degree necessary to continue progress towards the outcome when encountering current difficulties

---

A change in the scale or the pace of action – if the effect of the change is to move more slowly – can often be reassuring to people who know the individual person well, but have difficulties in accepting the notion of risk-taking. In such circumstances, the helpful 'compromise' overtones of the change should not present an ambiguous message if it is also clearly communicated that the wishes of the individual will continue to be pursued.

Debriefing and Reparation

The most effective risk management strategies cannot ensure that things will not go wrong. Mistakes are part of the process of learning for people with learning difficulties, as they are for everyone else. Occasionally, things will go badly wrong, and a high quality risk management process should anticipate this and plan to support people in such circumstances.

To develop and sustain a culture in which positive and creative risk training is encouraged and reactive responses are minimised requires a commitment to people who do take well planned risks and for whom things do go badly wrong, whether they are people with learning difficulties, or people who support them. Debriefing and reparation are crucial to this. Debriefing should:

- happen quickly (advance thought should have been given to who might provide support when it becomes necessary)
- involve people who have insight into and awareness of the wide range of post traumatic reactions
- allow for professional counselling support, where necessary
- be provided by people other than line-managers in cases where staff members are involved, as fear of repercussion is common, following a negative incident

- be adequately financially resourced to allow for professional help and for replacement cover should a staff member need to spend time coming to terms with a difficult experience
- should be provided for people with learning difficulties by people who are familiar, but have not been involved in whatever occurrence has led to the trauma.

Reparation, which clearly necessitates financial planning and financial resources is an important component of minimising the financial effects of a traumatic occurrence.

Reparation, along with debriefing, will only happen if careful strategic planning is applied to the risk management process, to ensure adequate resourcing including the availability of training and additional support where necessary.

INFORMATION

Regrettably, people with learning difficulties may be passive in response to the service they receive, and need particular assistance to register their disapproval and secure redress. In a number of instances, they will register their dissatisfaction by behaving in ways which are regarded as challenging.

In these circumstances, as in others where negative things occur, it is important to document specific incidents and to analyse them on a frequent basis. Without an overview, it is difficult to work towards maximising the occurrence of planned (positive and creative) risk and minimise the occurrence of unplanned risks. Good planning therefore requires a system of risk management which allows for:

- documentation of negative incidents
- analysis of what happened – and in particular what happened in the build up to the incident
- identification of particular trends and patterns, e.g. concentration of incidents in particular settings or particular times of the day
- planned action on the basis of the trends/pattern identified
- review of the effectiveness of the action.

There are distinct links with an effective quality assurance process here, though such a process would also usually identify not only matters which require preventative and corrective action but positive experiences, the features of which can be shared. Organisations need therefore to develop risk management processes which are not only effective in locating and analysing particular difficulties, but link into the broader quality assurance process which allows for the practice of managing challenges and risks to be audited regularly to ensure continuous improvement.

CONCLUSION

Many people with learning difficulties are vulnerable not only to everyday hazards, but to a lack of regard for their wishes and needs. Risk management is therefore of particular importance in breaking a negative cycle of consistently reinforced low expectations and assisting personal development. It also ensures advance planning, not only to minimise risk but to fulfil the needs of people providing support – particularly for security and freedom from harm.

As the availability of resources tightens, risk management processes take on a particular significance, as they focus the use of resources to secure identified and specific actions. They also act as a safeguard in ensuring that, where resources do become scarce, the specific level of risk created by potential reductions in resource levels can be made clear.

Virtually all policy statements regarding services for people with learning difficulties abound with the rhetoric of empowerment. Risk management processes offer organisations not only the opportunity to protect themselves, but to provide a clear, systematic and focused way of assisting people with learning difficulties to take risks which genuinely lead to more control over their own lives.

REFERENCES

Carson, D. (1994) 'Presenting risk options.' *Inside Psychologies 1*, 1, 3–7.

Wolfensberger, W. (1975) *The Origin and Nature of Out Institutional Models.* Syracuse, New York: Human Policy Press.

Wolfensberger, W. (1977) *Principle of Normalisation – A Foundation for Effective Services.* London: John O'Brien Values Into Action.

Wolfensberger, W. and Thomas, S. (1983) *Passing.* (p.395). Rating 214 Challenge/Safety Feature of Letting. Canada: National Institute on Mental Retardation.

Statutes

The following are sources of legal requirements referred to in this chapter:

Health and Safety at Work Act 1974

Control of Substances Hazardous to Health Regulations (1988)

Food Safety Act 1990

Food Hygiene (General) Regulations 1970

Manual Handling Operating Regulations 1992

Road Vehicles (Construction and Use) Regulations 1986 (Schedule 7)

Minibus (Conditions of Fitness, Equipment and Use) Regulations 1977 (Regulations 26–28)

CHAPTER 8

We Can Take It
Young People and Drug Use

Peter Argall and Ben Cowderoy

This chapter looks at the plight of some young people who become involved in drug use, tries to interpret the concept of risk taking in their lives and informs on a strategy for intervention and service provision within a Youth Service context in a busy Central London location through case studies and description of services. Within this we will look at those making active decisions and those finding the drug market attractive to their risk taking.

The world around us seems to change with such formidable rapidity that few of us are able to pretend that we can keep pace. New technology, changing legislation, a communications revolution, new drugs, all running hand in hand with a moral climate which seems to reach ever further into our lives to try and maintain a balance. Safety nets are being removed, open competition and high risk are the norm. Yet the most adaptable, the fittest, the most energetic, the young, are being increasingly legislated against and marginalised in some parts of our community.

How society identifies 'youth' and 'young people' is an important issue in a study regarding the younger age group. In most people's minds the age group probably refers to teenagers. In research documents pertaining to this group it is not always clear as to the age parameters of people targeted and we suspect that there is often a loose definition particularly when relating to groups. The Youth Service generally identifies young people as being between the ages of 16 and 25 and we would concur with that.

Youth as the separately identified group as we understand it today only really emerged in the post war period. In some senses it became viewed as an homogeneous group which transcended racial and gender lines. It can be argued that the main factor in the forming of this group was the result of a new prosperity through which youth focused cultures became more recognised. Youth appeared to become a driving force for societal change, creating new markets and opportunities. As a result being young has become synonymous with excitement. Looking for that excitement and taking risks has come to be seen as normal developmental behaviour. It is when this search for excitement takes individuals outside of society's norms, experimenting with drug use, for example, that fear is created. In some senses this new homogeneous group called youth has become a metaphor for social change and it could be argued that there has been a determination to use the young to shape society.

Unfortunately not all change is regarded as good and it can be seen that sometime ago society began to blame youth for the many dramatic and perhaps frightening changes it was experiencing.

There is a popular belief that people take drugs because they are in some way abnormal or because something has gone wrong with the 'normal' socialisation process. There is also an argument that groups of young people marginalised in our society, may look for opportunities to get back at society. The negative response of the establishment towards them may provoke those so alienated to take the very actions which have been stated as being unacceptable by wider society. In this context for some young people drug taking may be seen, not as is widely believed, as a passive response but as actively fighting back. The more that law and society reacts against them the more important their drug taking can become as a symbol of their struggle or difference.

Drug taking can be seen as a natural choice by this group in the same way that drinking alcohol or smoking tobacco is in broader society. In illicit drug taking they are clearly making a decision to be involved in risk taking behaviour and they can cultivate this 'exciting' image by being outside of the mainstream. Illicit drug taking in the young could be seen as an expression of being different from the rest of society and be the source of admiration amongst peers. The more the risk the higher the status which will be attached to the behaviour. Jock Young (1971) points out that as well as the attraction of the effects and availability of certain drugs young people would also be attracted to the most prohibited and feared of drugs as defined by the press and media, thus increasing the bravado and excitement involved in the experience.

This image of drug taking promotes so much fear in society that being involved can be seen as one way to go beyond the acceptable barriers. The excitement and deviance related to drug use and its attendant criminality may be particularly attractive to some sections of youth culture and may be seen as symbols of status and prestige. The young who have in the past been blamed for committing crimes for no reason may now be seen as having a sinister purpose.

Case Study A

Client E is a 17-year-old black male who operated on the peripheries of the local drug scene. What he found exciting was the lifestyle around his drug use which involved him in a range of high risk activities such as shoplifting and car theft. There was much bravado in him and pleasure in retelling the stories of his jaunts out to steal and he felt he gained some real status within the peer group through his exploits. Often he was stealing items of no real consequence and that which had no real resale value, often throwing things away once he had taken them. Over the period we knew him his drug use in fact remained fairly static but he felt he had a reason for his criminality which allowed him to justify it.

Fears about drug taking are most heightened when in relation to the young. Add an element of risk taking and we are confronted with what seems a volatile and dangerous combination that society finds difficult to deal with. On reflection we can see there is a crackdown on youth through stricter policing, exclusions from school, restrictions in the benefit system and the removal of their rights to gather in groups. These can be seen as attempts to manage them.

It is often young people from poorer neighbourhoods who receive the brunt of this reaction. It is in those areas where unemployment is at its highest, where there is little expectation amongst the young, that values are being forced to change. There is a danger that the highest status amongst young people will become attached to drugs and crime in place of a job and prospects. Here is where the relationship between young people and the surrounding community can be most fraught. Within this, alternative communities can be created, one of which may be a drug using community and often these will be seen to have greater stability and structures. An observation of the Basement Project's local drug using community or market place shows support for this.

The 'market' is situated in a central inner city area with a cosmopolitan mix of shops, fast food and other restaurants, clubs and pubs. The residential housing is a mixture of private rented, owner occupied, housing association, hostels and hotels often catering for homeless people but also for a large budget tourist population. The 'market' tends to be focused on heroin, with crack as a recent addition. Until the late 1980s the drug scene was contained in pubs but, after police activity over many years, has become more displaced onto the streets. The clientele of the 'market' include a large proportion of people who live locally and reach the 'market' on foot and use the drugs they buy at home. Overall the 'market' is seen as safe by our client group because there is a high level of stability and there are clear patterns of selling and buying. Relationships of trust within the market exist on three levels: between different sellers, between sellers and buyers and between different buyers. There is also a lot of information sharing at each of these different levels. Knowledge of 'market' functioning and changes are almost entirely passed on within the 'market'. Sellers inform one another of potentially difficult or untrustworthy customers, sellers inform buyers of changes in times and locations and buyers discuss between each other the quality and prices of their drugs. The lines of communication are maintained and strengthened as a consequence of the thriving street culture that exists in the area. This apparently more stable and coherent culture will undoubtedly be attractive to some.

Case Study B

Client P is a 20-year-old black male. He made many attempts to enter into the mainstream labour market but found his way blocked for a number of reasons. First he was a black man, second he had a poor educational experience and third he had a minor record for a drug offence. He was a person whose potential was ignored and who, as a result, found himself increasingly marginalised. As he found his access blocked he began to look at opportunities within alternative labour markets and began to move into the local drug industry. Here he began to find success and a structure not unlike that he would have found in any traditional employment site. First we saw him go through an apprenticeship as a 'runner' for more established dealers, then he became more attached to people who acted as mentors and began to be seen as someone who was known as trustworthy. As people were moved out of the 'market' by police he was able to fill those gaps and become an established dealer.

Constant activity by the police and modern surveillance techniques continues to ensure that this remains a high risk activity with rapid turnover of personnel, often attracting people who are able to be dynamic risk takers. One effect of this was that we saw this risk culture reflected in P's personal life and drug taking.

Most people would see having a sense of belonging as an important factor in young people's development. For the outsider the whole lifestyle of a drug using group can be seen as exciting, even more exciting than using the drug itself. We have observed that for anyone wishing to gain entry into such groups, taking drugs with them would be the only route to acceptance. The group tends to have clear roles for the individual and a leadership hierarchy

Case Study C

There is a kinship in such a group and this can be seen in the case of client M. A white male, he was from outside the area and finding it very difficult to stabilise his lifestyle within the locale. He found it very hard to access any sort of decent and safe housing and found the benefit system unsupportive and confusing. As a result he found himself increasingly on the street. What he found there, though, was the supportive drug using community who were willing to provide both a place to stay and camaraderie. The one cost to him was that he increasingly needed to be seen as a drug user to continue to access the 'good' that the group could provide. The risk to him was that his drug use became increasingly unmanageable but he found it very difficult to even consider moving out of the group as there seemed, in his terms, little alternative as his life was dominated by his economic realities.

that is driven by fiercely competitive economic realities. As shown in Case Study B this can make it attractive. As previously stated the action of police law enforcement ensure that vacancies appear. The novice drug user finds themselves in a group for whom high risk, safely negotiated brings rich rewards in credibility.

We therefore observe that risks around substance use can be taken in order to gain status and/or acceptance and support.

Excitement and adventure in societal terms are general ways of demonstrating toughness and masculinity. Certainly male dominance is a feature of local drug using youth groups. In our observations women in groups have a very different role and place. Street drug dealing and selling is male dominated and women may only operate on the periphery and in general never seem to have control of the substance. The risk taking female drug user has less status perhaps because women are expected to operate in the family.

Case Study D

Client L, a white woman, was a 20-year-old mother of two when she first contacted the Project. She was struggling in terms of her child care though achieving a great deal. Her housing was unstable but she was able to present at the Project on a daily basis. She was an alcohol user but operating at a distance from the general drug scene in the area. After a while she placed the children into voluntary care and being relieved of that responsibility began to make different choices about her substance use. In some aspects she was being portrayed as the bad parent but did not recognise this image of herself. It is interesting to note that her peer group were also quite hostile as a result of her handing her children into care. She seemed to have breached some unwritten rule about how the whole group perceived itself. As the struggle around this and with Social Services developed L began to take risks that defined her as she felt Social Services saw her – the bad, alcohol and drug using mother. This then began to develop its own momentum as L acted this out. She also saw it as a way of getting back at them, making them work on her behalf and gaining some status from that. It is interesting to note L's move into prostitution which gave her the status of a high earner and made her very much a part of the local scene. Obviously this was a risk activity but her earning status also linked her into the primary sellers and as a result she had a higher level of dependency. Consequently, she has become involved in a range of drug taking and is very much a part of the scene in the area and shows no desire to change her lifestyle having found a role that feels right for her, though perhaps shocking to society.

There is a lot of rhetoric and moralising about young people's drug taking which has had little effect either on their drug taking or on meeting their needs. Drug use amongst young people is widespread and there is in fact a distinct lack of service provision geared to the needs of young people; for example, residential rehabilitation units and prescribing services are often inappropriate. Educating young people to take substances in less harmful ways is politically difficult. All of this leaves young people in a naive and vulnerable situation.

If young people are determined to use drugs it is clearly difficult to stop them but many organisations find it difficult to offer a service to the current young drug user. Society will only accept prevention as an option. In our case prevention cannot be the only option as such a message in the first instance will certainly be lost on the client group. Pragmatic and sensible approaches such as harm reduction are offered to adult drug users but if offered to the young there will be a moral outcry.

It is within this context, though, that the Project operates and attempts to intervene with young people. It attempts to acknowledge and recognise the risk factors that young people are engaged in in terms of their lifestyle and find an intervention that will enable them to manage in more productive ways.

The main service delivery aspect of this is the placing of substance services within a broad youth work context. The agency has been able to develop a range of services to meet the needs of the agency's whole client group, not just those who take substances. It is this generic nature which has been effective, we believe, as the agency works with a client group that ranges from young refugees and asylum seekers through to older drug injectors. It places drug users within the context of the whole community within the area and does not attempt to isolate them and differentiate their needs.

We see this being effective for a range of young people and more particularly in Case Studies A,B and D where contact was made at a very early stage before their drug use was seen as problematic by them. It is doubtful that they would have made contact with a specialist drug agency at this stage in their drug using life.

As a result young people can feel the benefits of a community broader than just the substance using one and recognise the difference and possible advantages in that. There is also a lot of crossover learning from other clients. As a result they are able to begin to make a range of wider choices than would normally be available in their group. The agency is also able to offer a range of integrated services which contact people through a building base or street-work and provides advice, information, counselling, primary health care, complementary therapies and group work. This creates a process that takes people off the streets into the agency and then back into the adult world with issues resolved and structures and strategies in place.

Case Study E

We can see this process working in the case of client K. He is a young white man with a history of violence, both against him as child, and as a perpetrator as an adult. His drug use was consistently high. We first met through streetwork and began to develop a relationship with him there. He was very suspicious of accessing the agency and had very negative experiences from past access to services. Over a period of months we began to know him quite well and K ultimately felt able to come to the Project. When he first entered the agency he did it with such force and aggression that he frightened not only the workers but also other clients. This certainly provoked a response from the agency in its efforts to manage him as we told him about the unacceptability of his behaviour. In some ways K saw this as a negative response recognisable to him from his past and he seemed to be writing us off as well. What he found difficult though was that we did not reject him as we began to explain to him that there may be better ways to ask for contact with workers other than abusing them. At the time we were also helping him with some practical issues around housing and he could appreciate the work we were doing with him. Over a period of time K began to recognise that if he came and asked for help or assistance we would still give it to him and that the result may be more positive than our continually making reference to his behaviour. After a very hard year K was able to walk into the Project and seek help and begin the positive work on himself. Even though K has now left the area as a result of being rehoused elsewhere he still keeps in touch. He still 'uses' but his use is much more controlled and manageable, he has permanent accommodation, has entered into a relationship and finished a part time college course. Overall it felt that recognising him as the individual, bringing him into the supportive structure of the agency and working with him as a whole person enabled K to understand his behaviour and life pattern and assist him in slotting back into a lifestyle that he feels is more appropriate for him.

It is this holistic approach of seeing the whole person that we feel enables many young people to feel supported and 'cared' for enough.

The informal drop-in/streetwork context of the work also recognises that in the early part of a relationship prearranged meetings may not often happen. If we look at the case studies again we see clients whose lifestyles do not allow this to happen as they are not compatible with appointment based services. Yet there still needs to be a consistency that allows young people to define their own parameters of contact with us in both time and place. This is set up by the Project in terms of consistent opening times but also by sophisticated networking into the prospective client group. The young need to be provided with a framework within which they can become conscious of their situation and explore strategies to create change. Risk is a factor in any amount of change and the risk of failure is present in any strategy to achieve. For people who have suffered a series of failures great care needs to be taken not to set them up for failure again. Young people who feel set up to fail, particularly in the presence of their peers, may often express their frustration irrationally or violently. This can have serious consequences for them, for the Project and for the surrounding community. Thus it needs to be recognised that false starts, long stops and a seeming lack of continuity may often, in fact, be the appearance of the work, but we also see real results coming out of this as shown below.

Case Study A has now been rehoused out of the area. His drug use is now peripheral and there is therefore less need for him to involve himself in crime to fund his lifestyle.

Case Study B is still involved in the drug scene but has continued to keep in touch with the agency. He is also someone who introduces many new young people into the agency. Through our work with him he is also able to take out up to date information into the group and in that way acts as an informal peer educator.

Case Study D has now been accessed into drug rehabilitation and is in negotiation with Social Services about regaining contact with her last child.

This intervention is also based within some clear philosophical guidelines which we feel are important in the practice.

First, that the work operates within a client led, client centred approach which attempts to reflect the needs of the client. Second, the Project aims to provide a safe environment and safety in relationships. This is done through mutual respect and care of the young people in attempting to equalise the power relationship and in working with the young people's social and emotional needs. Third, the Project seeks to work through discussion and negotiation in our relationship with young people and within the staff team. The Project expects and encourages young people to take responsibility for their actions and to monitor their self development through access to their files. The Project also has a staff team and management structure that equates with the broader community. The staff team is composed of workers from a wide range of professional and personal backgrounds who carry areas of expertise. Within this though there is a shared workload with all workers undertaking generic work practice with the client group. Confidentiality is shared within the staff team and though this may be difficult for some clients it enables them to have a broad-based relationship with the whole agency and not just individual workers, enabling long term consistent practice to take place.

The issue that unites all the Project's client groups is their current and historical lack of access to services and it feels important that the agency does not collude with this. Hence the drop-in service which allows people to come in off the street and gain not so much instant gratification, but a feeling that they can be heard as the individual and not be treated as part of a larger bureaucracy. Also, the agency has taken part in street and outreach work for many years. This is a basic Youth Service process and enables the power structures in the work to be altered and therefore a better quality of relationship to develop. The success of this we can see with Case Study C who was initially contacted through the Project's street work. He has now been detoxed and through rehabilitation. He has moved into a broader community with a wider range of contacts and is now securely housed.

This going out to young people's 'spaces' enables the Project to have a clearer understanding of its clients' experience but also, we believe, gives the clients the view that they are important enough for us to come and provide services to them. Also it allows a range of information and services to be taken to young people in a way which may feel more user friendly and therefore be better retained.

As a result we can see a process of young people beginning to be heard within their own experiences, supported where they 'are now' and, we hope beginning to recognise ways of accessing mainstream society as opposed to confronting it. This, in itself, may seem difficult but for us it is important to remind ourselves that young people as a group are not necessarily radical and opposed to the mainstream societal norms but often just want a way of taking part.

BIBLIOGRAPHY

Arnison, E. (1994) *Speed: Kicking the Habit*. The Big Issue.

Burr, A. (1989) 'An inner city response to heroin use.' In S. McGregor (ed) *Drugs and British Society*. London: Routledge.

Channel Four Television (1994) *Critical Eye: The Lost Generation*.

Clarke, J., Hall, S., Jefferson, T. and Roberts, B. (1980) 'Subcultures cultures and class: a theoretical overview.' In S. Hall and T. Jefferson (eds) *Resistance Through Rituals: Youth Subcultures in Post War Britain*. London: Hutchinson.

Haralambos, M. (1984) *Sociology: Themes and Perspectives*. Slough: University Tutorial Press.

McRobbie, A. and Garber, J. (1980) 'Girls and subcultures: an exploration.' In S. Hall and T. Jefferson (eds) *Resistance Through Rituals: Youth Subcultures in Post War Britain*. London: Hutchinson.

O'Bryan, L. (1989) 'Young people and drugs.' In S. Mcgregor (ed) *Drugs and British Society*. London: Routledge.

Pearson, G. (1987) *The New Heroin Users*. Oxford: Basil Blackwell.

Willis, P. (1980) 'The cultural meaning of drug use.' In S. Hall and T. Jefferson (eds) *Resistance Through Rituals: Youth Subcultures in Post War Britain*. London: Hutchinson.

Young, J. (1971) *The Drugtakers: The Social Meaning of Drug Use*. London: Paladin.

The Basement Project, 4 Hogarth Road, London SW5 0PT (Tel: 0171 373 2335) is an independent charity in Earls Court (partly funded by the Royal Borough of Kensington and Chelsea). The Project aims to work with people 16–30 years old to provide an effective, confidential and free advice and counselling service on a broad range of issues, but more specifically around housing benefits, substance use and health.

CHAPTER 9

Alcohol
The Effects and Risks for Individuals

Pamela Askham

INTRODUCTION

This chapter will give an insight into working with drinkers who are finding both their lives and situations difficult. A drinker is someone who has found alcohol to be a problem to them and/or their everyday life – including family, friends, financial hardships and employment. I will show how the worker can facilitate the drinker making decisions about their life and their problem/s, and will give the worker knowledge of how to attempt various ways forward with more confidence using the different techniques and case histories.

WHAT IS ALCOHOL AND ITS EFFECTS?

Alcohol is a drug. It is suggested by the medical profession that sensible and low-risk amounts of alcohol would be 28 units for men and 21 units for women per week with two alcohol-free days (Health Education Authority). One unit is equivalent to a half pint of regular strength beer or lager, a pub measure of spirits, a glass of wine or a single sherry. Alcohol will alter the functions of the body, slow down the nervous system and affect the part of the brain controlling behaviour – taking only five minutes to reach and affect the brain. It is a depressant and brings deeper and unresolved feelings to the surface in a negative way. However, many people enjoy alcohol and know how much is enough for them. For people who may be becoming dependent on alcohol, it is similar to becoming dependent on a prescribed or illegal drug. For some, whilst using alcohol, their nervous system will adjust and cope with the effects of heavy drinking. If this happens and the drinker tries to go without for some time, they will feel shaky and may have 'flu-like symptoms. This will continue until the body re-adjusts to coping without alcohol.

For most people a dependence on alcohol will not happen; they will continue to enjoy alcohol for the following reasons:

- enjoyment for themselves and the social company experienced
- to relieve anxiety and/or tension
- internal/external pressures
- after a hard day at home/work

- relationship problems
- poor self image
- loneliness
- guilt
- coping with bereavement.

The above may be short-term drinking which may be heavy at times but not enough to cause dependence. After alcohol has been drunk it can give the feelings of increased confidence.

RISKS AND ALCOHOL

In order to consider the risks a heavy drinker may take it is necessary to understand him or her by observing behaviour. S/he will drink in order to gain or avoid something, that is the drinking is functional. It can lead to unpleasant consequences within the health, work, social life, family and housing situations of the drinker, which will be considered in relation to risk below.

Health

Weight can either be gained or lost; men can gain a 'beer belly', women may put weight on all over their body. The calorific and sugar content in alcohol is very high, but there is no nutritional value. The risk taken by the drinker is to cause damage to their health which could lead to liver damage and possibly death.

Work

Alcohol may be drunk before going to work, in which case there may be lateness leading to verbal/written warnings and later dismissal. Machinery becomes difficult to operate due to the alcohol affecting the brain. Accidents will almost certainly follow – these may be the cause of loss of limbs or be fatal.

Social Life

Although most people enjoy alcohol when going out for social occasions, heavy drinkers may need to have a few drinks *before* going out. They may approach the bar in the pub and order 'a quick one' whilst the other drinks are being poured. The need for alcohol becomes desperate at times and begins to interfere with the occasion. As the drinker begins to feel more at ease, s/he has the ability of saying and doing things that may embarrass others. The risk within a drinker's social life could turn to being arrested for drink-driving, being drunk and disorderly or causing a fatal accident involving a child. There does not appear to be a much worse scenario than the loss of livelihood due to drinking.

Family

Other members of the family and meals may be waiting to be shared at home and the drinker has not arrived home yet. Children can get irritable if they are expected to wait for a parent or caring adult. Often we do not explain to children why they are expected to be good and wait at the table. The rest of the family begin to eat earlier, so the drinker comes home and will have either nothing or something cold to eat. Time goes on and the family are becoming alienated from the drinker. This may not be a planned action but will happen due to the reluctance of the family to put up with this behaviour. Other events begin to suffer, for example the parents evening, the seasonal school play, sports day, important events for the partner of the drinker, and so the list goes on. The drinker will be full of remorse and promise this will not happen again. However, the next event is often just around the corner and the family live in hope that the drinker will be there.

If family members are aware of the drinker receiving help, they too may want to talk to someone – for example a counsellor or social worker (who shall be referred to below as the worker). If this happens the worker must not be led into talking about the drinker and his or her behaviour; the work being done with the drinker needs to remain confidential between the worker and the drinker. The other family members need to be heard, but they will need to be heard and helped by someone else. Drinking can create secrets within a family. It is important to try and enable the family to talk to each other and, just as important as talking, to help them to listen to each other. As suggested with the drinker, tasks can be undertaken with the friends or relatives. These tasks need to be shared and encouraged. This in turn will, hopefully, lead to more concrete communication within the relationships.

Housing

The rent, mortgage or similar financial commitments may not be being paid into the relevant organisations. Eventually, after negotiations with the land-lords, banks and building societies, etc., the money is promised to be there on time for the next week or month. Unfortunately, to some drinkers the money for their next drink is far more important than the money needed to keep the roof over their heads. This, in turn, can lead to becoming homeless – with the possibility of the family going separate ways.

ALCOHOL AND RISK ASSESSMENT

Alcohol becomes a problem when it fails to achieve the intended goal. This is when a risk assessment proves necessary in working with the drinker. As time goes on, the drinker will find him or herself drinking more and more to achieve the same effect as before when drinking much less. This can create a risk-centred environment. It is acknowledged that people and their situations may differ, however, when people are placed in a situation where there is a risk that they are more likely to act in a more dangerous way. For example, Pat came to see the worker with a broken arm. He always insisted on having a final whiskey; this always made him late for his bus. The previous week he was trying to beat the traffic as usual but unfortunately this time he was hit by a car. He had placed himself in a risk situation. He telephoned his partner, who went to the hospital to collect him. However, when she found out what had happened she suggested he make his own way home.

The risks of alcohol changing behaviour may be seen in:

- missing appointments
- forgetting people and/or things; losing things
- absenteeism from class or work
- poor standard of work
- offences committed whilst drinking
- court appearances
- custodial sentences
- mood swings
- depression
- financial hardship
- relationship problems
- child neglect or abuse
- domestic violence
- attempted suicides.

When helping a drinker with a drinking problem and undertaking a risk assessment, his or her story is very important. However, it is crucial that the worker listens to any other problems being presented by the drinker. Although these problems may not be alcohol related they need to be heard and evaluated for the risk assessment process. Listening is not only hearing verbally, it is listening to the drinker's tone of voice, hearing anxiety in the voice and interpreting the body language which is being presented. The worker should be asking him or herself "Does the body language match what is being said verbally?"

Before going into an assessment interview it is a good idea to have a checklist of questions. These will allow the worker to gain more knowledge about the drinker and his or her lifestyle regarding drinking. It is possible the drinker may give the worker much more information than has been asked for, in which case the worker needs to listen to other possible areas of risk that may be being given indirectly by the drinker:

- What are the reasons for drinking?
- Is there a pattern to the drinking?
- Does the drinker come from a family of heavy drinkers?
- Do the social groups attended by the drinker include heavy drinkers?
- Did the drinking evolve over a period of time or very quickly?
- What are the quantities of alcohol drunk in each drinking session?
- Has the drinker tried to cut down or stop before, if so with what effects?
- What does the drinker want to do about their drinking?
- What support will the drinker have during the period of cutting down or stopping?

The worker may need more than one session to complete the assessment and gain the answers to the following basic questions which underpin the assessment:

- Would you like to tell me how much you are drinking at the present time?
- Have you considered that alcohol may be contributing to what is happening in your life now?

These questions will give the worker some factual information about the drinker's drinking and life experiences. Although the first question is a direct one, the worker is asking the drinker to think about a problem that has probably been worrying him or her for some time. The second question may help to diffuse some of the drinker's confusion as to what is really happening to him or her while s/he is under the influence of alcohol. Other questions which need to be asked in a risk assessment are in relation to:

- cultural and religious environments
- present life style and family commitments
- work history with and without alcohol
- medical history, e.g. previous admissions to hospital for alcohol-related problems
- sources of enthusiasm
- aims and ventures for the future
- other problems being faced by the client
- time of day the drinking begins
- reasons for continuing to drink
- what the client wants to achieve regarding his or her drinking
- how realistic is the goal (does it need breaking down into more achievable goals?)
- positive aspects of drinking
- negative aspects of drinking
- where does the drinker see him or herself in six months time
- the reason for the drinker coming for help now
- what other key people think about the drinking.

The assessment is a time for obtaining the information regarding how much alcohol is being consumed. It is a time when the drinker has the opportunity to give the worker some idea of the risk(s) they are placing him or herself or family in with the drinking. A risk for one person is nothing more than a hiccup for others. The worker must not minimise the risk the drinker is offering in a risk assessment. For example, Alice never got sober. Her return home would put her partner at risk. She would be violent with kitchen equipment and risk hurting them both. Other risks included having the neighbours call the police, in turn this could bring police charges against Alice. A more detailed example is given in the case study below.

Mick's Story

Mick was living in a one-parent family situation for several years. His drinking had become heavy in the past ten months, especially in the mornings. The youngest of the three children, aged twelve, ten and six, had started school twelve months before, leaving Mick to sit and think about his past. Afternoons had always taken care of themselves in the past with shopping and preparing the evening meal which the family ate together after discussing everybody's day.

Mick began to feel lost, isolated and very lonely in the mornings since the youngest child had gone to school. He was unable to make friends and felt embarrassed when mothers asked if he would like to join them for coffee. He told the worker about going to the alcohol section in the supermarket and buying wine. He remembered enjoying a drink in the past before his wife had left. Mick had a personal rule of not drinking before 11.30 a.m, but as the weeks went on the drinking began earlier. In fact, as soon as all the children had left for school Mick would sit down and have some wine. Apparently other parents had noticed he was not at the gates as normal. Teachers were sending messages of concern. Mick was not functioning as he had done in the past, for example the children's meals were not ready at the usual times. The older children had begun to take over the household tasks of cooking, cleaning, etc and in fact there was role reversal taking place. Mick was being cared for by his children. The risk here was that others would begin to find out that there were problems and take matters into their own hands by forcing the issue of the children's health and welfare.

Mick discussed with the worker how alcohol helped and hindered his life. It helped him forget all the problems he faced – there was loneliness, trying to impress other parents, not having a friend with whom he could share problems and forgetting every negative memory he had. After the worker asked Mick where he saw himself in a few months time, his response was: 'If I carry on like this, not seeing my children growing up because I will have kicked the bucket'. They talked about ways forward and what Mick wanted to do about his drinking. He had never had a problem in the past and would like to return to having a family life as they had had previously. Mick assured the worker that stopping drinking was achievable as his children were the most important things in his life.

Mick had taken many risks with the children: not collecting them from school, leaving them to look after one another, not being there for them when they needed help and, most importantly, not listening to them sharing concerns about their father. It became obvious that Mick needed to have some time to get to know himself and the children again, to enjoy what was going on and give evidence to others that he was capable of taking care of his family and himself.

Other problems which Mick was facing were related to not letting the children talk about their mother and the pain they felt, not moving on for himself and asking for the help he needed. As Mick had been drinking heavily for so long, the worker discussed the idea of stopping slowly and over a period of time. This would not mean their lives would change dramatically but would begin to change over the next few weeks. Mick had reached three bottles of wine per day. After discussing what was possible within his drinking, he decided on going down to one bottle a day for a week. Mick risked experiencing certain symptoms – possible unsteadiness, feeling hot and cold and not being able to eat or sleep properly –at first. The reason for not sleeping well was that Mick had been having alcohol before going to bed. The alcohol had then helped him to sleep, so, without it, he may not sleep for as long or as peacefully.

It took seven weeks of talking and monitoring his drinking for Mick to be alcohol free and return to his normal behaviour. Understanding the reasons for his drinking was important but it was also crucial to visit other problems which had been around but had never been addressed.

In a risk assessment it is necessary to focus on the drinker's self-confidence and his or her ability to believe in him or herself. Friends, relatives and colleagues may have told the drinker that s/he will not have the willpower to either cut down or stop drinking. S/he may have been told that they have tried other things in the past and failed. The worker must help the drinker to recognise that this time does not have to be the same as any other. The drinker needs to be helped to understand that it is not going to be a self-fulfilling prophecy. People can change and so too can their behaviour. The drinker has come asking for help or the worker may have suggested that s/he could offer support in this area.

To do this, the worker must ask for different examples of how the drinker has succeeded in other changes s/he has made in his or her life. It is important to stay with the positive feelings. A check-list for the worker to help the drinker consider his or her past life changes is:

- What are the circumstances leading up to the drinker making decisions to stop drinking?
- Was the drinker the only person involved in making the decision to stop drinking? (People involved could be family members – partners, children and siblings – or friends, employers, employees and colleagues).
- What is going to take the place of alcohol?
- How could the drinker chart their progress during the next weeks/months?
- What rewards could there be in this change of behaviour?

At this stage the worker has more questions ready to be put forward to the drinker. S/he will also need a more accurate description of what is being drunk and where. This is when a drinker's diary would be a useful tool to use.

DAY	TIME	WITH WHO	WHERE	DRINK	MONEY SPENT
MONDAY					
TUESDAY					
WEDNESDAY					
THURSDAY					
FRIDAY					
SATURDAY					
SUNDAY					

Figure 9.1 A drinker's diary

The columns of the diary are easily understood. It is easier if the worker fills in the diary because the drinker may have literacy problems or maybe problems with concentrating on being involved in talking and writing at the same time. If the worker is filling in the diary, s/he must ensure that the drinker can see what is being written down. If the drinker does have any literacy problems, the worker should move the paper towards the drinker and give an explanation about what has been written at every opportunity. However, when completing the columns headed 'drink' and 'money spent', this involves asking the drinker what s/he had to drink and how much was spent in a drinking session. It can be a shock to the drinker to recognise what was drunk and indeed just how much s/he has spent on alcohol.

All the headings are a way of helping the drinker to monitor and gain some responsibility for his or her own drinking and the behaviour that goes with it. As the diary is being completed, the worker and the drinker may begin to see a pattern forming of times and days that are possible risk-problem areas. These patterns can be both negative and positive. After the full week has been recounted and the diary has been completed it will form a basis for the worker and the client to discuss the risks involved with the drinking. Some of the risks are finding that the drinker:

- drank much more than s/he had intended to
- is drinking more with certain people than others
- is going into the same places when s/he is drinking heavily
- gets into trouble on certain days of the week
- regrets how much they have drunk the day before.

ALCOHOL AND RISK MANAGEMENT

Having clearly established the present situation, it is time to move on from assessing risk to managing the risks in relation to changing the drinking pattern. Examples of high risk situations are:

- Negative emotional states – feeling angry, depressed, anxious and tense. This can lead to the drinker saying or doing things they would not normally do if s/he was not under the influence of alcohol. In the past, alcohol may have helped with the emotions listed above. However, they may now be seen as a high risk. If so, the worker must discuss how the drinker would act or react if s/he had not been drinking.
- Social pressure – the drinker may be introduced into a celebratory environment. It is usual for him or her to have thoughts regarding 'one won't hurt'; 'it wouldn't be polite to refuse a drink'; 'everyone around me is drinking, I don't want to feel left out'. The risk here is that s/he would have more than the one and put him or herself and other people at risk from embarrassment at not being able to revisit a place again.
- Testing personal control – there may be times, for example, when the drinker is being pressured by peers to have a drink. The peer group may offer statements such as: 'go on, it's been a long time since you

had a drink'; 'just the one won't hurt'; 'just the one won't lead to any more'. Being in such a high-risk situation may cause the drinker to stay and have drinks or to leave the place where s/he is at present and drink in isolation at a different venue.

Knowing that there are going to be hard-to-handle situations and environments means there is going to be a degree of risk involved with drinking in the future. The worker and drinker must together focus on one or possibly more of these situations and prepare better ways of coping. One exercise is to prepare for the risks by using a mental rehearsal in a role play scenario. The worker allows the drinker to practise what s/he would say in a risky situation. The worker then moves the drinker on to planning and rehearsing alternative thinking and behavioural patterns. The following case study illustrates this in more detail.

Dave's Story

When Dave went out in the evening, he would go to his local pub. On entering, the landlord would push a pint of beer along the bar saying 'the first is on me'. He would buy all further drinks himself. Dave did not join his peer group in buying 'rounds', he always seemed to drink more than they did. If he was in a round in the past, he would say he was going to the toilet. However, he did not go to the toilet, he would go to the bar and have one or two doubles. By doing this he would ensure he was getting as merry and, later in the evening, as drunk as the group were. The buying of rounds stopped when the others in the group told him he must have a weak bladder going to the toilet so many times in one evening. After that particular evening, Dave decided not to join in buying rounds in future. He would drink with them but buy his own alcohol. This had happened for years. The other regulars had been used to seeing Dave leave the pub drunk. He felt as though it was an expectation that he should leave the pub with a 'skin full'. Dave had decided 'enough was enough'. He was tired of being the pub fool but he did not know how to stop. After the worker asked what he would like to do, his response was 'to go to the pub and not have the landlord to already have poured the first pint'. The worker and Dave rehearsed what he could say. However, Dave kept saying he felt a fool and the landlord would not understand that he wanted to cut down his drinking. Dave decided the only way he could talk to the landlord was out of pub hours. Dave and the worker practised the role play with the worker being the landlord within the safety of the counselling room. There was no risk of failing or making himself look foolish there. Dave felt comfortable with what he had rehearsed. Some time later Dave was much happier. He had told the landlord he would like to cut down his drinking and the first drink he would like should be a low-alcohol beer. That way he felt no one would notice, whereas a soft drink might have brought whispers and ridicule by the regulars. He continued to go home having had a drink and went home more sober than he had done for a long time. This type of environment continues to be a high risk situation for Dave. However, he will happily rehearse using role play in front of the mirror.

It is at this stage that the drinker will need to be aware of other outside pressures and the possibility of being caught out. The worker can help the drinker by spending time with him or her and reviewing the benefits of sticking to the original commitment. In a sense it is moving forwards with the same idea as using the broken record in assertiveness. The worker allows the drinker to find a statement or phrase that s/he is happy with using; one that will be comfortable whether it is the first time or the fiftieth time s/he has used the same statement or phrase. For example, the drinker could use the following statements beginning with I am:

- taking antibiotics and am unable to drink alcohol whilst on them
- feeling a bit under the weather
- trying not to drink as much when I have the car
- buying my own, not a lot of cash right now.

If the drinker can own or feel comfortable with any of the above, or find another statement which s/he would continually feel okay with, then they have a much better chance of achieving the desired goal during that drinking time.

As the drinker begins to believe in him or herself and abilities, the worker can begin to offer tasks to be done outside the sessions, for example:

- keeping a drinker's diary every week
- drinking soft or low-alcohol drinks when thirsty
- trying not to drink on his or her own as much as possible
- practise the skill of refusing a drink with someone the drinker trusts and with whom s/he feels comfortable (not just in the safe environment of the room the worker and client use together)
- have something to eat before going out
- having one alcohol-free day in the coming week
- having space in the week for him or herself
- trying to replace one alcoholic drink with a soft drink
- starting the drinking later in the day
- not to drink at lunch times on certain days
- do something active while drinking
- make an achievable contract of units to be drunk in one day or in the week
- practise refusing alcohol when with friends
- ask a friend or relative to give support when going out to drink
- do not drink alone
- do not drink if feeling tense or anxious.

Together, the worker and the drinker will think of other tasks as they progress. The worker must remember that the drinker needs to feel comfortable with the tasks being set. These should be negotiated at all times. The drinker is in charge of his or her life and will be the best judge of what s/he can and cannot do. One task could be easy one week and the next it could be the most difficult thing s/he has ever done. This is where both negotiating and discussing the planned tasks will help. As the drinker begins to feel more at ease with the tasks the worker should ask him or her to think of a task s/he can achieve before the next meeting. The following case study will illustrate this.

Jo's Story

Jo had been drinking heavily for many months. In the past, Jo had always thought she had been fun to be around, happy and intelligent, now she was snappy and irritable. During her first visit she told the worker what life was like before she had started to drink heavily. After leaving school she had gone to secretarial college and worked extremely hard. Jo had always been excited about going to work in the mornings, until the day her manager left. She had always been an assertive person and coped well under pressure. However, her new manager was beginning 'to ask for the impossible'. To meet the deadlines set by him it meant her staying behind after work. All of a sudden she did not have the confidence to say she would tackle the work the following day.

A colleague suggested that they go to the pub as a reward for a long hard day. As time went on, Jo drank more often and lunchtimes were being spent in the pub. Whenever she felt tired, under pressure, got at or at risk of failing to present the work she was doing, she would have a drink. After a while her drinking became heavy and she began to shake in the mornings. To help her feel better she had a glass of vodka. Within seconds she was feeling much better and able to leave the house.

The day before Jo had come to see the worker she had had a verbal warning regarding her late arrival for work. Apparently there had been other warnings but none were given formally. The worker went through an assessment process. During this the worker, with the co-operation of Jo, needed to find out what the positive and negative aspects were about her drinking. Jo's list of these were:

The positive things about drinking:

- helps with the pressure at work
- work seems to flow and get done quicker
- gives confidence
- feels more assertive
- can relax more
- feel safe
- inhibitions are lowered
- can laugh again and be friendly with others
- able to talk to different people
- ability to sleep at night.

The negative things about drinking:

- costs too much
- dark circles under eyes, looking ill
- feeling ill
- people asking 'what's wrong?' all the time; people beginning to notice something is different

- getting depressed
- no other ways to unwind
- feeling guilty
- not having many good days
- family nagging about how much is being drunk.

As Jo had little support, the worker had to look at the risks associated with both her day and her evenings. She could be harming herself physically with this much alcohol, have been given a final warning before losing her job or have been involved in an accident, perhaps knocked down or fallen if she was not as sure footed as normal. She had nothing that would give her the same feeling that alcohol did. There was nothing else that would take the place of alcohol. If there is little or no support, the drinker will find stopping or cutting down very hard. The worker discussed the possibilities of her days being better than they were now and suggested that Jo visit her GP. There are times when the drinker needs medical help in order to stop or cut down on drinking. It was suggested that Jo should have five or six days off work. This would allow her body to get used to the idea of not having alcohol and, as suggested earlier, she needed time to re-adjust to life with no alcohol. Jo spent the first three days in the house with plenty of fluid, small meals when she felt like eating and people popping in to see her. After a time Jo felt the only option open to her was to find other work; possibly leave office work for a while. As this was a major move in her life the worker spent several sessions discussing what Jo could do. Jo moved jobs but continues to feel at risk when going into a pub at lunchtimes.

RECORDING/REVIEWING

Keeping records will help the worker organise his or her thoughts. They are an aid for the worker and drinker to continue planning achievable tasks. An important issue regarding recording is helping to provide evidence of drinking patterns – such as difficult times of the day or days of the week – which are beginning to become clearer. Records will also provide the worker and drinker with evidence of change during the period of time they have worked together. Alcohol can either be increased or decreased – this needs to be monitored. One way of doing this would be to look at the drinking diaries and compare the drinker's consumption. If the worker ceases work with the drinker for whatever reason and later resumes, it can be helpful for the worker to see where the drinker is now in their drinking and how this may have changed from any previous sessions. Recording is a personal issue. The worker knows how much s/he needs to remember about a particular issue being raised. The worker needs to remember that records may be accessed by others and used in court if the drinker has committed an offence. The length of time the records are kept is entirely up to the organisation for which the worker is providing the service.

Reviewing work with a drinker needs to be completed at regular intervals, initially every four weeks. This can change as and when both the worker and drinker feel it to be appropriate. The review should include:

- the amount being drunk, has it increased/decreased
- good things happening when not drinking as much
- negative things if drinking as much or more
- issues raised in the assessment interview
- issues being offered by the drinker that are important to him/her
- tasks that were agreed.

SUPPORT/SUPERVISION FOR WORKERS

The amount of time and number of sessions of supervision should be negotiated between worker and supervisor. Initially sessions could be after each session spent with the drinker if the worker feels the need, reducing to less often as time goes on. The worker needs to have trust in his or her supervisor as s/he will be helping the worker to implement ideas and plan for future sessions. The supervisor should always have more experience than the worker. The worker will need to explore his or her feelings about both the drinker and his or her drinking in supervision. The amount of time and frequency of sessions needed will depend on how much knowledge the worker has. If there are issues regarding alcohol that are hard for the worker and supervisor to understand, help may be found from a local alcohol advisory service. This will be support from another worker in the agency and not necessarily supervision. Support/supervision needs to be as useful to the worker as the worker is being to the drinker. The relationship is very similar to that of worker and drinker, a place where safety, respect and boundaries are discussed and agreed. Supervision should be negotiated throughout the alliance. If there comes a time that a supervisory alliance is not working then the worker should look towards finding alternative help.

CONCLUSION

Every drinker wanting help can be helped, but s/he must want to change patterns of thought and behaviour regarding alcohol. A drinker will need support, encouragement and time. It is important for a worker involved with helping a drinker to ensure that s/he has the right support and guidance. This chapter is a guide for workers who may find themselves dealing with drinkers and the problems drinking brings. I have tried to show that there is no single antecedent for alcohol problems and that improvement in a drinker's life is possible with the motivation to stop or cut down. Abnormal drinking patterns will take time to be re-adjusted. I show how time and understanding can be used by the worker to facilitate the recognition of old and new drinking habits.

Most drinkers with problems have responsibilities of family and employment, they are not homeless or without friends. Most of all, it must be remembered that drinkers create pain for themselves and their families and friends. This chapter will help the worker to piece together enough information to create the start of an alliance between them and enable the drinker to make sense of some of the decisions which need to be made in order to achieve a better quality of life for themselves, their family and their friends.

CHAPTER 10

Homelessness and Mental Health
Risk Assessment

Sue Lipscombe

The starting point for any discussion of risk assessment and risk management must be to examine the type of service and resource availability which will underpin the process. In the case of homeless people there is also a need to define terms – who do we describe as 'homeless'?

The answer to this question seems to depend on who provides it. Advocacy and campaigning groups understandably wishing to affect and improve national housing policy include not only those without shelter but all groups of people living in poor housing conditions. This would include staying with friends, families in bed and breakfast, occupants of sub-standard accommodation, hostel dwellers and street homeless. In these terms, clearly, the homeless are not an homogenous group.

Other classifications are made by drawing a distinction between statutory and non-statutory homeless using the criteria of the Housing Act 1985, which seeks to identify 'vulnerability' as a condition for housing assistance. Generally, by this definition most single people are classified as 'non-vulnerable' whilst families and pregnant women will be considered 'statutory homeless'. In practice a proportion of single adults are deemed vulnerable and others would be eligible if they presented for assessment to the local housing authority.

The Westminster Joint Homelessness Team (JHT) was set up in 1990 under the Government's Homeless Mentally Ill Initiative (HMII) to work with homeless mentally ill people who have little or no contact with mainstream health or social services. The team works on an outreach basis visiting hostels and day centres run by voluntary sector agencies. It also undertakes street work with long-term isolated rough sleepers who have no contact with either sector. Staff are drawn from the local mental health trusts and the local authority social services department. The objective is to improve mental health and access to appropriate housing, and the team has access to certain specific housing and residential care resources established through the Department of Health Initiative and the Housing Corporation.

In 1996 the team was expanded to undertake vulnerability assessments for the local authority of homeless applicants presenting to the housing department with mental health difficulties. In the first six months of operation the team assessed 237 single people, of whom 155 were found vulnerable against the criteria established under the Housing Act 1985. This would appear to indicate that the broad classification of single people as non-vulnerable is too simplistic and unhelpful.

The Royal College of Psychiatrists' working party report on Homelessness and Mental Illness (1991) (quoted in Bhugra 1966) has suggested three categories:

1. Single homeless.

2. Young single homeless (under 26 years of age).

3. Homeless families.

From an operational point of view this is a more convenient classification for clinical and social services practitioners, allowing a clear focus under statutory responsibilities such as Children's legislation, The Mental Health Act 1983 and the NHS and Community Care Act 1990. The age cut-off at 25 is also relevant to benefits regulations.

Scott (1993) has devised a classification of homeless groups which provides the likely level of incidence of mental illness associated with type of homelessness (Figure 10.1).

Suspected level of mental illness	Temporal classification	Geographical classification	Typographical classification
High			
		Street people	Street people
	Chronically homeless		
		Hostel residents	Chronic alcoholics
	Episodically homeless		
			Unconnected young
		Temporary accommodation	
			Women
			Families
		'Staying with others'	
Lower	Transiently homeless		Situational

Source: Scott (1993)

Figure 10.1 Classification of homeless groups

Attempts to classify people only according to housing status ignore other equally important aspects of their lives, for example social networks, employment status or education opportunities. Bachrach (1984) comments that most definitions of homelessness explicitly or implicitly involve not only an absence or inadequacy of a physical shelter but also elements of social isolation or dissatisfaction.

Broadly speaking, 'the homeless mentally ill' has come to refer primarily to the single homeless with mental health problems and those in couples without dependant children with mental health problems. The 1980s and 1990s have seen increasing numbers of visibly homeless in almost all European and American cities, a proportion of whom are mentally ill, with a growing number under 25 years of age.

SINGLE HOMELESS MENTALLY ILL PEOPLE

The proportion of the homeless population suffering from mental illness is the subject of much debate. Historically, most studies have focused on institutional populations in work houses and, more latterly, large hostels. There is some general consistency of findings which indicate that around 30% of occupants suffer from severe mental illness, probably schizophrenia, and a further third experience alcohol misuse problems. Almost all of these studies were of male populaces (Whiteley 1955, Lodge-Patch 1970, Priest 1976, Marshall 1989).

The late 1980s and 1990s has seen many of these large hostels close or become smaller and much improved in physical environment and general service provision. In London in 1981 there were still 9751 bed spaces in direct access hostels, 6000 of those in large traditional hostels for homeless people. By 1990 the numbers of direct access bed spaces had declined to around 2000 – a loss of over 7000 (Single Homeless in London 1986, 1995).

The Rough Sleepers Initiative (RSI) (Randall and Brown 1996), from 1990 onwards, has gone some way to improving this situation by the provision of some additional hostel places but it remains clear that this process of hostel closure, whilst welcome, has contributed to the increasing number of visibly homeless on London streets.

The popular belief that the closure of the large psychiatric institutions is also a major cause of this increase is not borne out by the experience of the HMII teams who reported only 2% of their clients with history of long-term care prior to homelessness.

It appears that the time lag in setting up and resourcing proper community alternatives to long-term care has been a further significant factor responsible for the increasing numbers of homeless mentally ill individuals. Craig et al. (1995) reported that 29% of homeless people assessed by the HMII teams had previously been housed in council accommodation as adults and their failure to maintain the tenancy appears to have been the result of lack of support and supervision.

Of course there have been other significant changes whose effect we are only now beginning to understand – namely economic recession, reduction in the availability of cheap housing and demographic changes in family composition and increasing family breakdown. One result of these recent changes has been to change the visible face of homelessness, characterised in the 1960s and 1970s by white middle-aged men, to a younger population with more women and a far greater ethnic mix. The under-25s are the fastest growing group of homeless people.

Whilst it is clear that the single homeless cannot be considered a homogenous group with identical needs, some general principles of good practice in health and social care service delivery can be identified and applied – whether as part of a specialist service specifically targeted at homeless people or as guiding principles in the delivery of a generic, mainstream service which is accessible to all. Most importantly, the threat of homelessness should always be identified by practitioners as a risk factor in all assessment and care planning activities.

MODELS OF SERVICE PROVISION

Much passionate argument takes place about the respective merits of specialist services versus improving access to ordinary mainstream services in health and social care for homeless people. It is argued, on the one hand, that specialist services exclude and marginalise homeless people and may lead to poorer standards, fewer resources and, worst of all, to stereotyping. The case for more accessible services open to all is based on the principle of equality of opportunity, responding to need rather than the 'status' of the individual. On the other hand, specialist services can be tailored to the circumstances of a smaller group and organised specifically to overcome the barriers to access usually experienced by homeless people.

Many practitioners now support the development of both complementary approaches (Pleace and Quilgars 1996) and regard both as having an important part in improving access to health care. Perhaps the most important element is the inter-relationship of service groupings, both specialist and mainstream, and the ability to refer between one and the other dependent on what the individual client may need at any one time. Thus a homelessness specialist mental health team may wish to refer a client who is no longer homeless and whose mental health is stable for support and monitoring to the local provider service. Equally, the local Community Mental Health Team (CMHT) may not be able to maintain contact with clients who are reluctant to keep appointments or come to a clinic but who may use resources for homeless people, where the specialist team has regular input and may be better placed to work with them.

KEY ELEMENTS IN RESPONSIVE SERVICE PROVISION

Accessibility

Few barriers like appointments, receptionists and delays. Simple informal contact process.

Location

Familiar location where client feels comfortable and can access other services, like cheap food and clothing and housing advice, in locations such as day centres, night shelters and hostels. A street work service is necessary where there are significant numbers of rough sleepers.

Flexibility

Staff are able to offer an initial contact at least to a wide range of clients.

Multidisciplinary Team

Should include mental health and social care practitioners, including housing workers. Practitioners should have core professional skills, e.g. nursing, social work, psychiatry, but have overlapping roles, which allows the client access to a wide range of assistance through one key professional who is the allocated case manager. Homeless people often present with a multiplicity of needs and staff must be prepared to take on a wider role than in more conventional teams.

ACCESS TO HOUSING AND COMMUNITY CARE RESOURCES

Many clients understandably regard their housing, practical and financial needs as being more urgent or at least as important as their mental health needs. It is vital that the team is as well placed as possible to respond to these needs by the creation of special access to hostel beds, registered care and a range of other forms of supported housing. Resources available through a care management assessment can be crucial to underpin any re-housing or support package and a fast-track assessment system for homeless people should be negotiated with the local authority in order to avoid delay in obtaining hostel places or other forms of shelter.

NETWORKING AND LIAISON

Most specialist mental health teams are located within the statutory sector, whilst many single homeless people rely on the voluntary sector for their essential provision. Specialist teams should provide a bridge between the two sectors, creating positive working relationships and good communication. Many teams offer training in mental health issues to voluntary sector agencies and draw up inter-agency guidelines for joint working, including referral arrangements and confidentiality policies. Increasingly, voluntary sector agencies have considerable experience and expertise in homelessness issues, which should be used to complement that of the mental health team. An example of more formal approaches to networking and liaison can be found in the Department of Environment's Rough Sleepers Initiative which set up consortia of agencies to co-ordinate work with rough sleepers on a geographical zone basis (Randall and Brown 1996).

'The key principle underlying good community care for mentally ill people is that caring for this group is not the job of one agency alone just as it is not the responsibility of one professional group alone' (Department of Health 1995, p.26).

This statement is nowhere more relevant than in work with homeless mentally ill people.

WHAT CONSTITUTES RISK?

There is much evidence to suggest that the state of homelessness itself constitutes risk to the health and safety of an individual, either by exacerbating existing conditions or exposing the individual to new risk factors.

Health

Bines (quoted in Pleace and Quilgars 1996) has compared the health of single people in Bed and Breakfast Hotels (B&Bs) and sleeping rough with that of the general population and has shown that chronic chest and breathing problems were twice as high amongst the B&B group and three times as high in the rough sleepers.

Keyes and Kennedy (1992) found that people sleeping rough were 150 times more likely to be fatally assaulted than the general population and that the average age of death for this group was 47 compared with an average of 73 for the male population in general. They also concluded that homeless individuals were 34 times more likely to commit suicide.

Mental Health

We have already seen that between 30 and 50% of any homeless population suffers mental health problems. Research from the HMII indicates that the most common diagnosis of clients was schizophrenia (50%) and that there was a high incidence of loss of contact with existing services. For 88% of clients their first episode of homelessness occurred after the onset of mental illness (Craig et al. 1995).

It would appear therefore that in the case of severe functional illness, it is more likely that the illness predates homelessness and that 'mainstream services had provided insufficient continuity of care for mentally ill people at risk of becoming homeless' (Craig et al. 1995).

There are, however, studies which indicate that the experience of homelessness can cause mental health problems in otherwise healthy people (See Pleace and Quilgars 1996).

Craig et al. (1995) also identified two broad groups within the population: the older group, with long histories of homelessness and co-existing chronic mental illness, and a younger group, with histories of institutional care or family breakdown characterised by high levels of stress-related disorders such as anxiety and depression.

Substance Misuse

Many studies indicate high levels of drug and alcohol misuse within the homeless population. Craig *et al.* (1995) found high levels of co-morbidity of 60% for mental illness and drug/alcohol abuse.

PREVENTION OF HOMELESSNESS

We can conclude that people with existing mental health problems, especially severe mental illness, are more at risk of becoming homeless as a result of service failure. Having become homeless, the individual is then further exposed to risks specifically associated with a homelessness environment. Recognition and awareness of this process and its implications should feature in any assessment of clients at risk of homelessness, for example those facing eviction from tenancies.

The point at which someone begins a pathway into homelessness is a key point for professional intervention. For those with existing mental health problems the longer the homelessness continues the more difficult it is for the individual to return to a 'housed' way of life. Grenier (1996) suggests a three-week period during which a person adapts in order to survive, after which it is more difficult to re-integrate into mainstream society. Resort to bed and breakfast or hostels usually involves moving away from a familiar locality and a severing of social networks and support; it may also mean loss of contact with mental health services. Over half the clients in the HMII study had become homeless from some form of independent accommodation (Craig *et al.* 1995):

> A significant proportion of homeless mentally ill people have 'fallen through the net' of social and psychiatric care. In approximately half the cases where clients had been lost to psychiatric care, this could be attributed to service failures. In addition, nearly a quarter of clients had been in council housing before their most recent episode of homelessness, and were known to mainstream services at the time. Despite this, such services were unable to prevent their homelessness and at times encouraged it, by rejection and misguided attempts to regulate behaviour through eviction. (p.3)

Eligibility criteria for housing lies with the Housing Act 1985, whilst that for community care is in the NHS and Community Care Act 1990. Thus, whilst housing is seen as an essential plank of any support and care arrangements, eligibility for one cannot guarantee eligibility for the other.

Many local authorities have initiated schemes to improve liaison and joint working between housing and social services and some of these are usefully described in Elsmore (1996) – an analysis of London Boroughs working practices with tenants with mental health needs. In areas with a relatively large homelessness population many boroughs now include homelessness as a high priority criteria for community care assessments.

THE ASSESSMENT PROCESS

Given the inherent risk factors involved in homelessness already described, an element of risk assessment is always present in the work of professionals working with homeless individuals. Ritchie, Dick and Lingham (1994) identified four key attributes of patients requiring 'special supervision':

1. Patients detained in hospital under the Mental Health Act 1983 on more than one occasion.

2. Patients who have a history of violence or persistent offending.

3. Patients who have failed to respond to treatment from the general psychiatric services.

4. Patients who are homeless.

Four per cent of the clients of the HMII teams fell into this category, while 59% met two of the criteria (Craig *et al.* 1995).

Engagement

The challenge for professionals is often to engage such clients in the first place – given their often poor previous experience of mental health services, their isolation and the suspicion with which such clients have come to view statutory services. This suspicion may be heightened amongst the younger age group, 40% of whom have had experience of the care system (Craig *et al.* 1996).

Services for homeless people must always be able to 'outreach' to where clients are to be found and where they may feel secure. Often this is in a voluntary sector day centre or hostel and for those most withdrawn and isolated people who have no contact with helping agencies, the setting will be street work. A regular and informal presence in such locations, with good liaison between the visiting team and centre staff or other outreach teams, helps in familiarising clients to the workers involved and makes positive initial contact more likely. The engagement process itself may be lengthy and may not touch directly on mental health issues for some while. Three-quarters of the contacts made by the HMII teams were described as 'social interventions' providing assistance with welfare benefits, improving accommodation and assisting with the problems of daily living. Until these basic needs of shelter, nutrition and finance have been considered, more specific medical or mental health needs cannot be addressed. The ability of one worker to respond positively to such a range of possible circumstances underlines the need for broad-based and overlapping job descriptions within the team.

As part of this process, assessment and provision go hand in hand but are often interspersed randomly depending on individual circumstances. Provision of some resources or advice may well come before full assessment, unlike the text book sequence of assessment, provision, monitoring and review. The process of engagement aims to develop a relationship of trust between the client and a case manager, which can be maintained even when a client crosses administrative and geographical boundaries.

Information Gathering

Information gathering is a particularly important activity with isolated homeless people. There may be no referring agency or person and the client may be unable or unwilling to divulge much. Unlike a housed population, there is rarely a partner, carer, neighbour or friend on hand to provide any background or, more importantly, to advocate for the client. Careful information gathering not infrequently turns up such a person who knows the client well and can provide essential information but is not part of the client's day-to-day environment. Often the person is a close relative from whom the client has become separated as a result of social deterioration and declining mental health but who has maintained contact of a sporadic nature.

Christopher Clunis was too readily dismissed as a wandering homeless person with no family ties, but he remained in contact with his sister who was extremely concerned for his well-being and could have provided essential information which may have enabled professionals to act more decisively. Enquiries with other agencies, both voluntary and statutory, also help to fill in the picture by giving information about any previous treatment and the likely response to particular types of intervention. In an area where there are a network of services for homeless people, clients are often known to several agencies. Good liaison and communication between them and the multidisciplinary teams can help to monitor and support vulnerable individuals. The 'Care Programme Approach' can be used to formally include voluntary sector agencies such as homelessness day centres and hostels in care planning and review.

CONFIDENTIALITY

Quite properly, confidentiality of information is a requirement of all helping agencies and the circumstances in which this can be compromised varies from organisation to organisation.

Many homelessness agencies emphasise the particular need to accord respect to homeless people who, by virtue of their position, have often been denied many other basic human rights.

Other agencies – usually those with statutory responsibility for risk assessment and monitoring – regard pro-active information sharing with the objective of positive intervention, improvement in the clients circumstances and risk minimisation as justifiable. An awareness of both perspectives and of the sensitivities involved is essential for joint working. Drawing up guidelines and policies to inform this difficult area of agency-to-agency interface can be invaluable.

TYPES OF RISK ASSESSMENT AND MANAGEMENT

Whilst assessment and management of risk are recurrent activities which form part of the everyday work of a mental health team, certain events or circumstances require a specific response with clear and measured outcomes.

The Risk Taking Approach

This approach has been well summarised by Ann Davis. She writes: 'risk taking is therefore an essential element of working with service users to ensure autonomy, choice and social participation. It is a means of challenging the paternalism and overprotectiveness of mental health services' (Kemshall and Pritchard 1996, p.114).

As we have seen, many homeless people are disengaged users of mental health services who are withdrawn and isolated – in extreme cases they lack even the bare essentials of life: shelter, food and adequate clothing. They are exposed to multiple risks which, in the main, are not measured and monitored by mental health services. These circumstances often give rise to the very marginalisation and stigmatisation which the 'risk taking approach' seeks to diminish. Once a client's circumstances do become known to an agency and the engagement process begins there is an immediate dilemma for the professional: clients who are 'habituated' to homelessness are often unable to respond to offers of accommodation or assistance. This may be the result of fixated delusional thinking, previous bad experiences with mental health services, previous bad experiences in hostels, being 'institutionalised' into street homeless culture or a mix of all or some of these.

The client's concerns and perspectives must be acknowledged and respected and the worker may be obliged to accept that his or her role may be initially limited to maintaining contact, building up engagement and monitoring any change in circumstances.

Experience in the Joint Homelessness Team has demonstrated that positive outcomes with people with long-term histories of homelessness often take place only after many months or years. Thirty-two per cent of cases had been known for between one and two years whilst 19% had been known for more than two years.

Positive outcomes are also dependent on the volume and range of resources available to support the work. This is particularly so in relation to housing, where there is a strong preference among clients for non-institutional accommodation. Independent units with dedicated off-site support teams are more acceptable to a majority of clients, although careful consideration must be given to those with the higher support needs.

MENTAL HEALTH ACT ASSESSMENTS

There may be obvious tensions in this long-term approach if the worker, or the team, have statutory responsibilities – for example under the Mental Health Act 1983 or possibly the Care Programme Approach. It may become necessary to consider formal assessments where an individual's circumstances deteriorate or in the interests of their health or safety.

ELECTIVE ASSESSMENTS

These are not usually undertaken in response to a crisis or sudden change of circumstance and can be planned and prepared. Some guidelines would be:

- Discuss with colleagues – where possible arrange informal assessment of the client by other professionals in the team.
- Careful and creative information gathering from all sources – small snippets of information given by clients can open up useful leads if persistently followed up. Check hospitals and social services records in any area mentioned by client as familiar to them.
- What links does the person have? Even the most isolated rough sleeper may be known to someone – another outreach team, a local shop keeper, the lavatory attendant in the railway station.
- Use this to see your client in a context. Homeless clients can appear anonymous, especially those who are long-term rough sleepers and do not have conventionally-recognised social relationships or geographical links.
- Try to establish, from contact with the client, your own observations and your information gathering, a bench mark in terms of mental health and presentation by which you can measure change in the client over time. This may include a very helpful indication based on documented evidence of previous levels of functioning. This is particularly important when justifying the need for intervention to a colleague from another team (Approved Social Worker or Psychiatrist) who may need to be part of the assessment team. Professionals who are unfamiliar with homelessness work sometimes need convincing that intervention is worthwhile.
- Try to involve the relevant Consultant Psychiatrist whose hospital bed you may need to use. Brief him or her well and ensure the team follow through with the client. Access to supportive housing on discharge, so that the client is not at risk of 'blocking a bed', is an advantage.
- Most importantly, consider whether there are any realistic alternatives that could be considered which have not already been tried.

Making the Decision

Finally, and sometimes the most difficult aspect of the decision making, be clear what the risk factors actually are which justify intervention. Where a person has been homeless for some while and, therefore, by definition, exposed to many risks, over time it may be on the basis of further deterioration – for example in physical health.

In other circumstances, where no obvious change has occurred, it may be that a judgement is reached in the team, over time, that the persistent and continuous level of risk experienced is beyond that which is acceptable. This can be an extremely difficult decision to arrive at, involving as it does professional and personal value judgements and weighing in the balance the issue of personal liberty versus every citizen's right to care and treatment. Although this is a situation not unfamiliar to mental health professionals in other circumstances, the quasi-romantic qualities sometimes attributed by some to long-term homeless people ('a chosen way of life'), and the lack of carers and advocates for the individual concerned, renders these decisions very complex for those involved.

In specialist teams, or in areas with relatively large populations of street homeless people, it is possible to compare the individual homeless mentally ill client with like others, rather than with a housed client, when making these decisions. As with housed people with mental health problems, some homeless mentally ill cope remarkably well and require little assistance, dealing with all their personal needs very adequately and creatively. Whilst continuing efforts should be made to encourage them to take up accommodation, coercive intervention is not appropriate. Other individuals are more distressed and disturbed by their mental ill health and unable to recognise and anticipate their own needs except in a very basic way. The following variables seem to offer a practical framework for assessment purposes in elective assessments:

- History, length and pattern of homelessness – Continuous rough sleeping over a period often indicates severe mental health problems, as does continuous, frequent and spontaneous moving from place to place
- Degree of isolation – From other homeless people. From other agencies.
- Degree of engagement with worker or other agencies – Client's ability or willingness to respond to contact from workers.
- Content of engagement – Client's ability or willingness to focus on issues central to homelessness.
- Client's ability to meet basic needs in the context of his/her environment – Ability to maintain adequate shelter, clothing, personal hygiene and nourishment adequately and systematically.
- Client's access to welfare benefits – It requires considerable motivation and organisation to maintain a claim as a homeless person. The less able or well a person is, the least likely they are to be able to do it.
- Family/Carer/Advocate – The location of a friend or relative may help to clarify facts and may be recognised by the client as an advocate.
- Mental state – It is often possible for long-term isolated homeless clients to become more severely ill than those in a housed situation before any intervention takes place. This is often because there is no family or carer to alert services to their need and, in isolated circumstances or an extremely tolerant or unstructured environment (rough sleeping), this goes unnoticed.
- Monitoring arrangements – Is it possible to monitor the client effectively or to implement any care plan aimed at minimising or reducing risk? Would this require a networking approach with other agencies such as day centres and street work teams?

SUICIDE AND SPECIFIC SELF HARM

The incidence of more specific and intentional acts of self harm in the homeless population is not widely recorded. Suicide attempts amongst young people under 25 were recorded by one-third of a sample homeless group, but only 9% of a comparison 'housed' group. Suicide attempts were also judged to have involved a greater threat to life with most dangerous methods and attempts at concealment (Craig *et al.* 1996). From a study of London Coroners Courts recording the deaths of 74 homeless people, 10 were judged to have been suicides (Grenier 1996).

As an obvious generalisation, it can be concluded that the risk of suicide or self harm is greater in the homeless population – whether as a result of pre-existing mental health problems or specifically as a response to the pressures of homelessness itself or a combination of both.

Loss, or the threat of loss, plus the absence of effective supportive networks are key indicators in the prediction of suicide and many homeless people have considerable experience of both.

RISK TO OTHERS

The publicity surrounding a small number of mentally ill offenders and the attention given to aspects of their care and treatment, including failures on the part of professional agencies, has created something of a public backlash against community care programmes. Sympathy for the mentally ill is now tempered with some caution, which may be magnified in the public mind if the person is visibly disordered, presents bizarrely and appears to be homeless.

The risk posed by the actions of homeless mentally ill people to others is poorly documented and understood. The Revolving Doors Agency Report, *People with mental health problems in contact with the Criminal Justice System* (1996), undertook a study of all custody records in two London Boroughs. Four hundred and ninety-nine people were identified as 'mental health cases' and 15% were recorded as 'No Fixed Abode'. Only 6% of the total had committed serious offences involving violence. In 75% of cases there were significant life events in the six-month period before arrest that might have alerted services to the subject's deterioration.

The Royal College of Psychiatrist's paper, *Assessment and Clinical Management of Risk of Harm to other People* (1996) lists the following features of previous history which overlap and build on the four high risks criteria identified in the Ritchie report of 1994 previously quoted. The standard psychiatric assessment should include:

- Previous violence and/or suicidal behaviour.
- Evidence of rootlessness or 'social restlessness', for example few relationships, frequent changes of address or employment.
- Evidence of poor compliance with treatment or disengagement from psychiatric aftercare.
- Presence of substance misuse or other potential disinhibiting factors, for example a social background promoting violence.

- Identification of any precipitants and any changes in mental state or behaviour that have occurred prior to violence and/or relapse.

Four per cent of the clients studied by Craig *et al.* (1995) and known to the clinical teams in the HMII met all four criteria identified by Ritchie for high risk, whilst three other factors were strongly associated with membership of this group:

- having been in local authority care as a child
- having previously lost accommodation because of behavioural problems
- having a greater number of housing changes in the previous six months.

Of those clients with a major mental illness *and* substance abuse, three-quarters also had two or more risk factors and 60% had at least three.

The very high significance of interrelated substance abuse and mental health problems in the high risk group presents enormous difficulties for statutory teams. The enquiry into the killing of Mr Frederick Graver by Michael Buchanan (North West London Mental Health Trust 1994) very ably describes the complexities of assessment and management of this group of homeless people, as well as the absence of consensus of treatment approaches. The report identified the lack of a long-term care plan for a patient with multiple admissions with psychiatric episodes interspersed with homelessness and offending behaviour. There was a notable absence of an effective multidisciplinary approach, with agencies working separately and in isolation. When a potential for persistent criminal activity is present, the report urges close involvement of the police and probation services.

Whilst risk assessment in general remains a rather blunt instrument for measurement and prediction, it can be said with some certainty that the homeless population appears to score highly for most current risk variables. It therefore behoves commissioners and providers in areas with significant populations of homeless people to create and sustain robust and innovative assessment systems.

There are several significant points of entry to mental health services where homeless people may be particularly prevalent.

The Mental Health Act 1983, section 136, allows the police to take a person who appears to require immediate care or control from a public place to a place of safety for assessment by mental health professionals. It is important that the assessing workers are familiar with issues of homelessness and are aware of alternatives to hospitalisation which may be available.

Entry into the criminal justice system by way of arrest may provide a vital opportunity for a homeless person's mental health needs to be addressed, as long as efficient mechanisms are in place with the local authority and health providers for their diversion into the health system and subsequent follow-up. The role of the 'Appropriate Adult' under the Police and Criminal Evidence Act 1984 is crucial and wherever possible the Appropriate Adult should be an Approved Social Worker (ASW) or Community Psychiatric Nurse (CPN) who can identify the circumstances when it is appropriate to use powers under civil sections of the Mental Health Act to divert the person from police custody or is able to intervene informally by arranging a place in a supportive hostel where further assessment can take place. A second level of 'diversion' can be provided at the point of appearance at Court for those individuals not already identified at the police station or where the nature of the offence may warrant an assessment in custody.

For such schemes to be fully effective careful consultation and planning needs to take place between social services (ASWs), health (acute beds and Section 12 Doctors), the police and magistrates, and for the scheme itself to liaise closely with locality providers – especially in the voluntary sector.

ACCIDENT AND EMERGENCY DEPARTMENTS (A&E)

Homeless people have traditionally made use of accident and emergency services, often in place of a GP if they cannot register with one or if they have moved away from the catchment area. Presentation at A & E with an associated health problem may present a window of opportunity to access other services, including referral to specialist agencies for housing advice or mental health follow-up. Attachment of CPNs and ASWs to busy A & E Departments can assist in the identification and assessment of vulnerable homeless people, as well as helping to access community alternatives to hospital admission.

CASE EXAMPLES

Tina

Tina was a 35-year-old woman who was referred to the specialist homelessness team by a local Church. She had been sleeping on the Church steps for 18 months and used the washing facilities in the Church hall. One or two members of the congregation had befriended her and gave her small amounts of money and food. She rarely moved far away from her sleeping area, but was reasonably warmly clothed for the cold weather.

The worker made contact with Tina who was reluctant to say much about herself initially. After several contacts she told the worker her name and that she was from the USA. The reason for her prolonged stay and persistent refusal of accommodation was closely related to specific delusional thinking.

The worker introduced the team psychiatrist to Tina and a medical certificate was issued and she subsequently agreed that a benefits claim could be submitted on her behalf (prior to Habitual Residency Test!). Eventually Tina gave the worker the address of her sister in USA. Contact was made and her sister made plans to come to the UK. She was also able to tell the worker of Tina's previous psychiatric history.

Before her sister arrived Tina became more actively disturbed and was finally admitted to hospital on Section.

Following a period of treatment she was discharged to a supportive hostel and she was reunited with her sister. After several weeks Tina decided to return with her to the USA.

Paul

Paul is a 67-year-old man who has been street homeless for probably ten years or more. He occasionally uses a local day centre. He is known to all the local street outreach teams and has been offered accommodation many times, which he always turns down. He is quite isolated but does spend time with other older rough sleepers.

He holds the strong belief that he must not apply for his pension and that punishment, possibly of a physical nature, may result if he does. It is difficult to elicit whether this is a delusion or has a factual basis based on a previous serious assault when he was also robbed. It is not clear where he spends his day or how he gets food. He rarely appears adequately clothed or equipped for cold weather (no blankets, sleeping bag).

Although welcoming of contact, he says very little about himself and his conversation is fragmented. He may be thought disordered. He has been known to the team for two years, during which time a monitoring network was developed between the mental health team, other outreach teams and the day centre so that any change or deterioration can be notified to the mental health team as lead agency.

Recently the team has traced a brother who has had no contact for several years but who was able to provide information about Paul which contributes to an ongoing assessment.

The worker involved is in the process of applying for appointeeship for his pension in the hope that Paul can be encouraged to take some money or accept clothing or equipment bought for him.

Paul is clearly very vulnerable on the street, by virtue of his age, and there is always considerable concern for his welfare in the winter. The team regularly review the grounds for intervention under the Mental Health Act and are arranging an informal assessment by a Psychiatrist with special interest in older people.

Andrea

Andrea is a 22-year-old woman who has been homeless since the age of 16. She has no contact with her family. The team have been working with her for three years. The first contact was made with her through a day centre when she was sleeping rough. The team worker arranged a place for her at a local women's hostel and supported her there until her mental health deteriorated and she was admitted to hospital. Andrea has a strong dislike of hospital treatment and medication, even though she is persistently tormented by critical voices.

On discharge the worker arranged a place at a specialist mental health hostel where she stayed for several months until she had a fight with another resident and disappeared. Andrea booked herself into a hostel in another borough and made contact with her team worker again after several weeks. Eventually he was able to find a supported bedsit for her and she has been there for a year. She periodically disappears and sleeps rough for a week or so. The home support team notify the team worker when she leaves and an alert is usually passed to other homelessness agencies and within the team. Contact with her is then re-established and Andrea is usually pleased to return to her bedsit. Her mental health problems continue to cause her considerable distress and the worker is also trying to help her with a cognitive behavioural approach to the hallucinations.

REFERENCES

Bachrach, L. (1984) 'The homeless mentally ill – a review.' American Psychiatric Association.

Bhugra, D. (1996) Homelessness and Mental Health. Cambridge: Cambridge University Press.

Craig, T., Baylis, E., Klein, O., Manning, P. and Reader, L. (1995) The Homeless Mentally Ill Initiative, An Evaluation of Four Clinical Teams. London: HMSO.

Craig, T., Hobson, S., Woodward, S. and Richardson, S. (1996) Off to a Bad Start – a Study of Homeless Young People in London. London: The Mental Health Foundation.

Department of Health (1995) Building Bridges – a Guide to Arrangements for Inter-Agency Working for the Care and Protection of Severely Mentally Ill People. London: HMSO.

Elsmore, K. (1996) Being There. Tenants with Mental Health Support Needs. London: Housing Unit.

Grenier, P. (1996) 'Still Dying for a Home' – the Links Between Homelessness Health and Mortality. London: CRISIS.

Kemshall, H. and Pritchard, J. (1996) Good Practice in Risk Assessment and Risk Management. London: Jessica Kingsley Publishers.

Keyes, S. and Kennedy, M. (1992) Sick To Death of Homelessness. London: Crisis.

Lodge-Patch, I. (1970) 'Homeless men: a London survey.' Proceedings of the Royal Society of Medicine 63, 437–441.

Marshall, M. (1989) 'Collected and neglected. Are Oxford hostels filling up with disabled ex-psychiatric patients?' British Medical Journal 229, 706–709.

North West London Mental Health Trust (1994) The Report of the Independent Panel of Enquiry Examining the Case of Michael Buchanan. London: HMSO.

Pleace, N. and Quilgars, D. (1996) Health and Homelessness in London – A Review. London: Kings Fund.

Priest, R. (1976) 'The homeless person and the psychiatric services: an Edinburgh survey.' British Journal of Psychiatry 128, 128–136.

Randall, G. and Brown, S. (1996) *From Street to Home – An evaluation of Phase 2 of the Rough Sleepers Initiative.* London: Department of Environment.

Revolving Doors Agency (1995) *People with Mental Health Problems in Contact with the Criminal Justice System.* London: RDA.

Ritchie, J., Dick, D. and Lingham, R. (1994) *Report of the Enquiry into the care and Treatment of Christopher Clunis.* London: HMSO.

Royal College of Psychiatrists (1996) *Assessment and Clinical Management of Risk of Harm to Other People.* London: RCP.

Scott, J. (1993) 'Homelessness and mental illness.' *British Journal of Psychiatry 162,* 314–324.

SHIL (1986) *Single Homeless in London.* London: SHIL.

SHIL(1995) *'Time To Move On' – A Review of Policies and Provision for Single Homeless People in London.* London: SHIL.

Whiteley, J.S. (1955) 'Down and out in London: mental illness in the lower social groups.' *Lancet 2,* 608–610.

CHAPTER 11

Risk, Residential Services and People with Mental Health Needs

Tony Ryan

INTRODUCTION

The term 'risk' frequently conjures up notions of fear and danger in the minds of those who work in health and welfare services. Risk has taken on mainly negative connotations during the 1990s and is perceived as being associated with harms, usually physical, and often concerned with injuries that one person may cause another. In social work this can be seen in relation to child abuse (Alaszewski and Manthorpe 1991), in the Probation Service through offending behaviour (Kemshall 1996) and in the mental health field in recent years the preoccupation has been with physical harm to self or others (Department of Health 1993, National Health Service Management Executive 1994).

In the mental health field at present there is a significant emphasis upon heavy end risks such as homicide and suicide yet a wider array of risks exist for people with mental health needs. Most risks are low consequence/high frequency risks such as being stigmatised or ostracised and apply to a greater number of people with mental health needs than heavy end risks (see Ryan 1996 for a review). Therefore it is worth noting that risk is not just about physical harms but also includes other concerns such as dignity and reputation.

The drive towards community care for people with mental health needs has seen a decrease in the total number of residential beds available in England in recent years (House of Commons Health Committee 1994). However, there has been an increase in the diversity of facilities now available, particularly in the private and voluntary sectors (Lelliott *et al.* 1996). Residential care in the mental health field has two principal concerns: accommodation and care. There is often differing emphasis placed on these two services and this usually relates to the type of facility.

The number of residential facilities, like the interest in risk, has grown in recent years. In order to set the scene on the risk issues present within these services, it is worth summarising what facilities exist and the services they offer. The typology given here should be regarded as a guide rather than an absolute classificatory system with facilities, along with client needs, being regarded as points on a continuum. At one end are people whose needs are complex, requiring high levels of input from a range of mental health professionals inside and outside the facility, and at the other are people with greater abilities and levels of independence. Whilst recognising that there are many residential services for people with mental health needs, this chapter is mainly concerned with those which are registered in one form or another.

RESIDENTIAL SERVICES

Nursing Homes Registered to Accept Residents Detained Under the 1983 Mental Health Act

The principal interest of these services is with the mental health needs of residents. Social functioning, accommodation and physical health are important but secondary concerns. Such places have trained mental health nurses on duty at all times with consistent input from a range of other mental health professionals, including psychiatrists. Many of these facilities were developed following the 'ward in the community' concept pioneered in the late 1970s (Wykes 1982, Goldberg *et al*. 1985). Today such facilities are available mainly for two client groups: first those undergoing rehabilitation and second as an alternative to long-term hospital care for people who are unlikely to live independently. Residents may be treated under the Mental Health Act 1983 within the home. This prevents residents having to be transferred to hospital when they become disturbed, which prevents the further distress of moving to an unfamiliar environment.

Registered Mental Health Nursing Homes

In a similar manner to the above homes, these facilities are also staffed by trained mental health nurses and are primarily concerned with the mental health needs of residents. However, they are not registered to detain people under the Mental Health Act 1983 or provide treatment against the wishes of the resident.

Registered Residential Care Homes

Usually, the social care needs of residents is the priority for staff working in registered care homes but monitoring residents mental health needs is also part of the work. Different staffing levels and systems of working may operate in these schemes. Sleeping night staff or on-call staff may form part of the team, depending on the needs of residents and whether the facilities are dispersed. As with nursing homes, there are registration and inspection teams who monitor these services.

Dual Registered Homes

Having some beds registered for nursing care and others for residential care, these facilities are able to provide flexibility. In some cases, for example core and cluster schemes, they may be dispersed with beds registered for different purposes.

Unregistered Care Homes and Supported Hostels

Often these facilities focus on either the provision of accommodation or care. This is usually dependent upon the aim of the organisation: housing associations lean toward the former whilst voluntary agencies the latter. Treatment or rehabilitation are rarely key components of care in these facilities, however many are exclusively for people with mental health needs. Some facilities are staffed over a 24-hour period whilst others provide less on site support. Most have someone available to supervise and support residents during office hours. The quality of these services can be variable as they are not subject to the strict regulation and monitoring of registered homes.

Common Lodging Houses

As hospital beds have closed over the last 30 years there has been an increase in the number of 'common lodging houses'. Many have been developed by private landlords providing little more than a bed, a roof and someone to collect the rent. For an increasing number of people these facilities provide residency, although the security of their tenancy can be rather vulnerable.

LEGISLATION, POLICY AND THE MANAGEMENT OF RISK

Definitions of risk which have been established from policy and recent legislation focus upon low frequency/high consequence events such as homicide and suicide. The Mental Health Act 1983 deals with people who are a danger to themselves or others. Supervision registers are concerned with tracking those who present a serious risk of violence to themselves and/or others or who may be at serious risk of self-neglect (National Health Service Management Executive 1994). Supervised discharge arrangements, which became law through the Mental Health (Patients in the Community) Act 1995, provide a framework for ensuring compliance with treatment regimes for people who fit into these definitions of risk and have been discharged after hospital detention. The Care Programme Approach (CPA) consists of a systematic assessment of health and social care needs, an agreed care plan, the allocation of a key worker and regular review of progress (Department of Health 1990). While all people who are accepted by specialist mental health services are subject to CPA, only those with the most complex needs will receive the input of a full multidisciplinary team (Department of Health 1996).

While the Mental Health Act 1983 is concerned with how people come into contact with mental health services and the treatment they receive, the principal concern of other initiatives is to ensure follow-up support. Where a person's mental health deteriorates, these policies are designed to ensure a speedy response for those who are regarded as presenting the greatest risk to themselves or others.

Table 11.1: A typology of mental health residential services

	Facility type	Client group(s)	Services	Provider types	Most relevant policy and legislation
Nursing homes registered to accept residents detained under the 1983 Mental Health Act	Nursing home	People with complex needs who may be detained or given treatment without their consent. Mental health needs may override social needs	Combinations of treatment, rehabilitation, supervision, respite care and accommodation	Private and voluntary agencies	Mental Health Act 1983, Mental Health (Patients in the Community) Act 1995, Care Programme Approach, Residential Homes Act 1984
Registered mental health nursing homes	Nursing home	As above but cannot be detained or treated without consent	As above although treatment cannot be given without consent of the resident	Private and voluntary agencies	Mental Health (Patients in the Community) Act 1995, Care Programme Approach, Residential Homes Act 1984
Residential care homes	Care home	Social needs may be greater than mental health needs	Rehabilitation, supervision, respite care and accommodation	Local authorities, private and voluntary agencies	Mental Health (Patients in the Community) Act 1995, Care Programme Approach, Residential Homes Act 1984
Dual registered homes	Nursing home beds and care beds	Able to meet changing mental health needs of residents	Treatment, rehabilitation, supervision, respite care and accommodation	Private and voluntary agencies	Mental Health (Patients in the Community) Act 1995, Care Programme Approach, Residential Homes Act 1984
Unregistered care homes and supported hostels	Care home	Stable mental health and good self-care skills	Supervision, social support, respite care and accommodation	Housing associations, private and voluntary agencies	Unregulated in relation to mental health policy
Hostels	Supported accommodation	Self-caring with uncomplicated and stable mental health needs	Social support and accommodation	Housing associations, private and voluntary agencies, private landlords	Unregulated in relation to mental health policy
Common lodging houses	Unsupported accommodation	May take a range of people with a variety of needs from simple to complex	Accommodation	Private landlords	Almost completely unregulated

RISK AND RESIDENTIAL MENTAL HEALTH SERVICES

Resident Risks

People with mental health needs experience a greater range of risks than they actually pose (Ryan 1996). Furthermore, there are additional risks to those which are dealt with through mental health legislation and policy. People with mental health needs are at greater risk of being made homeless (Leff 1993, Scott 1993, Timms and Fry 1989), imprisoned (Gunn, Maden and Swinton 1991) and committing suicide than the general population (Department of Health 1992). They are also likely to experience abuse of one form or another as a direct result of their illness. In some cases this abuse may be the result of public misconceptions and the social stigma associated with mental illnesses. These risks may be present within residential facilities, to varying degrees, for residents and may be influenced by the type of services offered and the availability of staff.

Physical, psychological, sexual and financial abuses have occurred when people with mental health needs have resided in hospitals (Department of Health and Social Services 1972, Department of Heath and the Social Services 1980, Department of Health and Special Hospital Service Authority 1992). People who live in residential care can also be vulnerable to similar institutional regimes – particularly if they are left unmonitored, which is the case in most unregistered facilities. This can lead to inappropriate staffing in respect of the number of staff on duty, their skills and experience – as in the case which resulted in the death of a volunteer worker at a hostel in Oxford (Davies et al. 1995).

The stigma of living in a mental health facility is frequently an inconspicuous risk which residents face. Whilst this often goes unobserved within the facility, this is not the case in the immediate locality. Despite studies of communities which show tolerant attitudes towards people with mental health needs (Brockington *et al.* 1993, Hall *et al.* 1993), many people are opposed to the development of new facilities within their own community (Gould 1992, Tissier 1993).

Staff Risks

Littlechild (1996) recognises that there is a significant difference between practitioners who work in residential and fieldwork settings when it comes to dealing with risk. Staff in residential settings are much closer to residents in every way. They live in the same facility for long periods, may share meals, their relationships can become blurred at times as they get to know about one another and they cannot walk away from situations. Living in such close proximity can have a bearing on particular risks. For example, the risk of violence toward a worker may increase whilst members of the community may be less exposed to this than if the resident lived in their own accommodation with less supervision.

Along with carers, professionals in the mental health field are most likely to be victims of violence from the people they work with (Estroff and Zimmer 1994, Whittington 1994). However, the majority of violence does not result in serious physical injury, although there can be a significant psychological effect upon the victim (Wykes and Whittington 1994, Royal College of Nursing 1994,

Rowett 1986). Where violence occurs to others at the hands of a resident in a mental health facility, there is the possibility, depending upon the circumstances, that staff may be held liable. Staff have a duty of care to exercise which can extend to members of the general public (Carson 1996). Should a resident assault a neighbour where the staff member could have been reasonably expected to intervene, they may be held to account for their inactions. As a result, staff run the risk of being disciplined, losing their position and, if professionally trained, having their licence to practice terminated.

Further personal risks faced by staff are those of 'burn out' and 'rust out' which depend on the nature of the work with residents. Where staff are working in very stressful roles over long periods, this can lead to 'burn out' even if they receive good support and regular supervision. No one in this field can be expected to work in a facility for years and remain fresh, enthusiastic and full of ideas. Conversely, if they do not face challenges in their day-to-day work, staff are likely 'rust out' which can lead to cynicism and low motivation. It can also lead to institutional practices which become task-orientated such as having meal times organised to suit staff duty rotas.

Risks to Others

An increasing number of people with mental health needs are receiving long-term support in community settings. Public concerns have been heightened as a result of a number of incidents which have culminated in serious injury or death (Sheppard 1995). The number of murders committed by mentally ill people is low and multiple murders extremely rare. The Confidential Inquiry into Homicides and Suicides by Mentally Ill People (1996) reported that during two periods, July 1992–December 1993 and September 1994–March 1995, it could only find 39 cases of homicide by people who had been treated by mental health services. Nevertheless, the minimisation of this risk has become an important theme for community mental health care in the late 1990s. As a result, it is important that residential services accept only those people with whom they are equipped to deal. Where an individual requires intensive staff support and there are insufficient workers to provide 24-hour supervision, this obviously increases the risk to local communities if, for example, the person has a history of violence. Additionally, it increases the risk to the resident of losing their liberty if they offend as the result of being accepted into inappropriate services. Finally, it also causes risk issues for the provider and their organisation as it can result in loss of good name and leave them financially vulnerable should liability claims be pursued.

RISK ASSESSMENT

Risk assessment is as much an art as it is a science and contains a strong element of detective work in gathering relevant information. Risk assessment is about predicting the future and the likelihood of particular events occurring; these will be both wanted and unwanted events. Inevitably the best predictions will employ a combined approach to assessing risk. One set of information will be concerned with past events of the resident. This will be combined with information about populations of similar individuals which will indicate factors which increase the likelihood of particular risks. For example, in relation to violence, an extensive research programme recently reported a link with people with mental health needs. The risk of violence increases significantly if additional factors to mental illness are present: if the person is young, male and abuses alcohol or other drugs (Steadman 1996). A further example is the case of suicide where mental illness is also a significant factor. Here the risk is increased if the person is a young or older man, they are unemployed or have a history of self harm (National Health Service Health Advisory Service 1994). It is important to note that whilst some demographic factors may highlight the risk within a broad population, they do not apply to all individuals who fit these profiles. Consequently, a combination of practitioner judgement about the individual and knowledge of variables which increase the particular risk is probably the best current method of reducing risk through assessment. This can be further improved through using specific tools, for example scales to measure anger in the case of potential violence (Novaco 1994) or instruments to measure hopelessness in the case of suicide (Beck et al. 1974), which are seen as key indicators in each of these areas.

There are a range of sources where information can be gained for a thorough risk assessment. These include the prospective resident, their relatives or advocate, practitioners currently involved with the person and any written reports, which may be historical or recent. The purpose of undertaking this work is threefold: assessment of client need and their goals, establishing whether the facility can meet that need and what other agencies or individuals will be involved in supporting the resident if they are admitted to the service.

It is essential to explore a range of issues within the assessment, including mental and physical health needs, any challenging or offending behaviours, alcohol or drug (mis)use and existing social networks. This may be supplemented with how prospective residents relate to others and particularly to the residents already in the facility. This should act as a screening exercise which establishes whether the needs of the person can be met in the home.

Prior to admission it will be necessary to establish who else will be working with the resident and what their roles will be. For example, if they have been detained under the Mental Health Act 1983 there will be a duty under Section 117 of the Act for all those involved with the resident to 'establish a care plan to organise the management of the patient's continuing health and social care needs' (Department of Health and Welsh Office 1993, p.106). Furthermore, aftercare may need to be supervised under the Mental Health (Patient in the Community) Act 1995 if they have been treated under Sections 3, 37, 47 or 48 of the 1983 Act and if there is a significant risk of them breaking down without close supervision. Consequently, the person can be required to reside at a specified place or to attend for medical treatment, occupation, education or training and a nominated person will be responsible for their supervision. The nominated person may be a psychiatrist but may also be a community psychiatric nurse, social worker or even a practitioner in the residential facility.

Although an assessment of risk takes place beforehand, the real process commences once the resident has moved in. As with other forms of assessment, the assessment of risk should be continuous. Changing the environment may bring various factors into the equation: new staff, other residents, a different location, numerous expectations and so on. These all affect risk assessment and management and consequently should be examined on an ongoing basis.

Table 11.2: Components of risk assessment(Adapted from Ryan 1994b)

Collecting information concerning the resident

Awareness of risks relevant to the resident and others

Awareness of risk factors

Communicating with all interested parties

Identification of all potential outcomes and their likelihood

Establish a plan to deal with the identified risks

Clarify individual responsibilities

RISK MANAGEMENT

It is impossible to remove all of the risks which may exist in relation to this client group in a residential setting. In part this is due to the fact than one risk may impinge upon another and to reduce or remove one risk may increase another. For example, it may be possible to drastically reduce the possibility of a resident self-harming by having very high staffing levels. However, this may increase the risk of violence towards staff since the intensity of very close supervision can create a stressful situation for the resident. It may also increase the risk of the facility going bankrupt and the residents having to leave. Despite this, there are basic approaches which can be taken in order to reduce the possibility of an untoward event occurring.

Resident Selection

A key factor in the management of risk is the selection of residents who will live in the facility. This will be influenced by the assessment prior to acceptance of the resident. In some cases it may be necessary for residents to move in gradually by spending increasing periods of time at the facility in order that they become acclimatised to the environment. Moving in can be a stressful time and a gradual introduction may reduce the possibility of a relapse in the mental health of the resident.

Staff Issues

Clearly, a key factor in the management of risk is the staff team who work with residents. If they do not have the abilities necessary to undertake the work being asked of them this is likely to increase the risk to the residents, themselves and others. Consequently, recruitment of staff is one of the most important areas of risk management (Ryan 1994a). If it is not carried out

Table 11.3: Factors to consider in selecting residents
Stability of mental health Other health needs Challenging or offending behaviours Alcohol or drug (mis)use Access to additional support Staffing levels and expertise Existing resident mix Applicability of mental health legislation and/or policy

correctly it will impact upon other areas of risk management since people will not be up to the task required of them. For this reason it is important for those recruiting staff to be clear about what they require from the people they take on and that they have clear methods of establishing whether or not the applicant can do this. There are many examples of people commencing in a position and everything working well for a while before deteriorating. One of the main factors for this is that they have not been supervised in their work. If staff are not guided through supervision then the risk of something going wrong increases. Many of the inquiries into abuse and neglect of people in care can be traced back to a lack of monitoring of what has been going on at the shop floor (Department of Health and Social Services 1972).

Table 11.4: Factors to consider in staff selection
Interpersonal skills Knowledge base Experience in the field Teamworking abilities Self awareness Attitude

Communication and Multidisciplinary Working

A pivotal feature in the management of risk in the mental health field is the degree to which different groups work together to assist residents to meet their needs. A significant finding in many of the recent inquiries concerning people with serious mental health needs has been the lack of co-ordinated working between the agencies involved (see Sheppard 1995). It is extremely rare that someone not in contact with mental health services will commit homicide, more often it has been the case that a vast array of people have been involved at some time or another. However, it is the communication between the professionals involved which has been the missing factor. Consequently, recent Department of Health guidelines have suggested that 'to make community care for mentally ill people work, networks of relationships need to be developed' (Department of Health 1996, p.43). Immediate and wider networks can include a very diverse range of services and people (see Table 11.5). Some of these networks may relate to the policy and legislation described above whilst others may be less formal yet just as valuable to the quality of life of the individual.

Table 11.5: Service networks for residential facilities (Adapted from Department of Health 1996)

Immediate service networks

Mental health services

Primary health care

Secondary health care eg. Accident & Emergency Departments and ambulance services

Child protection services

Probation

Police ambulance

Specialist alcohol and drug misuse services

Wider networks

Voluntary organisations

Social security offices

Local churches, mosques and temples

Employment and training services

Leisure and recreation services

Casenotes, systems of recording and communicating information and reviewing residents (preferably with them) all contribute to the ongoing processes of risk assessment and management. Although many of these practices have taken place in residential facilities for a long time, the idea that they should combine to form a system of risk assessment is relatively new. Additionally, the initial risk assessment which takes place when determining the suitability of a resident should not be the end of the risk assessment process. It should be seen as ongoing, dynamic and evolving as the resident progresses or declines. When viewed in this way the process of risk assessment also becomes an integral part of risk management.

Finally, open file systems encourage practitioners to analyse objectively what they are going to record and therefore make more accurate entries than they may otherwise do if the resident does not have access to their records. Where closed record systems operate this can lead to subjectivity and distrust. Consequently, the relationship between residents and staff can be poorer, which, in turn, can lead to inferior risk assessment and management as the staff will not know the residents as well as they otherwise might.

RISK TAKING

Any residential staff who are concerned with maintaining high standards will regard it as a basic principle that they empower residents through risk taking (Residential Forum 1996). For residents this leads to greater independence and empowerment whilst for workers it can provide immense satisfaction for workers to see this happen successfully (Ryan 1993). The downside to risk taking is that it can be stressful if not correctly undertaken. Where clear guidelines on assessment and planning are missing this can cause unnecessary anxieties for residents and the staff team. It can also lead to conservative practice where risks are not taken for fear that they will indeed go wrong and the worker will be scapegoated.

There are two reasons why people working with residents with mental health needs take risks. The first is to cut corners in the work and therefore make the job easier. The second, which is the concern here, is to enable the person to become more independent. The basic principle is similar to that which a mother may take with a young toddler in that a number of cuts and bruises are an acceptable trade-off for the development of the child as they learn from experience. However, there are some injuries which are not acceptable to the mother and where she will intervene to prevent those occurring.

The process of rehabilitation in the mental health field cannot occur without taking risks of some form or another. For some residents, perhaps those with long-term functional illnesses such as schizophrenia, rehabilitation may focus on learning skills which allow them to act more independently in everyday life. Here any risks which are taken are likely to be concerned with potential harms to the resident rather than to others. An example of risk taking here might be associated with a new resident going out unescorted when they are unsure of the area. It might be seen as an acceptable risk to let the person become lost in the locality once or twice in order that they learn about the area for themselves rather than escorting them around the area and risking a loss of dignity and confidence. However, it may not be so acceptable if the person does not have the necessary skills to cope with being lost in an unfamiliar environment. Where the team are unsure about the residents ability to cope in such situations many safeguards may need to be put in place to maximise the chance of a positive outcome from the risk taking. For example, the team might note the time the resident leaves and agree a time limit after which they will search the area. They may also ensure that they have a full description of what the resident is wearing and a recent photograph. A series of orientation trips with fellow residents or staff might take place before they go out alone for the first time. Contact numbers and a telephone card for the resident may also form part of the safety measures. Much depends on the abilities of the resident, the quality of the assessment by those involved and the safety measures set in place. Risk taking which involves the safety of people other than the resident is usually very different in terms of the potential consequences. Nevertheless, the method is very much the same even though the number and degree of allowable cuts and bruises may not be! Irrespective of the reason for risk taking, the process should be seen as a series of small steps without the possibility of major repercussions if they go wrong.

Each step should be thought through carefully with a clear understanding of the goal(s). Who the risk affects, how it affects them and the likelihood of something going wrong should be discussed openly. The resident should take an active part in the process along with other members of the (multidisciplinary) team. There may be risks to the resident, staff, local community or organisation running the facility. The discussion should decide which potential *risk loser* takes precedent if there are conflicts of interest. All potential outcomes, positive and negative, to the resident and others should be explored. Carson (1990) suggests that these should be rated in terms of their likelihood. Benefits should be discussed before disadvantages in order that practitioners think through positively exactly what they are aiming to achieve with the resident.

Safeguards should also be identified and set up in the event that something does go wrong as this will then minimise the effects of the undesired event. For example, it may be thought empowering that a resident looks after and administers their own medication. If they have a history of non-compliance with medication regimes there may be several outcomes to this. They may successfully manage their medicines, they may mismanage but not to a degree where their mental health is endangered, they may accidentally or purposefully overdose or they may stop taking their medicines. Following a discussion between the resident and the staff team it might be agreed that the resident keeps their own medications. Safeguards might include prompts from staff to take medicines, the resident being given a supply on a daily basis at first and some information/training for the resident on the effects of misuse.

Table 11.6: Risk dilemmas in residential mental health services

Are there circumstances where the management of risk may include informing residents of the history of a new resident?

In the event of a risk going wrong what evidence is likely to be persuade a court that a practitioner acted in the interests of all parties?

Under what circumstances might a practitioner involve the police in risk management?

Are there situations where confidentiality may be broken as good practice in risk management?

In what circumstances might practitioners be held liable for their inactions where a risk has gone wrong?

Are there circumstances where a practitioner may be liable for the actions of an ex-resident after the resident has moved out?

What factors might be considered in determining the authenticity of allegations made by a resident about abuse from a member of staff?

Are there situations where a prospective resident should not be involved in the process of risk assessment?

DILEMMAS AND FOOD FOR THOUGHT

Finally, since it is not possible to provide a handbook which gives practitioner responses to risk situations, it is useful to stimulate thought and discussion. Below are a series of questions, not exhaustive, which, given various scenarios, may produce diverse responses with different residents. The purpose is to highlight some issues which relate to the management of risk in residential mental health facilities in order that the reader may examine their own thinking in this area.

REFERENCES

Alaszewski, A. and Manthorpe, J. (1991) 'Literature review: Measuring and managing risk in social welfare.' *British Journal of Social Work 21*, 277–290.

Beck, A.T., Weissman, A., Lester, D. and Trexler, L. (1974) 'The measurement of pessimism: the hopelessness scale.' *Journal of Consulting and Clinical Psychology 42*, 861–809.

Brockington, I.F., Hall, P., Levings, J. and Murphy, C. (1993) 'The community's tolerance to the mentally ill.' *British Journal of Psychiatry 162*, 93–99.

Carson, D. (1990) 'Risk-taking in mental disorder.' In D. Carson (ed) *Risk-taking in Mental Disorder: Analyses, Policies and Practical Strategies.* Chichester: SLE Publications.

Carson, D. (1996) 'Risking legal repercussions.' In H. Kemshall and J. Pritchard (eds) *Good Practice in Risk Assessment and Risk Management.* London: Jessica Kingsley Publishers.

Davies, N., Lingham, R., Prior, C. and Sims, A. (1995) Report of the Inquiry into Circumstances Leading to the Death of Jonathan Newby (a volunteer worker) on 9th October 1993 in Oxford. Oxford: Oxford Health Authority.

Department of Health (1990) *Caring for People: The Care Programme Approach.* London: HMSO.

Department of Health (1992) *The Health of the Nation. A Consultative Document for England and Wales.* London: HMSO.

Department of Health (1993) Virginia Bottomley announces ten-point plan for developing successful and safe community care. *Press Release H93/908. 12 August.*

Department of Health (1996) *Building Bridges: A Guide to Arrangements for Inter-agency Working for the Care and Protection of Severely Mentally Ill People.* London: HMSO.

Department of Health and Social Services (1972) *Report of the Committee of Inquiry into Whittingham Hospital.* London: HMSO.

Department of Health and Social Services (1980) *Report of the Review of Rampton Hospital.* London: HMSO.

Department of Health and Welsh Office (1993) *Code of Practice: Mental Health Act 1983.* London: HMSO.

Department of Health and the Special Hospital Service Authority (1992) *Report of the Committee of Inquiry into Complaints About Ashworth Hospital.* London: HMSO.

Estroff, S.E. and Zimmer, C. (1994) 'Social networks, social support, and violence among persons with severe persistent mental illness.' In J. Monahan and H.J. Steadman (eds) *Violence and Mental Disorder: Developments in Risk Assessments.* Chicago: University of Chicago Press.

Goldberg, D.P., Bridges, K., Cooper, W., Hyde, C., Sterling, C. and Wyatt, R. (1985) 'Douglas House: A new type of hostel ward for chronic psychotic patients.' *British Journal of Psychiatry 147,* 383–388.

Gould, N. (1992) 'Public prejudice.' *Nursing Times 88,* 21, 36.

Gunn, J., Maden, T. and Swinton, M. (1991) *Mentally Disordered Prisoners.* London: Report of the Home Office.

Hall, P., Brockington, I.F., Levings, J. and Murphy, C. (1993) 'A comparison of the responses to the mentally ill in two communities.' *British Journal of Psychiatry 162,* 99–108.

House of Commons Health Committee (1994) *Memorandum from the Department of Health on Public Expenditure on Health and Personal Social Services.* London: HMSO.

Kemshall, H. (1996) 'Offender risk and probation practice.' In H. Kemshall and J. Pritchard (eds) *Good Practice in Risk Assessment and Risk Management.* London: Jessica Kingsley Publishers.

Leff, J. (1993) 'All the homeless people – where do they all come from?' *British Medical Journal 306,* 669–670.

Lelliott, P., Audini, B., Knapp, M. and Chisholm, D. (1996) 'The mental health residential care study: Classification of facilities and description of residents.' *British Journal of Psychiatry 169,* 139–147.

Littlechild, B. (1996) 'The risk of violence and aggression to social work and social care staff.' In H. Kemshall and J. Pritchard (eds) *Good Practice in Risk Assessment and Risk Management.* London: Jessica Kingsley Publishers.

National Health Service Health Advisory Service (1994) *Suicide Prevention: The Challenge Confronted.* London: HMSO.

National Health Service Management Executive (1994) *The Introduction of Supervision Registers for Mentally Ill people.* London: HMSO.

Novaco, R.W. (1994) 'Anger as a risk factor for violence among the mentally disordered' In J. Monahan and H.J. Steadman (eds) *Violence and Mental Disorder: Developments in Risk Assessment.* Chicago: Chicago University Press.

Residential Forum (1996) *Creating a Home From Home: A Guide to Standards.* London: Residential Forum.

Royal College of Nursing (1994) *Violence and Community Nursing Staff.* London: Royal College of Nursing.

Rowett, C. (1986) *Violence in Social Work.* Institute of Criminology Occasional Paper No 14. Cambridge University.

Ryan, T. (1993) 'Therapeutic risks in mental health nursing.' *Nursing Standard 7,* 24, 29–31.

Ryan, T. (1994a) 'All for one and one for all: Team building and nursing.' *Journal of Nursing Management 2,* 129–134.

Ryan, T. (1994b) 'The risk business.' *Nursing Management 1,* 6, 9–11.

Ryan, T. (1996) 'Risk management and people with mental health problems.' In H. Kemshall and J. Pritchard (eds) *Good Practices in Risk Assessment and Risk Management*. London: Jessica Kingsley Publishers.

Scott, J. (1993) 'Homelessness and mental illness.' *British Journal of Psychiatry 162*, 314–324.

Sheppard, D. (1995) *Learning the Lessons*. London: The Zito Trust.

Steadman, H.J. (1996) *The MacArthur Risk Assessment Study III: Risk factors for violence*. Paper presented at the MacArthur Foundation Research Network on Mental Health and the Law Conference: Violence, Competence and Coercion – pivotal issues in mental health law. Oxford: 4 and 5 July 1996.

Steering Committee of the Confidential Inquiry into Homicides and Suicides by Mentally Ill People (1996) *Report of the Confidential Inquiry into Homicides and Suicides by Mentally Ill People*. London: Royal College of Psychiatrists.

Timms, P.W. and Fry, A.H. (1989) 'Homelessness and mental illness.' *Health Trends 21*, 70–71.

Tissier, G. (1993) 'Neighbours.' *Community Care 14*, 998, 16–17.

Whittington, R. (1994) 'Violence in psychiatric hospitals.' In T. Wykes (ed) *Violence and Health Care Professionals*. London: Chapman and Hall.

Wykes, T. (1982) 'A hostel ward for "new" long-stay patients: An evaluative study of "a ward in a house".' In J.K. Wing (ed) *Long-Term Community Care Experience in a North London Borough. Psychological Medicine Monograph Supplement 2*.

Wykes, T. and Whittington, R. (1994) 'Reactions to assault.' In T. Wykes (ed) *Violence and Health Care Professionals*. London: Chapman and Hall.

CHAPTER 12

Community Care Homicide Inquiries and Risk Assessment

Michael Howlett

INTRODUCTION

Risk assessment in psychiatry, or what is sometimes better known these days as 'the clinical management of risk', has become increasingly important with the accelerated move towards community care in the context of the fast track hospital closure programme. Risk assessment has, consequently, come under increasing scrutiny, not least by the media, and its defective implementation is vulnerable to exposure. The once useful but now too narrow redundant adage that 'the only predictor of future behaviour is past behaviour' is still employed to excuse bad practice when, in reality, risk assessment research and risk assessment measures have become increasingly sophisticated and there is no longer any real clinical need to discharge a patient who may pose a threat to himself or others on a wing and a prayer, with a prescription in his hand. This chapter will explore some of the issues concerning risk and risk assessment from the particular perspective of a small mental health charity, which has been in existence for just over two years, and which has a particular focus on the practices and procedures of community care for the severely mentally ill. It will be helpful to describe the organisation – The Zito Trust – briefly, before moving on to the substantive issue with which this discussion is concerned.

THE ZITO TRUST

The Zito Trust was registered as a charity in January 1995, having been set up by Jayne Zito and Michael Howlett in July 1994. It was established following the death of Jonathan Zito and the subsequent Clunis inquiry to work for improvements in the provision of community care for the severely mentally ill, by providing a network of support for families and professional carers, by undertaking relevant and applicable research, and by providing training and consultancy to mental health services throughout the country. In short its objectives are to influence policy and improve practice in the field of community care for the severely mentally ill.

The Clunis inquiry was published in February 1994 (Ritchie, Dick and Lingham 1994) and it remains central in its importance in cataloguing failure and missed opportunities, in analysing the failure of services to communicate effectively in the delivery of care, and in highlighting a category of patients, like Clunis, who obviously require a more frequent and more intensive service than is currently available. The inquiry report made a number of crucial recommendations for improving practice, the majority of which have yet to be implemented.

While The Zito Trust supports the philosophy of community care for the majority of those patients who are discharged from hospital, it has made a point of insisting that adequate resources and facilities, including properly trained staff should be in place in the community *before* they are discharged. This is, in fact, the underlying principle of the Care Programme Approach (CPA), which has been a requirement since 1991 (Department of Health 1990) yet which is not yet fully implemented throughout the country by the responsible health authorities (Department of Health 1995). The resources must include as a bare minimum an effective key worker relationship with individual patients, 24-hour crisis intervention services and adequate provision of medium secure beds for treatment when needed.

The Zito Trust concentrates its energy and resources in two important areas of work, the provision of support for the victims of the failures of community care, including families, formal and informal carers; and in bringing together the recommendations from the independent inquiries into community care homicides in order to achieve its principal objectives.

There have been a number of key inquiries and reports since Clunis into the consequences of discharging the seriously mentally ill into the community without adequately resourced provision for them. Each of these inquiries (on individuals and on key areas in this field) contain recommendations which, if implemented, would certainly improve the provision of care and lessen the risk of failure. In January 1995 The Zito Trust published its preliminary report *Learning The Lessons*, which brings together the recommendations made by inquiries over the period 1969–1994. The second edition was published in July 1996 (Sheppard 1996) and contains the details of a further fifteen independent inquiries which have reported in the eighteen month interval between editions.

IMPLICATIONS OF COMMUNITY CARE FOR THE ASSESSMENT AND MANAGEMENT OF MENTAL HEALTH RISKS

Examples of the current weaknesses inherent in community care policy come to the Trust on a regular basis. A majority of these cases expose fundamental problems with the practical implementation of the policy and which, in clinical terms, are not particularly sophisticated or complex. The following vignette serves to highlight some of the areas where a process which begins badly may quickly deriorate:

A young woman contacted the Trust to complain about the increasing number of mentally ill and unstable residents being accommodated in neighbouring flats. Living alone, she felt vulnerable and described a number of verbal and physical attacks on herself and other residents. When pressed for further details, she described a group of former psychiatric patients supposedly subject to the care programme approach who had essentially been deposited by the various agencies responsible for their care and treatment in the community. There was, in addition, concern about alcohol and substance abuse in conjunction with a number of incidents of arson in an environment without a fire escape. Some of the patients were meant to take medication.

The response the Trust is able to give in such cases is limited in the same way that appropriate resources for the proper implementation of community care is limited, and there is a connection. Following letters to the various statutory agencies concerned in this case, and others like it, the only effective result was an expedited process enabling the (council) resident to move to a different area of the borough. The case highlights the following themes, however, which are of major importance:

Hospital Closures

With the accelerated closure of hospital beds since 1990 many inner city hospitals have occupancy rates as high as 150 per cent. This means that those who may still require acute care either cannot get it at all, or are discharged too quickly, and are required to live in the community without appropriate access to hospital care when they need it.

Accountability

The vignette describes patients discharged from hospitals which have closed or which are in the process of closing. Responsibility for such patients passes from the health authority to the local authority, that is to social services and then to housing. Housing will in many cases pass responsibility on to the voluntary sector, and so on. In effect this 'losing touch' is a very unfortunate by-product of the Care Programme Approach's fundamental philosophy which requires agencies to work together effectively in the interests of the patient in a style and culture for which there are no real precedents. And when things go wrong, responsibility is blurred in a way that would be unacceptable in other professions.

Housing

There is a drastic shortage of adequate housing for former psychiatric patients. They are, consequently, regularly accommodated inappropriately in whatever is available. Little or no help or education, or information, is given to other residents who may have to respond to a crisis for which they are unprepared, unskilled and unwilling. Increasingly, patients are being accommodated and cared for by the voluntary sector under service agreements. Many of the facilities here are staffed by young care workers without the necessary skills base or training to work with a client group that may, from time to time, pose a serious challenge to self or others. Tragedies have occurred, as in the Newby case (Davies, Lingham, Prior and Sims 1995).

Non-Compliance

It is estimated in the Confidential Inquiry into Homicides and Suicides (Royal College of Psychiatrists 1995) that non-compliance with medication is a significant management factor in 60 per cent of the independent inquiries into community care homicides. Even with the advent of new atypical neuroleptic medication (The Times 1996), with positive profiles and fewer side effects, compliance in the community remains and will remain a serious management and legal issue and one which has not been addressed adequately by any of the guidelines issued or legislation passed in response to community care failures.

Human Resources

Community psychiatric nurses (CPNs) and Approved Social Workers (ASWs) carry most of the responsibility for community follow-up care, outside of the sometimes overwhelming burden placed on families and relatives. CPNs work for the health authority, and have large, sometimes unmanageable, caseloads. ASWs work for social services. Apart from the burden placed upon these professionals by the sheer number of difficult patients, many of whom are actively non-compliant, the extent to which they can effectively work together, representing, as they do, health and social services, is minimal. There is evidence to suggest that CPNs have less experience working with difficult patients than they need, which raises the crucial question about skills and training in this area.

Risk Assessment

The vignette, which is not untypical, raises a number of important concerns and highlights a number of risk factors which need to be addressed before it is too late. Not least among these is alcohol and substance abuse in conjunction with other risk indicators which multiply the overall risk of violence by four (Monahan and Steadman 1994).

Briefly, the creation of inner city community care ghettoes by default is a consequence of policy implementation before adequate planning and resourcing, and shows how some of the incidents which lead to violent attack, suicide or homicide could practically be prevented. Although London often throws up the worst examples of its kind in this field, the Trust has cases from all over the country which suggest that the situation is not much better elsewhere. A recent account of Bristol's inner city mental health team working with very difficult patients without the benefits of an acute day-care centre, without properly staffed hostels and with too few supported housing schemes, indicates just how close to the edge many inner city services are (*The Observer* 1996a).

A summary of concerns expressed by The Zito Trust, and based on the direct evidence it receives, would begin with hospital beds. We have lost too many hospital beds too quickly and the necessary alternative facilities and resources are not in place in the community for those who need them, the severely mentally ill. It has already been stated that the CPA has yet to be universally implemented. Community care failures and shortcomings have received a good deal of publicity, compelling august institutions like the Royal

College of Psychiatrists at its 1996 Annual general Meeting to condemn the policy as being in a state of 'deep crisis'. The Government's responses have escalated from bland pronouncements about 'teething problems' to the regular issuance of guidelines, deadlines, and a timely intervention by the Prime Minister himself (*Independent* 1996), followed by the House of Commons statement in February 1996 by the Secretary of State for Health, with a raft of new measures, and even a new name for the policy, now known as the 'Spectrum of Care', and a promise of five thousand new twenty-four hour nursed beds, but no real new funding (Department of Health 1996a). There is new legislation on supervised discharge in the form of the Mental Health (Patients in the Community) Act 1995 which came into force in April 1996. Most recently, the Department of Health announced it would seek to pass legislation to remove the powers of hospital lay managers to discharge patients, following research by the Mental Health Act Commission which revealed that in seven hospitals chosen at random, one in twenty patients was discharged by the lay managers against the responsible medical officer's advice. A Green Paper is promised 'at the turn of the year', which is likely to propose unitary mental health authorities, or joint purchasing, and the implementation of rapid response teams which will deal with community care crises in the patient's home, and within hours, the intention being to keep patients out of hospital. A revised Code of Practice to the Mental Health Act 1983 is currently out for consultation (Department of Health 1996b).

In the meantime, as conditions in the remaining hospitals deteriorate, the use of the Mental Health Act increases (Department of Health 1996c), more money is spent on the private sector, hot-bedding becomes the norm for some hospitals and many psychiatrists are more engaged in fire-fighting and containment than therapy, such is the pressure on acute beds. Whether or not a professional working in this field ends up in an inquiry report into a patient's death is perceived, with some justification, as largely a matter of luck rather than judgement.

It is in this context that some health authorities, by no means confined to the inner cities, are drastically cutting their five-year community care budgets from 1997 to counter huge overall spending deficits (*The Observer* 1996b). In spite of the increased profile of mental health in recent years, it is usually mental health and non-essential surgery which bears the brunt of the cuts.

RISK ASSESSMENT AND THE CLINICAL MANAGEMENT OF RISK

If we look at the Clunis inquiry, in particular, and extrapolate from the report some of the basic information about his care between 1986 and 1992, we get the following picture:

- failure to acknowledge risk (poor communication)
- brevity of inpatient care
- too many diagnoses
- persistent reluctance to admit to hospital
- 35 different professionals involved in his care between 1986 and 1992.

The inquiry report was published in 1994. Many similar themes and issues emerge in the reports published since Clunis. A central theme running through all the inquiries concerns risk assessment, or the clinical management of risk. One of the most recently published inquiries, the Sinclair inquiry, published in July 1996 makes the following point:

> Certain features of a patient's mental state have been shown to be associated with seriously violent behaviour. Monahan (1993) has grouped these under the title of 'threat control override' symptoms. Shortly described, they comprise **delusions of control and passivity**, and associated hallucinatory experiences such as **command hallucinations**, especially if these occur as they commonly do, in the setting of paranoid illness. Other allied psychopathological experiences associated with dangerousness are **delusions of alien possession** and **delusions of jealousy**. A common thread running through all these experiences is that the patient feels that control of their behaviour and thoughts or those of someone with whom they identify very closely, has been **overridden by an external agency or force.** (Lingham, Candy and Bray 1996, p.66)

The report goes on to observe that:

> Recognition of any of the above symptoms places the patient, so to speak, on a lower rung of the **ladder of dangerousness**. In itself this calls for a full assessment of all the clinical and associated aspects of the case. If certain other features are present, then the patient moves up the ladder. These include **alcohol and other substance misuse, poor impulse control, low intelligence, a violent upbringing, a violent subculture, overcrowded and impoverished accommodation, and poor interpersonal relationships,** which for a person suffering from schizophrenia will include living in a 'high expressed emotion' household. In addition, two factors are of especial importance: **psychotic experiences which are directed towards particular groups or individuals,** where greater specificity means greater dangerousness, and **previous violent behaviour arising from such psychotic experiences.** (Lingham *et al.* 1996, p.66)

If at this point we return to the vignette involving former psychiatric patients unsupported in council accommodation, we can see that some, at least, of these patients are already some way up 'the ladder of dangerousness'. It would not be surprising to hear of an escalation of 'acting out', including the possibility of violence, suicide, even homicide, at some point in the future. It is appropriate here to bring in the distinction between *predictability* and *preventability*. Given the number of risk factors already in place, some increased form of violence to self or others can be predicted, although it is difficult to say when and no prediction can be absolute. However, even if one is advancing a quasi philosophical, semantic argument about prediction and inevitability in such a case, the concept of *preventability* has just as important a role to play in risk assessment, that is the clinical management of risk, and is practically easier if the appropriate systems are in place. In the vignette, some management structures could be (should be) implemented without delay to *prevent* the seeming inevitability of a serious incident from taking place.

Such as what? First, the former patients need adequate, supported housing; they need regular visits from the responsible CPN or ASW; they need to take their medication if medication is part of their care package; they need guidance and support on the dangers of substance abuse; they need something worthwhile to do, either educationally or occupationally, or both; and, finally, they need to have access to emergency hospital care if and when a crisis takes place for which immediate hospital care is indicated.

The key appropriate system which drives, or should drive, the implementation of these absolutely basic measures of support for patients living in the community is the CPA – the Care Programme Approach – which defines how the agencies are to work together in an integrated, structured and planned way for the benefit of the patient. But report after report (including the Department of Health's (1995) own report) has found that in a number of health authorities inspected the CPA had not been implemented and that there was very little effective inter-agency communication. This means, on one vital level, that lines of accountability are vague or absent so that seriously challenging patients like Clunis, Robinson, Sinclair, Mitchell, Buchanan and many others, can be lost to the systems, or *in* the systems, which have been designed on paper to look after them.

THE RISK OF VIOLENCE IN MENTALLY ILL PEOPLE

It is now possible to say with some degree of confidence that a sub-group of patients who may be diagnosed as severely mentally ill have an increased likelihood or predisposition to violence. This was not always the accepted view. As Gunn points out, research going back only a decade showed that mentally ill patients in hospitals were less likely than the general public to commit acts of violence (Gunn 1996).

The largest ongoing study on risk and the prediction of violence, led by Monahan and Steadman in the States, indicates that a number of key factors increase the risk of violence in mentally disordered patients in the community (Monahan and Steadman 1994) This research is supported by other major studies carried out in the United States, Sweden, Switzerland and the United Kingdom (Lindqvist and Allebeck 1990, Swanson, Holzer, Gunju and Jono 1990, Link, Andrews and Cullen 1992, Hodgkins 1992, Wessely, Castle, Douglas and Taylor 1994, Modestin and Ammann 1995) which have been analysed by Coid (1996). Recent research in Finland (Eronen, Tihonen and Hakola 1996) found that the risk of committing a homicide was about ten times greater for schizophrenia patients of both genders than it was for the general population. All but one of these studies show that people suffering from the major mental illnesses are more dangerous than the general public. Coid (1996) makes the point that 'It is…becoming increasingly accepted that the true potential for dangerous behaviour may have been seriously underestimated [and that] future mental health policy must come to terms with the emerging evidence that the overall risk of violence is still higher than that of the general population' (p.965).

A summary of clinical risk indicators can be made from a combination of the clinical research and from the independent inquiry reports. These include:

- history of violent behaviour
- concerns expressed by the family/relatives/carers
- poor impulse control
- clinical diagnosis/active symptoms
- non-compliance with medication
- substance/alcohol abuse
- homelessness or 'social restlessness'/lack of social support
- low socio-economic status/unemployment
- access to particular potential victims/specific threats
- history of obtaining weapons.

To this list can be added other factors, such as the consistent failure of professionals to make an assessment of risk, or to communicate information which would assist in this process, or their underestimation or denial of the importance of risk indicators taken discretely or as a whole.

Looking at the list of clinical risk indicators we can see, with the benefit of hindsight, in an analysis of some of the independent inquiry reports, how basic opportunities for making an appropriate assessment of risk were missed. The seminal inquiry report in this respect is Clunis (Ritchie *et al.* 1994) For example, Gunn (1996) has outlined a history of Clunis' violence during the period 1986 to 1992 which includes the following incidents:

1986 attempted to hit his sister

1988 hit another patient

found with a knife and threatened violence

1989 attempted strangulation

lunged at the police with a knife

threatened to stab a patient

threatened to stab a patient

punched a patient, grabbed a knife

1990 tried to gouge a patient's eye out

physical abuse to fellow employees

struck resident with walking stick

1991 chased residents with a carving knife

fight with another patient

punched nurse, broke glass, attacked patient

kicked and burned another patient

inflicted severe facial lacerations to resident

punched resident in the face

1992   set fire to a Bible, attacked resident with a knife

hit duty solicitor

tried to hit GP

hit stranger in the face, chased boys with a screwdriver
(9 December 1992)

stabbed and killed Jonathan Zito (17 December 1992)

Many of the attacks were aimed at the face. It is not really surprising to learn, therefore, that Jonathan Zito was stabbed in the eye at Finsbury Park tube station. He was standing with his brother at the very edge of the platform when Clunis approached from behind and stabbed Jonathan Zito over his head, when it would have been possible, and easier, to stab him in the back. The point of such graphic detail is not to sensationalise the incident but to suggest that Clunis's psychiatric history shows:

(1)   that it was likely he would kill

(2)   that he would probably use a knife, and

(3)   that were he to kill he would most probably stab that person in the face.

Hence the very basic need to take a full history of the patient, listen to the concerns being expressed by others, in particular the family (where possible), and to formulate and implement a management plan for the care and treatment of the patient.

An excellent model for such a psychiatric history, albeit one taken after the homicide, is included in *The Falling Shadow* (Blom-Cooper, Hally and Murphy 1995) where the index offence of the patient, Andrew Robinson, was committed in 1978. This index offence, when viewed in the context of the subsequent history, indicates that were Andrew Robinson to kill anyone it would probably be a young woman working in the caring professions. In 1993 Andrew Robinson killed occupational therapist Georgina Robinson (no relation) at the Edith Morgan Centre at Torbay District General Hospital. Georgina was 27 when she died.

A full, corroborated history has the potential to give enough information for the multi-disciplinary team to make a clinical *prediction* of risk which becomes the instrument for the *prevention* of future offending. Other published inquiry reports will support this contention. Tragically, in these cases, lessons are being learned too late to save lives.

OTHER INQUIRIES

Learning The Lessons (Sheppard 1996) summarises inquiry reports into mental health failures published since 1969. The reports published since 1992 are largely concerned with individual 'community care' homicides which are now mandatory under Department of Health (1994) guidelines.

Between 1992 and October 1996, there have been 22 inquiry reports into community care homicides involving 26 victims. Nearly half of these victims were strangers or healthcare professionals. The majority of defendants in this context plead guilty to manslaughter on the grounds of diminished responsibility, but there is a significant number not included in this category, and who may not be the subject of an independent inquiry because:

(1) they commit suicide after the homicide

(2) they are found unfit to plead

(3) they are found not guilty on the grounds of insanity

(4) they are found guilty of infanticide

(5) they choose to plead guilty to murder.

There is now considerable pressure to change the structure and process by which independent inquiries are managed. On the one hand, they are reporting with increasing regularity and impose an expense on health budgets which might usefully be re-directed. There is also a feeling that they have become so common that their impact has diminished accordingly. A further view is that the recommendations contained in the inquiry reports that have been published have yet to be fully implemented (and we can go back to Clunis to see the strength of such a view), and that there is no need for any more recommendations. On the other hand, inquiries are the only chance families have of coming to some kind of understanding about the circumstances of the homicide; they also provide a much-needed and continuing reminder that improvements over time have been patchy and inadequate; they also represent the appropriate, democractic response in terms of accountability and openness to an area of health and social policy in which mistakes can and do cost lives, with the consequence that the potential loss of investigative and independent rigour will inevitably be taken as official acceptance, either implicit or explicit, that the loss of x number of lives per annum is part and parcel of the operation of the policy, in the same actuarial way that expenditure on rail safety incorporates a figure for 'acceptable' loss of life through accidents.

In terms of risk assessment and the clinical management of risk, however, each community care homicide inquiry report raises different issues which could be said to provide a developing school of thought in this area, and one which will inevitably be of immense value to clinical work. Reference to a handful of the better known inquiries which have reported since 1994 will show the kind of risk indicators which played such a significant role in the homicide in question and how, when taken as a whole, there is contained here a potent seedbed for the development of multi-disciplinary learning materials and protocols.

(1) Jonathan Newby

Jonathan Newby was a volunteer worker at Jaqui Porter House in Oxford, a facility run by Oxford Cyrenians. He was the only person on duty when he was attacked and killed by patient John Rous in 1993. John Rous was born in

1946 and was first admitted to psychiatric hospital in 1965 for amphetamine psychosis, when a diagnosis of personality disorder was made. He had several admissions under the 1959 Act and a street life of some twenty years. The Report (Davies, Lingham, Prior and Sims 1995) lists the factors that were prevalent on 9 October 1993, the day Jonathan Newby was killed. These were:

(i)   John Rous had been under pressure to repay a loan of 20 which he did repay but was not pleased to do so.

(ii) Another resident's behaviour was affecting John Rous. He was upset and disturbed in Jacqui Porter House.

(iii) John Rous's medication was wearing thin. He was due to receive his depot injection on 8 October but this was postponed to 11 October at his request.

(iv) John Rous's appointment with his GP had been postponed and he was unhappy about this.

(v)   He had increased his intake of alcohol and possibly cannabis.

(vi) By 8 October 1993 John Rous was in a state of high expressed emotion. The skills of the volunteer staff were inadequate to deal with him.

(vii) The procedures and arrangements at Jacqui Porter House meant that the elements supporting John Rous in the days prior to Jonathan Newby's death were paper thin, and there was a total failure to provide a supportive environment for John Rous.

Thus a number of risk indicators were in place in an environment in which an unqualified, untrained careworker was working alone and without access to immediate support. In addition to this, John Rous phoned the police and made it clear that he was going to kill someone, but because of his abusive language the operator hung up.

(2) Jason Mitchell

Jason Mitchell was born in 1970. He was seen by a psychiatrist on a number of occasions while he was serving a period of two years' youth custody for robbery and other offences. In 1990 he attacked a cleaner at St Barnabas Church, Epsom, and was charged with attempted murder and other offences. He subsequently pleaded guilty at the central Criminal Court to common assault and possession of offensive weapons (two knives). He was made the subject of a hospital order with restrictions (ss 37/41, Mental Health Act 1983). In May 1994 he moved to shared accommodation run by MIND in Felixtowe but, following disruptive behaviour, was readmitted to hospital in Ipswich as an informal patient. On 9 December 1994 he left the hospital and failed to return. On 20 December 1994 he was arrested following the discovery by police of the bodies of his father and his father's neighbours Arthur and Shirley Wilson.

The Report (Blom-Cooper, Grounds, Guinan, Parker and Taylor 1996) highlights, *inter alia*, the absence of effective communication of information right across the various interlocking agencies and services responsible for the care and treatment of Jason Mitchell, the failure by clinicians to respond to and address the diagnostic implications of his psychotic symptoms, and the errors made by the Mental Health Review Tribunals in 1991 and 1993 which sanctioned his conditional discharge. There was also an important failure by the services to respond to Jason Mitchell's (unqualified) therapist's report which described his violent and homicidal fantasies.

(3) Anthony Smith

In August 1995 Anthony Smith, a diagnosed schizophrenic, killed his mother and ten-year-old step-brother in a frenzied and brutal attack in the family home four weeks after his discharge from Derby City General Hospital. The inquiry report (Wood 1996) concludes that 'The system markedly lacked the ability to react quickly to the warning signs. With hindsight, there are many concerned who would have acted differently and will deeply regret their failure to do so.' The particular indicators of risk that were ignored by the responsible services included:

(i)   the father's expressed concerns about the risk of violence posed by Anthony Smith to the family

(ii) Anthony Smith's refusal to take his medication following discharge from hospital

(iii) Anthony Smith's home-made weapons.

The Report states that it had soon become clear that enough was going wrong with Anthony Smith's care to justify a speedy review of his discharge, but weak communication and the lack of a clear chain of responsibility at the NHS trust concerned meant that this necessary review did not take place, with tragic consequences.

CONCLUSION

There is enough material available from research and from the independent inquiry reports to ensure that the number of mistakes leading to unnecessary deaths – homicides and suicides – with a mental health component is minimised. They can never be entirely eradicated. Effective and comprehensive training materials on risk assessment are now available (Alberg, Hatfield and Huxley 1996) which need to be widely employed across the range of professionals working in community mental health and multi-disciplinary teams in this field. This requires a structured and committed approach by health authorities and trusts, as well as the Department of Health, the Home Office, and other relevant statutory and voluntary agencies, to commit funds and energy to the proper training and supervision of people who work with some of the most challenging patients who may pose a threat to themselves or others if the right intervention, at the right time, based on the right evidence, is not taken.

The experience of The Zito Trust suggests that unless resources and time are devoted to across the board training in risk assessment and the clinical management of risk, the current level of community care homicides and suicides will increase.

BIBLIOGRAPHY

Alberg, C., Hatfield, B. and Huxley, P. (eds) (1996) *Learning Materials on Mental Health. Risk Assessment.* Manchester: The University of Manchester.

Blom-Cooper, L., Hally, H. and Murphy, E. (1995) *The Falling Shadow. One Patients Mental Health Care 1978–1993.* London: Duckworth.

Blom-Cooper, L., Grounds, A., Guinan, P., Parker, A. and Taylor, M. (1996) *The Case of Jason Mitchell: Report of the Independent Panel of Inquiry.* London: Duckworth.

Coid, J. (1996) 'Dangerous patients with mental illness: increased risks warrant new policies, adequate resources, and appropriate legislation.' *BMJ 312*, 965–9.

Davies, N., Lingham, R., Prior, C. and Sims, A. (1995) *Report of the Inquiry into the circumstances leading to the death of Jonathan Newby (a volunteer worker).* Oxford: Oxfordshire Health Authority.

Department of Health. (1990) 'Joint Health and Social Services Circular. Health and Social Services Development. Caring for People. The Care Programme Approach for People with a Mental Illness referred to the Special Psychiatric Services.' HC(90)23/LASSL(90)11. London: Department of Health.

Department of Health. (1994) 'Guidance on the discharge of Mentally Disordered People and their Continuing Care in the Community.' HSG(94)27. London. Department of Health.

Department of Health. (1995) 'Social Services Departments and the Care Programme Approach: An Inspection.' London: Department of Health, Social Services Inspectorate.

Department of Health. (1996a) 'The spectrum of care – a summary of comprehensive local services for people with mental health problems.' LASSL(96)16HSG(96)6. London: Department of Health.

Department of Health (1996b) *Code of Practice: Mental Health Act 1983.* London: Department of Health.

Department of Health. (1996c) 'In-patients formally detained in hospitals under the Mental Health Act 1983 and other legislation, England: 1989–90 to 1994–95.' Department of Health Bulletin 1996/10. London: Department of Health.

Eronen, M., Tihonen, J. and Hakola, P. (1996) 'Schizophrenia and homicidal behaviour.' *Schizophrenia Bulletin 22*, 1, pp.83–89.

Gunn, J. (1996) 'The management and discharge of violent patients.' In N. Walker (ed) *Dangerous People.* London: Blackstone Press.

Hodgkins, S. (1992) 'Mental disorder, intellectual deficiency, and crime: evidence from a birth cohort.' *Arch Gen Psychiatry 49*, 476–83.

Independent (1996) 'Major in mental health rethink.' 16 July 1996.

Lindqvist, P. and Allebeck, P. (1990) 'Schizophrenia and crime: a longitudinal follow-up of 644 schizophrenics in Stockholm.' *British Journal of Psychiatry 157*, 345–50.

Lingham, R., Candy, J. and Bray, J. (1996) *Report of the Inquiry into the Treatment and Care of Raymond Sinclair.* Maidstone. West Kent Health Authority.

Link, B., Andrews, H. and Cullen, F. (1992) 'The violent and illegal behaviour of mental patients reconsidered.' *Am Sociol Rev 57*, 275–92.

Modestin, J. and Ammann, R. (1995) 'Mental disorders and criminal behaviour.' *British Journal of Psychiatry 166*, 667–75.

Monahan, J. (1993) 'Dangerousness'. In J. Gunn and P. Taylor (eds) *Forensic Psychiatry: Clinical, Legal and Ethical Issues.* London: Butterworth Heinemann.

Monahan, J. and Steadman, H.J. (1994) 'Towards a rejuvenation of risk assessment research.' In J. Monahan and H.J. Steadman (eds) *Violence and mental Disorder. Development in Risk Assessment.* Chicago: The University of Chicago Press.

Ritchie, J., Dick, D. and Lingham, R. (1994) *The Report of the Inquiry into the Care and Treatment of Christopher Clunis.* London: HMSO.

Royal College of Psychiatrists (1995) *Steering Committee of the Confidential Inquiry into Homicides and Suicides by Mentally Ill People.* London: Royal College of Psychiatrists.

Sheppard, D. (1996) *Learning The Lessons: Mental Health Inquiry Reports published in England and Wales between 1969–1996 and their Recommendations for Improving Practice, Second Edition.* London: The Zito Trust.

Swanson, J., Holzer, C., Gunju, V. and Jono, R. (1990) 'Violence and Psychiatric disorder in the community: evidence from the epidemiologic catchment area surveys.' *Hosp Community Psychiatry 41*, 761–70.

The Observer (1996a) 'You're suffering, you're desperate – who cares?' 1 September 1996.

The Observer (1996b) 'NHS faces worst cash shortfall in 10 years.' 22 September 1996.

The Times (1996) 'Social cost of Schizophrenia.' 14 November 1996.

Wessely, S., Castle, D., Douglas, A.J. and Taylor, P.J. (1994) 'The criminal careers of incident cases of schizophrenia.' *Psychol Med 24*, 483–502.

Wood, J. (1996) *The Report of the Inquiry into the Care of Anthony Smith.* Derby: Southern Derbyshire Health Authority.

CHAPTER 13

Risk and Prison Suicide

Alison Liebling

Social death begins when the institution...loses its interest or concern for the individual as a human being and treats him as a body – that is, as if he were already dead. (Shneidman 1973, 159)

No...I wasn't on my own, I was in a cell with somebody else. He's in the hospital now with his nerves [laughs] – I must have lost nearly all my blood. (Prisoner)

I wouldn't say they're helpful – they're just worried. (Prisoner)

It was serious and not serious at the same time. It relieves the depression, releases it. Outside, I'd go out and get into trouble. In here, your head just get in bits. (Prisoner)

Was it serious? Partly. I knew it wouldn't help. I just thought, if I ask for help I'll just get thrown in strip cells, so what good does it do you? Either do it right, or don't do it. After, I felt even more depressed. It's just I'm not *bothered* if I live or die. The prison should look at your problems, look at the reasons why. (Prisoner)

Why do prisoners attempt suicide? Can suicide risk be identified – and reduced? Is there a relationship between suicide and self-injury, and what sorts of regimes would minimise risk to prisoners? These are the questions this chapter seeks to address.

Suicide and self-injury in prisons have been the subject of considerable research in recent years, both in England and Wales and elsewhere (see Liebling 1995 for a review). Prison suicide rates are relatively high and are increasing (however, for a discussion of the complexities of calculating relative suicide rates, see O'Mahony 1994). Large groups amongst the prisoner population share those characteristics associated with increased suicide risk in the community: adverse life events, negative interpersonal relationships, social and economic disadvantage, alcohol and drug addiction, contact with criminal justice agencies, poor educational and employment history, low self-esteem, poor problem-solving ability and low motivational drive (see, for example, Zamble and Porporino 1988, Walmsley, Howard and White 1992, Liebling and Krarup 1993). Arguably, the prison population is carefully selected to be at risk of suicide. Such a profile may be becoming even more concentrated as alternatives are found for those who have a greater hope of succeeding in the community, as social dislocation increases and as employment chances decrease. Partly because of this high presence of 'suicide risk' in the prison population (but for other reasons too) there are flaws in the traditional 'risk-management approach' to prison suicide. This chapter will set out the main qualifications to a 'risk-identification' approach to suicide prevention in prison. Having established the significance of these points, the chapter will then illustrate how suicide risk might be, first of all, *understood*, as both a potential and shifting feature of individuals and of situations in prison, and how such risk might be characterised, identified (where possible) and minimised.

QUALIFICATIONS TO A RISK-IDENTIFICATION APPROACH TO SUICIDE IN PRISON

Studies of suicide in prison have typically sought to establish a profile of the 'at risk' prisoner based on official data found in the records of completed suicides (see for example, Gover 1880, Smalley 1911, Topp 1979, Backett 1987, Dooley 1990a, Griffiths 1990, Phillips 1986 in the UK, Flaherty 1983, Hankoff 1980, Hayes 1983, Massachusetts Special Commission 1984, Orlowski 1985, Kennedy 1984, Correctional Services of Canada 1985 and Scott-Denoon 1983 in North America, Hatty and Walker 1986, Biles 1990 and Office of Corrections Resource Centre 1985 in Australia, Bernheim 1987, Spielman 1988, and Hammerlin and Bodal 1988 elsewhere in Europe). Such studies have provided a wealth of information, some of which is replicated in many studies, but much of which is contradictory. In practice, little improvement in the prediction of suicidal prisoners has been achieved. About 20% of prisoners who die by suicide in prison have been identified as being at risk whilst in custody. Whilst it is likely that a number of positively identified 'at risk' prisoners are successfully prevented from taking their own lives in custody, the stability of this figure relating to non-identified at risk prisoners over time suggests that progress in developing an accurate 'suicidal prisoner profile' has not been made.

The above studies conclude overall that the suicide rate in prison is high, that most completed prison suicides are male, that a disproportionate number are on remand at the time of death, that a third have a history of in-patient psychiatric treatment, that lifers are over-represented, most have previous convictions and that 40 per cent have been seen by a doctor in the week preceding death. Most completed suicides are accomplished by hanging, many have injured themselves before (often in custody), many have serious drug and alcohol problems and many completed prisons suicides are accomplished by the young (under 27). Studies disagree as to whether completed prison suicides are more likely to have been convicted of acquisitive crimes or crimes of violence. About a third of all prison suicides occur very early in custody (within the first week). Many – but by no means the majority – have previous in-patient psychiatric histories.

Whilst some of this information is useful, there are important explanations for the contradictory and limited findings of these sorts of studies. The major problems are as follows:

(1)   The inadequacy of official figures on suicides.

(2)   The inadequacy and inappropriateness of recorded information.

(3)   The lack of any control group.

(4)   Poorly understood links between suicide and self-injury.

(5)   The existence of different types of prison suicide.

(6)   The poverty of our conception of 'risk'.

(1) OFFICIAL PRISON SUICIDE FIGURES

> There is an important distinction between the knowledge that some-one...probably...committed suicide, and the *legal requirement* that one be *sure* that he (*sic*) both intended the outcome, and had the capacity to take the action. In a court of law, one must be satisfied of the *intent* and of the *capacity*. A suicide is – historically – the murder of oneself, and the law requires it to mean just that. (Coroner, cited in Liebling, 1992, pp.83–84)

Suicide figures and records, based as they are on prison records and the outcome of coroners' inquests, constitute an inadequate data source for analysis. A study by Dooley (1990b) illustrates this point. He found that many probable suicides are officially classed as 'open' verdicts or other non-natural deaths ('misadventure', 'accidental', etc.) and that there are differences be-tween those prison suicides which receive suicide verdicts at inquests and those which do not. Those self-inflicted deaths not receiving suicide verdicts at inquests were more likely to be female, young, to die by means other than hanging, to have injured themselves before and to have occurred during the day (Dooley 1990b; see also Liebling 1992 pp.82–93). In other words, only those suicides which 'look like' suicides (that is, which fulfil prior expecta-tions) are recorded as suicides. This limits the validity of research which takes such selective information as its starting point, as sociological critiques of suicide in the community have demonstrated (see, for example, Atkinson 1982, Douglas 1967, and Taylor 1982).

(2) THE NATURE OF RECORDED INFORMATION

Even where these issues have been recognised (the UK Prison Service now uses self-inflicted deaths, whether or not these deaths receive a suicide verdict at the inquest as its baseline) there are further problems with the nature of recorded information on which studies of prison suicide are based. Explana-tions of the death are sociologically 'constructed' rather than scientifically 'discovered' at inquests and other inquiries – evidence is selected, wide discretion is exercised, explanations are offered, situations are reconstructed – and the 'social facts' resulting from these complex, often emotional and sometimes conflict-ridden processes disguise the disagreements, contradictions and gaps existing in the 'real world' which official documents aim to represent. Such data sources are often attributed a credibility they do not deserve. Official records often masquerade as 'hard data' in research – their objectivity, accuracy and reliability should be thoroughly doubted (see Liebling 1992, pp.90–93). Prison records exist for very specific purposes which are unrelated to research. They fail to reflect the lived experience of prison life, they do not approach the subjective experience of the individual prisoner and they frequently do 'grievous harm to reality'.

(3) THE LINKS BETWEEN SUICIDE AND SELF-INJURY

> I wanted someone to stop me. But no-one stopped me. So I carried on. (Prisoner)

> It is like the blood is doing the crying for me... It's not a cry for help. It's a cry of pain. (Prisoner)

Half of all those who die by suicide in prison have injured themselves before – many in prison. Despite this overlap, suicide and self-injury are usually considered as separate issues with different populations engaging in each. Self-injury may be the first overt symptom of a level of distress only steps away from a final act of despair (see Liebling 1992 pp.59–67 and Sparks 1994, p.83). If there is no response to what can be seen as a 'last ditch' effort to change an unbearable environment, suicide may be extremely likely. Self-injury can incorporate a vast spectrum of 'harm' to the self, and there is no direct relationship between level of harm or seriousness of injury and the level of intent reported. Acts of self-injury are associated with feelings of 'melancholy tinged with self-contempt' (Cooper, 1971), depression, self-doubt and the search for relief (Toch 1975, Liebling 1992):

> It is a back-to-the-wall, dead-end desperation, an intolerable emptiness, helplessness, tension. It is a physical reaction, and a demand for release and escape at all costs. (Toch 1975, p.40)

Self-injury and suicide are 'expressions of a common suicidal process' (Goldney and Burvil 1980, p.2). The continuities between them (particularly in terms of motivation, cause and prevention) may be far more important than their differences (see Liebling 1992, pp.62–67 for a review). Both may be *reactive* rather than *purposive* and both may contain the cognitive ambivalence expressed by suicide attempters who live (see Diekstra 1987). It would be more useful to regard suicide – both in action and in intent – as a continuum along which the first step (which may be ideation) may prove to be the first stage along a pathway to despair. Responding at the first step, and providing alternatives – and support, and solutions – may divert prisoners from the destructive route along which they are setting.

(4) DIFFERENCES OF DEGREE: ESTABLISHING A CONTROL GROUP

The research reported in this section consisted of two separate projects. Both projects looked at prisoners who had attempted suicide and at prisoners drawn from the general populations in which the suicide attempters were drawn. Interestingly, these two studies of different populations (sentenced young male and female prisoners and all male prisoners) found that 18% of prisoners drawn randomly from the total populations being studied had thought about suicide during their time in prison (Liebling 1992, Liebling and Krarup 1993). To this extent, we can estimate that at any one time there may be up to a fifth of current populations who are, or who may have recently been thinking about suicide. This high proportion of prisoners in both studies confirms the point made earlier, that large numbers within *any* prison population are vulnerable. However, the studies also found consistent differences between suicide attempters and prisoners drawn randomly from the populations studied. Prisoners who made suicide attempts were found to differ in significant ways from other prisoners, showing poorer coping strategies and suffering from a greater degree of background disadvantage (Liebling 1992, Liebling and Krarup 1993). The prison experience was far more difficult for those prisoners who were not able to find their way into the best jobs, activities and social networks in prison (see Liebling 1992 and 1994).

The research – which was based largely on semi-structured interviews – grew out of a disenchantment with recorded information about suicide and suicide attempts in prison and with the traditional prediction approach to the problem. Serious methodological flaws in previous studies (as reported above) and a failure of research to contribute to developments in theoretical understanding signalled the need for a change of approach from a medical/psychiatric diagnostic exercise aimed at identifying and predicting suicide towards a more ethnographic approach aimed at understanding the real life world of prisoners at risk of suicide. The use of long semi-structured interviews, supplemented by observational methods, participation, statistical data and informal discussions with staff and prisoners were found to be a more appropriate approach to this type of research. In the first study, 100 prisoners and 80 staff from four young offenders establishments were interviewed. These interviews were supplemented by observation, participation in aspects of prison life (such as association, classes, visits to the health care centre, etc.) and informal discussions with prisoners and staff. Prison suicide inquests, training seminars and relevant meetings were also attended. The study demonstrated that important differences could be found between suicide attempters and other prisoners. Those differences relating to criminal justice histories and background characteristics were differences *of degree* – suicide attempters had suffered more severe disadvantage, violence and family problems in their histories and they had had more frequent contact with social services and criminal justice agencies. Suicide attempters were more likely to report multiple family breakdown, frequent violence leading to hospitalisation, local authority placement as a result of family problems (as opposed to offending), truancy as a result of bullying (as opposed to boredom or peer pressure) and very short periods spent in the community between custody. Suicide attempters were more likely to report experiences of sexual abuse and they were more likely to have injured themselves on a previous occasion. This information would not have been available from records, but only emerged in the descriptions prisoners gave of their lives.

Once in prison, the scale and quality of the differences between the two groups were more marked. On most questions relating to the prison experience, the suicide attempters both were and saw themselves as considerably worse off than their peers. They were less likely to be engaged in activities, less likely to have a job in prison, they were more likely to report difficulties with other prisoners and with staff. They were least likely to be receiving regular or helpful contact from outside, either from families and friends or from the probation service. Most important in terms of understanding their immediate vulnerability to suicide, they were unable to occupy themselves when left alone in their cells. It was this dependence on 'sustaining external resources' which left some groups of prisoners unable to cope in conditions of confinement and isolation. Prison was unbearable – for some.

Suicide attempters saw themselves as having problems – often related to their offending behaviour, but also relating to their families and relationships, job chances, etc. – and as needing help (although they were often unclear as to what sort of help they needed). They experienced custody as debilitating, painful and uncomfortable. They sometimes had difficulties expressing themselves clearly or asking for help directly, and were as a result often appearing a 'disciplinary' or 'medical' problem during their sentences, but not as 'vulnerable'. Again, this account of the variations between prisoners of their experiences of prison life was relatively easy to establish during a long interview but the information would not have been available from records.

The second project (on suicide attempts in male prisons) was funded by the Home Office following a request for further research in this area. It built upon the results of the first study above, and broadened the scope of the research to include all male sentenced and remand prisoners. Its methodology was similar, with an additional epidemiological component mentioned below. The results confirmed the findings of the first study, showing that suicide attempters were more likely to have had *more* violent or *more* troubled histories than their peers, and that they struggled in many respects with prison. On most demographic and socio-economic variables, few significant differences between suicide attempters and other prisoners emerged. Most were differences of degree. Prisoners from the general population could articulate their histories, their growth into crime, and the pain of their lives in words, and more of them had developed strategies for dealing with that world: a world where security, love, reward, opportunity and hope were notably absent. In their place, material gain, risk-taking, 'moonlighting', impulsivity and immediacy took root (see Zamble and Porporino 1988 for a discussion of prisoners' lives in the community). Once in prison, the scale and quality of the differences between the two groups were much more clear. Each indicator of life in prison confirmed this overall pattern. Lack of motivation or confidence to negotiate a place in education, in a workshop, or cleaning on a wing, was interpreted by staff as lack of interest. Not having anything to do was one of the most destructive aspects of life in prison, particularly for this group. More than half could think of 'nothing' to do to relieve their feelings of boredom and depression. Visits and contacts with families were unreliable and difficult. The suicide attempters looked for and needed more personal engagement with staff – saying during interviews that they wanted staff to listen to them more, take an interest in them, and try to understand them.

(5) TOWARDS A TYPOLOGY OF PRISON SUICIDE

Having argued that official figures are unreliable, cautiously treated figures on self-inflicted deaths in prison can still be used to make a start on establishing important aspects of the terrain we seek to explore – some types of recorded information are more reliable than others. Basic factual details, like frequency, time, method, age, etc. can be a useful starting place from which to launch deeper research questions. Explanatory or causally-inferred data is the least reliable, for the reasons outlined above. One way of improving upon previous attempts to search out a profile of 'the suicidal prisoner' is to abandon the search for a single profile, but to look more carefully at what the data shows us. What they show are different prisoner 'types'. There is no single profile, and there is no single explanation for suicide in prison. There may be broad patterns, particularly amongst particular groups of prisoners.

An exercise was carried out using data collected by the Suicide Awareness Support Unit in the UK on completed self-inflicted deaths in prisons in England and Wales between 1987 and 1993. Looking at the deaths separately, and categorising them as shown in Table 13.1 demonstrates that prison suicides can be conceptualised as at least three distinguishable groups with some distinct characteristics and causes. Table 13.1 shows that the three groups – the psychiatrically ill, life/long sentence prisoners and 'poor copers' – the vulnerable group discussed above – each have a different profile; with regard to the age, history, possible motivation and the types of situational factors which appear to contribute to their deaths, from the available information. It is important to note that the 'poor copers' or vulnerable prisoners discussed earlier in this chapter constitute the most numerous group of prison suicides and that the significance of the immediate prison situation may be most acute in these cases. It is also important to note that more of this group have attempted suicide or injured themselves before.

A second exercise which was carried out as part of the larger study of attempted suicides in male prisons, drew further distinctions between different prisoner groups, based on epidemiological data which aimed to provide important contextual material on the nature and frequency of suicide attempts in Prison Service establishments in England and Wales. It sought to improve upon existing data, which were known to be seriously flawed (see above; also Liebling 1992, HMCIP 1990, Liebling and Krarup 1993). A carefully chosen sample of 16 establishments providing a representative cross-section of the prison population was selected. The establishments consisted of six local and remand centres, four closed training prisons, four Young Offenders Institutions (YOI), one dispersal prison and one open prison. Contacts were made and maintained with each establishment throughout the period of the research (1990–1992) by visits, regular phone calls and letters. Each establishment was asked to complete a pre-coded 4-page form when a prisoner

	1. Poor Copers	2. Long Sentence Prisoners	3. Psychiatrically Ill
Table 13.1: A Typology of Prison Suicide			
Possible Motivation	fear/ helplessness distress/isolation	guilt/no future	alienation, loss of self control fear/ helplessness
Age	16–25	30+	30+
Proportion of Total	30–45%+	5–20%	10–22%*
Relevance of Situation	acute	chronic	varied
History of Previous Self-Injury	high	low	medium
Features	Often more typical of prison pop. i.e. acquisitive offences	often (76%)**on remand, after midnight; some well into sentence	psych. history present; single; NFA

* 13% for young offenders under 21.
** Dooley, 1990a

attempted suicide or injured himself[1] sufficiently gravely to require hospital treatment. Visits were carried out to each of the establishments asked to participate in the research in order to explain its aims and objectives and its potential significance for future policy and practice. Despite a high level of contact and the successful establishment of liaison personnel in each prison's health care centre, this exercise was difficult to complete. Staffing changes and absences, a reluctance to complete forms or to be seen as a 'top of the league' establishment, a resistance to define self-injury as 'serious' and time constraints, made this data collection exercise especially arduous (see Liebling and Krarup 1993, Ch 3).

Despite the above difficulties, details were received on 305 incidents carried out by 248 prisoners in 16 establishments between July 1990 and June 1991 inclusive. Most of the forms were completed by health care staff. The data received were not a complete sample: regular checking with local sources of information and record-keeping (such as hospital occurrence books) suggested that the data were unevenly incomplete for particular establishments and/or at particular times during the year. No incident forms were received from either the open adult prison or the open (YOI). Most of the forms received

---

1   There were no female establishments included in the second study. For an explanation of this, and for further detail on suicides amongst female prisoners, see Liebling 1994.

came from local and remand centres (60%). Twenty per cent came from YOI's and 20% came from the training and dispersal prisons. Forty three per cent of the prisoners were under 21 (the proportion of under 21s in the prison population in 1991 was 17% of the average daily population and 31% of annual receptions into custody). Forty per cent of the prisoners in the sample were on remand. Most of the incidents involved wrist-cutting (across and length ways). Eighteen per cent of the incidents involved self-strangulation. In 8% of cases, immediate transfer to outside hospital was required. An additional five per cent required transfer to prisons with full-time medical facilities. The remaining cases were treated locally, with stitches (between one and 120), steri-strip and plasters. A small number of prisoners refused stitches. Eighteen per cent of the incidents occurred within one week of arrival at the establishment. Almost a third (31%) occurred within three weeks. Most of the incidents occurred in 'normal locations' – a third in single cells and a third in shared cells (which may have been unoccupied by the prisoner's cell-mate at the time). Fifteen per cent of the incidents took place in health care centres, over half of these in single or unfurnished rooms.

The pattern of offences and charges for prisoners in the sample was not dissimilar from those of the prison population. Offences of violence (including sexual offences and robbery) were not significantly over-represented amongst the sample. Offences of arson and criminal damage appeared to be over-rep-resented, although the overall number of such offenders in the prison popu-lation is small. There was no over-representation of short or medium sentence prisoners, although the number of very short sentence prisoners (serving under four months) was slightly over-represented, probably reflecting the large number of under-21 prisoners in the sample.

Half of the prisoners had injured themselves previously – two thirds of these prisoners had done so in custody; 14% within one week of the current incident. Almost half of the prisoners (45%) were placed in seclusion as a result of their injury. Twenty three per cent were located in single rooms in the health care centre and nine per cent were accommodated in hospital wards or shared rooms. Less than a third were referred to a psychiatrist. A third of the sample had seen a Medical Officer less than seven days before the incident. Only 26% had been identified as being at some risk of suicide in the reception screening interview. Reasons given by staff completing the forms for the incidents were coded at the end of the research and included 'domestic' problems (break-up or threatened break-up of relationships, contact problems, bereavement, etc.) 'situational' problems (relating to the charge, frustrations, upset at being in prison, bullying and feeling unable to cope); 'strategic' reasons (wanting practical help, relating to changes in location, 'attention-seeking', etc.) and 'emotional' problems (depression, anger, distress, fear, etc.). Most of the staff attributed a mixture of the above reasons to each incident. 'Medical' explana-tions (such as mental illness, drug withdrawal, physical illness, etc.) were given rarely (less than 8% of cases).

A detailed analysis of the data collected was carried out, looking at different groups of prisoners and their suicide attempts. This analysis was supplemented by a re-analysis of the results from the qualitative study of suicide attempts reported above. This study compared suicide attempters with non suicide attempters drawn randomly from the same populations. Different types of 'at risk' prisoner were identified, whose suicide attempts seemed to be related to slightly different features of their personal histories and prison experience, such as prisoners on remand, long-termers, the young, first timers and those on Rule 43. Figure 13.1 illustrates the main distinctions between these groups (which may overlap; for more detail, see Liebling and Krarup 1993). What the figure shows is that the nature of suicide risk in different establishments may vary according to the populations concerned. These distinctions are *generalisations* only, and may serve as *guides* to risk management rather than 'predictors'. For young prisoners under the age of 26, it is the prison situation which is particularly important. Compared to older prisoners at risk of suicide, younger prisoners are less likely to be suffering from psychiatric illnesses, or from problems relating to shame and guilt. They may be unable to cope with the prison environment, often having problem histories (such as violence at home, sexual abuse, being bullied at school, etc.). They may be especially dependent on activity, structure and contact with family, staff, and others (that is, 'sustaining external resources'), and may be especially prone to boredom and/or bullying. Their need for support is marked, and their reactions to distress may be impulsive. Remand prisoners may be especially 'at risk', particularly in the very early stages of their time in custody (that is, within the first seven days).

This is in part because the remand population contains all the most vulnerable groups (the young, first timers, the psychiatrically ill) at a highly stressful time, under difficult circumstances, when the uncertainties of charge, conviction, sentence, family contact and allocation are at their greatest, and when feelings of guilt and shame may be acute. 'Family problems' can be especially distressing at this stage, and 'at risk' prisoners on remand expressed having problems with other prisoners, and not knowing how to get problems solved. First timers expressed severe difficulties in dealing with custody (many reported having been devastated by receiving a sentence). Amongst the 'first timers' those who attempted suicide were significantly younger and had fewer previous convictions than their peers. Their relative youth and inexperience meant that they were particularly dependent upon (and there-fore vulnerable to) outside contacts. Suicide attempts were more likely to occur at the weekends (e.g. after visits).

Short-term prisoners at risk of suicide showed distinct problems relating to lack of community ties and release plans. This group were most likely to have received news of separation or divorce, and had few plans for employ-ment or accommodation, and had few family ties. Amongst long-term pris-oners too, the suicide attempt group were significantly concerned about losing contact with their families. They were more likely to be receiving treatment for depression and they regarded staff as less helpful than their peers did. Suicide attempts occurred much longer after arrival than amongst other groups – and they had often been planned over long periods. Clearly the sex offender/'Vulnerable Prisoner Unit' population is a highly vulnerable popu-lation, their protected status reflecting the particular pressures of the prison environment for this group. The suicide attempters within this group had the most troubled histories, and were most likely to have injured themselves before. They were most likely to report difficulties with staff and other prisoners.

These brief descriptive 'typologies' can be represented by Figure 13.1. It makes useful conceptual distinctions, illustrating how different stages in the custodial process may expose particular groups of prisoners to different types and degrees of risk.

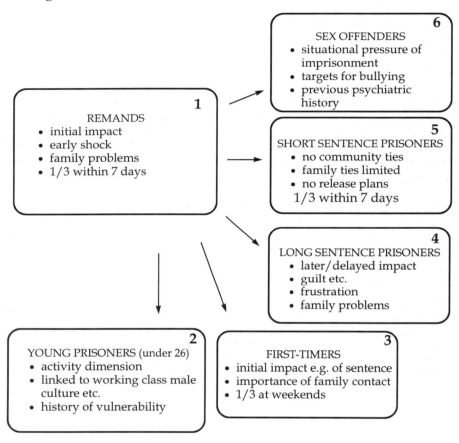

Figure 13.1: A differentiated model of prison suicide vulnerability

UNDERSTANDING SUICIDE RISK IN PRISON

> There was no-one to talk to...I felt lonely... There was nothing...I felt empty...I just felt so down...I'd had enough...I felt hopeless... No-one believed me...I couldn't answer the doctors questions... (quotations from several prisoners)

Prisoners interviewed by the author in two long-term research projects on suicide attempts in prison often could only build up to the 'real reason' for their attempts in stages, becoming most articulate at the very end of a long interview, when they finally felt that they were being believed. Their 'internal states' reflected fear, loneliness, loss and distress. Externally, their reactions were sometimes extreme, angry, and violent. A common theme was a sense of resourcelessness, bankruptcy, The self, the future, and the environment (Beck's 'cognitive triad') were all bleak (Beck 1976). Such states can be temporary, or potential, activated by immediate events – or in prison, activated by the lack of distraction and activity. Risk is not a permanent feature of the individual, identifiable upon reception into custody. It is a dynamic state, influenced by background vulnerability, long-term environmental conditions and immediate situational triggers. All of these dimensions play their part. The individual's current state may be reflected in their descriptions of prison life and their efforts to survive it, if these accounts are sensitively sought. This is one way of assessing risk – and may be our most important route towards addressing it, at both a general and an individual level. A model of suicide risk in custody may look as shown in Figure 13.2.

CONCLUSIONS

There are serious limitations inherent in the use of statistical data on prison suicide and suicide attempts. It is significant that there are different types of prison suicide, with distinct developmental pathways. The two studies referred to above showed that important differences could be found between suicide attempters and other prisoners. Those differences relating to criminal justice histories and background characteristics were differences *of degree*. The more important differences were found in their descriptions of life in prison, which was and was seen as more difficult for the suicide attempters in almost every respect.

Looking at completed suicides in detail demonstrates how distinct types of prison suicide can be identified for whom the significance of the immediate environment may differ. The main types are the psychiatrically ill, long-term prisoners or those charged with grave offences, and poor copers. The concept of 'poor coping' in prison has been under-researched. *Understanding* suicide risk is as important as, and may be a tool in, our strivings to predict it.

The situational aspects of suicide (such as bullying, lack of activity, isolation, the breakdown of relationships, parole refusal, an unexpected sentence or change in location, etc.) have been broadly acknowledged by policies aimed at minimising suicidal ideation in prison. The vulnerability of (particularly certain groups within) the prison population has not been considered outwith the narrow policy sphere of suicide awareness training in prison. The implications of a growing body of evidence illustrating the relative disadvantage and subsequent vulnerability of the prison population are massive (see Walmley *et al.* 1992 and Liebling 1995). Imprisonment is directed against highly selected and vulnerable groups who are least able to cope with the demands made by a largely unresponsive environment. The psychological resources of prisoners (and their variability over time) have been insufficiently examined.

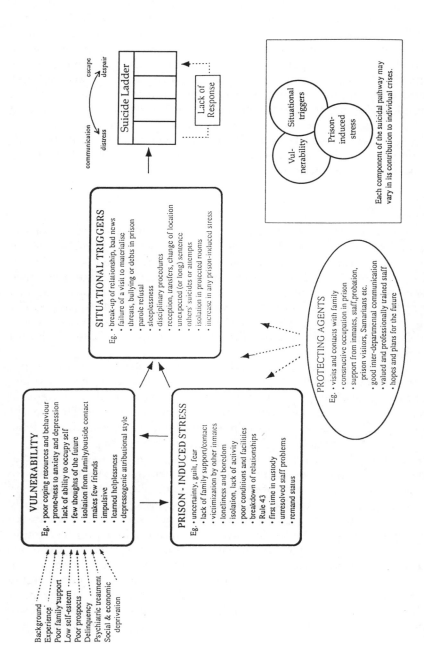

Figure 13.2 Diagrammatic representation of the prisoner's pathway to suicide

MINIMISING SUICIDE RISK IN PRISON

As can be seen by Figure 13.2, once suicide risk is understood as a dynamic feature of both individuals and situations, the sorts of preventive measures or 'protecting agents' appropriate to minimise risk in custody can be linked to this model. As the figure suggests, a good *throughcare* policy, with well thought-out programmes of planned activity, good communication between (e.g. probation, education, works, physical education, healthcare) departments, support from (supported and properly trained) staff, prisoner listener groups, Samaritans, Boards of Visitors and other visitors to establishments, along with good family contacts and future planning, may create an environment in which suicide risk is minimised. Programmes which aim to tackle offending behaviour (e.g. thinking skills, survival and life skills, communication and relationship skills) may also increase individuals' ability to cope with both prison and their lives outside. These are general preventive measures aimed at the level of the institution; as such, they are independent of any ability to identify risk in the individual. Making regimes constructive, and including all prisoners in the regime, is the first principle of good suicide prevention in prison.[2] At the individual level, the identification of suicide risk may require attention to 'unexpected' features of prison life, such as participation in activities, disciplinary infractions, relationships with staff and other prisoners, contact with family, as well as psychiatric or psychological assessment. Prison officers, works staff, education staff and other 'specialists' may have access to relevant information regarding prisoners' pattern of coping with different aspects of custody. An integrated, proactive and supportive approach to all prisoners may avert the sorts of crises many prisoners experience whether or not they are particularly vulnerable to suicide at the outset. Effective personal officer schemes are invaluable in this respect. Distinctions may need to be drawn between different prisoner groups: remands and sentenced, lifers, other long-term prisoners and others, young and adult, male and female, first-timers and others, those on Rule 43 or in vulnerable prisoner units, etc. when addressing risk. Suicide risk does not have a single causal pathway. Last resort 'situational prevention' measures (such as special watches), whilst sometimes necessary, may actually conflict with the therapeutic need for company, activity and support. Self-injury may be the first overt symptom of a level of distress only steps away from a final act of despair (see Liebling 1992 pp.59–67 and Sparks 1994, p.83). It has been demonstrated that those prisoners most likely to recover from suicidal feelings are those who feel they have some control over aspects of their environment (Dexter 1993). Taking (albeit cautious) risks may be necessary to the individual's recovery.

Investigating suicide risk in prison tells us much about where the prison environment may be contributing to suicidal feelings. Three broader ques-

---

2   It is arguable that current trends towards shorter core days, fewer gym, education, probation and works staff and provision, increased overcrowding, restrictions on association hours for prisoners not on enhanced levels, increased security, restrictions on temporary release and other efficiency savings are not conducive to these sorts of recommendations. Prison Service commitments to protect regimes 'in the current climate' should continue to be a priority.

tions should be asked about suicide risk, from the evidence reviewed in this chapter: does imprisonment damage already vulnerable populations further?; can (all, not just long-term) prisoners cope with what prison demands of them?; and what *does* prison demand of them? What resources does surviving prison require? To date, these questions have been asked and answered inadequately, particularly in the literature on prison suicide. We need to know more about what being in prison *feels like* and how far the prison experience exposes (or can repair) vulnerability. Those who are most vulnerable are exposed to a highly demanding environment in which survival skills are highly valued and indications of weakness or helplessness may bring about verbal and physical abuse, theft, taxing, sexual violence and psychological torment (see Liebling 1992 pp.145–149, McGurk and McDougal 1986, Feld 1977, HMCIP 1993, Liebling and Krarup 1993 pp.81–83). In this sense, risk may be situation-specific. Survival in prison demands recourse to a set of personal resources which may exceed the abilities of many of those it confines. Assessing risk in prison, and addressing it, requires a sensitivity to the subjective world of the prisoner, and a hard look at the nature of the regimes involved.

REFERENCES

Atkinson, J.M. (1982 edn.) *Discovering Suicide: Studies in the Social Organisation of Sudden Death.* London: MacMillan.

Backett, S. (1987) 'Suicides in Scottish prisons.' *British Journal of Psychiatry 151*, 218–221.

Beck, A.T. (1976) *Cognitive Therapy and Emotional Disorder.* New York: International Universities Press.

Bernheim, J.C. (1987) *Les Suicides en Prison.* Editions du Meridien: Canada.

Biles, D. (1991) 'Deaths in custody in Britain and Australia.' *Howard Journal 30*, 2, 110–120.

Biles, D. and MacDonald, D. (1992) *Deaths in Custody in Australia 1980–1989: The Research Papers of the Criminology Unit of the Royal Commission into Aboriginal Deaths in Custody.* Canberra: Australian Institute of Criminology.

Bukstel, L.H. and Kilmann, P.R. (1980) 'Psychological effects of imprisonment on confined individuals.' *Psychological Bulletin 88*, 2, 469–493.

Cooper, H.H.A. (1971) 'Self-mutilation by Peruvian prisoners.' *International Journal of Offender Therapy and Comparative Criminology 15*, 3, 180–188.

Correctional Services of Canada (1981) *Self-Inflicted Injuries and Suicides.* Canada: Bureau of Management Consulting.

Dexter, P. (1993) *Suicide Attempts at Highpoint Prison.* Unpublished MSc Thesis Submitted to Birbeck College.

Diekstra, R.F.W. (1987) 'Renee: chronicle of a misspent life, and Renee or the complex dynamics of adolescent suicide.' In R.F.W. Diekstra and K. Hawton (eds) *Suicide in Adolescence.* Martinus Nijhoff Publishers: Dordrecht: 25–77.

Dooley, E. (1990a) 'Prison suicide in England and Wales 1972–1987.' *British Journal of Psychiatry 156*, 40–45.

Dooley, E. (1990b) 'Non-natural deaths in prison.' *British Journal of Criminology 30,* 2, 229–34.

Douglas, J. (1967) *The Social Meanings of Suicide.* London: Routledge.

Feld, B.C. (1977) *Neutralizing Inmate Violence: Juvenile Offenders in Institutions.* Massachusetts: Ballinger.

Flaherty, M.G. (1983) *The National Incidence of Juvenile Suicide in Adult Jails and Juvenile Detention Centres.* University of Illinois: Urbana-Champagne.

Goldney, R.D. and Burvil, P.W. (1980) 'Trends in suicidal behaviour and its management.' *Australian and New Zealand Journal of Psychiatry 14,* 1–15.

Gover, R.M. (1880) 'Notes by the medical inspector, in Appendix No.19.' *Prison Commission Annual Report, 1880.* London: HMSO.

Griffiths, A.W. (1990) 'Correlates of suicidal history in male prisoners.' *Medicine, Science and the Law 30,* 3, 214–216.

Hammerlin, Y. and Bodal, K. (1988) *Suicide and Life-Threatening Activities in Norweigian Prisons During the Period 1956 Through 1987.* Norway: Ministry of Justice, Prison Department.

Hankoff, L.D. (1980) 'Prisoner suicide.' *International Journal of Offender Therapy and Comparative Criminology 24,* 2, 162–166.

Hatty, S. and Walker, J. (1986) *A National Study of Deaths in Australian Prisons.* Canberra: Australian Centre of Criminology.

Hayes, L. (1983) 'And darkness closes in… A national study of jail suicides.' *Criminal Justice and Behaviour 10,* 4, 461–484.

Hayes, L. (1994) 'Jail suicide prevention in the USA: yesterday, today and tomorrow.' In A. Liebling and T. Ward (eds) *Deaths in Custody: An International Conference.* London: Whiting and Birch.

HMCIP (1990) *Report on a Review by her Majesty's Chief Inspector of Prisons For England and Wales of Suicide and Self-Harm in Prison Service Establishments in England and Wales.* London: HMSO.

HMCIP (1993) Report of an Unannounced Short Inspection by H M Inspectorate of Prisons *HM YOI and RC Feltham.* London: Home Office.

Kennedy, D.B. (1984) 'A theory of suicide while in police custody.' *Journal of Police Science and Administration 12,* 2, 191–200.

Liebling, A. (1992) *Suicides in Prison.* London: Routledge.

Liebling, A. (1994) 'Suicides amongst women prisoners.' *Howard Journal 33,* 1, 1–9.

Liebling, A. (1995) 'Vulnerability and prison suicide.' *British Journal of Criminology 35,* 2, 173–187.

Liebling, A. and Krarup, H. (1993) *Suicide Attempts in Male Prisons.* London: Home Office.

Massachusetts Special Commission (1984) *Suicide in Massachusetts Lock-Ups 1973–1984.* Unpublished Final Report Submitted to the General Court: Massachusetts.

McGurk, B.J. and McDougal, C. (1986) *The Prevention of Bullying Among Incarcerated Delinquents.* D P S report Series II No. 114 (restricted circulation) London.

Office of Corrections Resource Centre (1985) *Suicide and Other Deaths in Prisons including Victorian Results from the National Deaths in Corrections Study.* Research Unit Office of Corrections: Canada.

O'Mahony, P. (1994) *Prison Suicide Rates: What Do They Mean?* In A. Liebling and T. Ward (eds) Deaths in Custody: International Perspectives Whiting and Birch: London pp.45–57.

Orlowski, R.J. (1985) *Suicide and Self-injury.* Unpublished paper presented to Michigan Department of Corrections.

Phillips, M. (1986) *Suicide and Attempted Suicide in Brixton Prison.* DPS Report: London.

Scott-Denoon, K. (1983) *B.C. Corrections: A Study of Suicides 1970–1980.* Corrections Branch: British Columbia.

Shneidman, E. (1973) *Deaths of Man.* New York: Quadrangle.

Smalley, H. (1911) Report by the Medical Inspector, in *Report by the Prison Commissioners.* London: HMSO.

Sparks, J.R. (1994) *Suicides in Prison.* By Alison Liebling, a Review in *British Journal of Criminology 34,* 1, 82–84.

Spielman, A. (1988) *Prison Suicides in the Grand Duchy of Luxembourg.* Council of Europe Prison Information Bulletin No.11 June 3–7.

Taylor, S. (1982) *Durkheima and the Study of Suicide.* London: MacMillan.

Toch, H. (1975) *Men in Crisis: Human Breakdowns in Prison.* New York: Aldine.

Topp, D.O. (1979) 'Suicide in prison.' *British Journal of Psychiatry 134,* 24–27.

Walker, N. (1983) 'The side-effects of incarceration.' *British Journal of Criminology 23,* 61–71.

Walker, N. (1987) 'The unwanted effects of long-term imprisonment.' In A.E. Bottoms and R. Light (eds) *Problems of Long-Term Imprisonment.* Aldershot: Gower.

Walmsley, R., Howard, L. and White, S. (1992) *The National Prison Survey 1991: Main Findings.* London: HMSO.

Zamble, E. and Porporino, F.J. (1988) *Coping, Behaviour and Adaptation in Prison Inmates.* New York: Springer-Verlag.

Chapter 14

Teenage Suicide and Self-Harm
Assessing and Managing Risk

Juliet Lyon

INTRODUCTION

In the course of growing up, many teenagers will think about dying. Some will have suicidal thoughts. Thankfully, comparatively few young people go on to kill themselves. There has been, however, a significant rise in the number of completed suicides amongst young men, and an increase in the incidence of self-harm amongst young women (Hawton, Fagg and Simkin 1996). This has to be of concern to all those who care for, and care about, young people.

This chapter will focus on young people and suicide risk in the context of normative adolescent development and risk taking. Why do young people take risks? What kinds of risks do they take? What effects does this behaviour have on the adults who are attempting to care for them?

Assessment of risk is not an exact science. It is not possible to predict which young people will kill themselves. Nor can a checklist spell away the real fears of either the worker or a distressed young person. However, it is possible to determine with some degree of accuracy which young people are particularly vulnerable. It is possible to identify the social circumstances, personal characteristics, situational variables and precipitating factors which combined could lead to suicide, or a suicide attempt. Even so, it is difficult to be wise before the event. One mother said of the news of her son's death 'When I heard the news then the connections all in a sense began to fall into place' (Coleman, Lyon and Piper 1995, p.13). It should be stressed too that, while risk factors can be documented, each individual will differ. How to assess risk both by objective measures and through the worker's own judgement, sense of a situation and knowledge of an individual client will be explored.

Much of what is known about assessing and managing suicide risk has been learned painfully during review and analysis following a suicide attempt or a death. The author would like to acknowledge the contribution made by families, bereaved parents, and troubled young people themselves, who generously agreed to be interviewed for a publication on teenage suicide and self-harm, commissioned by the Department of Health and produced by the Trust for the Study of Adolescence (Coleman, Lyon and Piper 1995). Reference will be made to their views and experiences throughout this chapter. Their wish was to increase awareness of suicide risk and to develop professional confidence and competence in helping distressed teenagers.

Ideally risk should be managed in partnership between the client, the worker and others concerned. In the course of looking at strategies to manage risk, emphasis will be placed on empowering the young person and providing appropriate support and help. Ways of building up coping skills and resilience will be discussed. The worker's professional responsibilities will be outlined. Work within the team, with allied agencies and with families will form part of this section. The concluding part of the chapter will explore the risks to those who work with troubled young people. The threat or fear of suicide, in particular teenage suicide, often leads to a kind of paralysis in the worker and professional isolation. How can staff cope and continue to work effectively? Risks to workers have to be acknowledged and managed. Maintaining staff mental health is a key to good practice with teenagers at risk of suicide.

ADOLESCENT DEVELOPMENT

An understanding of adolescent development is an essential normative reference point in work with troubled young people. Adolescence is a period of rapid change: psychologically, physically, socially and, often, environmentally. The belief that adolescence is a time of storm and stress has been challenged (Rutter 1989, Coleman and Hendry 1989). Adolescence is, however, characterised by mood swings. Many young people experience a confusing mixture of uncertainty and vulnerability together with a sense of change and opportunity. Important relationships are being formed with peers and family relationships are being re-negotiated. Young people are particularly sensitive to criticism. Adolescence is a time of identity formation. Teenagers are working out who they are and what they want to become. Risk taking is a characteristic of normal adolescent behaviour (Plant and Plant 1992). Questioning, experimenting, challenging, testing out and pushing limits are part of this process. Teenagers seek the freedom and independence they associate with adulthood. At the same time, they need and want the care and protection associated with childhood.

One source of understanding adolescence is the worker's own experience of being an adolescent. Whether consciously or unconsciously, professionals draw on their own past experience of the teenage years in their current work with young people. Memories of this time colour expectations and inform attitudes and opinions. Almost inevitably work with teenagers prompts us to 'bump into our own adolescence'. Troubled and troublesome adolescents, in particular, have a capacity to put staff in touch with past difficulties or unresolved issues in their own lives. Professionals should anticipate this process, and try to make some sense of their own transition from childhood to adulthood. Exercise 14.1 will help to do this.

Exercise 14.1 Risk Taking

Aims

- to gain insight into adolescence as a life stage by recalling the teenage years, events and the feelings which accompanied these events
- to think about risk taking behaviour from personal experience
- to use the insights gained as a resource for working with understanding and empathy

Method

Group members should divide into pairs to do this exercise. Each participant needs a few minutes to read through the questions. Allow 15 minutes for discussion in pairs and a further 15 minutes for feedback and discussion in the group. Times may vary. Trainers may wish to reduce these times and use the questions as a trigger or warm-up exercise. Flipchart paper and pens can be used to document key points.

This exercise can be done by individuals responding to and thinking about the questions on their own.

Instructions to participants

- Use these questions just to prompt memories
- Choose two or three to discuss with your partner

When you were a teenage did you ever...

- Stay up later than you were allowed to?
- Try to reduce or increase your weight?
- Push yourself past the limit in sport or physical exercise?
- Wear something that your parents or carers hated?
- Smoke at school?
- Get drunk at a party?
- Work under pressure to pass an exam or gain an award?
- Find it embarrassing or impossible to get contraceptives?
- Watch a film made for older people?
- Travel on public transport without paying your fare?
- Ride a bike or drive a car recklessly?
- Know people who took illegal drugs?
- Join in activities you did not like in order to be, or stay, accepted by a group of friends?
- Stand up against others for something you believed in?
- Avoid taking risks because...?

ADOLESCENTS IN SOCIETY

Although the process of moving from childhood to adulthood is similar to the one that workers will remember, it is important to bear in mind that today's teenagers are growing up in a different societal context. Arguably there are more risks and pressures. Young people face a much less certain future. (Coleman 1997). Youth unemployment has risen. Young people are less likely to leave school and go straight into work or an apprenticeship. Instead they will continue in education, enter job schemes or be unemployed. Family breakdown is widespread. One in four teenagers will experience the breakdown of their parents' marriage. The process of experiencing the disintegration of family life and other related changes such as new home, new school, new peer group, may place intolerable pressures on some young people. The period of time in which young people exist in limbo, as neither child nor adult, has lengthened considerably. Puberty now begins earlier. Many teenagers continue to live at home into their mid-twenties rather than leaving in their late teens. This lack of status has an impact on a young person's sense of identity and self-esteem. Other risks include the increased availability of drugs and the continuing availability of alcohol. Paradoxically, in an age of increased technological communication, there is more isolation. Young people are more likely to be occupied watching television, using computers or talking on the phone and less likely to communicate face-to-face.

COPING AND ADJUSTMENT

Why do some young people cope better with change or adversity than others? In part this depends on whether changes are 'normative stressors' such as puberty, leaving school, first sexual relationships or more stressful life events such as moving house, academic failure, loss of a parent through death or divorce. The nature and number of changes matter as does their synchronicity, whether they cluster or are spaced out. Temperament and coping styles vary. Some young people can be described as 'active copers'. They use social resources, strategy and planning, in other words they discuss the problem with friends, parents or teachers and work out what to do. Others are 'internal copers'. They use thought or analysis, that is, they think about the problem, what to do about it, list pros and cons and come up with solutions. Those more at risk may withdraw or deny there is a problem: they retreat or ignore it because they believe that they cannot change the situation. Finally, on the whole, those teenagers who seem resilient and cope comparatively well with stress and adjust to adversity are those who have someone to refer to and trust. They feel supported by a 'significant adult' or adults inside or outside the family, someone to turn to whose opinion they value (Seiffge-Krenke 1993). Evaluating and building up coping skills and on-going support are key factors in risk assessment and management.

ADOLESCENT SUICIDE AND ATTEMPTED SUICIDE

How common is suicidal behaviour? Suicide is thought to be under-reported in general and this is particularly true for young people below the age of 15 where coroners are reluctant to return a suicide verdict if there is any cause for doubt. The most recent mortality statistics for England and Wales relate to 1994 (Office of Population Censuses and Surveys 1995). These show that 65 young men and 12 young women, aged between 15 and 19 years, died as a result of suicide. Almost double this number, a further 64 males and 14 females, died from injuries where it was uncertain whether they were accidental or purposefully inflicted.

Attempted suicide is far more common than completed suicide. It has been suggested that around 19,000 young people between 10 and 19 years are referred to general hospitals in England and Wales following self-poisoning or self-injury (Madge 1996). The vast majority of these are young women. Other estimates indicate that as many as 44,000 young people reach Accident and Emergency Units each year, having harmed themselves in some way (Hill 1995).

SELF-HARM

It is important, though sometimes difficult, to try to distinguish between attempted suicide and deliberate self-harm. Most young people who hurt themselves do not do so with the intention of killing themselves. In fact, many of the young people interviewed by the Trust for the Study of Adolescence stated clearly that harming themselves was their way of coping with, and, surviving intolerable pressures. For others it was a way of ensuring that they got the help and attention they badly wanted. One young woman said:

> When I'm out in the community, especially when I'm really sort of lonely at night time, and I'm getting in a state, I feel like the only option I've got is to cut myself to get into casualty, to get help, 'cos I couldn't just walk into casualty without a problem. It sounds really sick but that's been the problem most of the time and here it's to be, it's all like heard and listened to. When you cut, you know, part of you wants to be patched up, that, the pain wants, needs patched up, to be patched up. (Coleman, Lyon and Piper 1995, pp.17–18)

It is still too common that self-harm is dismissed as 'attention seeking' or 'just a cry for help'. These behaviours have to be taken seriously in their own right. If a young person is hurting enough to damage herself or himself, then adults do have to pay attention. Young people who have harmed themselves in the past are at significantly increased risk of attempting suicide at a later date.

VULNERABILITY AND RISK

Are some young people more vulnerable than others? Gender is an important factor in assessing suicide risk. Young men are three times more likely than young women to kill themselves while for the incidence of self-harm these figures are reversed (NHS Health Advisory Service 1994) Male suicides in the 15–24 year age group increased by 78 per cent between 1980 and 1990 (Madge 1996). Rising unemployment, family breakdown and use of drugs and alcohol are factors associated particularly with this trend. Young men are considered less able to communicate their feelings and more likely to bottle up difficulties and distress (Samaritans 1995). One mother describes how she hoped that her son would communicate with someone.

> Desperate, the feeling that there must be something we could do and wanting to know what. Sort of trying to suggest that he phone the Samaritans – which he was totally unwilling to do. Talk to anybody – which he was totally unwilling to do. See a counsellor – which he was unwilling to do. Talk to friends or family which, on the whole, he was unwilling to do. (Coleman, Lyon and Piper 1995 Audiotape)

The Samaritans have developed Electronic Befriending, using the Internet as a way of giving young men who are more comfortable with this form of communication direct access to their services.

Gender differences are apparent too in methods of suicide or attempted suicide. Males tend to use more aggressive methods such as hanging or jumping, where females are more likely to overdose. Increased use of paracetamol by young women is 'a worrying trend in view of the profound liver damage this drug can cause' (Kerfoot 1996). Particular groups of young people have significantly higher incidence of suicide and self-harm. Those who are in the care of their local authority, many of whom will have a chaotic history of broken placements and sudden moves, are likely to be less anchored than other young people from more stable backgrounds. One young man said:

> I was mucked about too much by the authorities. I was moved about from pillar to post and I didn't feel that anything was going on in my life apart from I was just being moved all the time and I was very unhappy and I couldn't see anything good going right. I couldn't see anything positive for the future so I just thought 'What the hell. I've, there's nothing worth living for' and that was it. (Coleman, Lyon and Piper 1995 Audiotape)

Young prisoners, particularly those held on remand, are at risk of suicide. They are significantly more likely than other young men of their age to try and kill themselves (Liebling 1992).

Gay young men and women are a vulnerable group, not because of their sexual orientation, but because of the lack of acceptance they experience and the difficulties they may have in communicating with family and friends about their sexuality. Those teenagers who have been victims of abuse, particularly sexual abuse, may have a strong sense of worthlessness and self-loathing. Although members of many ethnic minority groups will have developed a strong racial identity, for some it is difficult to maintain this in the face of racism or racial abuse. Some young people, particularly Asian young women, may find having to balance two cultures – that of their family and that of their friends – creates extra stresses and difficulties (Kingsbury 1994). Social class is not a factor usually associated with suicide risk but there are increased risks for young people living in poverty. Geographical location is important, with those in isolated rural areas being more vulnerable.

Drug users are another group at risk of suicide because the use of some illegal drugs increases impulsiveness and lowers the awareness of consequences of actions. In addition, many have to resort to risky or criminal behaviour in order to fund their drug habit. A high proportion of those who commit suicide do so while under the influence of drugs or alcohol.

> The implications for prevention and intervention are clear: focusing on drug and alcohol abuse would have a greater impact on adolescent suicide rates than any other primary prevention programme. (NHS Health Advisory Service 1994)

Finally, mentally ill young people pose a particularly high suicide risk. Depression is strongly associated with deliberate self-harm (Andrews and Lewinsohn 1992). Young male schizophrenics, especially those who are unemployed, are very vulnerable (Alberg, Hatfied and Huxley 1996). Sleep difficulties, self-neglect, confusion, cognitive rigidity, hopelessness and helplessness are common signs of poor mental health. One mother said:

> He gets so low sometimes that you can't seem to bring him out of it, what ever you do, whatever you say, you just, you can't bring him up. (Coleman, Lyon and Piper 1995 Audiotape)

The common themes which link these vulnerable groups are:

- isolation
- lack of support
- low self-esteem
- sense of powerlessness/helplessness
- uncertain futures.

Their implications for risk management will be considered later in this chapter.

DAMAGING CULTURES

As well as being alert to the individual young person, one needs to be alert to the prevailing culture in an institution. It is also important to notice signs of increased risk within a family or a peer group.

Specifically a culture may develop where self-destructive behaviours become accepted as a method of communication, a way of showing distress and, in some cases, seeking help. Without devaluing the seriousness of these attempts, ways must be found to avoid self-destructive acts becoming a valid, or valued, currency within an institution or culture. For example, one young woman who was interviewed in prison said of the staff: 'They just don't take no notice of you. You just have to cut up or kick off or smash up your cell' (Lyon and Coleman 1996).

Where a group of troubled or troublesome young people come together, particularly in a residential institution, staff have to be aware of the process of extremely negative communication developing which often involves harm to self and/or others. Staff hostility and withdrawal in the face of work with very difficult clients or client groups has itself been documented as a factor in suicide risk (Watts and Morgan 1994).

Self-destructive behaviour can seem more acceptable to young people if it is seen as widespread. For example a young woman who had taken a serious overdose at school following a broken relationship said

> It was like, about a month before it was like something that happened, loads, everyone done it. About four of my friends done it.

The interviewer asked what effect her overdose had had on her friends.

> It didn't really, apart from Sam. She was really shocked and that and she was, like, really nice. Apart, the rest of my friends, like it didn't affect, like, my cousin, and, like, a little group of girls I hang around with and that. It didn't really affect them 'cos they've all done it before and they, like it's nothing surprising to hear that I'd done it. (Coleman, Lyon and Piper 1995 Audiotape)

Simply seeing these actions as 'copy cat' incidents is not helpful. Staff or team meetings should be used to share information, document the extent of the problem, examine any connections between incidents of self-harm, look at staff and peer group responses in each case. Understanding this process will provide pointers for how to intervene and create a more positive climate where it is possible to express distress and gain help in less destructive ways.

PRECIPITATING FACTORS

What leads a young person to attempt suicide? For vulnerable teenagers 'living on the edge' what factors might propel them towards suicide? It is rare for one single event to be the cause of a serious attempt. Instead for each person a different constellation of factors will have led up to this point. Together with a generalised feeling of isolation, despair, hopelessness or helplessness a bad experience or stressful event may prove to be the 'last straw'. 'The best evidence suggests that risk factors include both personal characteristics and situational variables. Often a combination of circumstances, perhaps triggered by a final rejection of some kind, provides the best possible explanation in individual cases' (Madge 1996).

A common precipitating factor, or stressor, is the experience of loss. In the majority of cases it is the loss of an important person which can tip the balance. Broken relationships are the reason most often given by young women after they have attempted suicide. Other losses might concern the death of a grandparent, suicide of a sibling, loss of contact with father following family breakdown, or the experience of termination of a pregnancy. Many young people who have been abused will have suffered a profound loss of trust coupled with the loss of a sense of themselves due to sexual abuse or neglect within the family. The loss of a cherished ambition or of a job or failure to meet their own, or others' perceived expectations, together with low self-esteem and an increasing sense of isolation, may lead a young person to try to kill himself or herself. One young woman said:

> I just feel totally disgusted with myself. I don't feel like, I feel totally worthless. I don't know. If people aren't listening to me or taking me seriously, I'm very rejected and lonely. Very disappointed with myself

that I can't achieve what I really want to achieve, that I know I've got the potential but I can't, you know. (Coleman, Lyon and Piper 1995 Audiotape)

For young people under the age of 16 a serious disagreement with a parent or parents may be the most influential factor. In a study of 100 children who were admitted to hospital following an episode of deliberate self-poisoning, 47 per cent identified a serious disagreement with a parent (within the previous 24 hours) as the main reason (Kerfoot 1988). Family dysfunction is one of the primary causes of suicidal behaviour. Other precipitating factors include physical or sexual abuse, rape, bullying or threats, poor physical or mental health, exam stress or failure, being under investigation or in police custody.

REPEATED ATTEMPTS

For those concerned with the safety of young people, it is painful to acknowledge that primary prevention is not always effective. Teenagers particularly likely to commit suicide are those who have already made a serious attempt on their lives. If a member of a young person's family or a friend has either attempted or committed suicide then that young person is personally at increased risk of suicide. In addition, it is a myth to assume that those who talk about suicide will not kill themselves. Where suicidal ideation or behaviour is in some way 'familiar territory' for a young person, then there is an increased risk. This risk is particularly marked in the first few years following a serious attempt or exposure to suicidal behaviour within the family or peer group. This level of increased risk, however, needs to be put in its proper context. Ten per cent of young people who attempt suicide will make at least one other attempt on their lives (Kerfoot and McHugh 1992). Approximately one third of teenagers who kill themselves have a history of previous attempts (Marttunen, Aro and Lonqvist 1993).

A suicide attempt by a young person can be seen as a sign of extreme distress and hopelessness. If the attempt leads to:

- a recognition and understanding of this distress by those who matter to the young person
- sustained help from professionals
- an increase in the young person's own capacity to cope with difficulty or distress

then the risk of subsequent attempts will be reduced. But it should be remembered that attempted suicide is often a marker of severe social, interpersonal or psychiatric difficulties such as depression and/or behavioural problems. These concurrent problems may persist.

Paradoxically, at a time when a young person seems to be emerging from a state of depression, perhaps presenting as being more sorted out, this may be a time to be especially alert. One bereaved mother said,

When they begin to get better it's the most risky time... I just hadn't a clue. All the doctors, all the psychiatrists, who we'd been in contact with

–why didn't they tell me that? They all said that afterwards, but nobody told me at the time (Coleman, Lyon and Piper 1995, p.14)

So, for some young people being 'well enough' or ready to make a second attempt is clearly a time of risk.

ASSESSMENT OF RISK

From the onset of work with a vulnerable young person, a worker will be assessing risk. This will be done in the course of getting to know the teenager, becoming aware of his or her circumstances and understanding his or her concerns.

An everyday knowledge of the young person helps to assess significant changes in behaviour, thoughts or situation. For example, the worker will notice if a teenager who is normally outgoing and communicative becomes isolated and withdrawn. It is more difficult if the young person is not known to the worker, for example on first admission to hospital or first contact with a duty social worker or drop-in service counsellor. Whether the young person is well known or not, some general principles still apply. The worker needs to be aware of his or her own levels of concern about the teenager and, if possible the concerns of colleagues. Assessment of risk should not be made by one individual without adequate consultation with colleagues preferably from different disciplines such as psychiatry and social work.

Assessment of risk cannot be made on a single dimension; for example, a psychological evaluation of the individual. For assessment to have any validity, the complex interaction between all the factors has to be explored and evaluated. Exercise 14.2 will help this process.

ASSESSMENT OF INTENT

If a young person has harmed himself or herself or made a serious suicide attempt, an assessment interview should try to discover the young person's level of intent:

- Was he or she alone when he or she made the attempt, with others or were there others nearby?
- Was the attempt timed so that intervention was likely or not?
- Were active precautions taken to avoid discovery?
- Did the young person try to gain help either during or after the event?
- Was there any evidence that the attempt was planned: hoarding of medication, careful consideration of means, suicide note, giving away possessions?
- Did the young person talk to anyone about intending to commit suicide or communicate in any way?

Other ways to assess seriousness of intent include exploring the young person's own views on whether he or she thought that the attempt would succeed. Was there any ambivalence? Was the method thought to be lethal? Was it thought of as reversible if medical help was given?

Exercise 14.2 Mapping Risk

Aim

- to document risk factors
- to see how these risk factors interact
- to identify protecting agents
- to develop a holistic view of the client and the service provided.

Method

This exercise can be done individually, or preferably with a group of colleagues. If trainers are working with a group it is useful to subdivide into small groups or pairs. Each group or pair to work on one of the 4 questions for 15 minutes. A map can then be assembled by bringing together each small group's response on A4 or flipchart paper in roughly the same order and spatial relationship as shown in Appendix 14.1. The group should take 15 minutes to discuss what can be learned from this map. Trainers can use this exercise to focus more generally on a particular client group rather than an individual teenager.

On completion of this part of the exercise the individual, or group of colleagues should take a further 15 minutes to consider which of the factors identified in response to questions 2 and 4 are open to change in any way. In what practical ways can stress be reduced in their institution or service? Are there protecting agents or buffers which are lacking, or exist within the service but could be miximised? These should be chart listed.

Instructions to participants:

Think of one teenager at risk and answer these questions in as much detail as possible:

(1) **Vulnerability**
What are the personal and social factors which together indicate that this young person, is vulnerable to suicide? e.g. poor coping resources, drug use, family problems.

(2) **Institution or Service-induced Stress**
What are the factors within the service you provide, or in your institution which could increase a young person's level of stress? e.g. being bullied, lack of family support, inconsistent care.

(3) **Situational Triggers**
What are the situational triggers or precipitating factors which could prove the final stressor or last straw in the young person's life? e.g. broken relationships, loss.

(4) **Protecting Agents**
What are the protecting agents which could reduce or provide a buffer against the pressures you have identified? e.g. supportive supervision by staff, future plans.

Sadly, for a minority of young people it may have been impossible to determine that they had suicide in mind. A mother of a girl who killed herself at home said:

> I think it's fair to say that we, the teachers, her friends, we didn't see that she was in such a dreadful state. It wasn't as if she had obvious signs, she didn't hurt herself, she didn't have sleepless nights, there were no apparent signs of acute distress. (Coleman, Lyon and Piper 1995, p.13)

ASSESSMENT PROCEDURES

Employing authorities, prison or probation services, voluntary agencies, vary tremendously in relation to risk assessment procedures. For example, detailed suicide risk assessment forms have been developed by Northern Birmingham Mental Health Trust and Birmingham City Council Social Services Department (Alberg, Hatfield and Huxley 1996, pp.64–68) and by the Prison Service. Guidelines and checklists have been produced by the Health Advisory Service (Appendices 14.2 and 14.3). It is vital that the worker is aware of the relevant policy and formal requirements within the service or institution. It is essential that information is documented and shared within and across agencies if risk is to be identified, assessed and managed effectively.

Following a suicide attempt, the overall aims of a detailed risk assessment are:

- to gain understanding of why the young person made the attempt
- to learn what sort of help is wanted
- to influence the young person to consider other means of coping in future and less destructive ways of communicating distress.

Prior to making an assessment, the worker should clarify what confidentiality can be offered to the young person and should explain the reasons for sharing information with colleagues. The assessment interview itself should be conducted so that it is part of establishing a therapeutic alliance with the young person. The worker and the client are working together to understand what has happened and what needs to be done. It is difficult to get this right. A distressed and vulnerable young person will all too easily feel powerless in a situation such as this, bombarded by questions and objectified. It is extremely useful both to practice conducting assessment interviews with colleagues or to co-work with a supervisor and get feedback.

Risk assessment interviews are likely to include the following:

Present History

- Circumstances of the attempt – events preceding and following it. Degree of suicidal intent. Motivation. Previous attempts.
- History of any recent difficulties or problems as given by the young person. Explore psychological, physical and social difficulties (children, employment, housing, financial, alcohol...) Whether any help has already been provided and what agencies are involved.

Medical/Psychiatric History
Family History

Parents, siblings, other important relatives and significant others. Family history of psychiatric difficulties including suicide and attempts.

Personal History

Childhood and development, physical/sexual/emotional abuse, schooling, employment, sexual orientation, marital, children. Alcohol and drugs.

Usual Personality

Personality traits and habits. Interests and hobbies – recent loss of. Prevailing mood – variations? Degree of self-esteem. Existing coping resources. Plans for Future? Ability to establish and maintain relationships. Body image/eating habits. Sleep. Appetite. Weight change?

Mental State at Interview

Appearance, behaviour and rapport; mood, including suicidal ideas; talk; thinking and beliefs; insight.

MANAGEMENT OF RISK

Assessment is an intrinsic part of risk management. Listening with empathy and understanding to the young person is the first step. The worker needs to use the process of assessing intent, or conducting a risk assessment interview, as a way to help to steady the young person, to contain the risk and to establish a relationship with the young person where the young person and the worker together can begin to plan how to manage the risk posed. How risk is managed will depend to a large extent on the needs of the individual and on the setting in which the worker operates and the resources known to be available. If the risk of suicide is very great, then arranging admission to hospital, possibly under the Mental Health Act 1983, is likely to be the safest course of action. However, in most cases, and certainly following an emergency admission, a plan needs to be made with the young person about what on-going help is needed and how it can be provided. The worker should focus on attaching the young person both by establishing a therapeutic alliance and by arranging a series of follow-up meetings. Ideally, with the young person's agreement, a plan for care and support should be made with relatives and/or friends. It may be important to liaise with the young person's GP to discuss a prescription for anti-depressants. Check that the young person knows how to get help quickly from services at any time of the day or night.

If the young person is living at home, life is likely to change there. Most parents will feel anxious and protective. In the short-term increased monitoring and supervision is a good idea. One strategy which has been found to be effective is the removal of the means to commit suicide This can serve to put a brake on impulsive acts as well as giving the young person the message that someone is concerned about their safety. A 14-year-old young woman said of her attempts:

> It just causes so many problems at home. Like, your life has to change totally and that, they can't trust you with nothing no more. You have to, you're like padded in cotton all the time. (Coleman, Lyon and Piper 1995 Audiotape)

In the longer term the emphasis has to be on enabling a young person to cope and to take more responsibility for his or her own life. There is no evidence to suggest that 'wrestling away' the idea of suicide is effective, rather it is important to acknowledge that while that is one possibility there are other ways of coping with difficulty. The role of the worker is to:

- listen and take seriously
- help the teenager to describe the problem as he/she sees it
- promote consideration of alternative strategies
- help the young person to feel more in control of the situation
- build up confidence and self esteem by identifying strength and existing coping skills.

Schemes which encourage young people to identify risk for themselves and to seek help in an appropriate way have been found to be successful. 'Coloured card' schemes, which operate in some hospitals, enable a young person to receive treatment, and to gain admission if necessary without having to resort to self-harm. Within institutions young people can be supported to help one another. Good examples include peer counselling in schools and Listener schemes in prisons.

Where it is possible, the involvement of the family in risk management is recommended.

> Parents of teenagers are often the last group to be seen as a resource, and yet they are, more than any other group of adults, the first line of defence. More attention should be directed to educating and supporting parents in caring for distressed or troubled adolescents (NHS Health Advisory Service 1994, p.58).

An effective system of brief work with families has been developed and piloted in Manchester. The intervention is short-term, focused, intensive and home based. It aims to increase understanding and to improve communication.

It enables the development of co-operative relationships and shared problem-solving within the family, which responds to the isolation and sense of alienation that so often precedes the suicide attempt (Kerfoot, Harrington and Dyer 1995, p.566).

RISKS TO THE WORKER

In considering how to manage risk in work with troubled young people it is essential to pay close attention to managing the worker's own mental health and wellbeing. Close work with adolescents at risk is bound to lead to risks for the worker (Lyon and Coleman 1996). Inexperienced staff are particularly vulnerable and likely to absorb disorder and distress. If experienced staff assume immunity to this process then this in itself may be a form of denial or disconnectedness. Essentially, to manage risk and to keep work in perspective, there must be systems which support professional work. Risks to the worker include:

(1) Staff will be challenged

Young people are able to expose uncertainty, inconsistency, and anything they consider to be a weakness in adults. As part of establishing their own identity, and experiencing rapid change and confusion themselves, young people challenge adults. Challenging authority and needling adults are common processes in institutions. Young people are likely to set up unproductive confrontations and to get into conflict with staff.

(2) Staff may be rejected

Disturbed young people often feel compelled to repeat past experiences. If they have been abused or rejected before, they may be quick to be the one who does the rejecting now. It could be that the closer they get to an adult the more worrying this feels. The worker needs to make sure that the young person knows that he or she is there. The worker should be consistent and steady but not intrusive.

(3) Staff get too involved

Vulnerable young people are bound to be very needy and demanding. While they may be suspicious and wary of making relationships with staff, they may well be looking for trust, understanding and warmth. Sometimes disturbed teenagers may seek more from the worker than he or she is able to give. It is sometimes very difficult for staff to keep within professional boundaries, particularly in relation to work with suicidal young people. In a confiding and close relationship it is easy for the worker to feel that only he or she can deal with the young person's problems. This is a common, seductive, and sometimes frightening experience for staff when they start working in this field. Workers have to remember that they must share responsibility with colleagues. The worker's job is to enable the young person to cope and take responsibility for him or herself.

Exercise 14.3 Managing Risks to Staff

Aim

- to explore strategies for minimising professional risk
- to examine personal and organisational ways to reduce stress

Method

This exercise can be done by a group, ideally colleagues, or individually. Twenty minutes should be allowed to consider the questions. Key points should be listed or charted up. Trainers should allow a further 10 minutes for discussion.

Instructions to participants:

Consider and respond to these questions as fully as possible.

- How can we remain effective in our work with distressed young people?
- How can we keep stress to a reasonable level?
- From personal and professional experience list individual strategies for managing the work and doing a reasonable job.
- List organisational policy and practice issues which are designed to enable staff to manage stress and to work effectively.

MANAGEMENT OF RISK TO WORKERS

(1) Maintenance of professional boundaries

Staff need to be as clear as possible about their professional role and responsibilities. Staff should be aware of the overall aims and objectives of the institution or service and of their aims and objectives with individual young people. They should be fully aware of all formal requirements in relation to assessment and management of risk. It is important to acknowledge possibilities and limitations: what can and cannot be done.

(2) Proper system of support in the work environment

All staff who work with distressed young people need professional support to do their job effectively. Good management and team work, on-the-job coaching or supervision and on-going professional training all help to make work manageable and satisfying.

(3) Knowledge of Adolescents

Young people can be very demanding. The more needy or lacking in self esteem the young person is, the more demanding he or she will be. Staff have to balance listening and responding to a young person's needs with a professional requirement to work in a considered way and not just to react. One characteristic of adolescents is their impulsiveness, and this can erode the need for staff themselves to stop and think, to keep things in perspective and to be consistent.

(4) Awareness of stress

People under stress may lose perspective, work in a reactive manner, and fail to plan ahead. It is important for staff to be able to recognise signs of stress in themselves, and to learn to pace themselves in their job. In general, the more personal insight staff have, the more aware they are of their strengths and weaknesses, attitudes and emotions, the more confident and effective they will be in their work. Stress is not just an individual problem. Above all it is an organisational one. An awareness of stress and how it can be reduced should be an important concern for managers, planners and policy makers. (Jee and Reason 1989)

This concluding section has focused on assessing and managing risk to workers because young people, particularly troubled young people, need adults. They need adults who they can turn to for protection, support and guidance. The adult worker is undoubtedly a primary source of help for a suicidal young person. Care is needed in the selection, training and on-going management of workers so that they can work closely alongside young people in extreme distress. Each individual and each set of circumstances will differ. One mother of a suicidal teenager said:

You want people to be sympathetic but not say too much, but everybody's different and have got their own way, but as long as people say they're there to support you in whatever way you need, that's all you really need (Coleman, Lyon and Piper 1995 Audiotape).

At the beginning of the chapter the impossibility of accurate assessment of suicide risk was acknowledged. If, however, the worker can develop an understanding and an awareness of what constitutes suicide risk, she or he will be able to face this impossible task with increased confidence. A preparedness to seek help is essential. Just as the young person needs to find a way of expressing distress and seeking help, so the worker has a duty to seek help from and consult with colleagues. Finally, to manage risk effectively the worker has to find an acceptable way of enlisting help from the troubled young person. Problems can then be faced together and the young person will be supported to find his or her own ways of coping.

Appendix 14.1. The Pathway to Suicide

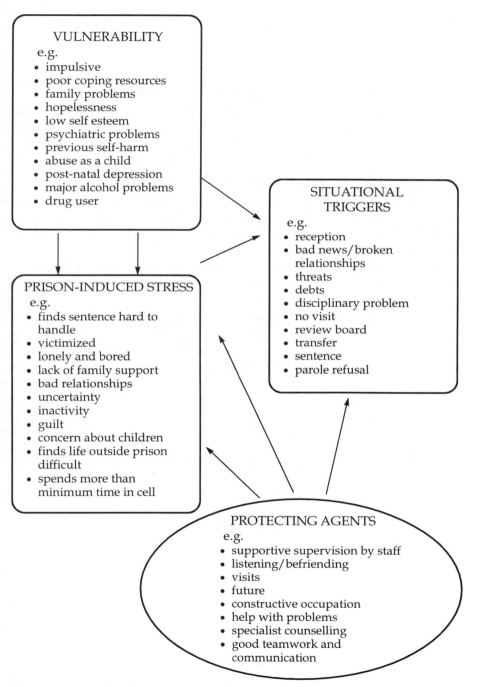

VULNERABILITY

e.g.
- impulsive
- poor coping resources
- family problems
- hopelessness
- low self esteem
- psychiatric problems
- previous self-harm
- abuse as a child
- post-natal depression
- major alcohol problems
- drug user

SITUATIONAL TRIGGERS

e.g.
- reception
- bad news/broken relationships
- threats
- debts
- disciplinary problem
- no visit
- review board
- transfer
- sentence
- parole refusal

PRISON-INDUCED STRESS

e.g.
- finds sentence hard to handle
- victimized
- lonely and bored
- lack of family support
- bad relationships
- uncertainty
- inactivity
- guilt
- concern about children
- finds life outside prison difficult
- spends more than minimum time in cell

PROTECTING AGENTS

e.g.
- supportive supervision by staff
- listening/befriending
- visits
- future
- constructive occupation
- help with problems
- specialist counselling
- good teamwork and communication

Source: Lyon and Coleman (1996). Developed from the work of Alison Liebling for the HM Prison Service.

Appendix 14.2

CHECKLIST

Questions Relating to Suicide Risk in Adolescents

(1) Does this patient have the potential for self-harm?

Here the question has to do with whether the patient presents with one or more risk factors in his or her history or current life experience. For example, is there a family history of suicide, or has the patient been exposed to the suicidal behaviour of a peer?

(2) Might this person possibly harm himself or herself?

The possibility of suicide increases substantially where there is evidence that death or suicide is on the individual's mind. Additional factors here are cognitive rigidity, and evidence of social isolation or alienation.

(3) If self-harm is possible, what is the probability of such behaviour, and what are the circumstances, the degree of lethality and imminence involved?

Whether suicidal intent will be acted upon depends on a number of situational factors, including conditions of threat or stress, the availability or accessibility of method, and often a particular trigger or event which has a high level of personal meaning for the individual.

(4) Are there continuing provocative factors?

The individual's living circumstances need to be considered, in particular whether there are any deficits in care and supervision.

(NHS Health Advisory Service 1994, p.111)

Appendix 14.3

ASSESSMENT OF DELIBERATE SELF-HARM (CHILDREN AND ADOLESCENTS)

Circumstances of the Episode of Deliberate Self-harm

- method used
- source of agent
- availability
- likelihood of discovery
- suicidal communications
- motives
- precipitants
- previous acts of deliberate self-harm.

Social Life and Activities

- network of relationships
- out of school activities
- casual or close friendships
- dating
- leisure activities
- degree of freedom from parental authority and intrusion.

School (where applicable)

- time in school
- changes of school
- attendance record
- work record
- behaviour in relation to staff and peers
- bullying.

Problems and Coping Strategies

- current problem behaviours, eg delinquency
- anxieties, eg school, running away, physical, sexual or emotional abuse
- alcohol or drug abuse.

General Health

- previous significant medical history
- present health status

- psychiatric status including specifically:
- variation in sleep patterns
- appetite
- mood
- health contacts, eg GP, clinic or hospital appointments
- current treatments.

Family Structure and Relationships

- marital status of parents
- composition of family
- rating of relationships within the family
- emotional climate in the home
- expressed emotions (EE)
- frequency and pattern of arguments
- past or present abuse.

Family Circumstances

- level of income
- housing
- environmental problems
- family pathology, eg crime, mental illness
- family history of suicide
- physical or mental disability
- contacts with social agencies.

Other High Risk Items

- others not present or nearby at the time
- intervention unlikely
- precautions taken against discovery
- suicide note
- problems for longer than a month
- episode planned for more than three hours
- feeling hopeless about the future
- feeling sad most of the time prior to the act of deliberate self-harm
- contributing social or family adversity
- use of alcohol or drugs.

(NHS Health Advisory Service 1994, p.109).

REFERENCES

Alberg, C., Hatfield, B. and Huxley, P. (eds) (1996) *Learning Materials on Mental Health: Risk Assessment.* University of Manchester.

Andrews, J.A. and Lewinsohn, P.M. (1992) 'Suicidal attempts among older adolescents: prevalence and co-occurrence with psychiatric disorders.' *Journal of American Acad. Child Adolescent Psychiatry 31,* 655–662.

Black, M., Erulkan, J., Kerfoot, M., Meadow, R. and Baderman, H. (1992) 'The management of parasuicide in young people under 16.' *Bulletin of Royal College of Psychiatrists 6,* 182–185.

Coleman, J. (1997) *Key Data on Adolescents.* Brighton: Trust for the Study of Adolescence.

Coleman, J. and Hendry, L. (1989) *The Nature of Adolescence.* London: Routledge.

Coleman, J., Lyon, J. and Piper, R. (1995) *Teenage Suicide and Self-Harm.* Brighton: Trust for the Study of Adolescence: Audiotape.

Hawton, K., Fagg, J. and Simkin, S. (1996) 'Deliberate self-poisoning and self-injury in children and adolescents under 16 years of age in Oxford 1976 – 1993.' *British Journal of Psychiatry 169,* 741–7.

Hill, K. (1995) *The Long Sleep. Young People and Suicide.* London: Virago.

Jee, M. and Reason, L. (1989) *Action on Stress at Work.* Health Education Authority.

Kerfoot, M. (1988) 'Deliberate self-poisoning in childhood and early adolescence.' *Journal of Child Psychology and Psychiatry 29,* 335–343.

Kerfoot, M. and McHugh, B. (1992) 'The outcome of childhood suicidal behaviour.' *Acta Paedopsychiatrica 55,* 141–145.

Kerfoot, M., Harrington, R. and Dyer, E. (1995) 'Young suicide attempters and their families.' *Journal of Adolescence 18,* 5, 557–568.

Kerfoot, M. (1996) 'Suicide and deliberate self-harm in children and adolescents: a research update.' *Children and Society 10,* 236–241.

Kingsbury, S. (1994) 'The psychological and social characteristics of Asian adolescent overdose.' *Journal of Adolescence 16,* 121–140.

Liebling, A. (1992) *Suicides in Prison.* London: Routledge.

Lyon, J. and Coleman, J. (1996) *Understanding and Working with Young Women in Custody.* Brighton: Trust for the Study of Adolescence.

Madge, N., (1996) *Suicidal Behaviour in Children and Young People.* Highlight No. 144 London: National Children's Bureau.

Marttunen, M.J., Aro, H.M. and Lonqvist, J.K. (1993) 'Adolescence and suicide: a review of psychological autopsy studies.' *European Child and Adolescent Psychiatry 2,* 10–18.

NHS Health Advisory Service Review. (1994) *Suicide Prevention: The Challenge Confronted.* R. Williams and H.G. Morgan (eds) London: HMSO.

Office of Population Censuses and Surveys (1995) *Deaths in 1994 by Cause.* London: OPCS Monitor DH2 95/1.

Plant, M. and Plant, M. (1992) *Risk Takers: Alcohol, Drugs, Sex and Youth.* London: Routledge.

Rutter, M. (1989) *Helping Troubled Children.* London: Penguin.

Samaritans (1995) *Behind the Mask: Men, Feelings and Suicide*. Slough: Samaritans Central Office.

Seiffge-Krenke I. (ed) (1993) 'Stress and coping in adolescence.' Special Issue of *Journal of Adolescence 16*, 3.

Watts, D. and Morgan, G. (1994) 'Malignant alienation: dangers for patients who are hard to like.' *British Journal of Psychiatry 164*, 11–15.

BOOKLIST

Alberg, C., Hatfield, B. and Huxley, P. (eds) (1996) *Learning Materials on Mental Health: Risk Assessment*. University of Manchester.

An information and training pack which covers characteristics of risk, intervention and management, legislation and policy and ethical issues. It focuses on risk of violence and risk of suicide.

Arnold, L. (1995) *Women and Self Injury*. Bristol Crisis Service for Women.

A booklet which explores and explains self-injury in a non-judgmental way and looks at strategies for helping.

Burningham, S. (1994) *Young People Under Stress. A Parent's Guide*. London: Virago Press.

This helpful book explains many of the stresses and mental health problems that young people may experience. It explores sources of help and support for teenagers and for parents themselves.

Coleman, J., Lyon, J. and Piper, R. (1995) *Teenage Suicide and Self-Harm*. Audio tape and booklet. Brighton: Trust for the Study of Adolescence.

This is a useful booklet for families and professionals. This booklet covers Understanding Suicide and Self-harm; Recognising Risk; A Suicide in the Family; Helping Distressed Young People; The Way Forward for Parents and Carers. The audiotape consists of extracts from interviews with young people who have harmed themselves or attempted suicide, and parents, some of whom are bereaved.

Graham, P. and Hughes, C. (1995) *So Young, So Sad, So Listen*. London: Gaskell.

This useful book is written for parents and teachers to help increase their understanding of depression in childhood and adolescence. It focuses on what adults can do to help young people. Available from the Royal College of Psychiatrists, 17 Belgrave Square, London SW1X 8PG.

Harding, C. (1995)*Not just black and white*. Information pack about mental health services for people from black communities Good Practices in Mental Health: London.

This information pack raises important issues about culture, race and mental health. It documents good practice and includes a useful list of mental health projects for ethnic minority groups. It is now available from the University of London.

Hill, K. (1995) *The Long Sleep: Young People and Suicide*. London: Virago Press.

This excellent book combines current research and interviews with young people and their parents to illustrate the complex routes which lead young people to a point where suicide seems the only solution. This book explores how to respond to the young and suicidal. It offers valuable information and insights to parents and professionals.

Home Office (1984) *The Work of the Coroner.*

Free leaflet which explains the work of the Coroner and the process of an inquest. Available from London, Home Office Publications Department. 0171 273 4000.

Keir, N. (1986) *I Can't Face Tomorrow: Help for Those with Thoughts of Suicide and Those who Counsel Them.* London: Thorsons.

This book, written by an experienced volunteer with The Samaritans, considers what makes people suicidal, how to recognise the warning signs, the effects on those left and what family, friends and colleagues can do to help the potential suicide.

MIND (1995) *Understanding Self-Harm.* London: Mind Publications.

MIND (1995) *How to Help Someone who is Suicidal.* London: Mind Publications.

Booklets written in a straightforward way to increase understanding about suicide and self-harm and what practical steps can be taken to help people in distress. Available from MIND Publications, Granta House, 15–19 Broadway, Stratford, London E15 4BQ.

NHS Health Advisory Service Review (1994) *Suicide Prevention: the Challenge Confronted.* R. Williams and H.G. Morgan (eds) London: HMSO.

Thorough going review and recommendations. Chapter Eleven focuses on children and adolescents.

Rioch, S. (1994) *Suicidal Children and Adolescents.* Durham: Celia Publications.

Crisis and preventative care are the subjects of this book. This short book sets out to give information and advice to those concerned with suicidal young people and their families.

The Samaritans (1995) *Behind the Mask: Men, Feelings and Suicide.*

Free booklet summarises current research on men and suicide. It explains the work of the Samaritans and looks at ways of coping with suicidal feelings. Available from The Samaritans, 10 The Grove, Slough SL1 1QP.

Young Minds (1996) *Mental Health in Your School.* London: Jessica Kingsley Publishers.

This book is helpful for teachers interested in creating a whole school approach to mental health.

Wertheimer, A. (1991) *A Special Scar.* London: Routledge.

This book explores the experience of people bereaved by death by suicide through a series of sensitive interviews.

USEFUL ADDRESSES OF SPECIALIST ORGANISATIONS

Bristol Crisis Service for Women
PO Box 654, Bristol BS99 1XH

Support and advice for women who self-injure. Research, training and publications.
National Helpline: (0117) 925 1119.

ChildLine,
2nd Floor, Royal Mail Building,
Studd Street,
London N1 OQW.
Tel: 0171 239 1066.

Any child or young person can call ChildLine at any time about any problem on 0800 1111. The call is free and will not show up on itemised phone bills. ChildLine counsellors help callers to talk about any feelings of pain or loss, anger and unhappiness without being judged. ChildLine publishes a free leaflet on Suicide and Young People.

Cruse (for all those who have suffered a bereavement),
Cruse House, 128 Sheen Road,
Richmond, Surrey.
Tel: 0181 940 4818.
Helpline counselling service
0181 332 7227.

Provides a service of counselling, advice and opportunities for social contact for all those affected by bereavement. Some local branches have specialist groups for those bereaved by suicide.

The Compassionate Friends
53 North Street, Bristol
BS3 1EN.
Helpline: (0117) 953 9639.
Admin/fax (0117) 966 5202.

A national self-help organisation of bereaved parents offering each other friendship, comfort and understanding. Shadow of Suicide (SOS) is a group within The Compassionate Friends for the parents, and families, of children who have ended their lives. Support is offered by telephone, visits to the family, group meetings. The Compassionate Friends publishes leaflets and has an extensive postal library.

Inquest
Ground Floor,
Alexandra National House,
330 Seven Sisters Road,
London N4 2PJ.
Tel: 0181 802 7430.

Offers a support and information and legal advice service for families and friends facing an inquest. Inquest is particularly concerned with deaths in custody, death in psychiatric hospitals or following discharge.

Lesbian and Gay Bereavement Project
Vaughan M Williams Centre,
Colindale Hospital,
London NW9 5HG.
Tel: 0181 200 0511.
Helpline 0181 455 8894.

Offers advice and information to lesbians and gay men as well as to families, friends and caring professionals. It has a telephone helpline offering advice and emotional support to people bereaved by the death of a same-sex partner. Support is also given to parents, brothers and sisters and other family members.

NAFSIYAT
278 Seven Sisters Road,
London N4 2HY.
Tel: 0171 263 4130.

Offers specialised therapeutic help to people from ethnic and cultural minorities. It was set up to provide a specialist inter-cultural psychotherapy service for individuals, families, children and adolescents experiencing psychiatric problems, emotional strain and sexual problems.

Papyrus
Clough End House,
Clough End Road, Haslingden,
Rossendale,
Lancs BB4 5AN.
Tel: (01706) 214449

Papyrus is a Nationwide Voluntary Organisation of Parents, who have lost a young person through suicide and who wish to use their experiences in an effort to reduce such tragedies in the future. The main aims of the group are as follows: to promote public awareness; to co-operate with professional and voluntary bodies; to encourage the inclusion of mental health education in the school curriculum; to ensure that adequate mental health services for young people are available; where a suicide has already occurred to ensure that appropriate support is readily available for those closely and traumatically affected

Samaritans
General Office:
10 The Grove, Slough
SL1 1QP.
Tel: (01753) 532713

The Samaritans offer confidential emotional support at any hour of the day or night to anyone who is passing through a personal crisis and in danger of taking their own life. Helpline 0345 909090. Training information and advice available to volunteers and professionals.

Survivors Speak Out
32 Osnaburgh Street,
London NW1 3ND.
Tel: 0171 916 5472.
Information Service Tel: 0171 916 6991.
Staffed 1.30pm-5pm Monday, Wednesday and Friday but with an answerphone at other times.

The term 'survivor' was chosen to portray a positive image of people in distress and people whose experience differs from, or who dissent from society's norms. The main aim of Survivors Speak Out is to promote self-advocacy. A nationwide information service is available about groups and events within the survivor movement. Publications include books on Self-Help Alternatives to Mental Health Services and perspectives on self-harm.

Trust for the Study of Adolescence
23 New Road,
Brighton,
East Sussex,
BN1 1WZ.
Tel: (01273) 693311

TSA is an applied research organisation which also provides training and consultancy, conferences and publications. This charity has a particular focus on adolescent mental health and has been commissioned by the Department of Health to produce materials on teenage suicide and self-harm and to organise a national training initiative.

Who Cares? Trust
Kemp House,
152–160 City Road,
London EC1V 2NP.
Tel: 0171 251 3117

The Who Cares? Trust works to improve the experiences and opportunities of young people in residential and foster care throughout the UK. The Trust works in partnership with other organisations, particularly in the areas of health, education and employment. It publishes the quarterly Who Cares? magazine which is received by over 27,000 young people via Social Services department. It also runs a helpline for young people in care. Freecall 0500 564 570.

Young Minds
102–108 Clerkenwell Road,
London EC1M 5SA.
Tel: 0171 336 8445

This is the national children's mental health charity, and works to promote the mental health of children, young people and their families. As well as aiming to increase understanding about children's mental health, and lobbying for the provision of multi-professional children's services, Young Minds runs an information and advice service for parents and carers. Young Minds' publications include a series of leaflets about different aspects of child and family mental health.

Youth Access
1A Taylor's Yard,
67 Alderbrook Road,
London SW12 8AD

Provides addresses of the nearest counselling and advice services for young people.

CHAPTER 15

Risk and Parole
Issues in Risk Assessment for Release

Hazel Kemshall

INTRODUCTION

Risk prediction and parole have a long, if somewhat chequered history. E.W. Burgess' work (1928, 1936) stands as one of the earliest attempts to formulate a reliable prediction method for safe parole release. The most notable parole risk prediction tool of recent times is Nuttall's 1977 model here in Britain, and Nuffield's 1982 model in Canada. Despite positive evaluation of Nuttall's model by Sapsford (1978) and Ward (1987), its impact upon the work of Probation through-care officers in assessing risk in reports has been limited, and the work of Local Review Committees pre-Carlisle in parole decision making was often idiosyncratic (Glaser 1962, 1973). By the late 1980s the parole system was under review, leading to the Carlisle Report in 1988.

It was the Carlisle report which placed risk as the central, most explicit concern of the parole procedure. Whilst earlier notions of 'earning a reprieve', coupled with satisfactory reports of institutional behaviour had been influential in the largely subjective and case by case decision making of LRCs (Carroll 1977, Flynn 1978), risk was now to be the deciding issue. Whilst outside the institution, rehabilitation and resettlement had often been central to the parole concerns of Probation Officers, explicit attention on risk was now a requirement. The proposed new procedure for parole decisions was envisaged as unproblematic and easy to utilise, as stated by Carlisle in Recommendation 35:

> The simplest and most defensible method of distinguishing between those prisoners who should be released after a fixed proportion of their sentence and those whose release should be conditional on a careful risk assessment is by sentence length. (Carlisle 1988, p.122.)

In this statement, and one presumes in subsequent parole decisions, sentence length, seriousness and risk were meshed. This was given further emphasis by the legislative concerns of the Criminal Justice Act 1991 on sexual and violent offenders (section 1(2)(b), Wasik and Taylor 1991), again implicitly classifying the risk concerns of both parole boards and through-care officers. The agenda for parole risk has been clearly set as the risk of physical or sexual harm to members of the public from the reoffending of parolees. This has been mirrored in the Probation Service by the Inspectorate's recent thematic concern with 'dangerous' offenders which has utilised a similar classification of risk (HMIP 1995).

It is perhaps appropriate to consider why this classification of risk has become so central to the parole process. In a paper entitled: 'Classification for Risk and Supervision – A Preliminary Conceptualization,' Flynn (1978) noted that when prison populations expand and incarceration rates outstrip resources:

> the search is on for new techniques designed to reassess the use of corrections and detention institutions and to find ways to reduce the populations in a manner consistent with public safety. (p.133–134).

The accurate identification of risk is now central to the economic, efficient, and safe use of criminal justice resources, particularly of custody. Risk assessment for parole is now being conducted in a particular economic, political and social climate. This climate can be characterised by the increased 'commercialization of crime control' (Christie 1993) in which cost-benefit analyses, market forces, privatisation, economy, efficiency and effectiveness concerns have all impinged upon the management of criminal justice including Probation. This approach to criminal justice has been recently labelled the 'new penology' by Feeley and Simon (1992, 1994), and exhibits the following key trends:

(1) the management of justice and thereby the management of offenders

(2) the targeting of increasingly limited resources at those most risky to public safety, and

(3) a policy of selective community surveillance of those deemed to be 'less risky' in order to diminish both prison overcrowding and prison costs.

In addition to posing risk as the central concern, Carlisle also supplanted the anecdotal and largely subjective decision making of LRCs (Flynn 1978, Glaser 1962,1973) with Recommendation 54 in the hope that greater clarity would thereby follow:

> ...it does seem to us right in principle that those who have to take decisions affecting the liberty of the individual and the safety of the public should be absolutely clear about the responsibility which is theirs and about the criteria they are meant to apply. (Carlisle 1988, p.78, para 317)

Centralised decision making is viewed as a mechanism which can ensure both consistency and appropriateness. Carlisle further states that a parole decision will:

> ...be based upon an evaluation of the risk to the public of the person committing a further serious offence at a time when he would other wise be in prison. (Carlisle 1988, p.79, para. 321)

In Carlisle's view the Parole board should comply with:

...the risk-based test which is central to the scheme which we have proposed. (Carlisle 1988, p.79, para. 324)

In essence, paras 317, 321, and 324 of Carlisle have produced the twin concerns of predicting reoffending and, more important, predicting violent crime recidivism.

Sadly the demise of the Nuttall predictor has been well documented by Polvi and Pease (1991), and they state that the Carlisle report 'devotes just one of its 500 paragraphs' to the issue of recidivism prediction. Carlisle specified a task for Parole Boards and through-care probation officers, but the means to deliver the task remained largely unarticulated. However, the 1990 White Paper (Home Office 1990) was quite clear on how parole decisions should be made:

(1) Is the prisoner likely to commit further serious offences, while under supervision?

(2) Would his early release sometime after half his sentence rather than after two thirds significantly increase the risk of serious harm to the public?

(3) Is he willing to cooperate with his supervisor and is it likely that extended supervision in the community would reduce the risk of his reoffending in the future. (p.33, para. 6.20)

However, how Boards and Probation Officers were to reliably answer these central questions was unclear.

Policy around Temporary Release has also become increasingly risk driven. On November 18th 1994 the Home Secretary announced a 40 per cent reduction in the number of prisoners released on home leave and temporary release. Emphasis was placed upon public safety, with governors instructed to consider: the risk of reoffending, the risk of absconding or failure to comply with licence requirements, and the suitability of accommodation arrangements. More important, governors were also required to consider 'whether the reasons for granting temporary release are likely to be acceptable to reasonable public opinion' (Penal Affairs Consortium 1995). The views of the police and victims were to be sought on the riskiness of release. These instructions to governors were followed in due course by Probation Circular (PC/84 1994) to Area Services, designed to influence the practice of those officers involved in through-care.

ASSESSING PAROLE RISKS AND POTENTIAL DANGEROUSNESS

Risk is a term prone to various meanings and interpretations (Kemshall 1995, 1996a, Royal Society 1992), but can be understood as a calculation under conditions of uncertainty as to whether a loss, damage or harm will occur (Brearley 1982). The identification and measurement of risks posed to others or the public by individuals or groups has become a central preoccupation of all agencies of the criminal justice including the probation and prison services. This has led to the intensive development of technologies of identification, assessment and management of risk (Kemshall *et al.* 1995, Parton 1996). Risk is now understood in criminal justice as a negative phenomenon, that is as a calculation of the likelihood of potential negative outcomes. These calculations can either be expressed as statistical probabilities of outcome based upon actuarial data, that is data derived from large groups of persons of a similar type, or as clinical judgements based upon clinical assessment techniques of interviewing, observation and collections of social histories. Risk is the probability or possibility that harm will occur, it is not the harm itself. Harm is the impact or consequence of the risk having occurred. Harm is the negative outcome which is feared. The term danger describes the actual or potential exposure to harm, and when used about offenders/prisoners it is about the propensity of these individuals to present harm to others.

Monahan (1981) notes that the terms dangerousness and risk are often used synonymously, leading to a lack of clarity about what is being assessed and predicted. As Monahan observes, this can confuse 'what one is predicting with the probability one is assigning to its prediction' (p.25). In essence, the dangerous behaviour and the probability that it will occur are assessments of two different things: the first is about the type of behaviour of concern, the second is about the risk or likelihood that it will take place. This raises the important question of how dangerousness is to be defined and understood. Monahan and Streadman (1994) note that the broad definition within American criminal justice is 'risk of behaviour harmful to others' (p.1). Walker (1996) associates dangerousness with the presentation of harm to others but notes that the question 'How serious must the harm be to justify preventive measures?' (p.1) is fraught with difficulty, not least in providing an accurate answer and the subsequent ethical issues which arise from this. In addition, how does this propensity to harm others present itself? Is it 'a characteristic of behaviour' or 'a reified personality trait'? (Monahan 1981, p.25). Scott's (1977) early definition of dangerousness as an 'unpredictable and untreatable tendency to inflict or risk irreversible injury or destruction or to induce others to do so' (p.28) implies that dangerousness is an immutable personality trait. The Butler Committee (1975) widened the understanding of harm from physical to include lasting psychological, but did not entirely resolve how dangerousness was to be understood. Difficult questions still remain, such as whether dangerousness is an endemic condition of certain individuals or a capacity to harm which presents only under certain circumstances? Whilst the concept of harm may itself be open to varying definitions due to political, social and economic values (Monahan and Hood 1978, Monahan 1981, Megargee 1976) the use of the concept does enable an identification of what it is we may wish to minimise or prevent. The Butler Committee (1975) used the harm reduction or prevention principle in order to define and identify dangerous mentally disordered offenders prior to release. More recently the Criminal Justice Act 1991 has used harm reduction or prevention as a key objective for the imposition of a custodial sentence: 'to protect the public from harm from him or preventing the commission of further offences' (CJA 1991, s.1(2)(b), Wasik and Taylor 1991). The Carlisle Report also embodied this concept (Carlisle 1988) as did the the subsequent early release arrangements. Section 2(2)(b) of the CJA 1991 also allows for protective sentencing upon the principle of preventing risk to the public, enabling sentences non-commensurate with the seriousness of the offence (Hirsch and Ashworth 1996). The concept of harm, and more particularly of harm reduction or harm prevention, is now rooted in both current penal policy and legislation.

Whilst decision makers are often resistant to actuarial methods of risk prediction (Carroll and Payne 1976, Carroll 1977, Glaser 1955, 1962, 1973, Kahnemann and Tversky 1973, 1984, Nisbett *et al*. 1976, Shah 1978a, 1978b), actuarial methods for predicting parole risks are now well established. A number of actuarial risk indicators have an established history for the prediction of success or failure upon parole. Burgess' (1928) study has been emulated numerous times, principally by Ohlin and Duncan (1949), Mannheim and Wilkins (1955), and the Gottfredsons who have a lengthy track record in this area of work (e.g. Gottfredson and Gottfredson 1993). The principles outlined by Burgess (1928, 1929) still form the core of actuarial parole prediction, and the following factors have been the most replicated in subsequent studies:

- nature of the offence
- nature and length of sentence
- age at conviction
- number of previous convictions
- personality type
- social factors such as accommodation, marital status, social background.

These factors are applied to parole cases to determine which of them relate to success or failure upon parole, and then the generation of sum probabilities for success or failure in each case studied. An 'experience table' demonstrating violation rates is then constructed and applied both to those cases with a low expectancy of parole violation and to those with a high (Burgess 1936, pp.228–229). In this way the indicators of parole success or failure can be retrospectively validated and reapplied in terms of statistical probabilities. This technique is still applied today with some slight adaptation of the key indicators (Copas, Ditchfield and Marshall 1994).

This methodology has gained currency in the assessment of parole risks, and a number of the risk indicators have stood the test of time such as: previous criminal record, age upon conviction, number of previous custodial sentences, offence type, and gender (Copas and Tarling 1986, Copas *et al*. 1994, Farrington and Tarling 1985). However, such parole predictors have been plagued by an accuracy barrier of the base expectancy scores of around 40 per cent (Arthur 1971, Gottfredson and Gottfredson 1993) resulting in high levels of false positive and false negative predictions. Such errors raise ethical, moral and credibility issues for criminal justice personnel. False positives, that is predictions of parole violations which do not in fact occur can result in longer than necessary custodial sentences being served with the consequent infringement of liberty and waste of resources. False negatives, that is prediction of no parole violations which turn out to be wrong can have disastrous effects upon the credibility of criminal justice personnel particularly where the public perceive risk to have been mis-assessed or mis-managed. Both sets of errors are very costly.

The limits of actuarial parole prediction have been well documented with the most notable issues being accuracy of prediction (Arthur 1971, Gottfredson and Gottfredson 1993, for example), an over dependence upon static risk indicators at the expense of the increased accuracy gained by the inclusion of situational and environmental factors (Harris 1994), and an inability to capture the changing nature of risk over time (Clark, Fisher and McDougall 1993). In addition, such risk indicators have been criticised as potentially discriminatory (Ryan 1971). They have the power to stigmatise, exclude, and curtail the liberties of certain sections of the population based upon key demographic factors and historical facts. This is particularly difficult for the parole population where the crucial issue is not solely pre-custodial behaviour in the past but behaviour which may occur in the future and under what circumstances and conditions.

Clark *et al.* (1993) piloted a new methodology for parole risk prediction at HMP Wakefield in an attempt to alleviate these difficulties. In essence they wished to monitor and assess risky behaviour over time and to combine the use of traditional indicators with knowledge and observation of behavioural traits, personality characteristics and situational factors. At the same time, they acknowledged the limits on assessing risk in an institutional setting due to difficulties in selecting the appropriate variables to monitor, the difficulty of obtaining objective and consistent recording of what is monitored, and making the monitoring specific enough to the individual in question so that situational and individual factors are captured (p.439). They claim that these difficulties can be overcome by combining knowledge of 'behaviours, characteristics, and situational aspects which contributed to the original offence with institutional monitoring' (p.439). Following the work of Zamble and Poporino (1990) who found that the responses to situations and problems which prisoners had prior to conviction were often maintained in custody, Clark *et al.* (1993) took this as a starting point for their risk assessment tool. In effect, after establishing the behaviours and the relevant situational factors which precipitated the risky criminal act for which they are incarcerated, prisoners are then monitored within the institution to determine whether these are still in place or have diminished. Whilst situational factors may be more difficult to monitor as the environment is different, Clark *et al.* (1993) argue that the interaction between some behaviour traits and significant environmental cues can be examined. For example, prisoners who have committed crimes of violence out of frustration that their desires were not met are likely to meet similar situations in custody.

Clark *et al.* claimed an accuracy level of 65 per cent for this methodology in 1993. The methodology also represents a constructive attempt to combine traditional risk indicators, behavioural traits and environmental stressors, and to develop a more dynamic assessment of a prisoner's risk potential upon release. However, the methodology is labour intensive, requiring detailed observation and recording of behaviour over time and high levels of integrity of application, as assessors must rigorously apply the same observation and assessment criteria to ensure consistency. A causal connection between the specified risk criteria and future behaviour is inferred rather than proven, with many of the criteria utilised being highly context specific. Law (1993) in a retrospective evaluation of the efficacy of the HMP Wakefield risk assessment model demonstrated that whilst an accuracy level of 45 per cent could be achieved for predicting prison behaviour the assessment tool could not predict accurately the rate of recall based upon the specified risk factors.

PAROLE RISK ASSESSMENT AND THE PROBATION SERVICE

Actuarial parole risk predictors have gained currency in the difficult decision making of parole release. Whilst guaranteeing higher rates of accuracy than clinical assessment alone (Kemshall 1996b), as with the application of any actuarial scale transferability of statistical information about groups to the probable behaviour of a specific individual is problematic. There are always exceptions to the rule and the risk of false negatives or false positives in any decision. The key issue is how the risk assessments of individual through-care officers on individual prisoners can credibly contribute to the risk decision making of parole boards. Through-care officers have a role in adding their professional judgement of risk to the largely actuarially based decision making of boards, and more importantly in proposing how the risks identified can be monitored and minimised through community supervision. The actuarially based risk assessment can only state a probability score of risk, it cannot identify individual exceptions to the rule nor can it offer risk minimisation interventions.

This raises the issue of the most appropriate role and function for through-care officers in parole risk assessment, and how their contribution to risk assessment can best be formulated. The recent sentence planning unit project on risk assessment (Biddle and Wincote) is likely to equip prison personnel to apply a parole risk predictor well founded in current parole recidivism/predictor research (Copas et al. 1994, Copas, Marshall and Tarling 1996) and it is this calculation which is most likely to inform the initial parole board assessment of risk. The through-care officer's report is likely to be only one piece of information in this decision making process, and whilst it is appropriately an individual assessment of an individual's risk level it is important that it is not written in ignorance of the relevant actuarial factors or is totally dependent upon an idiosyncratic clinical assessment. Such reports are likely to be easily dismissed by boards.

In order to have both credibility and influence in the parole decision making process, through-care officers will need to be aware of the relevant actuarial factors utilised by boards and reports will need to address them. These factors will be of two kinds: those related to parole recidivism and those related to the commission of further harmful offences. Those relating to parole recidivism are well documented (Burgess 1928, 1936, Copas et al. 1996, Gottfredson and Gottfredson 1993) and have been expressed by Copas et al. (1996) as factors affecting survival time on parole:

- **Age at conviction** – risk decreases with age.
- **Gender** – women reoffend less often than men.

- **Employment status at time of offence** – greatest risk for those unemployed or in casual jobs. Lowest risk for those employed or retired.
- **Time in last job** – risk decreases the longer the time in last job.
- **Marital status at time of release from prison** – the highest risk for prisoners who are single.
- **Type of offence** – highest rate of reoffending is for theft.
- **Age at first conviction** – risk decreases with age.
- **Number of previous convictions for property offences** – risk increases with number of previous convictions for property offences.
- **Number of youth custody sentences** – risk increases with number of such sentences.
- **Number of adult custodial sentences** – risk increases with number of such sentences.
- **Number of supervision orders** – risk increases with number of supervision orders. (From Copas *et al.* 1996)

Through-care officers will have an important role in their report writing in identifying which of these are pertinent to the future behaviour of the prisoner, and which, if any may have changed. Of particular concern to through-care officers must be the immutable nature of many of these indicators, and how reports can make a case for risk reduction strategies in the light of the risk levels which these indicators will suggest for many prisoners. In addition, through-care officers will also have to address not only the risk of recidivism which is a key concern of parole boards, but also the more crucial issue of whether recidivism on parole will lead to offences of 'serious harm to the public' (CJA 1991 in Wasik and Taylor 1991).

Estimations of harm, or 'dangerousness' as it is sometimes labelled, are more problematic than estimations of recidivism per se. Brooks (1984) has suggested a conceptual framework for assessing dangerousness which has the notion of harm at its core. He suggests that any assessment of dangerousness should assess:

(1) the nature of the harm involved;

(2) its magnitude;

(3) its imminence;

(4) its frequency;

(5) the likelihood or unlikelihood that it will occur;

(6) situational circumstances and conditions that affect the likelihood of harm occurring;

(7) ...balancing between the alleged harm on the one hand and the nature of society' intervention on the other. (p.295)

Harm reduction was embodied as a key principle of the Carlisle Report (1998) and the subsequent early release arrangements of the CJA 1991 (Wasik and Taylor 1991). Harm or 'serious harm' is explicitly framed by the CJA 1991 as sexual or physical harm (section 1(2)(b)) or as persistent psychological harm, with violent offending prioritised over property crime (Home Office 1990). Assessments of harm must therefore focus upon a specific description and evaluation of the potential behaviour in question, its likelihood, impact, and consequences of the behaviour should it take place. As with actuarial and clinical assessment of recidivism, assessment of future harmful behaviour, particularly of violent behaviour has also been plagued with difficulty (Monahan 1981). However, Limandri and Sheridan (1995) provide a useful overview of the indicators most often invested with predictive utility in the study of violence. They acknowledge that violence prediction is limited by low base rates generally and reiterate the point that violent behaviours are often infrequent within the population as a whole (Monahan 1981, Scott 1977) and that this affects the accuracy of prediction (Lambert, Cartor and Walker 1988). However, Limandri and Sheridan (1995) note that:

> ...predictions can be made more accurately when evaluators take into account such interactive factors as gender, marital state, concomitant use of disinhibiting agents, and availability of victims and weapons... (p.10)

This suggest that officers will have to make holistic assessments of both recidivism, *and* what impact such recidivism might have and with what consequences and upon whom. These assessments will need to utilise both actuarial factors and careful professional judgement grounded in sound clinical techniques, enabling a dynamic and interactive assessment of: key demographic factors, predisposing personality and behavioural traits, situational and environmental factors, and particular conditional triggers and stressors. Officers could utilise the assessment process shown in Figure 15.1 to ensure that an integrated approach to all the likely risk factors is taken.

1.	Antecedents (Patterns)	– previous convictions – history of behaviours
	Is it likely?	Use of actuarial data
2.	Behaviour	– behavioural traits
	Is it likely?	– learned responses
	Why is it likely?	Use clinical
		Partially actuarial
3.	Conditions	– 'situational triggers'
	Is it likely?	– 'stressors'
	Why it is likely?	– 'predisposing hazards'
	When and under what conditions	Use clinical

Figure 15.1. The ABC of risk assessment

The model encourages the use of actuarial data as a base line by focusing upon antecedents, history and patterns. The next focus is upon particular behavioural traits and dispositions which the officer will have accessed through the use of clinical assessment over time, but the risk potential of which can be evaluated by reference to the available actuarial and research data. The final focus is upon the conditions and circumstances under which the behaviour potentially will take place. Officers can access this information again through clinical assessment, for example by using Weist's (1981) technique of 'getting the offender to walk through the crime', and by establishing under what conditions harmful behaviours have usually taken place in the past. Parole reports have much to offer in the area of detailed assessment around behaviour and conditions, but more important in establishing what Weist (1981) described as 'treatability'. This has been more recently expressed as 'responsivity' (Andrews 1995, Andrews and Bonta 1994, Andrews, Bonta and Hoge 1990), that is in classifying and appropriately matching offenders for the most effective intervention programmes. Through-care officers will have a crucial role in focusing the attention of parole boards on this crucial issue, and in convincingly arguing how the identified risks can be effectively dealt with by parole supervision and the likelihood of the prisoner to respond to the identified programme.

In convincingly arguing for appropriate interventions, through-care officers will also have to identify the potential harmful behaviours of concern under the Brooks (1984) framework. This will require assessments of detail and great specificity. General statements of danger, or imprecise predictions of future violence will be both unhelpful and potentially prejudicial.

Scott's (1977) assessment model of: **Offender + Victim + Circumstances = Offence** is a useful starting point for estimating the likelihood of a violent act occurring. This can be extended to include Megargee's (1976) combination of behavioural traits and situational factors, creating a multi-dimensional model in which the physiological and personality characteristics are combined with demographic factors and critical situational triggers such as the environment in which the behaviour occurs, who is targeted, the type of weapon used, and the time period in which it took place (Mulvey and Lidz 1984, 1993). Webster *et al.* (1994) have also outlined a multi-dimensional approach combining both clinical and actuarial assessment, utilising both statistical knowledge and a psycho-social assessment. Such a multi-dimensional model for Probation use would comprise:

Offender (including analysis of predisposing personality and behavioural traits), plus

Victim (access to, proximity to and grooming of), plus

Availability of Weapons (access to, preparedness to use), plus

Circumstances (environmental factors, conditions, circumstances and situational triggers), equals the:

Violent Offence.

This kind of approach has been pursued in more recent assessment models for violent behaviour, for example the MacArthur risk assessment study (Steadman *et al*. 1994) which utilises four basic 'domains' for use in predicting violence: '(a) dispositional factors, (b) historical factors, (c) contextual factors, and (d) clinical factors' (p.302). Walker (1991, Shaw 1996) adds to this a typology of dangerousness which usefully incorporates the notion of progression:

- The individual who harms others only if sheer bad luck brings him/her into a situation of provocation or sexual temptation.
- The individual who gets into such situations not by chance, but following inclinations.
- Individuals who are constantly on the look-out for opportunities.
- Individuals who do more, and who create opportunities. (Shaw 1996, p.170).

Such a typology assists in identifying those who are a 'chance, one off', those who have an initial predisposition, those who are actively grooming, and those for whom committing the dangerous act is their sole 'raison d'etre'. This can aid judgements of repetition, escalation, and amenability to intervention.

Following this in-depth assessment, the indicators of potential harm can be used to match interventions by literally plotting these indicators and targetting those which can be addressed by probation case based interventions or group work as shown in Figure 15.2:

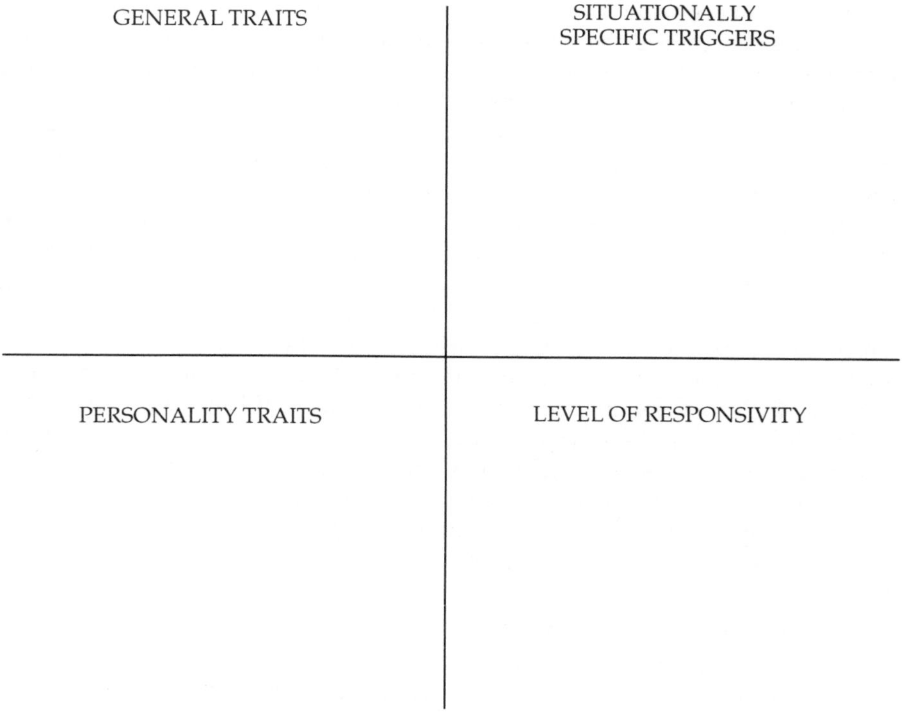

GENERAL TRAITS	SITUATIONALLY SPECIFIC TRIGGERS
PERSONALITY TRAITS	LEVEL OF RESPONSIVITY

Figure 15.2 Identifying appropriate intervention

Through-care officers could use the grid to ensure that programmes are appropriately matched to the risk factors identified and that this is convincingly presented in parole reports. Scarce through-care resources will need to be targetted on the basis of the responsivity principle and at those factors most likely to be changed or minimised by intervention. Parole conditions requiring additional resources should be argued for on this basis.

MANAGEMENT AND TRAINING SUPPORT FOR PRACTICE

Through-care officers are regularly involved in the complex task of assessing risk, particularly the risk of harmful or dangerous behaviours to the public in cases which will often attract public and media attention if 'things go wrong'. These decisions need to be of the highest quality if they are to be subsequently defended to public, media or inquiry teams (Carson 1995, Kemshall 1996b). Management has a crucial role in informing and enhancing the decision making of staff in the area of risk. This can be done through accessible and informative risk policies and guidance to staff, which are well grounded in research and the current reliable indicators of risk of recidivism and risk of harmful behaviours. Regrettably this is not always the case in Probation current risk policies (Kemshall 1997a, 1997b) which are too often lacking in the available actuarial data and make little reference to the extensive literature on theories of violent behaviour and violence prediction. This is however, exactly the knowledge base that through-care officers and their immediate supervisors need in order to do the task effectively. In addition, officers and their managers also need to be well informed about the data and assessment techniques that parole boards are using to make these decisions and the place of parole reports in this arena. There is a danger of the prison service and the probation service working to differing sets of risk prediction data and differing assessment techniques. The dual assessment of risk by both agencies in a dynamic way throughout the sentence and as a key objective of the sentencing planning process needs to be re-asserted. It is possible that each agency has slightly differing contributions to make to this process, the prison service to the production of actuarial base line assessments of risk, and the probation service to the assessment of specific harms, responsivity and to matching appropriate interventions to the risk factors likely to result in harms. The probation service will also have the primary responsibility for the delivery of such intervention programmes in a manner which can contribute to public safety. Whilst this has not been the primary focus of this chapter, such work will require skills and knowledge in addressing violent and sexually harmful behaviour, an increased knowledge of criminal psychology, and a consistent use of the those methods which have a proven track record of effectiveness such as cognitive behavioural programmes (McGuire 1995).

These practice demands suggest a training agenda covering at least the following:

- risk and harm/dangerousness assessment
- knowledge of and ability to apply the relevant actuarial and clinical indicators of risk of recidivism and risk of violence/harm

- knowledge of and ability to apply the relevant effective case based or programme interventions to respond to risk of harms and risk of reoffending
- knowledge of the parole boards decision making process
- knowledge of the sentence planning process, the role of risk assessment and risk management within this, and of the differing roles and responsibilities of prison and probation service personnel
- additional training on motivational interviewing in order to establish responsivity, and training in effective interventions based upon the 'What Works' research literature.

CONCLUSION

Risk is now becoming the 'core business' of the probation service. Whilst the probation service cannot guarantee to prevent risk (Kemshall 1996a) it can and should demonstrate an ability to respond to offender risks with consistency, reliability and credibility. This will be important in all aspects of its work, but certainly in respect of assessing and managing those offenders who would otherwise be the subject of incarceration. Victims, media and public are likely to become increasingly intolerate if the 'risk based test' of Carlisle is mis-applied, and the probation service risks a 'backlash' against its staff and against offenders if risk is perceived to be mismanaged. This will require high levels of knowledge and skill from staff and managers and the application of risk assessment and risk management techniques well grounded in empirical research.

REFERENCES

Andrews, D.A. (1995) 'The psychology of criminal conduct and effective treatment.' In J. McGuire (ed) *What Works: Reducing Offending: Guidelines from Research and Practice.* Chichester: John Wiley and Sons.

Andrews, D.A. and Bonta, J. (1994) *The Psychology of Criminal Conduct.* Cincinnati: Anderson.

Andrews, D.A., Bonta, J. and Hoge, R.D. (1990) 'Classification for effective rehabilitation.' *Criminal Justice and Behaviour 17*, 19–51.

Arthur, R. (1971) 'Success is predictable.' *Military Medicine 136*, 539–545.

Biddle, D. and Wincote, T. (1995) *Risk Assessment and Sentence Planning. Draft document.* The Sentence Planning Project. H.M. Prison Service.

Brearley, C.P. (1982) *Risk and Social Work: Hazards and Helping.* London: Routledge and Kegan Paul.

Brooks, A.D. (1984) 'Defining the dangerousness of the mentally ill: involuntary commitment.' In M. Craft and A. Craft (eds) *Mentally Abnormal Offenders.* London: Balliere Tindall.

Burgess, E.W. (1928) 'Factors making for success or failure on parole.' *Journal of Criminal Law and Criminology 19*, 2, 239–306.

Burgess, E.W. (1929) 'Is prediction feasible in social work?' *Social Forces 7*, 533–545.

Burgess, E.W. (1936) 'Protecting the Public by parole and parole prediction.' *Journal of Criminal Law and Criminology 27*, 491–502. As reprinted in Cottrell, Jr., L.S., Junter, A. and Short, Jr., J.F. (eds) (1973) *Ernest W. Burgess on Community, Family, and Delinquency.* Chicago: University of Chicago Press.

Butler Committee, Home Office and Department of Health and Social Security (1975) *Committee on Mentally Abnormal Offenders.* Cmnd. 6244, London: HMSO.

Carlisle, Rt. Hon Lord of Bucklow (1988) *The Parole System in England and Wales. Report of the Review Committee.* London: HMSO.

Carroll, J.S. (1977) 'Judgements of recidivism: conflicts between clinical strategies and base-rate information.' *Law and Human Behaviour 1*, 2, 191–198.

Carroll, J.S. and Payne, J.W. (eds) (1976) 'The psychology of the parole decision process: a joint application of attribution theory and information processing.' In J. Carroll and J. Payne (eds) *Cognition and Social Behaviour.* Hillsdale, NJ: Erlbaum.

Carson D. (1995) 'Calculated risk.' *Community Care*, 26 October – 1 November., 26–27.

Christie, N. (1993) *Crime Control as Industry.* London: Routledge.

Clark, D.A., Fisher, M.J. and McDougall, C. (1993) 'A new methodology for assessing the level of risk in incarcerated offenders.' *British Journal of Criminology 33*, 3, pp.436–448.

Copas, J.B. and Tarling, R. (1986) 'Some methodological issues in making predictions.' In A. Blumstein, J. Cohen and C. Visher. *Criminal Careers and 'Career Criminals'.* Washington DC: National Academy of Sciences.

Copas, J., Ditchfield, J. and Marshall, P. (1994) *Development of a New Reconviction Score.* Research Bulletin 36. London: HMSO.

Copas, J., Marshall, P. and Tarling, R. (1996) *Predicting Reoffending for Discretionary Release.* Home Office Research Study 150. London: HMSO.

Farrington, D.P. and Tarling, R. (1985) *Prediction in Criminology.* Albany State Press.

Feeley, M. and Simon, J. (1992) 'The new penology: notes on the emerging strategy of corrections.' *Criminology 30*, 4, 449–475.

Feeley, M. and Simon, J. (1994) 'Actuarial justice: the emerging new criminal law.' In D. Nelken (ed) *The Futures of Criminology.* Sage.

Flynn, E. (1978) 'Classifications for risk and supervision.' In J. Freeman (ed) *Prisons Past and Future.* Cambridge Studies in Criminology.

Glaser, D. (1955) 'The efficacy of alternative approaches to parole prediction.' *American Sociological Review 20*, 283–287.

Glaser, D. (1962) 'Prediction tables as accounting devices for judges and parole board members.' *Crime and Delinquency 8*, 3, 239–258.

Glaser, D. (1973) *Routinizing Evaluation.* Rockville Maryland, National Institute of Mental Health.

Gottfredson, S.D. and Gottfredson, D.M. (1993) 'The long-term predictive utility of the base expectancy score.' *Howard Journal 32*, 4, 276–290.

Harris, P. (1994) 'Client management classification and prediction of probation outcomes.' *Crime and Delinquency 40*, 2, 154–174.

Her Majesty's Inspectorate of Probation (1995) *Dealing with Dangerous People: The Probation Service and Public Protection. Report of a Thematic Inspection*. London: Home Office.

Hirsch, A. and Ashworth, A. (1996) 'Protective sentencing under Section 2 (2) (b): the criteria for dangerousness.' *Criminal Law Review*, 173–183.

Home Office (1990) *Crime, Justice and Protecting the Public*. Cm. 965.

Kahnemann, D. and Tversky, A. (1973) 'On the psychology of prediction.' *Psychological Review 80*, 237–251.

Kahneman, D. and Tversky, A. (1984) 'Choices, values and frames.' *American Psychologist 39*, 4, pp.341–350.

Kemshall, H. (1995) 'Researching risk in probation practice.' *Practice Matters 7*, 1, December 1995.

Kemshall, H. (1996a) 'Offender risk and probation practice.' In H. Kemshall and J. Pritchard (eds) *Good Practice in Risk Assessment and Risk Management 1*. London: Jessica Kingsley Publishers.

Kemshall, H. (1996b) *Reviewing Risk: A Review of Research on the Assessment and Management of Risk and Dangerousness: Implications for Policy and Practice in the Probation Service*. A report for the Home Office, Research and Statistics Directorate. Forthcoming, London: Home Office.

Kemshall, H. (1997a) *Risk in Probation Practice: Training Issues. A Report on the National Survey into Risk Training*. Home Office Probation Training Section/Association of Chief Officers of Probation, London.

Kemshall, H. (1997b) *Risk Management Workshops for Probation Service Senior Managers*. Home Office Probation Training Section/Association of Chief Officers of Probation.

Kemshall, H., Parton, N., Walsh, M. and Waterson, J. (1995) 'Concepts of risk as core influences on organisational structure and functioning within the personal social services.' Paper for ESRC Risk in Organisational Settings at the White House, Regents Park, London. 16th–17th May 1995.

Lambert, E.W., Cartor, R. and Walker, G.L. (1988) 'Reliability of behavioural versus medical models: Rare events and danger.' *Issues in Mental Health and Nursing 9*, 31–44.

Law, K.M. (1993) *A Retrospective Study looking at the Efficacy of the HMP Wakefield Risk Assessment Proforma with Life Licencees*. Unpublished dissertation for the MSc in Applied Criminal Psychology, H.M. Prison Service.

Limandri, B.J. and Sheridan, D.J. (1995) 'The prediction of intentional interpersonal violence: An introduction.' In J. Campbell (ed) *Assessing Dangerousness: Violence by Sexual Offenders, Batterers, and Child Abusers*. Interpersonal violence: The Practice Series. London: Sage.

Mannheim, H. and Wilkins, L.T. (1955) *Prediction Methods in Relation to Borstal Training*. London: HMSO.

McGuire, J. (ed) (1995) *What Works: Reducing Reoffending. Guidelines from Research and Practice*. Chichester: John Wiley and Sons.

Megargee, E. (1976) 'The prediction of dangerous behaviour.' *Criminal Justice and Behaviour 3*, 3–21.

Monahan, J. (1981) *The Clinical Prediction of Violence*. Beverley Hills, CA: Sage.

Monahan, J. and Hood, G. (1978) 'Ascriptions of dangerousness: The eye (and age, sex, education, location, and politics) of the beholder.' In R. Simon (ed) *Research in Law and Sociology.* Greenwich, Conn.: Johnson, 143–151.

Monahan, J. and Steadman, H.J. (1994) *Violence and Mental Disorder: Developments in Risk Assessment.* Chicago, IL: The University of Chicago Press.

Mulvey, E.P. and Lidz, C.W. (1984) 'Clinical considerations in the prediction of dangerousness in mental patients.' *Clinical Psychology Review 4,* 379–401.

Mulvey, E.P. and Lidz, C.W. (1993) 'Measuring patient violence in dangerousness research'. *Law and Human Behaviour 17, 3,* 277–288.

Nisbett, R., Borigda, E., Crandall, R. and Reed, H. (1976) 'Popular induction: Information is not necessarily informative.' In J. Carroll and J. Payne (eds) *Cognition and Social Behaviour.* Hillsdale, N.J.: Erlbaum.

Nuffield, J. (1982) *Farole Decision Making in Canada: Research Decision Guidelines.* Ottawa: Ministry of the Solicitor General, Communications Division.

Nuttall, C.P., with Barnard, E.F., Fowles, A.J., Frost, A., Hammond, W.H., Mayhew, P., Pease, K., Tarling, R. and Weatheritt, M.J. (1977) *Parole in England and Wales.* Home Office Research Study No. 38. London: HMSO.

Ohlin, L.E. and Duncan, O.D. (1949) 'The efficacy of prediction in criminology.' *American Journal of Sociology 54,* 441–451.

Parton, N. (1996) 'Social work, risk and "the blaming system".' In N. Parton (ed) *Social Theory, Social Change and Social Work.* London: Routledge.

Penal Affairs Consortium (1995) *The Reduction of Home Leave and Temporary Release Opportunities.* Penal Affairs Consortium.

Polvi, N. and Pease, K. (1991) 'Parole and its problems: A Canadian-English comparison.' *The Howard Journal 30, 3,* 218–230.

Probation Service Division (1994) PC/84 1994 *Risk Assessment for Temporary Release Prisoners.* Home Office, Probation Service Division.

Royal Society (1992) *Risk: Analysis, Perception and Management.* London: Royal Society.

Ryan, W. (1971) *Blaming the Victim.* New York: Random House.

Sapsford, R.J. (1978) 'Further research applications of the "Parole prediction Index".' *International Journal of Criminology and Penology 6,* 247–254.

Scott, P. (1977) 'Assessing dangerousness in criminals.' *British Journal of Psychiatry 131,* 127–142.

Shah, S. (1978a) 'Dangerousness and mental illness. Some conceptual, prediction and policy dilemmas.' In C. Frederick (ed) *Dangerous Behaviour: A Problem in Law and Mental Health.* NIMH. DHEW Publications No. (ADM) 78–563, Washington, D. C. Supt of Docs., Govt. Print. Off. 153–191.

Shah, S. (1978b) 'Dangerousness: a paradigm for exploring some of the issues in law and psychology.' *American Psychologist 33,* 224–238.

Shaw, R. (1996) 'Supervising the dangerous in the community.' In N. Walker (ed) *Dangerous People.* London: Blackstone Press Limited.

Steadman, H.J., Monahan, J., Appelbaum, P.S., Grisso, T., Mulvey, E.P., Roth, L.H., Robbins, P.C. and Klassen, D. (1994) 'Designing a new generation of risk assessment research.' In J. Monahan and H.J. Steadman (ed) *Violence and Mental*

Disorder: Developments in Risk Assessment. Chicago, IL: University of Chicago Press.

Walker, N. (1991) 'Dangerous mistakes.' *British Journal of Psychiatry 158*, p.752.

Walker, N. (ed) (1996) *Dangerous People.* London: Blackstone Press Limited.

Ward, D. (1987) *The Validity of the Reconviction Score.* Home Office Research Study No. 94. London: HMSO.

Wasik, M. and Taylor, R.D. (1991) *Blackstone's Guide to the Criminal Justice Act.* Blackstone Press Ltd.

Webster, C.D., Harris, G.T., Rice, M.E., Cormier, C. and Quinsey, V. (1994) *The Violence Prediction Scheme: Assessing Dangerousness in High Risk Men.* Toronto: University of Toronto Centre for Criminology.

Weist, J. (1981) 'Treatment of violent offenders.' *Clinical Social Work Journal 9*, 4, 271–281.

Zamble, R. and Poporino, E.J. (1990) 'Coping, imprisonment and rehabilitation.' *Criminal Justice and Behaviour 17*, 1, 53–69.

Thanks are extended to the through care officers and seniors of South East London Probation Service who contributed to the development of some of these ideas in various workshops throughout 1996. However, the views expressed are entirely the responsibility of the author.

The author is currently in receipt of an Economic and Social Research grant to investigate 'Risk in Probation Practice' grant number:L211252018. The author has also recently completed a review of risk assessment and risk management interventions for risk and dangerousness sponsored by the Home Office Research and Statistics Directorate. The sponsorship of the ESRC and the Home Office is gratefully acknowledged.

Appendix

SOUTH EAST LONDON PROBATION SERVICE

THROUGHCARE

PRE-RELEASE **SENTENCE PLAN CONTRIBUTION**	**POST-RELEASE** **SUPERVISION PLAN**
INITIAL ☐	INITIAL ☐
REVIEW ☐	REVIEW ☐
TRANSFER ☐	TRANSFER ☐
	FINAL ☐

Date Completed: Date of Next Supervision Plan:

1

Name:

DOB: Prison No:

Home Address:

Other Relevant Address:

Tel No:

Offence:

Length of Sentence:

2

Date of Sentence: Court:

CRD/ARD: PED:

NPD: LED: SED:

3 Prison Establishments:

1.   2.

3.   4.

4 <u>Home Circumstances/Family Perspective:</u>

(a)   **How supportive is the family/friendship network of an offending-free life-style?**

non-supportive ☐ ☐ ☐ ☐ ☐ ☐ ☐ ☐ ☐ ☐ supportive

(b)   **Information in support of rating:**

(c)   **Has there been independent family contact?**

by standard letter ☐; telephone ☐; home visit ☐; no contact at all ☐

5	**Overall Pattern of Offending (see pre-cons)**	**In Frequency**	**In Dangerousness**
	Accelerating	☐	☐
	Decelerating	☐	☐

Stable ☐   **Chaotic** ☐   **One-off** ☐

Comment on overall pattern:

6 | **Details of Most Serious Current Offence:**

7 | **Victim's Perspective**
Attitudes to victim:

Victim Charter complied with?   yes/no/na

Victim assessment/perspective:

Area Where Offence Committed:

2

8   Factors Contributing to Offending:

Contributing Factors (Factors relating to Offence List)	Ranking
	1
	2
	3
	4
	5

Comment on contributing factors:

9   Effects of Disadvantage or Discrimination:

10   Details of Risk Posed by This Client:

☐   What behaviour is of concern?

☐   To whom?

☐   When?

☐   What is the probability that it will happen again (if nothing changes)?

☐   Under what circumstances?

☐   **What would be the consequence of it happening?**

☐   **How aware is the client of these factors?:**

aware ☐ ☐ ☐ ☐ ☐ ☐ ☐ ☐ ☐ ☐ **unaware**

☐   **What factors in the client's situation and personality reduce this risk?**

---

11 | **Overall Risk of Re-offending:**

Client's View	**Officer's View**
1 2 3 4 5 6 7 8 9 10	1 2 3 4 5 6 7 8 9 10

12 | **Client Motivation to Change:**

Client's View	**Officer's View**
1 2 3 4 5 6 7 8 9 10	1 2 3 4 5 6 7 8 9 10

13 | **Decision to Include in Potential Dangerous Offenders Register**   yes/no

14 | **Action Plan (to reduce identified risk):**

Pre-Release	**Post-Release**
Appropriate Prison-based Programmes	**Appropriate Core-Programmes**

4

	Detail of Action Plan:
15	**Significant Developments Since Last Plan:**
16	**Final Review**
	Name of Probation Officer **Telephone No:** **Probation Office**

Client's Signature ....   **Date:** ....

CHAPTER 16

Rights Versus Risks
Issues in Work with Prisoners

Brian Williams

Prisons have always been involved in risk assessment and management. A balanced discussion of prisoners and risk must consider not only the risks presented by serving and released prisoners but also the dangers posed to individuals by their imprisonment. This chapter introduces these issues and begins by looking at the threats to individuals' rights posed by the process of risk assessment in prisons.

RISK ASSESSMENT AND PRISONERS' RIGHTS

The level of risk presented by prisoners is assessed in private, using techniques inaccessible to the lay person. This gives rise to several concerns, including questions about prisoners' rights and issues in relation to the level at which decisions are made. Abstract assessment instruments may remove decisions about the risk presented by individuals a considerable distance from the prison staff who know the individual best, and 'the intrusion of abstract systems, especially expert systems, into all aspects of life undermines pre-existing forms of local control' (Giddens 1991, p.137).

In the prison setting, the introduction of objective methods of risk assessment (supposing that these actually existed) might lead to greater respect and attention being paid to prisoners' rights, but there is little sign of such considerations having influenced the trend towards the increased use of technical assessment measures. Rather, prison systems around the world have responded to the advent of the 'risk society' by reorganising themselves in ways intended to exploit existing knowledge about individuals and the risk they present and to recognise, and if possible avoid, 'the political potential of catastrophes' (Beck 1992, p.24).

This is not to deny that prisoners do present risks to others. It would be irresponsible not to attempt, in managing prisons, to minimise such risks to other prisoners, to staff and to the public. Whatever one's views about the rise of what Feeley and Simon (1994) have called 'actuarial justice', this is already deeply entrenched in many criminal justice systems. New forms of expertise have begun to replace those traditionally involved in assessing risk:

> Instead of social workers and sociologists, the new experts are geographers and psychologists; instead of prescribing treatment, expertise is now being used to calculate risk. Risk of reoffending and risk of victimization are now the key issues on which social science expertise is being addressed. (Hudson 1996, p.154)

In England and Wales the Probation and Social Services Inspectorates have been engaged in the discourse of risk for some years (see Parton 1996, Her Majesty's Inspectorate of Probation 1995). Interestingly, the Prisons Inspectorate has remained relatively aloof from this process, criticising some aspects of the prison service's approach to risk management. The Prisons Inspectorate's 1995 inspection report on Leyhill prison, for example, bemoaned the reduction in the number of prisoners able to work in the community as part of their resettlement plans, attributing this to the introduction of stringent new risk assessment procedures in 1994 and saying that Leyhill's future as a resettlement prison for lifers and long-term men was threatened. In other reports, risk to prisoners was highlighted: the risk from male intruders at Drake Hall women's open prison, high rates of self-mutilation at Young Offender Institutions and sloppy suicide management at Deerbolt (Her Majesty's Inspectorate of Probation 1995, Fielding and Fowles 1995, 1996).

The actuarial approach to the distribution of risk in criminal justice is likely to be with us for some time and is to some extent institutionalised in the 1995 Prison Rules (Creighton and King 1996), but its application in prisons in England and Wales illustrates some of the issues it raises. There is a need for vigilance on two levels; the 'new risk penality' (see Hudson 1996) has important consequences for criminal justice in general, as well as for the rights and welfare of prisoners. In the prison setting, as elsewhere, the discourse of risk has an ideological function: 'dangers (real dangers) are being used to give automatic, self-validating legitimacy to established law and order' (Douglas 1992, p.29).

The fact that there are some prisoners whose escape would present genuine dangers to sections of the public is used to justify the whole system of secure custody, however unjust it might be to apply it to the majority of relatively minor offenders who present little risk. It is therefore important to engage with those who believe they can control the distribution of risk, both by challenging their fundamental approach and by questioning individual assessments of risk. Otherwise, an instrumental approach to risk will come to prevail, allowing prisons (and other institutions) to: 'adapt procedures and self-presentation in order to secure or repair credibility, without fundamentally questioning the forms of power or social control involved' (Lash and Wynne 1992, p.4).

In other words, the debate about risk should be linked, in the prison context, to the wider debate about the legitimacy of prison (Sparks 1994). Every challenge to an assessment of the risk posed by an individual prisoner takes the protagonists into the arena of such debate. It is also important to question prison procedures ostensibly aimed at minimising risk, although this is a difficult area. Rules designed to protect inmates and staff may, if inflexibly applied, cause new problems and risks – and prison officers tend, in situations where they are not trained or encouraged to use discretion, to follow the rule book. This can result in injustice and discrimination. The dilemma for prison-based probation officers is whether to defend their professional values or to maintain their credibility with prison staff by failing to question prison routines. While respecting prison officers' professionalism, and their right to decide matters relating to security, probation staff must also defend their own claim to professional expertise and values.

There can be no doubt that the new risk culture impinges upon prisoners' rights. To take only two recent examples: the prison service in England and Wales has embarked upon risk assessment on a massive scale with reference to sexual offenders and to release on temporary licence. Refusal by lifers to engage in 'voluntary' assessment for the Sex Offender Treatment Programme, according to one prisoner, 'guarantees at least a two-year knockback... Lifers put on the SOTP are angry and bitter. We will go through the motions only because it is Home Office policy, not because we think we need the course' (Casey 1996, p.24).

There have been cases of long-sentence prisoners being assessed as need-ing to join the Sex Offender Treatment Programme even though they have no record of sexual offending, and Casey's article outlines some of the physical risks incurred by prisoners moved in and out of Vulnerable Prisoner Units to undergo such assessment and treatment. They also have to be transferred between prisons for assessment and then 'treatment', with all the disruption to their visits such moves involve (Sampson 1994). They face dilemmas about the disclosure of previously unknown offences and about the degree of openness with which they participate in the programme 'by revealing just how often they have offended and how ingrained their problems are, offend-ers may reveal the fact that they pose a far greater danger to society than had been previously thought' (Sampson 1994, p.200).

All applications for release on temporary licence quite properly involve an assessment of risk. The criteria for such releases have, however, been consid-erably tightened in recent years (see Creighton and King 1996 for details of the 1995 changes). Despite the introduction of standard forms, the process remains highly subjective. In completing the risk assessment required by Circular Instruction 36/1995, prison officers: 'are required to make entirely subjective assessments (on the likelihood of recidivism) and are also supposed to give details of the known views of victims. The level of reporting will vary considerably from prison to prison depending on the skill of the reporting officer and the time available in which to complete the assessment' (Creighton and King 1996, p.17).

The quality of information available to prisons about victims' views will also vary considerably. Probation practice in relation to this duty is enor-mously varied from one county to another (Williams 1996a). In terms of prisoners' civil liberties, these inconsistencies raise the spectre of 'justice by geography'. The sudden tightening of the criteria in 1995 also illustrates the close connection between political decisions taken at the centre and assess-ments of supposed risk in individual cases.

Similar issues arise in relation to the risks arising from drug misuse in prisons – the stated rationale for introducing random drug testing was partly one of harm reduction (Her Majesty's Prison Service undated) and an implicit aim was to reduce the incidence of drug-related violence (see, for example, Phillips 1996, Williams 1991). The outcome has been a radical change to prison regimes with large numbers of inmates testing positive and receiving disciplinary 'awards' affecting their eventual release dates. Prison regimes which had tolerated widespread drug misuse suddenly introduced random urine testing and individual prisoners took the consequences.

Probation officers in prisons are expected to inform security staff of anything which might prevent a security risk. They use the Security Information Report (SIR) system fairly routinely to ensure that information is shared efficiently, for example in cases where individuals are being bullied or 'taxed' because of drug-related debts. In such a case this is entirely proper but the SIR system raises important issues of civil liberties: the prisoner who is the subject of such a report never knows about it in most instances and certainly has no right to see what has been said about his or her conduct.

PRISON SUBCULTURE, THE PAINS OF IMPRISONMENT AND INDIVIDUAL RISK

Some of the dangers involved in being in prison have already been touched upon. Without labouring the point, it is important to understand that prisoners are daily at risk by virtue of being in prison. They are placed at greater risk of suicide, self-mutilation, physical and sexual assault and many kinds of psychic damage than their counterparts in the outside community (Williams 1991). Any just risk reduction strategy must give these types of risk due attention.

Particular sub-groups are susceptible to greater risks. Young offenders and women, for example, are particularly liable to suicide and self-harm (Liebling 1992, 1994, Morris et al. 1995). Although intimidation, assaults and bullying occur at all levels of the prison system, young and elderly prisoners seem to be at greater risk and may cope less well than young adults in a violent institution (Phillips 1996). Sexual offenders and those segregated for their own protection within mainstream prisons are also more vulnerable to violent attack than prisoners in the general population. While the prison service has done a great deal to reduce the vulnerability of, and the risks to, these groups of prisoners, such initiatives have more impact in some prisons than in others. The Chief Inspector noted in his 1995 annual report, for example, that 'Most establishments were in the process of adopting the latest suicide risk identification system... But we found considerable variation in how much training staff had in its use and how well it was being used' (Her Majesty's Inspectorate of Prisons 1995, p.10). Again, these variations are indicative of varying degrees of priority being given to the risks that prisoners daily endure. A consistent risk reduction strategy would seek to rectify such disparities.

Prisoners who are HIV Positive, those who have AIDS and any thinking of being tested for the virus need, and cannot always obtain, independent, confidential, professional counselling. The official figures suggest that only a tiny proportion of UK prisoners has AIDS, but there is little incentive to be tested for the virus and good reasons not to. The figures probably under-estimate the size of the problem substantially. Thus, a serious risk is being neglected, although progress is now being made in involving outside agencies in the support of HIV Positive prisoners (Williams 1996) and improving the medical services inside (Ralli 1994).

POST-RELEASE SUPERVISION

Since the publication of new National Standards and of a critical report by the Probation Inspectorate in 1995, the probation service has paid greater attention to the assessment and management of risk. The Inspectorate recommended that 'risk assessment must be carried out in every case' (Her Majesty's Probation Inspectorate 1995, p.15), and the Association of Chief Officers of Probation have also issued guidance (Association of Chief Officers of Probation 1994). As a consequence, there is now a requirement in some local services that all clients making contact with probation should be the subject of risk assessments, including casual callers. This has primarily involved staff in form-filling rather than in any process of reflection or training about risk issues. Perhaps unsurprisingly, the quality of the risk assessments made has been variable (Kemshall 1996c).

The Inspectorate report made other strong statements about risk issues: for example, it asserted that: 'public protection takes priority over the right to confidentiality of those with whom the probation service is involved' (Her Majesty's Probation Inspectorate 1995, p.17). This presumably means that public protection takes priority over *offenders'* right to confidentiality (ignoring the probation role in working with *victims of crime*, whose right to confidentiality is not always respected by the prison system (see Williams 1996b). While one can understand that public protection would normally have a higher priority than client confidentiality in cases involving serious offences or the protection of children and other vulnerable people, it is a remarkably strong and categorical statement. 'Public protection' is defined in the document, in a strangely circular way, as 'the desired outcome of risk assessment and risk management' (Her Majesty's Probation Inspectorate 1995, p.13).

Taken literally, this would mean that protecting the public from serious risk should always override any commitment to clients' rights to confidentiality. This would involve a radical change to the ethos and values of the probation service, to say the least. The probation service is in danger of becoming the custodian of a whole new system of labelling, with 'risk' replacing the former concerns with 'moral degeneracy', 'social inadequacy' or 'incorrigibility' (see Sumner 1994). This suggests that the optimism arising from recent research findings about 'what works' may be misplaced, if the discourse of risk is to override the existing values of probation work. For offending behaviour to be effectively challenged, there needs to be a degree of trust between client and worker. Offenders may in future need to be warned at the outset of their period of supervision of the possible consequences of sharing information with probation officers. Until now, such warnings have not been routinely given but clients have usually understood that there is a limit to the protection afforded by professional confidentiality (Williams 1995). The Inspectorate seems to be wanting to bring a much greater proportion of confidential discussion between probation officers and clients into the public domain, in the name of public protection.

The Inspectorate, not for the first time, is trying to steer the probation service in a particular direction. The Chief Inspector, Graham Smith, used the phrase 'community corrections' in his annual report at a time when uncertainty about the future role of the probation service was rife (Her Majesty's Probation Inspectorate 1993). At the time, many observers took this as a deliberate strategic alignment of the Inspectorate on the side of the new, right-wing Home Office ministerial team. In this case it might be argued that an attempt is being made to redefine the types of deviance to which the service should give priority. If probation work is to become dominated by the assessment and management of risk, what previous areas of work are to be displaced? The increasing dominance of risk work would seem to imply a reduction in the service's former commitment to the assessment and management of client need and the discourse of risk thus coincides with the move towards correctionalism and away from social work.

When prisoners are released they move from being subject to the assessments made by prison personnel (including prison-based probation officers) and become the subject of assessment by field probation officers. The Inspectorate criticised the low level of probation staff awareness of risk issues and the lack of systematic risk assessment of one-third of the individual clients whose files were inspected in its 1995 report, as well as deploring probation officers' continuing reluctance to make custodial proposals in the Pre-Sentence Reports (PSRs). While staff understanding of the issues may not have greatly increased, risk assessment forms have proliferated rapidly in response to the report and PSRs have been redesigned to ensure that they include risk assessments. By the time a prisoner becomes subject to post-release supervision, the degree of risk he or she presents is likely to have been assessed many times. Where that assessment indicates high risk, many areas now require a fresh risk assessment quarterly during the course of the client's statutory contact with the service.

It may be that this can be done unobtrusively by experienced staff, but there is a danger that risk assessment will become the be-all and end-all in post-custody supervision of serious offenders. If so, those under probation supervision after their release from prison will, in the fullest sense, be serving the remainder of their prison sentence in the community. Whether such an approach to supervision will in fact 'help offenders lead law-abiding lives' (Prison Service undated) needs full and urgent discussion.

CURRENT BRITISH PENAL POLICY AND RISK TO THE PUBLIC

Penal policy in the UK is at present based upon a high-risk political strategy; it generally responds to perceived popular concerns about law and order in preference to academic or professional advice. The policy of incarcerating more people for longer periods is presented by politicians as part of a strategy of reducing risk to the public, but in some respects it arguably increases the level of such risk. Offenders are increasingly likely to leave the impoverished regime of an overcrowded prison embittered and ill-equipped to cope with a crime-free way of life. The degree of risk they present to the public may thus have increased as a result of their prison experience. Prisons are managed more reactively than in the past, with half an eye to political pressures, and the expertise and judgement of staff are under-valued. Risk to the public can easily be overlooked in such a climate.

After being sacked as director of the prison service by Michael Howard in the wake of revelations about security lapses leading to escape attempts from a high-security prison, Derek Lewis accused the Home Secretary of constantly interfering in the running of the system. Such direct and frequent intervention was, perhaps, a result of the lack of trust between two particular individuals, but there does seem to have been an increase in direct political involvement. The changing climate within which daily decisions are made in the prisons is more important in the long term, but it is bound to be influenced by politicians' pronouncements. In a culture where everyone is 'minding their backs', those managing risk successfully receive little praise (Shaw 1996).

If these influences lead to greater caution in assessing risk, it might be thought that this would automatically lead to improved protection of the public. However, over-cautious risk assessment does not necessarily enhance public safety. Sampson (1994) notes that the Sex Offender Treatment Programme was funded on the understanding that it would lead to a significant reduction in reoffending rates:

> Such expectations of success may be misplaced... Moreover, the use of reoffending rates as a criterion of success is a questionable policy, since very few offences are ever reported, and very few of those reported ever result in convictions. An apparently successful programme therefore, may simply be one that teaches offenders how to offend without getting caught.' (p.201)

The style of prison management so far adopted in this country depends to a considerable extent upon the consent of the prisoners. In the USA, where prison staff are armed and prepared to use deadly force if challenged, this is less of an issue. The legitimacy of the American prison system is undermined accordingly, not only in the eyes of the prisoners but also of the wider public. It seems to me that the kind of issues raised by risk assessment, including those discussed above, have an important relationship to the question of the legitimacy of our own prison system. The reforms proposed in the Woolf report proceeded from his identification of 'a generally shared sense of injustice' and his 'implicit recognition of some entrenched legitimation problems' (Sparks, 1994, p.20). His proposed solutions have largely been jettisoned in favour of approaches drawn from the new 'risk penality'. Mechanistic risk assessment will inevitably lead to false positives, whereby people will be kept in custody because they are assessed as presenting a risk. This is bound to fuel a sense of injustice and a deliberately-overcrowded system becomes much difficult to manage as the number of resentful, angry and desperate inmates rises.

Risk assessment is also linked to a more general bureaucratisation of decision making in prisons, which has occurred as part of the managerialist trend. As Garland (1990) has pointed out, this has been going on for a century or more but its logic is to displace the role of the public in penal decision making, making penal administration less open to public scrutiny and less accountable. The danger of this, as Garland goes on to argue, is that the public becomes more susceptible to misinformation and more likely to form judgments on the basis of sensational headlines.

In the field of risk assessment some of these trends are illustrated by the case of the two ten-year-olds convicted of murdering James Bulger. The trial judge recommended that they serve a minimum of eight years in custody, the Lord Chief Justice recommended ten years and the Home Secretary, after a campaign in the tabloid press, announced that he had increased the tariff to fifteen years. One of the grounds for the Court of Appeal declaring the Home Secretary's tariff decision illegal was that he had been influenced by irrelevant information – namely petitions urging that the boys remain in prison for life and coupons sent to his office by readers of the *Sun* Newspaper. The appeal judges argued that the circumstances of individual young offenders ought to be taken into account in deciding whether and when to release them (Dyer 1996). Such holistic assessments of the likely risk posed by offenders are in danger of being supplanted by media campaigns, leaving penal professionals isolated and defensive.

THE ACTUARIAL SOCIETY

In prisons, as noted above, decision making can come to be dominated by the need to 'cover one's back'. In such a climate, border-line cases are determined cautiously. Prisoners are thus refused early release, home leave, lower security categorisation and other discretionary goods. The system is based upon individual cases but discretion is systematically exercised in accordance with bureaucratic rules formulated in the light of the ruling political ideology, and policy can change even without any conscious decision being made to alter its direction.

The growing hegemony of the discourse of risk creates an ideal climate for such developments. The mission of the prison service in England and Wales has changed in recent years from an emphasis on disciplinary techniques to a greater reliance on actuarial practices. Simon's point about the criminal justice climate more generally is apposite here: 'Rather than seeking to change people ('normalize them', in Foucault's apt phrase) an actuarial regime seeks to manage them in place' (Simon 1988, p.773).

As Hudson (1996) (see also Taylor 1995) has pointed out, the American 'war on drugs' illustrates the consequences of such a shift in the area of sentencing policy – which is reflected in more austere prison regimes and in the increasingly disproportionate rate of imprisonment of members of racial minority groups. The 'justice model' at least strove to eliminate the discrimination involved in allowing irrelevant factors such as race to influence sentencing. In the 'new risk penality': '"Non-legal factors" such as race, employment record, homelessness and single parentage, which the "justice" reforms of the 1980s sought to remove from sentencing decision-making, are reintroduced as "risk factors"' (Hudson 1996, p.155) (see also Creamer and Williams 1996).

This is dangerous both in terms of the increasing difficulties of managing overcrowded prisons whose inmates question the legitimacy of the system and in terms of its injustice. As Hudson goes on to argue, 'New Right' criminology and the 'new risk penality' share a distaste for the notion that people can change and a belief in an irredeemable underclass. In the prison context such attitudes have explosive potential. As Cohen (1994) has noted:

> In the crime control business, we see an ascendancy of managerial, administrative and technocratic styles. The old liberal ideologies (treatment, rehabilitation, social reform) are discredited... If people cannot be changed and societies cannot be transformed, then theories become less ambitious and lose their critical edge or indeed any social context. (p.72)

The responsibilities of the prison and probation services overlap when it comes to making decisions about the risk involved in releasing prisoners. It is precisely in such situations that conflicting organisational values are exposed: 'Where different social organisations share responsibility for common risks there is a potential for disagreement and conflict over the existence, nature and extent of the risk' (Kemshall 1996b, p.5).

Mechanistic predictive instruments may be used with a critical understanding of their limitations by staff in one setting, but seen as objective measures in another. There is also scope for misunderstandings and conflict between organisations wedded to a clinical model of assessment, and those more familiar with actuarial approaches (see Kemshall 1996b).

In prisons, the organisational cultures and values of the various professions involved in decision making are likely to lead to different perceptions of risk among members of multidisciplinary meetings reviewing the progress of individual prisoners. Thus, a psychologist might feel that a probation officer has become over-involved with a prisoner in the process of designing a release plan or that a chaplain is incapable of objectivity when advocating the release of an inmate who has experienced personal growth as a result of counselling or of spiritual development. This could be an example of a clash between the clinical and actuarial models of assessment: the psychologist questions the predictive validity of his colleagues' individual knowledge of a prisoner. Similarly, a prison officer might favour an optimistic assessment of a model prisoner while the probation officer might argue that the man's behaviour and attitudes during a group work programme indicate that his attitudes towards women remain unmodified and that prison behaviour is a poor predictor of conduct after release.

These examples are not intended to suggest that all members of the occupational groups concerned generally favour particular predictive models but rather to demonstrate the complexity of any attempt to predict future human behaviour. Indeed, it is probably misleading to think in terms of professionals consistently espousing either a clinical or an actuarial method of risk assessment. Much of the literature argues for the use of holistic methods of prediction (Kemshall 1996a, 1996b, 1996c, Cowburn and Modi 1995) but, in the present state of knowledge, we have to accept that: 'what people think about risks is as much a matter of value as of fact' (Floud and Young 1981, p.5).

It is important that these value questions are made explicit: only then will truly holistic assessments of individuals be made, because: 'Determinations of risk straddle the distinction between objective and value dimensions. Moral standards are not asserted openly but in quantitative, theoretical and causal forms' (Parton 1996, p.109).

It will not be easy to insist that the probation perspective is incorporated in risk assessments made in prisons (not least because of the current struggle over the value-base from which probation operates and the decimation of the probation presence in many prisons as a result of budget cuts). The seductiveness of the 'expert's reality', which appears to embody an abstract rationality superior to the rich, socially constructed reality of individual professionals, means that professional opinions can be swept aside (Smallman 1996). It is vital that practitioners engage in this struggle, however, and that they find allies to join with them: otherwise decisions will be made without the benefit of any effective contribution by those working in prisons who maintain a belief in individuals' ability to change.

The advent of the 'risk society' (Beck 1992) raises important challenges for the social work profession. Not least, it is clear that there is a good deal of intellectual work to be done. Can a genuinely holistic form of risk assessment be devised or will expert systems be allowed to dominate? Is the probation perspective on individual offenders valuable as part of that assessment process? It is clear that prison-based probation officers will play an important part in deciding the answers to these questions. They will need to assert the importance of the probation contribution to the assessment of risk and to insist upon the relevance of social work expertise. To do so effectively they will need strong support from field colleagues and probation managers, who in turn will require a full understanding of the moral and technical complexities of assessing and managing risk.

REFERENCES

Association of Chief Officers of Probation (1994) *Guidance on Management of Risk and Public Protection*. Wakefield: Association of Chief Officers of Probation.

Beck, U. (1992) *Risk Society: Towards a New Modernity*. London: Sage.

Casey, M. (1996) 'Lifers and the sex offender treatment programme.' *Prison Report 34*, 24.

Cowburn, M. and Modi, P. (1995) 'Justice in an unjust context: implications for working with adult male sex offenders.' In D. Ward and M. Lacey (eds) *Probation: Working for Justice*. London: Whiting and Birch.

Creamer, A. and Williams, B. (1996) 'Risk prediction and criminal justice.' In G. McIvor (ed) *Working with Offenders*. London: Jessica Kingsley Publishers.

Creighton, S. and King, V. (1996) 'The law relating to prisoners.' *Legal Action*, March, 16–18.

Douglas, M. (1992) *Risk and Blame: Essays in Cultural Theory*. London: Routledge.

Dyer, C. (1996) 'New blow for Howard over Bulger.' *The Guardian*, 31 July.

Feeley, M. and Simon, J. (1994) 'Actuarial justice: the emerging new criminal law.' In D. Nelken (ed) *The Futures of Criminology*. London: Sage.

Fielding, N. and Fowles, T. (1995) 'Penal Policy File no. 57.' *Howard Journal 34*, 2.

Fielding, N. and Fowles, T. (1996) 'Penal Policy File no. 60.' *Howard Journal 35*, 1.

Floud, J. and Young, W. (1981) *Dangerousness and Criminal Justice*. London: Heinemann.

Garland, D. (1990) *Punishment and Modern Society*. Oxford: Clarendon.

Giddens, A. (1991) *Modernity and Self-identity: Self and Society in the Late Modern Age*. Cambridge: Polity.

Hudson, B.A. (1996) *Understanding Justice*. Buckingham: Open University Press.

Her Majesty's Inspectorate of Prisons (1995) *Report of the Chief Inspector of Prisons for England and Wales, April 1994-March 1995*. London: House of Commons Papers no. 760.

Her Majesty's Inspectorate of Probation (1993) *Annual Report 1992–93*. London: Her Majesty's Inspectorate of Probation.

Her Majesty's Inspectorate of Probation (1995) *Dealing with dangerous people: the Probation Service and public protection*. London: Her Majesty's Inspectorate of Probation.

Kemshall, H. (1996a) 'Offender risk and probation practice.' In H. Kemshall and J. Pritchard (eds) *Good Practice in Risk Assessment and Risk Management*. London: Jessica Kingsley Publishers.

Kemshall, H. (1996b) *Reviewing Risk*. London: Research and Statistics Directorate, Home Office.

Kemshall, H. (1996c) 'Risk assessment: fuzzy thinking or "decisions in action".' *Probation Journal 43*, 1, 2–7.

Lash, S. and Wynne, B. (1992) 'Introduction.' In U. Beck, *Risk Society: Towards a New Modernity*. London: Sage.

Liebling, A. (1992) *Suicides in Prison*. London: Routledge.

Liebling, A. (1994) 'Suicide amongst women prisoners.' *Howard Journal 33*, 1, 1–9.

Morris, A., Wilkinson, C., Tisi, A., Woodrow, J. and Rockley, A. (1995) *Managing the Needs of Female Prisoners*. Research and Planning Unit, Home Office.

Parton, N. (1996) 'Social work, risk and "the blaming system".' In N. Parton (ed) *Social Theory, Social Change and Social Work*. London: Routledge.

Phillips, J. (1996) 'Crime and older offenders.' *Practice 8*, 1, 43–54.

Her Majesty's Prison Service (undated) *Drug Misuse in Prison*. Home Office.

Her Majesty's Prison Service (undated a) *National framework for the throughcare of offenders in custody to the completion of supervision in the community*. Home Office.

Ralli, R. (1994) 'Health care in prisons.' In E. Player and M. Jenkins (eds) *Prisons after Woolf: Reform Through Riot*. London: Routledge.

Sampson, A. (1994) 'The future for sex offenders in prison.' In E. Player and M. Jenkins (eds) *Prisons after Woolf: Reform Through Riot*. London: Routledge.

Shaw, R. (1996) 'Supervising the dangerous in the community.' In N. Walker (ed) *Dangerous People*. London: Blackstone.

Simon, J. (1988) 'The ideological effects of actuarial practices.' *Law and Society Review 22*, 4, 772–800.

Smallman, C. (1996) 'Risk and organisational behaviour: a research model.' *Disaster Prevention and Management 5*, 2, 12–16.

Sparks, R. (1994) 'Can prisons be legitimate?' *British Journal of Criminology 34*, Special issue, 14–28.

Sumner, C. (1994) *The Sociology of Deviance: an Obituary.* Buckingham: Open University Press.

Taylor, J.M. (1995) 'The resurrection of the "dangerous classes".' *Journal of Prisoners on Prisons 6*, 2, 7–16.

Williams, B. (1991) *Work with Prisoners.* Birmingham: Venture Press.

Williams, B. (1995) 'Probation values in work with prisoners.' In B. Williams (ed) *Probation Values.* Birmingham: Venture Press.

Williams, B. (1996a) *Counselling in Criminal Justice.* Buckingham: Open University Press.

Williams, B. (1996b) 'The Probation Service and victims of crime: paradigm shift or cop-out?' *Journal of Social Welfare and Family Law 18*, 4, 461–474.

The advice and help of Liz Dixon, Hazel Kemshall, Nigel Parton and Sue Roberts in preparing this chapter is gratefully acknowledged.

CHAPTER 17

Risk, Domestic Violence and Probation Practice

Katherine Beattie

Since the imposition of the Criminal Justice Act 1991, the Probation Service has increasingly operated under a new centrally-led agenda, shedding its 'rehabilitative' focus and taking its place '...as one of the five agencies of an increasingly centralized and managed justice system.' (Kemshall 1996, p.113). The service provided to the courts and the public has been placed before the needs of the offender (Home Office 1992, Kemshall 1996). Probation Officers are now required to make regular risk assessments whilst supervising community sentences and pre-sentence reports (PSRs) must include assessments of the risk of reoffending and of harm to the public (Kemshall 1996b, Home Office 1995a). The assessment and management of risk, particularly in relation to violent offenders, has become a central concern for the Probation Service (Her Majesty's Inspectorate of Probation 1995, Kemshall 1996a).

It is in this climate that there has been the awakening of what Stelman (1993) describes as a 'sudden interest' in domestic violence. Prior to this the general view within the service was that domestic violence was a family problem and peripheral to its work (Sleightholm 1994, Morton 1994). Following a study by Smith (1989) the Home Office issued a policy statement (Home Office circular 60/1990) which was vital in leading the way for the criminal justice agencies, including the probation service. Domestic violence was for the first time viewed officially as seriously as other forms of violent crime, meaning that agencies had to begin to recognise domestic violence perpetrators as 'serious' offenders. Police services began to establish domestic violence units (DVUs), and the Crown Prosecution Service (CPS) published guidelines for prosecution (1993). The Association of Chief Officers of Probation (ACOP 1992) concluded that 'women have not attained equal opportunities in society, and there is a need to examine probation practice to find out how far it contributes to these inequalities.' The inter-agency circular on domestic violence (Home Office 1995b) sealed the position for the probation service, placing it firmly alongside other key statutory and voluntary agencies in 'tackling' domestic violence. Hearn (1996) makes the important point that whilst many agencies have involvement with male domestic violence perpetrators '...few specialize in, or have men's violence as their main concern.' (p.111).

Whilst focusing more clearly on public concerns, the service has had to conduct its work with 'due regard for the safety of victims' (Home Office 1995b) rather than concentrating exclusively on offenders (Home Office 1996, Probation Circular 77/1994, Home Office 1994a,b). In 1993 the Home Affairs Select Committee concluded that the probation service is in a unique position within the criminal justice system to work with survivors and perpetrators of domestic violence (Sleightholm 1994, Stelman 1993). The inter-agency circular (Home Office 1995b) noted that 'Probation staff come into contact with abused women under supervision, and the partners or mothers of abusers under supervision.'

Before continuing it is important to define what constitutes domestic violence. Stordeur and Stille (1989) refer to the controversy surrounding attempts to define what is meant by the terminology. There is not the space here to review the debates but, in retaining the use of the term 'domestic violence', I note some of the specific criticisms that have been made. Domestic violence has been criticised as vague or ambiguous, victims can be seen as equally responsible as the perpetrators. It has also been used pejoratively to separate violence in the home from other crimes, the view that it is only a domestic has been difficult to eradicate. The term 'domestic violence', also obscures the fact that violence is directed predominantly at women, and children, by men (Heidensohn 1989, Pahl 1985, Smith 1989, Stordeur and Stille 1989, Dobash and Dobash 1992, Pence and Paymar 1993). Physical and sexual assault is '…one act in a continuum of controlling behaviours whereby a male maintains power over his female partner in a relationship.' (Stordeur and Stille 1989, p.20). Pence and Paymar (1993) use the power and control wheel to demonstrate the tactics perpetrators use:

> A batterer's use of physical assaults or sexual abuse is often infrequent, but it reinforces the power of the other tactics on the wheel (e.g. emotional abuse, isolation, threats of taking the children) that are used at random and eventually undermine his partner's ability to act autonomously. (p.2).

It is therefore important that any definition of domestic violence should include the variety of controlling behaviours used by male perpetrators. To this end the definition used by the Women's Aid Federation (1992) in their evidence to the Home Affairs Select Committee is useful:

> Domestic violence may, and often does, include a range of abusive behaviours, not all of which are in themselves inherently violent. Violence can mean among other things: threat, intimidation, manipulation, isolation, keeping women without money, locked in, deprived of food, or using (and abusing) her children in various ways to frighten her or enforce compliance. It can also include systematic and belittling comments…sometimes the abuser's behaviour fluctuates wildly; he may offer rewards on certain conditions, or in an attempt to persuade his partner that the abuse will never happen again. (p.97).

I do not deny that violence may take place in lesbian or gay relationships, or that women may be violent, but, given the overwhelming evidence that most domestic violence is perpetrated by men in heterosexual relationships, it is vital that we first consider the risks to women and children in this context. In addition, I recognise the claim by women to be described as survivors rather than victims (Marchant 1993, 1993a). Physical assaults include spitting, pinching, slapping and hair pulling, as well as the more 'severe' forms: choking, punching, and stabbing (Stordeur and Stille 1989, Pence and Paymar 1993). Sexual assaults include '...physical attacks on the victim's breasts or genitals, coerced sexual activity accompanied by threats of violence, or sexual assault or rape.' (Stordeur and Stille 1989, p.8 (see also Hester and Radford 1996)). Stordeur and Stille also note that legal definitions in most cases focus only on assaultive acts that lead to visible injury. Hester and Radford point out that '...there is very little in the way of legal remedy or professional understanding of the effects of emotional, psychological or verbal abuse.' (p.7).

The Leeds Inter Agency Project has adapted a model describing '...types of violence carried out on prisoners in concentration camps to divide the types of domestic violence perpetrated by men.' (Ingram 1993, pp.18–19). Stelman (1993) identifies four respects in which domestic violence differs from other types of crime, these must be considered by practitioners when assessing risks. First, the offence occurs within the home, the '...most private of institutions.' Second, the offender has total control over the environment in which the violence occurs. Third, the offender and victim share the '...closest possible relationship.' This relationship will add to the complexities faced by the woman. Fourth, escape for the woman is difficult or impossible, she may be forced to leave her home if she is to get away from the violence. I believe that there is a fifth dimension in that alongside sexual crime survivors have to live with suggestions that they may be at fault in some way and experience less understanding than, for example, the victim of a random violent attack perpetrated in public by a stranger. Given all of these factors, it is hardly surprising that survivors have specific needs and to get free takes a long time (Victim Support 1992).

Domestic violence is not a chance occurrence with causes that can simply be located with individuals. Pro-feminist theorists argue that it is a historic legacy of the relationships sanctioned by the justice system, our religious bodies and the community (Dobash and Dobash 1992). Those relationships seen as acceptable are based on the unequal divisions of society, particularly along lines of gender. It was not until 1878 that the legal right of a man to beat his wife with a stick no thicker than his thumb was removed (Smith 1989, Kennedy 1992, Hearn 1996). That year Francis Power Cobbe said: 'The notion that a man's wife is his property in the sense in which a horse is his property...is the fatal root of incalculable evil and misery.' (Smith 1989, p.4).

Despite the removal of a man's legal right to chastise his wife physically, cultural approval remains (Hague and Malos 1993, Pence and Paymar 1993). Women have campaigned against this approval and its consequences throughout this century, beginning with the suffragettes in the early 1900s (Smith 1989, Hearn 1996). Later, women focused on the family (Eaton 1986) and the legal system (Smart 1989, Heidensohn 1989, Carlen 1990). However, mistakes have been made and Black women have criticised the women's movement as focusing only on issues relevant to White women, forcing feminists to re-evaluate some of their core principles (Bryan, Dadzie and Scafe 1985, Mama 1989, 1992, Bhatti-Sinclair 1994). It is clear that Black and South Asian survivors have to face the additional oppression of racism on a daily basis. Their difficulties will only be compounded if they encounter practitioners who uphold damaging and oppressive stereotypes, and fail to allow them to define their needs.

To more accurately assess risks we need actuarial data (Kemshall 1996a). The identification of accurate numbers of perpetrators amongst the population is not an easy exercise. The figures we do have relate to the numbers of victims. Domestic violence is the most under-reported crime (Smith 1989, Morley and Mullender 1994). Figures of incidence have been obscured by the way that crimes are classified and researchers and campaigners are conclusive that any figures we have represent only the 'tip of the iceberg' (Edwards 1989, Dobash and Dobash 1992, Tuck 1992, Stelman 1993, Hearn 1996). This is confirmed by Dobash and Dobash (1992) who suggest that only two per cent of assaults are reported to the police, and the Women's Aid Federation who believe that a woman will be assaulted up to thirty five times before seeking help. Every week two women are murdered by current or ex-partners (Harwin 26/6/96). Home Office figures suggest that one in four women has been struck by her partner, and domestic violence accounts for a quarter of all reported violent incidents in the United Kingdom (NCH Action for Children 1994, Labour Party 1995). Risks to women increase whilst they are pregnant; violence may first occur or increase during pregnancy and can result in bleeding, miscarriages and premature births (Dobash and Dobash 1980, Morley and Mullender 1994, Hester and Radford 1996).

So what is known about perpetrators? Stordeur and Stille (1989) argue that: 'Batterers have been found to come from all socio-economic backgrounds, occupations, races or religions.' (p.21). They believe that a significant number commit violent offences outside the home and in other relationships with women. This must be considered in a risk assessment. Very few men will admit to perpetrating domestic violence, the number and gravity of assaults and level of their controlling behaviours. Stordeur and Stille (1989) cite a study by Briere (1987) who sampled a 'normal' population of male college students and found that 79 per cent said they would use physical violence against their wives or partners in at least one given context. As a result of this study, Briere (1987) suggested a correlation between endorsement of the use of force against women and negative attitudes towards women, attitudes supporting wife abuse and attitudes supporting interpersonal violence (Stordeur and Stille 1989, p.21).

RISK AND CHILD PROTECTION ISSUES

It is a myth that domestic violence is an activity kept discreet from children, indeed studies have begun to argue that '...In all probability [woman] battering is the single most important context for child abuse.' (Stark and Flitcraft 1985, p.165). Child protection is an area where professionals have grossly underestimated the risks to children by locating the problem of violence very firmly with women. Children have been used to persuade mothers to stay with violent men, as professionals have believed that the men do not pose a risk to anyone other than their partner. This has, on occasion, led to child deaths (Children's Legal Centre 1992, O'Hara 1993). For those children who survive, studies highlight the damaging consequences of their experiences of domestic violence (NCH Action for Children 1994, Saunders 1995, Morley and Mullender 1995, Hester and Radford 1996). In her study, Maynard (1985) found the following entry in a social work case file: 'She was thinking of leaving her husband again. Pointed out that she had Christopher [son] to consider in this and her husband's feelings for the baby and herself. Reminded her that she had married and had to accept the consequences.' (p.130). According to Maynard this response was not unusual. O'Hara (1993) cites a study that found that men who beat their wives also physically abused their children in 70 per cent of cases where children were in the home. Stordeur and Stille (1989) cite a number of suggested figures, ranging from 12, to 57 per cent. Hester and Radford (1996) interviewed 53 women in England, and found that 21 reported that their children had been physically or sexually abused by fathers. Where evidence of direct physical or sexual abuse does not exist, studies have made some findings of great concern, for example Morley and Mullender (1994) cite one finding that '...almost all the children they interviewed could give detailed descriptions of violence that their parents were not aware they had witnessed.' (p.8).

Dobash and Dobash et al. (1985) found that there are a number of inhibitors that prevent women from seeking help from the statutory (formal) services. Maynard (1985) argued, similarly, that lack of knowledge about formal agencies, and the fear that their children will be removed, often prevents women from disclosing that they are subjected to violence. Bhatti-Sinclair (1994) found that Black women have their experiences marginalised and receive even less support than their White counterparts. In my own experience whilst supervising women on probation, who are survivors living with a violent partner, a number have told me that it is too painful to them to fully acknowledge the effects of their partner's violence on their children as they know that when they do they will have to leave. Harwin (ACOP 1994) has argued that in the end it is an over-riding concern for their children that prompts many women to leave their violent partner. Probation Officers can face dilemmas when considering child protection issues. When I undertook a study within the West Midlands Probation Service (WMPS), I found that whilst officers acknowledged that they had some issues of concern if children were present when a man was violent towards his partner, there was little acknowledgement of risk if they were not physically injured and were in a different room. But how do we really know that children are safe? Do we take the perpetrators word for it when he says the children are always in bed or in another room when he is violent? And even if they are, we know that it is likely they will hear what is happening to their mother and see the other forms of controlling behaviour exhibited by her partner. Furthermore, Hester and Radford (1996) found that children of all ages had intervened to try to stop their father's violence or were forced to take part in the abuse of their mother despite their protestations and crying. We do need to be clear who poses a risk to the children. O'Hara (1993) disputes the tendency to assume that battered women pose the greatest risk to their children:

> ...suggests that generally non-abusing parents are one of the best sources of support for children recovering emotionally from abuse... When both children and their mothers are being abused it is in the children's interests for child protection professionals to try to make an alliance with the mother and give her practical and emotional support in protecting both her children and herself... (p.19).

I have supervised women clients who have had their children placed on the child protection register after a culmination of violent acts by their partner and have co-operated in the hope that they will at last receive specific support in dealing with their experiences of violence. The notion of forming an alliance with mothers is important, however I believe that support needs to come early and be specific. Agencies are beginning to work more closely together but there is room for improvement (I will return to this later). If we can answer the questions, what is the risk? To whom is it posed? And if we consider the overwhelming evidence of the impact of domestic violence on children, then it is clear that we should have the protection of children as a primary concern. This may result in competing priorities: do we protect the mother's needs over her children's needs? Can we deal with the discomfort we experience if the answer to this is no? In the end best practice must involve the building of an alliance with the mother in an environment where she can receive a co-ordinated and supportive service from local agencies enabling her, where possible, to make the decisions regarding protection.

CASE STUDY

John is allocated to a probation officer as a throughcare case. He is serving an eighteen-month custodial sentence for an offence of assault occasioning actual bodily harm (AOABH). He has previous convictions for AOABH, drive excess alcohol and drive whilst disqualified. The Pre-Sentence Report indicates that John's offence took place outside a night-club and that alcohol has been a feature in each of his offences. John has a partner, Andrea, a son aged four, Tom, and Andrea is expecting a baby. The officer notes from the case records that John's previous throughcare officer responded to numerous requests by him to visit Andrea but did not return as she was hostile.

The officer visits John. He perceives himself to be a victim of the system, feeling that his sentence is unfair. He talks of this at length and blocks any attempts to examine his violent behaviour. John insists he is not a violent man, this was a one-off, he was drunk and was acting in self-defence. John asks the officer to visit Andrea. He says she is having difficulty in coping without him, particularly as she cannot control Tom who is very naughty. Andrea has a history of depression and has been given tranquillisers. He feels that she might be becoming ill again. He requests a full 'report' of the officer's impressions after the home visit.

When the officer meets Andrea, in contrast to the image that John has created, she presents as relaxed and well. The home environment is very peaceful. Tom is playing quite happily. The officer notices that Tom is reluctant to talk about his father but decides it is because he misses him. Andrea tells the officer that she has not taken anti-depressants for some time and seems surprised at John's suggestion that she is becoming ill again. She feels she is coping very well in John's absence and says Tom is settling well into nursery. Her only wish is that she was not so isolated, she has lost contact with her friends and family since moving to the flat with John. Andrea says that she would like the officer to visit her again and seems keen on the suggestion that she is linked with a volunteer.

The officer feels that the case is 'ticking along nicely' until John applies for home leave so that he can be at home when the baby is due. When undertaking the enquiry the officer visits Andrea, who is distressed and anxious. She says that she is frightened at the prospect of John coming home but cannot tell him she wants to end the relationship. She knows that the officer does not think he is violent, but he has beaten her for years; the abuse began within a week of them living together. She indicates that the attacks have increased in severity and last time he attempted to strangle her. The police have come out numerous times and the neighbours have complained about 'the rows' to the housing department. Their son has witnessed some of the assaults, including an incident when John raped her. He has told his teacher that he does not like his daddy because 'he hurts mummy.' Andrea says her loss of contact with family and friends is due to John's behaviour. He does not like her talking to anyone except him and times her when she goes out. During his sentence Andrea says John has telephoned her at random intervals; she has had to explain herself if she has not answered the phone. In addition, he has questioned her at length about her conversations with the probation officer. She asks the officer not to tell John that she has said these things about him, but is there anything that can be done to help her?

ASSESSMENT AND INTERVENTION ISSUES

In recent years there have been a number of groupwork initiatives established to work with domestic violence perpetrators (Scourfield 1995). Many are based on North American models such as that developed by the Domestic Abuse Intervention programme (DAIP) in Duluth (Pence and Paymar 1993), for example the Stirling Change project (Dobash *et al.* 1996), West Midlands Probation Service (WMPS) domestic violence intervention group Wolverhampton (Davies *et al.* 1996) and Devon Probation/Icthus domestic violence intervention (Annual Report 1996). As an intrinsic part of this work, full risk assessments are made of perpetrators. However, there are a significant number of domestic violence perpetrators within probation caseloads who are in effect 'hidden' – men whose index offence is not domestic violence, who may never have been convicted of such an offence, but are perpetrating this crime. A case-scan undertaken by Merseyside Probation Service (1992) labelled these cases as 'informal.' The results of a small study I undertook within the WMPS suggested a correlation between officers' interest and level of awareness of domestic violence with the numbers of men they suspected of perpetrating domestic violence. Though some officers are identifying the issue, it seems that probation services have yet to fully accept the levels of risk posed by hidden perpetrators. If we accept that known perpetrators present a risk to their partners, children and the public, then it follows that hidden perpetrators will pose the same, if not greater, risk as they are unlikely to be receiving the appropriate and necessary intervention. Undoubtedly there would be resource implications if services were to identify hidden perpetrators on a larger scale and respond to the levels of risk they pose. There is a flipside to this as: 'Showing that domestic violence will not be tolerated and helping women and their children to escape from it, could be the most important crime prevention strategy that society could undertake.' (Tuck 1992, p.131).

So how can we identify hidden perpetrators and make a more accurate assessment of risk than John's officer made ? The following suggestions are based on models used by Megargee (1976), Monahan (1981), Stordeur and Stille (1989), Limandri and Sheriden (1995) and Kemshall (1996a, 1996b). If we begin with Kemshall's proposed model of risk assessment, it is clear that John's probation officer used a clinical assessment of risk and focused on his rehabilitative needs rather than focusing on public safety. Thus it was impossible to predict future violence more accurately (Kemshall 1996a). Workers need to question and scrutinise their values and beliefs to ensure they are not 'supporting' violence in any way (Dobash et al. 1985, Stordeur and Stille 1989, Pence and Paymar 1993). John's probation officer has taken his information at face value and, in fact, he has lied. As a result, the relationship between them has become collusive. Increasingly, links are being made between the similarities in working with sex offenders and domestic violence perpetrators (Scourfield 1995). Literature on both identifies the congruency of beliefs and attitudes held by clients and male workers (Stordeur and Stille 1989, Mark 1992, Perry 1993, Pence and Paymar 1993). Male workers and clients share the patriarchal power base but the difference between them is the degree that clients hold the stereotypical beliefs and attitudes and the extent to which they use them to inform and justify their behaviour. Pence and Paymar (1993) suggest that 'the tactics used by batterers reflect the tactics used by many groups or individuals in positions of power.' (p.2).

One male Probation Officer in my study said:

> There's a degree of comfortableness if you're being supervised by a white male, and you are a white male who has abused your partner. I think you have to flag up very early and very consistently I'm not going to sit here and listen to you use inappropriate language and descriptions, and I'm not going to allow you to marginalise the victim which men can do very well. (Beattie 1994, p.68–69)

Collusion may not be a male phenomenon. Women officers I interviewed in my study identified three forms of collusion, two related to lack of confidence or not challenging where domestic violence was suspected. There may be complex reasons for this stemming from officers own experiences or feelings of intimidation and fear engendered by perpetrators. Perrott (1994) highlights the impact of working with perpetrators on women staff. The third identified the pressure of a high caseload and said:

It's hard to discuss any issues of men's abuse of women. I think we're just like anybody else, we can cop out when we want to, it makes it easier. On a Monday when I see ten people…if I want to channel them in and out as quickly as possible I don't want to be having in depth discussions. I want to have a quick session, focus on offending behaviour, set some homework, and sod them off out of the office, and see the next person…I've got to bring them up, bring them down, and get them out of the office in such a way that they don't go home angry about talking about violence towards their partner, and then beat her… (Beattie 1994, p.69)

There has been some discussion as to the most appropriate methods of intervention with domestic violence perpetrators. Pro-feminist theorists argue that group work is the most suitable method and warn against couple counselling, which enables perpetrators to continue their abuse overtly and covertly (Stordeur and Stille 1989, Hague and Malos 1993, Pence and Paymar 1993). One-to-one work as a method of intervention is criticised: 'By its nature individual therapy tends to be a supportive environment. In effect, counsellors may end up colluding with batterers and supporting their justifications and continued use of power' (Stordeur and Stille 1989, p.56). If services were to adopt a policy of co-working all domestic violence cases, at which point would a co-worker be introduced if a client was a hidden perpetrator? Kemshall (1996) has argued that actuarial data alone is insufficient in predicting violence and notes the criticisms of the use of violence predictors. Violence predictors can never be 100 per cent accurate, however I would argue that they do provide us with a starting point to analyse a case and, used with a combination of clinical and actuarial information, enable us to assess risk. The following headings are a combination of those suggested by Monahan (1981, 1984), Limandri and Sheriden (1995) and Stordeur and Stille (1989).

Previous Behaviour

John has a previous conviction for violence. Without his antecedents, a list of previous convictions alone will not give us an indication of the race or gender of his victims. The probation officer would need to explore this. John has maintained his current offence is a 'one-off' despite his previous conviction. From the information supplied by Andrea, and the actuarial data regarding the repeat victimisation of domestic violence survivors, we can assess it likely that John will perpetrate further offences of domestic violence. Furthermore, Andrea is at increased risk of violence from John whilst she is pregnant (Dobash and Dobash 1980, Morley and Mullender 1994, Hester and Radford 1995). This risk can only be reduced with appropriate intervention and, in basic terms, an acceptance by John of his own responsibility for his violence. It will not be reduced by Andrea leaving him as John will pose a risk to any other women with whom he has relationships. Exploration of John's attitudes towards Andrea, and other women, would reveal useful information for an assessment. It is suggested that: 'Many assaultive men do have a set of stereotypic attitudes and beliefs related to what men are supposed to be like and how women should be subservient to men. They also appear to have a callous attitude toward others pain and suffering.' (Stordeur and Stille 1989, p.52, also Pence and Paymar 1993).

Substance Misuse as an Associated Factor

Some perpetrators attribute their violent behaviour to alcohol or drug misuse. However, rather than being a causal factor, men who are already predisposed to violence are more likely to behave violently when misusing substances (Stordeur and Stille 1989, Pence and Paymar 1993). De-toxification treatment will not remove a man's propensity to violence. Furthermore, it is argued that substances fulfil a useful role for perpetrators and give them a feeling of power. Stordeur and Stille (1989) suggest that: 'Batterers also admit that they sometimes use alcohol in some situations in order to batter. Not only does the alcohol provide a disinhibiting influence, but after the incident these men can blame their abusive behaviour on the alcohol.' (p.42).

For officers assessing risks there are factors that need to be considered. Men are likely to inflict more serious injuries whilst under the influence of alcohol or drugs. It has also been found that substances can be administered to women by perpetrators in an abusive way as an additional means of diminishing their control, for example during a sexual assault (Mezey 1995).

Availability of Weapons

We know that domestic violence attacks generally increase in severity over time. Stordeur and Stille (1989) argue that the use of weapons is significant if assessing the lethality of a situation and give detailed questions that practitioners should ask. For example, how life threatening has his violence been, does he typically use weapons, what kinds of situations have been triggers for his most severe abuse? Hester and Radford (1996) found in their study that: 'Some of the men, particularly in rural areas in England, had access to firearms and had threatened to use these on the women.' (p.7). However, what we define as a weapon is important. I have worked with survivors who have been assaulted with a range of household items including bottles, cutlery, and pans; in addition to belts, chains, knives and guns. One of the perpetrators I worked with admitted to using a telephone to assault his partner, another used a car jack. Stordeur and Stile (1989) also point out that part of our assessment must include questioning if the perpetrator has been in situations where violence is 'normalised' and he has received training, for example in the armed forces or as a bouncer/doorman.

Proximity to Victims

The proximity that perpetrators have to their victim is one of the factors that makes this offence different (Stelman 1992). We have to assess a partner as potentially at risk whenever she is near the perpetrator. Kelly (1988) describes some of the coping mechanisms women adopt in order to deal with the level of risk they face from their partner and the uncertainty about when he will next be violent. Even if a man is not violent for a length of time, his partner will never know for sure he is not going to assault her; he can maintain this level of fear with overt or covert threats. Research has shown that the risks to women continue after separation, they '...may be most at risk of domestic homicide directly after separating from the abuser.' (Jones 1991, p.8). Hester and Radford (1996) point out that post-separation violence is usually linked to child contact and happens at a time when women are '...least likely to be given support or protection from Court Welfare Officers and other professionals involved in child contact.' (p.8).

Race and Gender

The race or ethnic origin of a perpetrator does not provide us with a violence predictor, however I would suggest that it can provide officers with a specific set of factors to consider in assessment and intervention. Mama (1989) points out that none of the world's major religious texts actively challenge the abuse of women, but neither do they condone it. Yet despite ACOP (1992) warning against the notion that violence towards Black women or women from minority ethnic communities is acceptable because of 'quasi-cultural' factors, I found in my study that a significant number of White officers felt their service delivery was affected if perpetrators came from a different racial, cultural or ethnic background to themselves. The following words of one officer reflect their responses: 'A particularly difficult client group to work with is those who have come to Britain to live, after being raised in a country where violence to women considered to be misbehaving is the norm.' (Beattie 1994, p.51). Officers who believed this indicated that they did not challenge Black and South Asian perpetrators, or those from a minority ethnic community, because of a 'lack of understanding' of their racial, cultural or ethnic background. The responsibility for clear communication was placed very firmly on the client, with officers indicating that they believed perpetrators were using 'language barriers' to avoid challenge. There seemed to be little sign of the use of appropriate interpreters despite a provision for this service. I would argue that this is a dangerous stance to take, because to become 'bound up' in quasi-cultural and racist mythologies results in the adoption of: '...spurious rationales for justifying violence as a convenient means of allowing it to continue, rather than facing the difficulties and complexities of seeking its elimination.' (Dobash and Dobash 1992, pp.53–54). I have already argued that in White western cultures, domestic violence has traditionally been condoned and accepted. Research has shown that the criminal justice system operates along racist and oppressive lines, resulting in disproportionate numbers of Black people being imprisoned (NACRO 1986, Smellie and Crow 1991, Stern 1987). If, in the case study, John was Black, his experiences of racism may have shaped his belief that he was a victim of the system. However, this would not make his violence towards Andrea acceptable. Furthermore, it has been found that Black women and women from minority ethnic communities may be reluctant to contact the police or other 'White authorities' to disclose that they are being subjected to domestic violence: 'Experience has told them to expect racist treatment, and they may feel that they have 'betrayed' their whole community if they talk about the abuse they have received from their partners.' (Women's Aid Federation 1992, p.98, see also Hague and Malos 1993). Perhaps Andrea's reluctance to disclose she was subject to domestic violence was compounded by this reason. Thus for Black women, or women from other minority ethnic communities, who are subjected to violence by 'hidden perpetrators', officers need to be aware that disclosure will carry additional difficulties and they and their children will need services that are culturally sensitive to their needs. In addition to oppression on a personal level, they will also have experiences of racism on an institutional level, for example the 12-month immigration rule that means women from minority ethnic communities without British citizenship face deportation if they leave a violent marriage in the first twelve months. Best practice will mean that officers do not make assumptions about any survivors needs, particularly those based on stereotypes (Mama 1989, Women's Aid Federation 1992, Hague and Malos 1993, Bhatti-Sinclair 1994).

For reasons argued earlier, this chapter has only focused on male violence against women in heterosexual relationships. The pro-feminist theorists I have cited argue that it is in this context that women are most at risk of violence. More recently, the subject of women who perpetrate abuse – particularly of a sexual nature against children – has prompted a debate amongst feminists (Cameron 1996, Platt 1996). For example, Cameron (1996) says: '...Rose West challenges *everyone's* most cherished beliefs about women, and for feminists she poses a particular dilemma. Assuming we do not think she was wrongly convicted, what does it mean that these horrific crimes were committed by a woman.' (p.22). Women who perpetrate abuse are seen as either mad or evil figures because they have departed from their ascribed gender roles (Cameron 1996, Platt 1996). There is not the space in this chapter to open up this debate. However, in discussing the difficulty many people have in accepting that women can and do abuse, Platt (1996) suggests that '...The sticking point is the question of whether women initiate abuse or are forced into it by men.' (p.21). This is particularly pertinent in a domestic violence situation. Pence and Paymar (1993) argue that: 'Most men who live with women who are violent are abusing the women who have assaulted them and can end the violence against them by stopping the violence or leaving the relationship.' (p.6). This is clearly a controversial point. There has been a pattern amongst the women I have worked with who have been violent towards a male partner, or in some cases killed him, that their actions have been in response to sustained violence perpetrated by him. Survivors in this situation have frequently told me that they blame themselves, believing they would not be beaten if they were more placid and compliant. We do not have research evidence in this country suggesting the numbers of women who do perpetrate violence against their female, or male partners, or the reasons for their behaviour. However, I would argue that whilst the debate regarding women perpetrators must inevitably take place, it needs to be discussed separately to the issue of male power, control and violence against women; otherwise it can be used to distort and detract the focus away from what is, in fact, a huge social problem.

Socio-Economic Status

We have already seen that women from all socio-economic backgrounds are at risk of domestic violence from their partners. John's employment status prior to his prison sentence is not given. However, if he were unemployed there would be a number of factors that would inform risk assessment. Stordeur and Stille (1989), in reviewing studies on the subject, have found that in some cases domestic violence has been associated with unemployment. There may be a number of reasons for this. Alongside social services departments (SSDs) the probation service tends to have most contact with clients from the most disadvantaged sectors of society, who have less access to stable employment and incomes. Men who are unemployed are likely to spend greater amounts of time at home, increasing the opportunity for violence. Believing they should be the family breadwinner, some men may feel that their status is undermined by unemployment. If their partner has a job giving her contact with other people or she has superior skills, this will be perceived as threatening their ability to control (Stordeur and Stille 1989).

Behavioural Traits

These will be divided into two distinct areas: psychological defence mechanisms, and individual traits or personality characteristics. 'Most batterers use some form of the defence mechanisms of minimization, denial, and projection of blame onto others of their circumstances.' (Stordeur and Stille 1989, p.41). Thus they can abdicate responsibility for their behaviour and avoid feeling guilty or ashamed. In John's case, his portrayal of himself as a victim of the system was a defence mechanism. Officers in my study within the WMPS identified a number of different defence mechanisms that perpetrators used on a one-to-one basis – including attempts to charm the officer, personal racist and sexist comments, verbally abusive language and intimidating and physically threatening behaviour.

INDIVIDUAL TRAITS/PERSONALITY CHARACTERISTICS:

Whilst suggesting these characteristics, Stordeur and Stille (1989) caution practitioners not to assume that they will be demonstrated by all perpetrators.

DEPENDENCY AND JEALOUSY

Perpetrators often have difficulty in forming equal, mature friendships and are therefore overly dependent on their partners (Stordeur and Stile 1989). Survivors talk about 'mind games' that are a form of emotional abuse, for example they are told what to wear and then criticised or they may be constantly accused of having an affair; perpetrators will use jealousy to justify their actions. By making accusations and objectifying their partner, they give themselves permission to assault her (Pence and Paymar 1993). Many survivors say that they find emotional and verbal abuse harder to cope with than physical violence. Hester and Radford (1996) point out that 'mental torture' does not leave physical signs and is '…not often seen or heard by others.' (p.7). When supervising survivors of domestic violence, officers will not be able to apply national standards rigidly. I have supervised women who have been timed whilst out of the house or have arrived at the office closely followed by their partner who has stood just outside. A focus on the safety of women survivors in all my interactions has also been vital as I have found that their partners have demanded to know what they have talked about whilst with me.

DEPRESSION

In reviewing a number of studies, Stordeur and Stille (1989) suggest that:

> ...the depression we see in assaultive men tends to be related to the remorse they present on entering treatment, or to separation, or the threat of losing the person to whom they are dependent. When batterers manage to convince their partners to return to the relationship the depression lifts quickly. When experiencing this panic however, these men may be suicidal. (p.47)

In the case study, Andrea had some history of depression. However, John used this to manipulate the officer into visiting her out of concern. Domestic violence has been linked to the high numbers of women receiving tranquillisers; one in four survivors are prescribed them. Thirty per cent of suicide attempts are made by survivors and 25 per cent of women admitted for emergency hospital treatment are experiencing violence from known men (all figures from Ingram 1993/4). Au and Bau (1991) identify domestic violence as one of the factors behind a high proportion of Bengali women being admitted to a London hospital for psychiatric treatment.

SELF-ESTEEM

The abusive behaviour of domestic violence perpetrators is directed at eroding the self-esteem of their partners (Pence and Paymar 1993). Many perpetrators initially present as overly confident, but on close examination: '...their sense of inadequacy becomes apparent.' (Stordeur and Stile 1989, p.35). It is argued that low self-esteem does not lead to battering, though it is believed to be linked to the dependency of perpetrators and their need to control. However it is suggested that '...battering lowers self-esteem.' (Stordeur and Stille 1989, p.35).

'JEKYLL AND HYDE'

When describing their initial attraction to their partner, many of the survivors I have worked with recall a time when he was loving and caring. They have told me: 'I know what he is doing is wrong but I know he has a nice side.' Stordeur and Stille (1989) believe that the charming side of perpetrators is one of the methods they use to manipulate women. 'At times this charm almost appears to be a parody of true affection, and often reflects a traditional, stereotypic notion of romance, rather than intimacy.' (p.49). Many women see the 'Hyde' element of their partner's character once they have moved in with them – it might be within days, weeks or months. After a violent incident perpetrators will frequently adopt their charming side to manipulate the woman again and persuade her to stay. This method of manipulation will also be used with practitioners.

Situational Triggers

In making a risk assessment we might assume that we should identify possible situations that might 'spark' violence. However, this is falling into a position of collusion with the perpetrator. Violent men identify external factors that prompt them to perpetrate violence, for example unemployment or oppression due to racism. They may identify more individual 'triggers', for example 'she winds me up, she knows I don't like her friend/mother coming round, the house was a mess, and my dinner wasn't ready'. These are not triggers for violence but are all connected to the perpetrators attitudes, behaviour, and justifications. Stress is often identified as a cause of violence – in reality, perpetrators use violence as a means of temporarily reducing stress. They may experience a physiological high, thus increasing their sense of power. However, 'Battering cannot be explained by the pressure of stress. Focusing on stress reduction (with short-term benefits) is not likely to be a long term solution.' (Stordeur and Stille 1989).

RISK ASSESSMENT, INTERVENTION AND MULTI-AGENCY RESPONSES TO DOMESTIC VIOLENCE

It has been recognised that because domestic violence is a widespread social problem, from Central Government downwards no department or agency can deal with it in isolation (Smith 1989, ACOP 1992, Stelman 1992, Women's Aid Federation 1992, Victim Support 1992, Hague and Malos 1993, Home Office 1995b). Whilst the probation service will have an active role in the legal sanction and punishment or challenge of perpetrators, this alone will not improve the position of survivors. Indeed, the North American models of work with perpetrators, for example the Duluth model (Pence and Paymar 1993), are based upon a solid foundation of co-operation between agencies with a shared aim and common purpose. At the centre of this multi-agency model are the refuges and services for survivors. It is recognised that multi-agency work is not always straightforward. Agencies may have conflicting philosophies, aims and competing resource constraints (Hague and Malos 1993). Women's campaigners, such as the Women's Aid Federation, have long argued that services for survivors must be the priority and hope that multi-agency work is not being promoted by the government as a cheaper alternative to proper provision for women and children (Hague and Malos 1993). Whilst there is no single model for a successful multi-agency initiative, Hague and Malos (1993) believe that there are certain provisos for its success. Voluntary sector agencies, particularly those who take full responsibility for services to survivors, must not be marginalised. Multi-agency work must improve direct services for abused women, raise public awareness and provide a '...firm public message that domestic violence is unacceptable.' (Hague and Malos 1993, p.176). Clear aims, objectives, structures and a sense of purpose are vital, in addition to a focus that is tailored to the requirements of the community.

Inter-agency co-ordination has been the '...appropriate formal and officially sanctioned response' in child abuse cases (Hague and Malos 1993, p.174). As we have seen, it has taken some time for woman abuse to be considered as an issue of concern in child protection. I am struck by the number of times professionals at case conferences have, for the first time, shared information about the dynamics in the relationship between parents. Putting together these pieces of information is vital in identifying 'hazards'. If we look again at the case study, the probation officer could have liased with a number of agencies including the police, local authority housing department, possibly a health visitor or midwife and Tom's school. Each of these agencies would have had information about John's violent behaviour and its impact on Andrea and Tom. Even when women do disclose, I have found that they are sometimes reticent or reluctant to provide a full picture. In addition, these agencies and others would be able to provide a valuable source of support for Andrea. With her agreement, and with the right to attend a network meeting convened by the probation officer, taking on an advocacy role might pre-empt the need for child protection intervention later. In my study officers who were interested in domestic violence as an issue identified a desire to form networks but had difficulty in finding the time to liaise effectively with colleagues in other agencies. I have found the networks I have formed through my involvement with the local domestic violence forum invaluable. It has certainly been easier to advocate for survivors with a known worker in another agency rather than speak to an anonymous official, but has required an initial 'investment' in terms of time. The sharing of knowledge and resources is also valuable within teams, though again I have found through experience and in my study that domestic violence is rarely given space on busy team meeting agendas.

CONCLUSION

Throughout this chapter I have argued that hidden domestic violence perpetrators pose a great risk to their partners, children and to wider society. This risk is currently ignored, or at least is avoided, much of the time. As we have seen, the probation service cannot deal with domestic violence or improve the position of survivors in isolation. However, it can take a valuable role in being part of a multi-agency movement, signifying to society that violence against women and children is unacceptable.

The probation service needs to re-classify the clients to be included within the category of those seen as violent and posing a risk to society. Included within this category of offenders must be men whose index offence is not domestic violence but who are clearly perpetrating this crime. A starting point would be for services to undertake two forms of research: first, to evaluate the numbers of women survivors amongst probation caseloads. Second, to evaluate the numbers of hidden perpetrators currently subject to supervision. I would suggest that morally, once the figures were known, services could not continue to avoid dealing with this issue. Clearly, to 'lift the lid' on hidden perpetrators carries resource implications but services can develop multi-agency initiatives and form links with agencies that can also work with survivors. On an individual level, officers need to be given time to form networks in their local areas as a necessary, indeed vital, aspect of their work. This can be developed so that teams form close links with the services for survivors in their areas and are able to provide women with up-to-date information regarding the support they will receive, for example from the refuge or Domestic Violence Unit. In areas with very little in the way of services for survivors, teams could become more closely involved in working with other agencies to campaign and take responsibility in developing a provision. Services could consider partnership money for agencies who already provide support for survivors or to enable new services to be developed where the need dictates.

The probation service also needs to focus on the training and support of staff working with domestic violence perpetrators and survivors. As Kemshall (1996) has argued '...Training and practice guidance will need to be supported by adequate management systems and appropriate supervision of officers.' (p.142). Because of its nature, domestic violence is an area of work that can impact strongly on workers. It was noticeable whilst undertaking my study that many of the officers I interviewed disclosed that they had personal experiences of domestic violence as children or adults. My study also demonstrated that there are officers with an interest in domestic violence who are working very hard, often in isolation, to support survivors and challenge perpetrators on a one-to-one basis. This is far from ideal. Services need to reconsider methods of intervention with domestic violence perpetrators and establish specific groups (with a pro-feminist theoretical base) and co-working practices.

All probation officers need to be asked to undertake training in domestic violence issues, thus enabling them to take on an advocacy role for survivors and to assess risk and supervise perpetrators effectively. Services need to include clear guidelines on child protection, enabling officers to discuss the issues and dilemmas. Hague and Malos (1993) suggest that one-off training courses must not be seen as the 'miracle cure.' As a starting point, courses would need to be aimed at raising officers' awareness, defining what constitutes domestic violence, providing actuarial data and ensuring that officers are not operating within racist or oppressive stereotypes and myths. Officers need also to be given information to enable them to assist survivors, such as those from minority ethnic communities, who will have specific needs. Services would need to provide training on an annual basis, therefore encouraging officers to develop and improve their practice. Clearly 'basic' training would not meet the needs of everyone. Officers who already have a level of knowledge and expertise would need to be provided with the opportunity to develop their practice further; the use of their skills should be valued and supported.

REFERENCES

Association of Chief Officers of Probation (1992) *Position Statement on Domestic Violence*. London: ACOP.

Au, S. and Bau, H. (1991) 'Hope after hospital.' *Social Work Today* 14.11.91,18.

Beattie, K. (1994) *The Hidden Crime – a picture of Domestic Violence in Probation Officer caseloads within the West Midlands Probation Service*. University of Birmingham: Unpublished.

Bhatti-Sinclair, K. (1994) 'Asian women and violence from male partners.' In C. Lupton and T. Gillespie (eds) *Working with Violence*. London: BASW Macmillan.

Briere, J. (1987) 'Predicting self-reported of battering: attitudes and childhood experiences.' *Journal of Research in Personality* 21, 61–69. cited in R.A. Stordeur and R. Stille (1989) *Ending Men's Violence against their Partners: The Road to Peace.* London: Sage.

Bryan, B., Dadzie, S. and Scafe, S. (1985) *The Heart of the Race – Black Women's Lives in Britain.* London: Virago.

Cameron, D. (1996) 'Wanted: the female serial killer.' *Trouble and Strife 33,* 21–28.

Carlen, P. (1990) *Alternatives to Women's Imprisonment.* Milton Keynes: Open University Press.

Children's Legal Centre (1992) *Children and Domestic Violence.* Report to the Home Affairs Committee Inquiry. London: Children's Legal Centre.

Crown Prosecution Service (1993) *Domestic Violence: A Statement of Prosecution Policy.* London: CPS.

Davies, H., O'Sullivan, E., Sharman, D. and Wallace, C. (1996) *Evaluation of the Domestic violence Perpetrators Programme, Wolverhampton January-April 1996.* Birmingham: West Midlands Probation Service.

Dobash, R.E. and Dobash, R.P. (1980) *Violence against Wives: A Case against the Patriarchy.* Shepton Mallet: Open Books.

Dobash, R.E. and Dobash, R.P. (1992) *Women Violence and Social Change.* London: Routledge.

Dobash, R.E., Dobash, R.P. and Cavanagh, K. (1985) 'The contact between battered women and social and medical agencies.' In J. Pahl (ed) *Private Violence and Public Policy.* London: Routledge Keegan and Paul.

Dobash, R.E., Dobash, R.P., Cavanagh, K. and Lewis, R. (1996) *Re-Education Programmes for Violent Men – an Evaluation.* Research Findings No.46. Research and Statistics Directorate. London: Home Office.

Domestic Violence Intervention (1996) *Annual Report.* 24 Wyndham Square Plymouth PL15EG. St Peters-Icthus.

Eaton, M. (1986) *Justice for Women, Family, Court and Social Control.* Milton Keynes: Open University Press.

Edwards, Susan S.M. (1989) *Policing Domestic Violence: Women the Law and the State.* London: Sage.

Hague. J. and Malos, E. (1993) *Domestic Violence Action for Change.* Cheltenham: New Clarion Press.

Harwin, N. (1994) *How do Women Experience Domestic Violence? What Effect can the Probation Service have on their Situation.* ACOP Transcribed papers Domestic Violence Conference 24.12.1994, 15–22. London: ACOP.

Harwin, N. (26.6.96) *Challenging Violence against Women: Multi Agency Initiatives to tackle Domestic Violence.* Address to conference. Bristol University School for Policy Studies.

Hearn, J. (1996) 'Men's violence to known women: historical, everyday and theoretical constructions by men.' In B. Fawcett, B. Featherstone, J. Hearn and C. Toft (eds) *Violence and Gender Relations: Theories and Interventions.* London: Sage.

Heidensohn, F. (1989) *Crime and Society.* London: Macmillan.

Her Majesty's Inspectorate of Probation (1995) *Dealing with Dangerous People: The Probation Service and Public Protection. Report of a Thematic Inspection.* London: Home Office.

Hester, M. and Radford, L. (1996) *Domestic Violence and Child Contact Arrangements in England and Denmark.* University of Bristol: Policy Press.

Home Office Circular (1990) 60/90. London: Home Office.

Home Office (1992) *Three Year Plan for the Probation Service.* London: HMSO.

Home Office (1994a) *Three Year Plan for the Probation Service.* London: HMSO.

Home Office (1994b) *Probation Circular 77/1994.* London: Home Office.

Home Office (1995a) *National Standards for the Supervision of Offenders in the Community.* London: Home Office.

Home Office (1995b) *Inter-Agency Circular on Domestic Violence.* London: Home Office.

Home Office (1996) *Victims Charter.* London: Home Office.

Ingram, R.L. (1993/1994) 'Violence form known men.' *Open Mind Volume 16,* 18–19, December 93/January 94.

Jones, A. (1991) *Women who Kill.* London: Victor Gollancz.

Kelly, L. (1988) *Surviving Sexual Violence.* Cambridge: Policy Press.

Kemshall, H. (1996) 'Offender risk and probation practice.' In H. Kemshall and J. Pritchard *Good Practice in Risk Assessment and Risk Management.* London: Jessica Kingsley Publishers.

Kemshall, H. (1996a) *Reviewing Risk. A Review on the Assessment and Management of Risk and Dangerousness: Implications for Policy and Practice in the Probation Service.* London: Home Office.

Kennedy, H. (1992) *Eve was Framed – Women and British Justice.* London: Vintage.

Labour Party (1995) *Peace at Home.* London: Labour Party.

Limandri, B. and Sheriden, D.J. (1995) 'The prediction of intentional interpersonal violence: an introduction.' In J. Campbell (ed) *Assessing Dangerousness: Violence by Sex Offenders, Batterers and Child Abusers.* London: Sage.

Mama, A. (1989) *The Hidden Struggle – Statutory and Voluntary Sector Responses to Violence against Black Women in the Home.* London: Race and Housing Research Unit.

Mama, A. (1992) 'Black women and the British state – race, class and gender analysis for the 1990s' In P. Braham, A. Rattansi and R. Skellington (eds) *Racism and Anti-Racism, Inequalities Opportunities and Policies.* London: Open University Press/Sage.

Marchant, C. (1993) 'Within four walls.' *Community Care* 14 January, 7.

Marchant, C. (1993a) 'Countering violence.' *Community Care* 15 July, 7.

Mark, P. (1992) 'Training staff to work with sex offenders.' *Probation Journal 39,* 1, March, 7–13.

Maynard, M. (1985) 'The response of social workers to domestic violence.' In J. Pahl (ed) *Private Violence and Public Policy.* London: Routledge Keegan and Paul.

Megargee, E. (1976) 'The prediction of dangerous behaviour.' *Criminal Justice and Behaviour 3,* 3–21.

Merseyside Probation Service (1992) *Domestic Violence: Caseload Study.* Unpublished.

Mezey Dr.G. (18.10.95) *Domestic Violence the Victim and the Perpetrator.* Address to Conference. St Georges Hospital Medical School, London.

Monahan, J. (1981) *The Clinical Prediction of Violence.* Beverley Hills, CA.: Sage.

Monahan, J. (1984) 'The prediction of violent behaviour: towards a second generation of theory and policy.' *American Journal of Psychiatry 141,* 10–15.

Morley, R. and Mullender, A. (1994) *Preventing Domestic Violence to Women.* Home Office, Police Research Group, Crime Prevention Unit Series, Paper 48.

Morton, F. (1994) *Domestic Violence, Community Safety and Justice for Women.* London: London Action Trust/Inner London Probation Service.

National Association for the Care and Resettlement of Offenders (1986) *Black People and the Criminal Justice System.* Report of the Race Issues Advisory Committee. London: NACRO.

NCH Action For Children (1994) *The Hidden Victims – Children and Domestic Violence.* London: NCH-Action For Children.

O'Hara, M. (1993) 'A fistful of power.' *Social Work Today 2,* 5, 4 February, 18–19.

Pahl, J. (ed) (1985) *Private Violence and Public Policy.* London: Routledge Keegan and Paul.

Pence, E. and Paymar, M. (1993) *Education Groups for Men who Batter – The Duluth Model.* New York: Springer.

Perrott, S. (1994) 'Working with men who abuse women and children.' In C. Lupton and T. Gillespie (eds) *Working with Violence.* London: BASW Macmillan.

Perry, T. (1993) 'Congruent behaviour: male worker and sex offender.' *Probation Journal 40,* 3, 140–143.

Platt, S. (1996) 'Women do abuse.' *Community Care 21,* 21.

Saunders, A. (1995) *It Hurts Me Too' Children's Experiences of Domestic Violence and Refuge Life.* Bristol/London: WAFE, Childline, NISW.

Scourfield, J. (1995) *Changing Men: U.K. Agencies Working with Men who are Violent Towards their Women Partners.* University of East Anglia: Social Work Monographs.

Sleightholm, D. (1994) *How Does the Probation Service respond? – How can it Improve its Response?* ACOP transcribed papers Domestic Violence Conference. 24.12.1994. 9–13 London: ACOP.

Smart, C. (1989) *Feminism and the Power of the Law.* London: Routledge.

Smellie, E. and Crow, I. (1991) *Black People's Experience of Criminal Justice.* London: NACRO.

Smith, L.F. (1989) *Domestic Violence: an Overview of the Literature.* Home Office Research Study 107. London: HMSO.

Stark, E. and Flitcraft, A. (1985) 'Woman battering, child abuse and social heredity: what is the relationship?' In N. Johnson (ed) *Marital Violence.* London: Routledge Keegan and Paul.

Stelman, A. (1993) 'Domestic violence: old crime, sudden interest.' *Probation Journal 40*, 4, 193–198.

Stern, V. (1987) *Bricks of Shame: Britain's Prisons.* London: Penguin.

Stordeur, R.A. and Stille, R. (1989) *Ending Men's Violence Against their Partners: The Road to Peace.* London: Sage.

Tuck, M. (1992) 'Domestic violence matters.' *Magistrate 48(7)*, 131–132.

Victim Support (1992) *Report of a National Inter-Agency Working Party: Domestic Violence.* London: Victim Support.

Women's Aid Federation (1992) *Memorandum 22, Report to the Home Affairs Inquiry on Domestic Violence.* Bristol: WAFE.

CHAPTER 18

Throughcare Practice, Risk and Contact with Victims

Peter Johnston

INTRODUCTION

At a time of tight financial control, the probation service is increasingly focusing its reducing resources on those offenders who have committed serious offences, especially those of a violent or sexual nature. If the service is to survive as a significant part of our criminal justice system, its work must be seen as enhancing public protection through the management of serious offenders and the risks they present.

After sentence to imprisonment, and before release of potentially dangerous offenders, the service is involved in contributing to a release decision and planning how rehabilitation in the community can most effectively take place within the restrictions on liberty felt to be appropriate for each offender. Recent government initiatives (detailed below), requiring service staff to have direct contact with victims or their relatives, after sentence and before release, bring another dimension to the risk assessment process. This new area of probation practice is not without its own particular challenges, but victim contact, and the information it provides about the victim, the offence and the offender, will become increasingly important to risk assessment and the rehabilitation planning process as confidence in practice develops.

Risk assessment and victim contact work by probation staff have, however, developed along separate tracks due to the traditional focus of the service on the offender and an initial reluctance by probation services to engage positively with the new requirements to contact victims. There needs to be a shift in probation values away from commitment to work with and provide services for offenders to a position where the needs and rights of offenders are balanced with those of victims. This shift can take place through the medium of risk assessment, in which victim information assists the service to prepare release plans which take account of victim information as well as the proposals put forward by offenders.

Without such a change of reference point to victim contact work, progress within the service in terms of staff perceiving the value of this work will be slow. Consequently, the service will remain vulnerable to Home Office driven initiatives over which there will be little influence and which may lead to areas of victim work not appropriate to the role of the service in the criminal justice system.

The Victim's Charter (Home Office 1990), a statement of victims' 'rights', was the first government initiative which required probation services to make direct contact with the victims or their relatives before the release of a prisoner. If focused attention on the life-sentence prisoner. Probation staff were required to find out if victims or their relatives had any concerns which should be heard, including where the prisoner would work, live or go on release. Probation circular 61/95 (Home Office 1995) reinforced this process, but extended its scope to include all prisoners who have committed serious offences of a violent or sexual nature and directed that contact by the probation service with victims or their relatives should begin immediately after sentence (within two months) and continue throughout the sentence, if the victims and/or their relatives wished, until the point of release.

The revised Victim's Charter (Home Office 1996) now talks of 'Service Standards' (rather than 'rights') which victims of crime can expect from criminal justice agencies. It reinforces probation service early contact with victims following the prison sentence and the requirement for probation services to have access to victims' views and concerns before serious offenders are released.

Information about the prisoner's release date and address, however, can only be given to victims with the prisoner's consent. The new charter advises victims or their relatives how to complain if the probation service in their area does not meet the required standards of service delivery.

The purpose of direct contact by probation staff with victims during the prison sentence of a serious offender, defined in the Home Office circular 61/95, is to give information to victims about the custodial process and receive information from them about any anxieties they may have about the prisoners eventual release. The victim information may *contribute* to decisions made about the conditions of release but may not always be acted upon and will not influence the decision whether to release or not. Curiously, the circular excludes from the victim contact process those cases where the offender has received a Hospital Order, unless the responsible medical officer agrees to the contact being initiated. It must remain a matter of speculation why implementation of the Victims Charter requirements should be subject to the discretion of the Responsible Medical Officer in Hospital Order cases but, as I hope to show later, the use also of such discretion by the probation service in the process of victim contact work in life sentence and other cases could also become a cause for serious concern for victims and their representatives.

The probation service faces a major management problem with the implementation of these new requirements. Whilst victims or their relatives clearly wish to be contacted and receive information (and the experience in my own and other probation services suggests some life and parole licences will not be signed until attempts are made to establish contact), senior managers have faced many dilemmas in facing up to this significant change in practice (see Johnston 1994). Some services have yet to implement the new requirement in a consistent way and others have sought partnerships with independent (voluntary) organisations to deliver the work on their behalf.

My own research, referred to above, found that many probation chief officers felt direct contact with victims and/or their relatives by probation personnel would damage victims, cause them more distress, re-open old wounds and possibly cause distress for the probation personnel involved too.

The practical reality, however, is one in which the expectations of the public at large, victims (or their relatives) and organisations representing victims, have been raised through the issue of the 'Charters' referred to above. The service will be expected to take forward victim contact work in a positive way and to meet the required 'standards' now established in terms of when contact will take place. The Association of Chief Officers of Probation has recognised this and in its position statement *Probation Services and Victims of Crime* (ACOP 1996) seeks to advance the work on victim issues. It establishes key principles which should underpin a victim perspective in all aspects of probation practice. These include [a] victims should receive respect; recognition; support; compensation and protection as appropriate to need and circumstances, [b] victims should be relieved of direct responsibility for decisions relating to the offender, [c] victims should be offered timely information and an explanation of events and [d] victims should be able to communicate with the offender, subject to the offender's informed consent, proper supervision and safeguards.

The Association of Chief Officers of Probation principles relate very closely to those victims 'rights' promoted by Victim Support (see Victim Support 1995). However, the ACOP position statement makes a significant addition. For prisoners who have committed 'serious' offences, victim contact is not only to give and receive information but victim information is now seen as crucial to the *assessment* of offenders who may pose a risk to the public on release.

This is an important new development which probation services are now beginning to recognise is critical to the acceptance by probation staff of the place of victim contact work in their throughcare with potentially dangerous prisoners. Re-framing victim contact work from a practice which is a good thing itself and a 'right' of victims to one which is an integral part of the risk assessment process, will greatly benefit the release planning work of probation staff and therefore establish victim contact work as a key element in probation practice.

The service now has a unique opportunity to develop a much greater victim perspective in its work with prisoners through (a) taking account of victim's feelings, wishes and concerns before serious offenders are released and (b) incorporating victim information into the decision making process which will make judgements on the current or future levels of risk and what may be done to reduce the level of assessed risk.

These significant changes to probation practice however, require each probation service to develop strategies and practice guidance for staff which will provide a framework within which decisions regarding allocation of resources can be made and through which managers can monitor and evaluate the work of practitioners. Victim contact after sentence and before the release of serious offenders is a complex, sensitive process which needs to be undertaken carefully. It consumes resources in terms of staff time, training requirements and supervision of those staff responsible for tracing and having direct face-to-face contact with victims or their relatives.

RESOURCING VICTIM CONTACT WORK IN THE THROUGHCARE PROCESS

The service now faces critical choices in the way it allocates resources of all aspects of its work and victim contact work is no exception. Home Office guidance referred to above requires services to focus victim contacts on life sentence and other determinate sentence prisoners who have committed 'serious' violent or sexual offences but leaves open the question which violent or sexual offences fall into the 'serious' category. Pressure on service resources will inevitably lead to assessment of future risk of harm as the key to targeting resources on this work in determinate sentence cases. To focus on the index offence alone will not be sufficient to inform managers if they need to devote staff time and other resources to the victim contact process. Assessment of risk before serious offenders are released from institutions is a matter of judgement about the predicted level and nature of risk once released and toward whom any future harm may be directed. It requires both an analysis of historical information about the offender and his/her current needs, attitudes and circumstances which, if addressed appropriately, may reduce the chances of future hazard or danger. These judgements are increasingly seen as a multi-agency responsibility and not just the preserve of the individual supervising officer. The Inspectorate of Probation Report *Dealing with Dangerous People: The Probation Service and Public Protection* (HMIP 1995) advised that risk assessment on the basis of the offence or type of supervision alone was unsatisfactory and found that where other factors, such as patterns of previous offending and current attitudes, were taken into account, supervising officers were in a much stronger position to manage risk and protect the public. Although the HMIP report made a brief reference to links with Victim Support in terms of 'shared working' on some cases, it failed to see the importance of probation service direct victim contact in providing information which could enhance the risk assessment process.

Each probation service is now being encouraged to develop assessment procedures which define those determinate sentence prisoners who pose a significant risk to the public on release. Life sentence prisoners, as noted above, are automatically included in the victim contact process but probation services will also have to concentrate victim contact work on determinate sentence cases where qualitative judgements about the offender, his/her background, present circumstances and proposed release plan indicate a significant level of predicted future risk. Consequently, some offenders who have committed 'serious' offences of a violent nature may not be considered sufficiently high risk on release to attract victim contact work by the local probation service. It is here that the discretionary element in victim work referred to earlier comes into play.

Some victims may feel vulnerable or 'at risk' because of the offence suffered by them, but their local probation service may decide this risk is not sufficiently high enough to merit scarce resources being devoted to victim contact work. Victims of determinate sentence prisoners will not define which are the 'serious' offences or which offenders pose the most risk on release. Service managers will have to make difficult decisions when allocating service resources to this work and be prepared to explain their decisions to individual victims or their representatives.

In West Yorkshire Probation Service we have developed, in recent years, a risk assessment process which grades future predicted risk on release for prisoners serving life and determinate prison sentences (West Yorkshire Probation Service 1995). Index offence, past offending, background, current circumstances, attitudes and proposed release plan are key elements in determining the level of future predicted risk to the public at large or to particular individuals. All life sentence cases attract victim (or relative) contact work. Where a determinate sentence prisoner, no matter what length of sentence being served, reaches a certain point on the risk assessment scale, decisions are taken regarding if and when victims should be contacted. These decisions are normally taken as part of multi-agency risk assessment conference which plans the work to be undertaken with the offender and victims or relatives. We are increasingly recognising the value in preparing risk assessments shortly after sentence and becoming more aware of how (as will be seen below) the information received from victims and/or their relatives can inform the ongoing assessment of the risk the offender may pose on release. In a small number of cases, victim contact work has also informed judgements on risk to the offender if the proposed release plan was allowed to go ahead.

Throughout the development of risk assessment and victim contact work in West Yorkshire, we have liaised closely with Victim Support, SAMM (Surviving Murder and Manslaughter) and other interested parties. Our approach to this area of probation practice is well understood and there is a real sense of working together and respect for each agencies particular role and contribution. We work with Victim Support and understand their position. The probation service locally is responsible for contacting victims or relatives and directly giving and receiving information but Victim Support will advise us on the process and in some cases may be present with victims or relatives if they request it. Each service nationally will have to develop its own model for victim contact work in terms of which staff should undertake the contact, based on its resources and expertise. I will return later to this issue as it presents some dilemmas for the service as a whole.

VICTIM INFORMATION AND THE RISK ASSESSMENT PROCESS

The Home Office three-year plan 1996–99 (Home Office 1996) for the probation service details, among other responsibilities, those of minimsing risk to the public, challenging attitudes and behaviour of offenders, effective supervision in the community of released prisoners and assisting to reduce the effects of crime on victims. Since March 1993, in West Yorkshire Probation Service, we have undertaken victim contact work with victims or relatives of life sentence and assessed 'high risk' determinate sentence prisoners. Accounts of this work are detailed elsewhere (see Johnston 1995 and Johnston 1996). We have found, in more than 100 such cases, a definite contribution from the information given by victims or relatives to meeting the responsibilities noted above. Meeting these responsibilities in throughcare cases depends on the integration of information received into the risk assessment process.

Victim contact work in West Yorkshire has assisted those responsible for the prisoner's release plan to assess:

- the risk of further danger to particular victims or their relatives
- the risk of not only physical harm but emotional re-victimisation if the release plan involves residence near to, or possible contact with, victims or their relatives
- the risk to the public at large where the crime was committed and victims or relatives still reside.

The reader is referred to the case summaries (Appendix I) for two examples of this work (West Yorkshire Probation Service 1994).

Experience of victim contact work relates directly to answering what Prins (1995) calls the 'unaskable questions', which all managers and supervising practitioners must consider in the risk assessment process (I have adapted these slightly to fit the issues currently under discussion):

1. Have the facts of the offence been adequately addressed and understood? Victim information often reveals dimensions to the offender's behaviour not previously known to the supervising officer, i.e. the use of fear and force.

2. What are the key stressors/precipitants in the offender's background? Victim contact work may reveal use of drugs or other forms of substance misuse not known before to the probation staff or prison authorities.

3. What is the offender's current capacity to cope with provoking events? Release plans have been changed because of victim concern in West Yorkshire and offender reaction to these situations has given good information to throughcare officers on how far the prisoner has progressed in coping with difficult situations.

4. How well has the throughcare officer appraised the offenders self-image? Victim information, which can be put to the prisoner if the victim agrees, can assist here. This is especially important when testing just how vulnerable and fragile is the sex offender prisoner who is facing release.

5. Is the behaviour person specific? Victim contact can help assess if there is still 'unfinished business' between offender and victim, especially when the victim informs of unwelcome contact by the prisoner (through letters or other sources) which was not previously known of by probation or prison staff.

6. Does the prisoner still feel threatened or persecuted? Again, victim information which can be shared with the prisoner (subject to the victim's agreement) can assist with this part of the assessment.

7.   Has the prisoner come to terms with what they did, why they did it and its consequences for the victims? Victims views on the release plan, which can be shared (subject to victim agreement) with the prisoner, may help assess if he/she 'blames' the victim, or do they show genuine understanding of the victim's feelings and are prepared to accept that these feelings should be heard and taken into account?

MANAGING VICTIM CONTACT AND RISK ASSESSMENT

I have already mentioned above a number of issues which the probation service must grapple with as victim contact work develops. There are several others which should also be highlighted.

Training for staff who have the responsibility to contact victims or their relatives will be of major importance. The training material produced through the co-operation of Home Office Probation Training Unit, ACOP and West Yorkshire Probation Service will hopefully assist this process. These materials will include modules on the place of the victim in the criminal justice system, victim awareness and the impact of crime on victims and their relatives, the probation service role in relation to contacting the victims, practise issues, identification of existing skills and how they can be applied to the unique context of meetings with victims or their relatives.

There remains, however, a fundamental question which each service has to answer before training can be implemented. Which staff should contact victims or relatives in order for the service to discharge its duties and obtain the best possible information? Is this work part of the throughcare officer role or should another member of staff undertake the contact on behalf of the responsible probation officer.

In West Yorkshire the contact is fulfilled through highly trained and experienced victim contact specialist workers (non probation officer grade) reporting to the throughcare officer. This model of practice is based on a recognition that it could be very difficult for the throughcare officer to balance the role of probation officer to the offender/prisoner with direct responsibility for victim contact. There could be considerable role tensions here. Probation officers may well have the necessary skill base on which to build victim contact practice, but can the throughcare officer combine responsibility for offender risk assessment and rehabilitation with the direct victim contact work? Victim information enhances the risk assessment management and rehabilitation process, but is there merit in the approach that the direct contact with victims or relatives should be undertaken by a probation staff member not directly involved with the offender? Staff whoseek out and approach victims of serious offenders need to assure the victims they are there to listen to them, not to represent the offender, in order to carry out service duties. They need to assure victims they will pass on their needs, wishes or concerns to those who are more closely involved with responsibilities for the offender's release planning and rehabilitation. From our experience in West Yorkshire, this model of practice appears to work in terms of supplying good quality victim information to the throughcare officer who is responsible for incorporating it into the risk assessment process. Other probation services have recognised this and another member of the team or service (at Probation Officer or Senior Probation Officer grade) acts as the victim contact worker for the throughcare officer. However, my personal contact with a large number of services also reveals some examples where the throughcare officer is undertaking both responsibilities to offender and victim(s) as an integral part of their role.

These developments in practice require comparative evaluation to assess what model is most effective in terms of providing the required standard of service to victims and in gaining information which contributes to the work of those making key decisions regarding release of potentially dangerous offenders.

Practice is developing quickly and each service must, at present, make its own arrangements on the basis of knowledge of good practice and available local resources. What is also known is that Victim Support will assist probation staff in victim contact work but will not relieve the service of its duties (see Victim Support 1996). The possibilities for 'contracting out' victim contact work are therefore limited. Surely the time is now right for the Probation Inspectorate to review practice nationally and advise on the difficult question of allocation of resources to this new growth area in probation work.

Tough decisions will still have to be made, even if the appropriate procedures are developed to define those cases in which we can afford to do this work. Offenders who have committed crimes of a serious violent or sexual nature and will present a significant risk to the public may have several victims. How far does the local service go in trying to contact all the victims or their relatives? Should we put limits on the numbers to be included, and how do we choose? It could be argued that all such victims should be heard as a 'right' but in a climate of tight budget control there may be a case to be made for limiting contact to those who we think can provide us with the information we need to make sound risk assessment judgements prior to the offender's release.

A major challenge for the service managers at all levels is to hold the balance between the control and management of potentially dangerous offenders on the one hand and our traditional commitment to the rehabilitation of the individual offender on the other (Kemshall 1996). Victim contact has the potential to impact on both these elements of our work with offenders who pose a substantial risk to the public on release. We must avoid offender management and control functions eclipsing individual offender work aimed at positive change. Victim contact work can act as a bridge between these two essential aspects of our work with offenders. If victim contact is initiated shortly after sentence, and victim or relatives consulted at key stages throughout the sentence (as defined by Probation circular 61/95), this process will not only assist the continual review and assessment of the level of risk but inform the work to be done with the prisoner throughout sentence to reduce the level of risk on release. We must assist the prisoner to think about the consequences of their past actions on others and how their future plans might also have major effects on the victims of their crime or their relatives.

Further thought must be given, however, to the issues surrounding confidentiality of victim information. From my own experience as a manager responsible for the development of victim contact work in West Yorkshire, I am always surprised just how individual is the experience of the impact of serious crime on the victim or their relatives and how reactions to an approach for victim contact varies between victims. Some will want the prisoner to know in detail how the crime affected them, others may be very frightened of the consequences should the prisoner have access to the information given. The present arrangements (under Probation circular 61/95) preserve confidentiality of offender information to the extent that release date, release address and details of treatment programme or location of the prison where the sentence is being served can only be disclosed to the victim or their relatives with the prisoners consent. Victim information, however, will be made available to the prisoner unless it is decided that there is an unacceptable risk to the victim. The victim or relative may ask for non-disclosure when the probation staff member contacts them, but there can be no guarantee that once their information is passed into the prison system it will not be disclosed to the prisoner.

Applications for non-disclosure can be made to the prison Governor in the first instance but, here again there is the danger of Governors' individual decision making increasing the already high level of discretion operating to limit the control and influence the victim has in the process. There needs to be a centralised decision making process for each type of prisoner (Lifer – discretionary or mandatory – Discretionary Release and Automatic Conditional Release) which will establish coherent procedures for assessing such requests and providing consistency of response to probation staff who have the direct face-to-face contact with victims or their relatives. I am aware of a number of cases where victims have been reluctant to allow crucial information to be written down and passed into the prison system for fear of reprisal if disclosure to the prisoner took place. This information could, however, be crucial to the risk assessment and pre-release planning process.

VICTIM CONTACT, RISK ASSESSMENT AND MEDIATION

The Association of Chief Officers of Probation principles for victim contact noted above acknowledge that for some victims they may wish to communicate with the offender. We have experience in West Yorkshire of a small number of cases where victim contact under the Home Office requirements before the release of a serious offender from prison have lead to requests from victims or relatives for mediation. West Yorkshire Probation Service has provided victim offender mediation services since 1985. We define mediation as a process of communication between the victim and offender in which the victim can express to the offender their feelings about the offence and have questions answered, and the offender hears what the victim has to say, takes responsibility for their actions and attempts to put right, as far as possible, the wrong committed. This process can take place directly, face-to-face, facilitated by specialist mediators or indirectly with the mediator travelling between victim and offender, communicating the views of the parties to each other.

Our experience of victim contact leading to requests for mediation is not unusual, other probation services are also experiencing a small number of such requests. The process of mediation, if conducted with skilled workers and conducted under the principles of Restorative Justice (see Wright 1996), has intrinsic value for both the victim and offender and can create an alternative positive way in which the criminal justice system accommodates the particular needs of some victims or relatives. Assessment of risk, however, is one of the three key elements to be considered early in the pre-mediation process (risk of physical or emotional damage to either party) along with genuine willingness to participate without pressure from others and full acceptance of guilt by the offender.

We have found that where such a process is requested by the parties, and takes place under the conditions described above, it can also have considerable value in the risk assessment process with regard to the viability of release plans for both sides. Issues and problems which could cast doubt on the release plan being successful, especially if there may be contact, planned or unplanned, between victim and offender on release, can be explored within a framework designed to allow the parties to resolve their conflict wit the assistance of a neutral third party who can facilitate the process.

The Association of Chief Officers position statement on victims (ACOP 1996) supports intervention based on the principles of Restorative Justice, but with probation services facing severe budget restrictions in the coming years, it is far from clear how many services will have the resources available, either within their own organisations or through partnership arrangements, to meet the needs of some victims or relatives for mediation, either before or after the release of the prisoner.

CONCLUSION

Through the requirements to have direct contact with victims or their relatives after sentence, and before the release of prisoners who have committed serious offences of a violent or sexual nature, probation services have been given a central role in the re-establishment of the link between the criminal justice system, the offender and the victim. The driving force behind these recent developments has not just been a political strategy but a recognition by agencies working with victims or their relatives that they have a 'right' in terms of 'good practice' to be heard in an appropriate manner. We are now learning, however, just how important their information may be for the risk assessment process. Victim contact can give the probation personnel who will supervise the prisoner on release a clearer picture of issues which will require attention before release and will assist in the process of re-integration of the offender into the community. In so doing, victims or their relatives will be given a chance to have their anxieties, wishes and concerns taken into account by those who make the final decisions.

As the primary agency involved in the supervision after release of potentially dangerous offenders, the service needs to have the confidence of the public at large in its operations. As victim issues in the criminal justice system achieve greater prominence, there will be increased expectations that victims will be contacted by probation staff and victims' views on release plans of prisoners taken into account. This is one way in which the public can feel confident in the service and, therefore, in the criminal justice system as a whole. However, the service does not have unlimited resources and hard choices regarding targeting the resources available will have to be made. It is anticipated that probation services will make such judgements on the basis of assessed future risk to the public at large or to particular individuals.

This relatively new area of work poses many challenges for managers and practitioners. The future of the service will depend in no small part on how we are perceived to have integrated the needs and wishes of victims into our work with those dangerous prisoners whose attitudes and behaviour we seek to change in order to minimise further risk to the public. The probation service thus has a key role to play in restoring the legitimacy of a crucial part of the criminal justice system with the public at large and, as a consequence, our own place within that system.

Appendix I

Extract from Leeds Victim Offender Unit Bulletin (West Yorkshire Probation Service 1994).

POST SENTENCE LIFER CASE. OFFENCE – MURDER

This referral was received by the specialist Victim Offender Unit in Leeds, West Yorkshire a month following sentence at Crown Court. The offender had been convicted of murdering his girlfriend. They had periodically live together, although the relationship was cooling and the victim was living with her mother.

The victims' parents live separately and our service contacted both parents simultaneously by letter to offer information about the life sentence process and establish a point of contact for the future.

Both parents were pleased to have contact and keen to take up the appointments offered. The victim enquiry worker later visited them at their homes. They asked how the life sentence would progress and what tariff date had been set. The enquirer was able to discuss the life sentence systems with them, leaving a specially developed leaflet, and agreed to obtain information on the tariff setting. Reports on the initial contacts were submitted, with their consent, to the through care officer outlining their wishes to be kept informed of significant developments in the sentence. The enquirer later returned with the tariff information.

Our service will contact and consult the family in relation to developments in the sentence. This will be particularly relevant when considering any future temporary release on licence or permanent release on life licence plan.

PRE-RELEASE LIFER CASE. OFFENCE – MURDER

This referral was received prior to an application for home leave of a Category D Life Sentence Prisoner.

The offender had been convicted of the murder of the one-year-old child of his co-habitee. Leave was to be taken at a West Yorkshire hostel near to his home area. The offender was hoping to be allowed to return to his home area upon release. The child's natural father lived a short distance away from the hostel.

Our service made enquiries in line with the Victim's Charter as to any concerns the victim's family may have about the eventual release of the prisoner. Very strong feelings about the offender were expressed and any decision to return the offender to the area would affect and be strongly opposed by the family. The enquirer was able to answer some of their questions and misunderstandings about the progress of the sentence. Untrue rumours existed in the area, ie that the offender had already been released. The family were honest in sharing some vengeful feelings, which were considered when assessing the appropriateness of the release/home leave plan. In addition to the effect of these plans on the victim's family and community, risk to the offender needed to be considered.

The family were informed, as requested, of the progress of the case. A new home leave and release plan were formulated with the offender. This did not include visits or settlement to the home area as this was now considered inappropriate.

REFERENCES

Association of Chief Officers of Probation (1996) *Probation Services and the Victims of Crime*. London: Association of Chief Officers of Probation.

Home Office (1990) *Victim's Charter: a Statement of the Rights of Victims of Crime*. London: HMSO.

Home Office (1995) *Probation Service Contact with Victims*. Probation Circular 61/95. London: Home Office.

Her Majesty's Inspectorate of Probation (1995) *Dealing with Dangerous People: the Probation Service and Public Protection*. Report of a Thematic Inspection. London: Home Office.

Home Office (1996) *The Victim's Charter: a Statement of Service Standards for Victims of Crime*. London: Home Office.

Home Office (1996) *Three Year Plan for the Probation Service*. London: Home Office.

Johnston, P.H. (1994) *The Victim's Charter 1990 and the Release of Life Sentence Prisoners: Implications for Probation Service Practice, Value and Management*. West Yorkshire Probation Service.

Johnston, P.H. (1995) 'The victim's charter and the release of long-term prisoners.' *Probation Journal 42*, 1, 8–12.

Johnston, P.H. (1996) 'Probation contact with victims – challenging throughcare practice.' *Probation Journal 43*, 1, 26–28.

Kemshall, H. (1996) 'Risk assessment: fuzzy thinking or "decisions in action".' *Probation Journal 43*, 1, 2–7.

Prins, H. (1995) *Offenders, Deviants or Patients*. London: Routledge.

Victim Support (1995) *The Rights of Victims of Crime*. London: Victim Support.

Victim Support (1996) *Newsletter. April 1996*.

West Yorkshire Probation Service (1994) *Leeds Victim–Offender Unit Bulletin*.

West Yorkshire Probation Service (1995) *Potentially Dangerous Offenders – Management of Risk and Public Protection*.

Wright, M. (1996) *Justice for Victims and Offenders – a Restorative Response to Crime*. Waterside Press.

CHAPTER 19

Risk
The Role and Responsibilities of Middle Managers

Christine Lawrie

BACKGROUND

This chapter discusses the role of first-line managers in providing an adequate public protection focus to the work for which they are responsible. It is relevant principally to probation service middle managers but many of the points apply in other settings where staff work with potentially dangerous people. The chapter is based on first-hand experience in the probation service and the probation inspectorate. The examples given in the text are real but details have been changed so that individual cases cannot be identified.

Public protection in this context is the prevention of serious harm. Serious harm is physical or psychological harm which is traumatic and whose effects are long lasting. The Butler Committee (1975) have described this as 'serious physical injury or lasting psychological harm' and the Scottish Council on Crime (1975), 'serious and irremediable personal injury' (1975, Scottish Council 1975).

Agencies such as the probation service have long had a responsibility to try to prevent all further offending by everyone under supervision. This duty was emphasised by the 1991 Criminal Justice Act which enshrined in law probation services' duty to protect the public from offenders subject to community sentences (other than community service orders) and the Home Office's three-year plan for the probation service 1996 – 1999 (Home Office 1996) lists reducing risk to the public as one of six priorities for the service. National Standards for the Supervision of Offenders (Home Office 1995) provide guidance on the legislation and require services, *inter alia*, to assess whether offenders are likely to re-offend and thus harm others and to take steps to reduce the likelihood of this happening.

The prevention of *serious* harm, however, is of particular importance and requires special policies and practices to ensure effectiveness. This chapter is therefore mainly concerned with the management of those people under statutory supervision who have been assessed as likely to 'seriously harm' others because their past actions or current behaviour indicate they pose such a threat.

There is currently insufficient information to be able to state definitively how many people under the supervision of the probation service pose a threat of serious harm to others. Data may be become available in due course as more services develop systems for registering potentially dangerous offenders. However, in its inspection of the probation service's public protection role (Her Majesty's Inspectorate of Probation 1995) the probation inspectorate calculated that around 14,000 offenders per year are placed under statutory supervision having been convicted of a serious offence of violence, a significant number of whom pose some threat of repeating their offence. Information collated by the Home Office from reports submitted by probation services of serious incidents by offenders under supervision suggests that at least 16 supervised offenders each month seriously harm someone else.

GOOD PRACTICE IN PUBLIC PROTECTION

There are some overarching principles for working with a public protection focus. Most importantly, the public interest takes priority over a person's rights to confidentiality and to the receipt of services. However, being assessed as potentially dangerous may entitle the person to special help or access to particular facilities. It is also important to protect an individual's civil liberties, as long as this is compatible with ensuring the protection of others. Second, the responsibility for the management of people assessed as having the potential to seriously harm others is always an agency responsibility and involves first-line and senior managers as well as the operational staff members who hold cases. Finally, successful case management requires an individualised approach in which high quality supervision is based on the unique characteristics and progress of each case, within the overall policy and practice framework of the agency.

Good practice in public protection at individual case level comprises the following essential elements. An accurate risk assessment should be made to identify who may seriously harm others and to establish who may be at risk of what kind of harm from them. Case management should meet the standards set locally and nationally covering contact with the offender and enforcement of the order or licence to which he or she is subject. High quality, well planned, individually tailored professional intervention must be implemented to tackle and reduce the causes of offending which may cause serious harm to others. Careful monitoring is essential so that indicators that the person poses a threat of dangerous behaviour can quickly be identified. This recognition of alarm signals may initiate action to forestall dangerous behaviour. Finally, although it may be regarded defensively, or as a chore, good record keeping is vital so that understanding, responsibility and accountability can be demonstrated.

The quintessential test of good practice is not whether a person under supervision seriously harms someone else, it is whether the quality and content of work is appropriate on the basis of the known facts about the case. In essence this can be encapsulated in the question: can it be demonstrated that everything is being, or has been, done to try to prevent harm occurring?

If the answer is yes, then the practice is or was satisfactory, irrespective of the actual outcome of the case (Carson 1996).

This is sometimes a difficult concept to accept because it appears to deny the central aim is the prevention of harmful behaviour, but it is important that agencies, and individual staff, are held to account primarily not for outcomes but for the quality of their practice (though clearly there is a connection between the two which in some cases is critical). Many factors which are beyond the control of a statutory supervisor influence behaviour. Thus a case in which a person harms another may have been managed in an exemplary way and another which terminates with no harm done may have been supervised poorly. Therefore, to facilitate good practice, managers should have an involvement in the day-to-day management of individual cases as well as taking an overview of the work of staff and of the team.

In practice this means that first-line managers should know 'inside out' each case involving a potentially dangerous person held by staff members accountable to them. They should be involved in key decisions relating to the management and supervision of such cases and have the professional skills, knowledge and expertise to advise staff, endorse or guide the direction supervision takes and coach them to enhance their professional skills. They should have the professional confidence to liaise and negotiate with other professionals, and with senior managers in their own agency, to ensure that resources are available to provide high quality supervision, that staff receive adequate training and supervision and that the agency's framework of policy and practice guidance is sufficient.

In the probation service the skills and knowledge which managers are required to demonstrate in this area of work have been laid out as part of a national document *Core competences for senior and middle management* (Home Office 1994). Managers are required to be assessed annually against the performance criteria it specifies.

That's all very well, you say, but I am a busy first-line manager whose team supervises a wide range of people. I understand the importance of public safety but I have to make decisions on a day-to-day basis in the real world which is populated by difficult and demanding offenders and hard-pressed staff of varying abilities, skills and experience. As a team we have a hundred and one things to do. Public protection is important but it is one function among many. My work as a manager often feels more like continuous crisis management than the implementation of a well-oiled cycle of planning, achievement and review. Although we do our best to anticipate and prevent harmful behaviour by the people on our caseload, it sometimes seems we avoid disaster more by luck than judgement. Sometimes I worry about whether I would be supported by my employers if anything went wrong. What should I do in practice?

Be Interventionist!

Probation officers are generally regarded as professionals who, as long as legal requirements and agency policy are met, are expected to make their own decisions about professional intervention in each case. Often colleagues are used for mutual support and problem solving, but this is not the same as sharing the responsibility for a case with a manager who has the authority to endorse practice or require it to be changed. For this reason, many staff prefer the 'interventionist' manager, as long as it is someone whose professional views they respect.

In describing managers they admire as 'interventionist', staff generally mean they inspire trust and confidence, are encouraging, are informed about the content and demands of the work undertaken by their staff, are technically skilled and assured about using their knowledge to give professional advice, are constructively critical in a tactful but forthright way, know what they want from staff and are secure about making requirements of them. They intervene but they also maintain an 'open door' and staff feel able to approach them for advice, which they experience as useful. These managers combine the ability to establish a friendly rapport with their staff, based on a sense of shared purpose, with the maintenance of a distance appropriate to their respective roles and responsibilities. It is debatable whether such managers are born or made and, in describing their managers thus, staff seem to include a person-ality component which is difficult to describe or quantify, but it seems that the closer a manager reflects these characteristics the more likely they are to be effective.

Read Records

The critical first step to effective managerial intervention is to read case records thoroughly. Managers do not always do this and sometimes miss basic and vital information. The introduction of computerised case records has also made it easier sometimes to focus on those aspects of supervision which can be counted rather than on the text which describes the content of supervision. One new member of staff found that one of his caseload, transferred from a colleague, had been dead for some time but the case had never been closed. He therefore remained a live case, as it were; clearly no-one had checked the records recently. In another case a probation officer 'lost' a man on life licence but this was not picked up by managers. The lifer was only 'found' when he was arrested for a further offence.

Although apparently time consuming, reading a record 'cover to cover' is an effective way to learn a lot about a case relatively quickly. It almost certainly gives a broader and more complete picture than you could build up from case discussions with the supervising officer alone. It provides an overview of progress and enables patterns of behaviour and developments to be seen in context and in perspective.

A separate, informed, authoritative opinion helps you to genuinely share responsibility and be accountable for the handling of the case. It makes case discussions with the supervising officer potentially more penetrating and useful and can be helpful, and in some instances critical, in spotting signs of potential trouble or in seeing a more effective way of supervising the offender. You may see things which the supervising officer has missed or interpret aspects of the case differently. This is not to imply that supervising officers tend to make mistakes while managers are always right but to emphasise that cases, particularly those involving potentially dangerous offenders, are often complex and supervisors can necessarily be too 'close to the action'. One male offender had a history of harmful behaviour beginning, as a child, with cruelty to animals and then other children. As an adult he injured others, usually during fights at pub closing time, and was on supervision following such an incident. Supervision was superficial and infrequent on the basis that he was 'just another pub brawler'. His probation officer failed to see the pattern of violence, with sadistic elements, which indicated that he was a continuing and serious threat to others.

'Listen' to your instinctive reactions to what you read. While intuition should never, of itself, influence how you require a case to be managed, it can be a prompt to look more closely at particular aspects of it. Check whether your instincts are pointers to worrying aspects of the case or, indeed, to good practice.

Reading records provides a reminder of why the person is known to the agency – often, particularly in the case of people under long-term supervision, the original offence, or reason for referral, is forgotten. A case record on a man who was several years into a life sentence for murder had been divided into two to make it easier to handle. Only 'volume one', covering the earlier part of his sentence, referred to the offence but it was filed away. It was impossible to know, from the supervising officer's 'working file', which covered a considerable period of time, why the man was in prison.

Records also illustrate good practice and reassurance for the manager that a case is being handled well. One probation officer was supervising a man convicted of sex offences against children. He had developed the practice of mentally 'running through' each meeting with the offender immediately it finished to check whether there had been any warning signs, however faint, that he might re-offend. Each entry on the record concluded with a note of this mental check. This not only helped alert the officer when the offender did show such signs by talking about a place where the probation officer knew children might be unsupervised by adults, it also provided an example of excellent practice which could be used in other cases.

A common feature of many case records is a tendency to record only factual information and to avoid using the record as a working tool to record impressions, hypotheses and tentative concerns. Staff understandably want records to be accurate and are wary of using the record as a notebook in which to record unproven suspicions or developing views of the case. They are also often concerned about what will happen if the subject of the record reads it and reacts critically to the contents. This applies especially in those organisations with a policy of client access to records and where information is governed by the Data Protection Act. However, externalising concerns by writing them down helps to put them into perspective. It ensures they are not forgotten and it enables patterns in behaviour to be charted. It makes it more likely that early indicators of potentially dangerous behaviour will be highlighted and that preventative action can be taken. Also, in the event of an enquiry, it provides evidence that staff have been alert to public protection issues even if ultimately they were unable to prevent harm occurring. Staff should be encouraged to log concerns, however tentative, on the case record.

Coach Staff and Discuss Cases

Staff are sometimes reluctant to ask their manager for professional help. The reasons for their hesitation are varied but may include a wish not to seem incapable, a belief that they 'know best', a desire not to trouble a busy manager and a concern that the manager may require work which they feel unskilled or unable to carry out. It may also be that they have no confidence in the manager. It can seem simpler to do nothing, live with anxieties about the case and hope that nothing untoward happens.

There has also been an emphasis in recent years on meeting standards governing frequency of contact and the enforcement of court orders. To an extent this has diminished the importance of what used to be called 'casework', which stressed the sensitivities of the process of supervision. Though such an emphasis was sometimes at the expense of a proper focus on outcomes, it is clear that the quality of the process of supervision, that is the techniques and methods used and the style of the supervisor, are fundamental to the eventual outcome of supervision and there is no substitute for practical, personal, case-focused discussion to enhance and develop supervision style and technique.

Coaching in the workplace, as the probation inspectorate found in its inspection of appraisal arrangements for managers (Her Majesty's Inspectorate of Probation 1992), is a vital element in the development of good practice. A first-line manager who knows both the case and the case supervisor, and who shares responsibility for the work, is in the best position to help the supervisor refine his or her understanding and techniques.

The involvement of first-line managers in the conduct of cases is usually welcomed by operational staff even if they hesitate to ask for it. Especially with cases who have been assessed as likely to pose a threat of serious harm to others, supervising staff often want to talk about their work – for recognition, reassurance and to consider alternative methods of supervision. A probation officer supervised an arsonist who often talked about fire raising. Although the officer judged it unlikely that he would translate his thoughts into action, he lived with a nagging worry, which he discussed with no-one, about whether he was right. He later said he wished he had spoken to his manager because he thought this might have saved him 'many sleepless nights' of worry about the case. Another officer received bizarre and abusive letters from an offender. The entries on the case record showed she was unsure how to respond but she kept her worries to herself and the case file was not read by the middle manager. A third officer asked a manager for advice about how to handle what she knew would be a potentially explosive interview. Her manager talked her through the likely course the meeting would take, providing what she described as 'a script' for the interview, which enabled her to manage it successfully.

Sometimes staff may feel, consciously or instinctively, that concerns about a case are either too trivial, or too difficult to validate, to be raised, but often these 'nagging concerns' are the first indicators of problems. Just as writing down concerns and hypotheses about a case helps set them in perspective or highlights what might otherwise be missed, so discussing the details of a case helps draw out and register features which might otherwise be overlooked.

An informed and involved manager, who knows his or her staff and their work well, can do this effectively. As with reading records, 'listen' carefully to your reactions to what you hear.

Joint Decision Making

Joint decision making between manager and case supervisor is generally the key to more reliable decision making. However, managers carry a particular responsibility for the way the case is managed. If, after discussion, you disagree with the supervising officer about the way the case should be handled, you have an obligation, and the authority, to require your views to take precedence. Taking such an approach also helps supervising officers, who are then clear that they do not carry alone the burden of responsibility for the conduct of cases. A probation officer described how it was both a demand and a relief to have a manager who actively held her to account for her work and shared responsibility for it. If in doubt, consult your own line manager, who also has a responsibility, on behalf of the agency, for the way cases are managed.

Competent managers encourage and enable staff to discuss with them some of the stress and anxiety which can arise in dealing with potentially dangerous, risky cases. While no one would advocate treating staff as though they are inadequate or inevitably likely to be upset by the pressure of this kind of work, there is undoubtedly at times a need to take account of such factors. Be alert to pointers that the supervising officer is struggling with the case or cases. People will often not admit to difficulties but may show strain through illness or working in a superficial way. A previously competent probation officer, whose caseload included many potentially dangerous offenders, told his managers he could give only limited attention to individual offenders because he had too much work. In reality he carried a modest caseload but was shocked and anxious through having been seriously physically assaulted by a casual caller when he was on office duty and these feelings had translated into a generalised fear of engaging properly with offenders. His complaints about workload were an indirect way of saying so, but, though his managers recognised this, they seemed unable to help him and he had become labelled as a 'weak link' in his team.

Even those staff who have had no bad experiences, or who are professionally assured, will experience pressure managing potentially dangerous people. One experienced, confident and robust probation officer described how she 'psyched herself up' to each interview with a highly dangerous and manipulative man who characteristically tried to control the supervision process through threats to his supervising officers. He also repeatedly threatened to harm again the victims of his previous offence. The concern about what he might do to others, the unpleasantness of undertaking interviews with him and the tension of staying alert to, but unaffected by, his manipulations all added to the demands of supervising him. Managers at middle and senior management level recognised the problems posed and gave the probation officer a good deal of useful formal and informal support and guidance during the period the man was under supervision. The selection of a supervisor for each case should be made carefully, bearing in mind account skills, experience and any specialist training or knowledge. In many cases the gender or ethnic origin of the supervisor should also be taken into account.

Ensure Adequate Administration and Case Management

Terms of any statutory order should be implemented and contact with the offender, and the administration of the case, should meet agency policy and practice requirements. Thus records should be complete and contain whatever information local practice expects. They should be up to date and completed quickly after significant events have occurred. If there is a requirement to register certain categories of case, this should be done. Standards relating to frequency of contact and the enforcement of statutory orders or licences should be met.

Good case management ensures that information necessary to plan work and demonstrate accountability is recorded and is accessible to the supervising officer and his or her manager. It guarantees regular contact with the offender, a prerequisite for undertaking effective work, and that he or she receives services to which he or she is entitled. The implementation of a sentence of the court is, in itself, also clearly imperative.

Meeting rigorously the requirements of courts and agencies is also necessary for what might be called the 'worst case situation'. Usually statutory supervision is a fairly private matter between the agency and its clients, but when things go wrong, and in this context that means when a client of the agency seriously harms another person, a public, or semi-public, enquiry is almost inevitable. If the case is notorious there may also be a media 'witch hunt'. If there is an investigation into the handling of the case, failures to comply with agency requirements will be pin-pointed and will raise doubts about whether everything was done to prevent the incident. Public enquiries have criticised statutory agencies after people known statutorily to them have caused personal injury or death and some agencies have been successfully sued when their negligence has allowed those in their care to harm others (Carson 1966). Even if poor work was demonstrably unconnected with the client's actions, it leaves an impression of an unreliable or unprofessional service and question marks about the management of other cases and the supervision of staff. Can the public rely on a service which fails to implement its own policies or the terms of statutory orders?

If the policy and practice framework for the supervision of potentially dangerous people in your organisation is inadequate, raise this with your line manager. He or she shares responsibility with you and your operational staff for the proper management of cases and should be made aware of shortcomings. If there are serious failings, put your concerns in writing.

Be Alert to Signs that the Offender Poses a Threat of Harm

Never ignore indicators of likely harm and do not worry about seeming to over-react. Whatever the situation, it is important to decide what to do based on a thorough consideration of the evidence, and to record your decision and reasons for it. This ensures that everyone is clear about what is being done and why, but it will also be valuable evidence if things go wrong and there is an investigation. Note that investigators have the advantage of hindsight and may interpret critically what you regard as reasonable actions (Carson 1996). Always provide a complete picture of what happened, what was done and why so that you and your staff can be judged on the basis of information available at the time. If there is nothing you can do, say so and why.

Know Your Own Professional Requirements

Do not carry alone the burden of managing staff and overseeing their cases. The agency and its senior managers also have responsibility for the work and you should use them for advice and help in the same way as your staff should use you.

A MANAGER'S CHECKLIST

As you supervise cases ask yourself:

- Is the supervising officer on top of the case? Do you think he or she has the measure of the offender or are they intimidated or misled, perhaps allowing the offender to dictate the pattern and content of contact? Who is making the running?
- Does he or she understand the public protection role or is he or she inclined to put the interests of the offender first?
- Is there an assessment of whether the offender will cause harm to others, including, if relevant, who is at risk of what sort of harm and in what circumstances? Does the information on the record legitimise the assessment? Do you think the supervising officer has got it right? Has he or she over- or under-estimated the risk of harm? Has he or she ignored the question of future harm altogether?
- Does the supervising officer (especially in cases where there is a likelihood that serious harm may result) keep the risk of harm in mind? Has he or she 'forgotten' the original offence or reason for referral? Does supervision now focus largely on unrelated issues? Do you think he or she is alert to the possibility that the offender might harm someone?
- Is the professional intervention satisfactory? Does it deal adequately with precipitating factors in the person's offending? Does the supervising officer have the skills, knowledge and experience to handle this case properly? Should the supervising officer be given training or coaching? Would it be managed better, and would public safety be better assured, if the case was allocated to someone else?
- Is the offender's behaviour or attitude changing in ways which may make them likely to harm others in future? Are patterns, or similar patterns, of behaviour being repeated which preceded previous incidents of harm to other people? Is there evidence that the offender may be about to cause harm?
- Are there signs that the officer feels unduly pressured or is struggling to manage the case effectively? Has he or she shown signs

of stress? Has he or she been the subject of physical or verbal violence in the course of work? Do you know the details of what happened? Did the organisation give him or her adequate support or was the incident ignored or otherwise badly handled?

- Is there evidence on the case record to show that the supervising officer had done everything possible to contain and reduce the chance of harm occurring? Is there evidence of poor work, of policy or practice requirements or the requirements of court orders not met?
- If this case became the subject of an official investigation, or if a member of the public sued your employer because of harm caused by the person under supervision, could you demonstrate good practice?

DOES IT WORK?

It would be easy to conclude that public services should develop their public protection role mainly as a defence against criticism when things go wrong, but there is evidence that good practice can make a difference – even though it can be very hard to demonstrate that harm would have occurred but for professional intervention. The most obvious and dramatic examples tend to be those cases in which services alert the police to specific threats made or where probation officers have instigated recalls to prison when an ex-prisoner's behaviour has deteriorated dangerously. There are also countless instances of staff controlling or changing the behaviour or attitudes of offenders in less spectacular ways.

The probation inspectorate found in its inspection of public protection (Her Majesty's Inspectorate of Probation 1995) that staff often underestimated their own skills, knowledge and abilities despite testimonies from other agencies to their competence and effectiveness in dealing with potentially dangerous people. Probation officers, and other professionals who work with such people, develop considerable skills in assessing and managing them. Where practice needs improvement it is often not so much a question of needing to acquire or develop skills or experience but of needing to enhance professional self-assurance and belief in one's ability to manage potentially dangerous people. First-line managers have a vital part to play in helping operational staff maximise their professional skills and confidence.

Bibliography

Butler, Lord (Chairman) (1975) *Report of the Committee on the Mentally Abnormal Offender. Cmnd 6244*. London: HMSO.

Carson, D. (1996) 'Risking legal repercussions.' In H. Kemshall and J. Pritchard *Good Practice in Risk Assessment and Risk Management*. London: Jessica Kingsley Publishers.

Her Majesty's Inspectorate of Probation (1995) *Dealing with Dangerous Offenders: the Probation Service and Public Protection*. London: Home Office.

Her Majesty's Inspectorate of Probation (1992) *The Appraisal of Management Grade Staff*. London: Home Office.

Home Office (1994) *Core Competences for Senior and Middle Management.* London: Home Office.

Home Office (1995) *National Standards for the Supervision of Offenders in the Community.* London: Home Office.

Home Office (1996) *Three Year Plan for the Probation Service 1996–1999.* London: Home Office.

Scottish Council on Crime (1975) *Crime and the Prevention of Crime.* London: HMSO.

The Contributors

Pamela Askham is an independent trainer and counsellor. Whilst working in the alcohol field for 11 years, Pamela has provided training for professionals, volunteers and client groups and has supervised workers in both the statutory and voluntary sectors. She is now working independently with a commitment to the development of individuals and groups, to help them express themselves, to listen to others and to work more effectively together.

Peter Argall, who is co-ordinator for The Basement Project, is a qualified youth worker with counselling and postgraduate management qualifications who has worked with young people for the last 18 years.

Katherine Beattie is a probation officer working in the West Midlands Probation Service. She has a practice and research interest in domestic violence, and in work with survivors and perpetrators.

Sheila Byrne is a child placement consultant with British Agencies for Adoption and Fostering. She has a wide experience of child care including residential work, specialist adoption and fostering, training and consultancy. She is the author of *Learning from Disruption* (1994) and has a particular interest in child development and the practice implications for all aspects of caring for separated children.

Ben Cowderoy is a drugs and alcohol worker for The Basement Project. He is a qualified youth worker with a Diploma in Drugs and Alcohol Studies who has worked in the drugs field in a variety of statutory and voluntary sector settings for the last 12 years.

Stephen Hicks is a Lecturer in Social Work in the Department of Applied Community Studies at the Manchester Metropolitan University. He is also doing postgraduate research at the University of Lancaster, looking at the social work assessment of lesbian and gay foster and adoptive carers. Previously he was a social worker for children under eleven at a voluntary organisation in Manchester. He is founder member of the Northern section of Lesbian and Gay Foster and Adoptive Parents Network, and with Janet McDermott is currently co-editing a collection of personal accounts by lesbians and gay men who have fostered or adopted children.

Michael Howlett is a founder director of The Zito Trust, a charity focused on the implementation of Community Care policy for the severely mentally ill, and which advocates for improvements in the provision of community care services in the mental health field. He has practice, management, and training experience in work with the mentally ill, and is the author of numerous publications on mental health and forensic risk assessment.

Peter Johnston is a senior probation officer with West Yorkshire Probation Service, with lead responsibility for work with victims. He has developed both practice and policy in work with risk and victims and has written articles on risk assessment and victim perspectives.

Hazel Kemshall is a Lecturer at the University of Birmingham. She is presently the holder of an Economic and Social Research Council award to investigate 'Risk in Probation Practice', and has carried out work on offender risk assessment for the Home Office. She has ten years' experience as a probation practitioner and manager in a range of fieldwork and specialist settings.

Christine Lawrie is a member of Her Majesty's Inspectorate of Probation, and was responsible for the 1995 inspection on dangerous offenders. She has contributed to HMIP guidance to probation services on risk assessment and risk management.

Alison Liebling is a Senior Research Associate at the Institute of Criminology, the University of Cambridge. She has extensively researched prison suicide for the Home Office, and has addressed both policy and practice issues in this area. She is the author of numerous publications on the issue of prisoners, vulnerability and suicide.

Sue Lipscombe is a social worker and manager of The Joint Homelessness Team, Westminster which is a service commissioned by Kensington and Chelsea and Westminster Health Agency.

Juliet Lyon is Associate Director of the Trust for the Study of Adolescence. She has worked as a teacher in charge of an Adolescent Unit school. She has worked for 10 years with the Richmond Fellowship and managed its therapeutic communities for young people. She holds an Honorary Research Fellowship in the School of Psychology at Queen's University, Belfast.

Anne van Meeuwen is a Principal Policy and Practice Officer with Barnardos, where her main areas of responsibility are family placement and child sexual abuse. She has over 20 years' experience of local authority social work including 15 years as a family placement manager. She is trustee of the Post-Adoption Centre in London.

Hilary Owen is currently Child Protection Specialist Adviser with Community Health Sheffield. She is chair of the Training Sub-Committee of Sheffield Area Child Protection Committee. Hilary worked as court social worker for five years and as a social services child protection co-ordinator for seven years. She administered the inquiry into the employment by Sheffield City Council of a residential social worker who sexually abused a large number of children in his care and has prepared a number of reports into children's deaths for Sheffield Area Child Protection Committee.

Jacki Pritchard is a freelance trainer, consultant and researcher. She qualified as a social worker and has worked as a practitioner and manager both in fieldwork and hospital settings. She is also an accredited practice teacher. Her main interest is in the concept of 'abuse' and working with both children and adults. She is currently working on The Vulnerable Adults Project for Wakefield Community and Social Services Department and undertaking postgraduate research into the life experiences of older survivors of abuse at Nottingham University.

Tony Ryan has worked within the field of mental health since 1982 in a variety of practitioner and managerial positions, including both the public and 'not for profit' sectors. He is currently Area Manager for the mental health charity Turning Point. He is also Honorary Research Fellow at the University of Lancaster where he is researching risk in relation to people with mental health problems.

Robert Strachan is a senior practitioner and lecturer with Bradford Social Services. He has practice and research experience in the decision making processes used by professionals in risk assessment, and with Chris Tallant has published on the impact of framing on risk decision making by both workers and clients.

Chris Tallant is a probation officer working with West Yorkshire Probation Service involved in the design and delivery of intensive probation programmes. He has practice and research experience of how offenders frame their risky behaviour and the link between framing and effective risk management strategies. He has published in this area with Robert Strachan.

Bob Tindall is the Director of Community Care for United Response, a national voluntary organisation providing small scale community based services for people with learning difficulties and people with mental health difficulties. His organisational responsibilities include the quality of support given to users of services and health and safety.

Brian Williams is a lecturer at the University of Keele. His research interests include service delivery to prisoners, and he has numerous publications on probation practice with serving prisoners. He has experience of the probation service as an officer and as a probation tutor.

Subject Index

abilities 12
absconding 72
abuse, children's homes
    66–7
  by residents 74–5
  physical 72–4
  sexual 70–2, 75
accessibility, service
    provision 144–5
accident and emergency
    services 155–7
accommodation 110–13
accountability,
    community care 176
actuarial methods
    237–8, 239, 242, 256
Actuarial Society 262–4
addresses 230–2
administration,
    probation service 308
adolescents
  coping and adjusting
    208
  deliberate self harm
    225–6
  development 206
  knowledge of 221
  in society 208
  suicides 208–9
adopters, tasks for 46
adoption and fostering
    52–65
  disruption 61–3
  introductions 60–1
  linking 60
  placements 61
  planning for
    permanence 55–9
  post placement 63–4
  short term care 52–4

see also family
    placements;
    lesbian and gay
    carers
agencies
  probation service 301
  responses, domestic
    violence 281–2
  responsibilities 12–13
  risk policies 11–12
AIDS, prisoners 258–9
alcohol 127–40
  effects of 127–8
  records and reviews
    139–40
  risk assessments
    129–35
  risk management
    135–9
  risks of 128–9
  social workers and
    supervisors 140
amendments, risk
    assessments 114–16
appropriate adult, role
    of 154
approved social
    workers (ASWs) 154,
    155, 177, 180
area child protection
    committees 76
aspirations 12
attachment 42, 58
availability bias 21

bad practices 98
behaviour
  alcohol 130
  domestic violence
    279–80
bias 19–26
birth families, working
    with 55–6
Bristol Crisis Service for
    Women 230
bullying 75

care homes 160–1
Care Programme
    Approach 149, 150,
    161, 175, 176, 177, 180
carers
  gays and lesbians
    27–39
  recruitment and
    assessment 45–7
  working with 57–8
case examples
  alcohol abuse 132–3,
    136–8, 138–9
  domestic violence
    272–3
  drug use 119, 121, 122,
    124
  fears, residential
    homes 88–9
  framing 17–18
  heuristic biases 22
  homelessness 155,
    156–7
  mental health failures
    183–5
  reactive assessments
    107, 108
  risk taking 91, 93
case management 302,
    306, 308, 309–10
case meetings,
    residential homes
    94–5
casenotes, mental
    health services 168
checklists
  case management
    309–10
  teenage suicide 224
chemicals 111
child development 42
child protection 9–10,
    270–3
ChildLine 230
children
  black, adoption and
    fostering 53

deliberate self harm
  225–6
disabled 73–4
domestic violence
  270–3
working with,
  placements 55
Children Act (1989) 10,
  27, 69, 75, 78
children's homes 66–79
choice 12, 87
citizenship 11, 87, 105–6
clinical management,
  risk 153–4, 174,
  178–80
clinical risk indicators
  181–2
Clunis Inquiry 175,
  178–9
cognitive theories 43
collusion, domestic
  violence 274–5
common lodging
  houses 161
communication, mental
  health services 167–8
community care
  homicide inquiries
    174–87
  inquiry reports 182–5
  policy 175–8
  psychiatric risk
    assessments 178–80
  violence, risk of 180–2
  Zito Trust 174–5, 177,
    185–6
legislation 10, 11–12
resources, access to 145
settings 113–14, 164
community corrections
  260
community psychiatric
  nurses (CPNs) 154,
  155, 177
Compassionate Friends
  230
concurrent planning 54

confidentiality
  homelessness 149
  vs. public protection
    259–60
  victim information 296
confirmation bias 21–4
contact
  with families 78
  post placement 63
  see also victim contact
Control of Substances
  Hazardous to
  Health Regulations
  (1988) 110
corporal punishment 73
corruption theory 29
cost/benefit analysis,
  placements 47–8
counselling, domestic
  violence 275
crime control,
  commercialization
  234
Criminal Justice Act
  (1991) 10, 233, 236,
  267
Cruse 230
culture, teenage
  suicides 211–12

danger, defined 82
dangerousness 235–9,
  240
Dave's story, alcohol
  abuse 136–8
day services 113
de-biasing 24
debriefing 115–16
decision making
  elderly, residential
    care 94–5
  homelessness and
    mental health
    151–2
  prisons 262, 263
  probation officers 239,
    307–8

dementia 97
dependency, domestic
  violence 279
depression
  domestic violence 280
  self harm 211
dignity 11, 87
disagreements, suicide
  risks 213
disruption 61–3
domestic violence
  267–87
  agency responses
    281–2
  assessment and
    intervention 273–81
  child protection 270–3
  defined 268
  dimensions of 269
domiciliary services 113
drugs
  medication
    administration 112
  misuse, prisons 257–8
  users, suicide risks
    210–11
  young people 118–26
dual registered homes
  160

education, lack of 76–7
elderly, residential care
  80–102
  decisions and case
    meetings 94–5
  defining risk 80–6
  fears 87–9
  policy and procedures
    89–90
  risk assessments 90–4
  risks in 89
  specific problems
    95–100
elective assessments
  150–2
electrical equipment 111

Electronic befriending 210
emotional states, alcohol 135
emotional support, lack of 69–70
empowerment 13
engagement, homelessness 148
environment, learning difficulties 110–14
exercises
elderly, residential care 83–6
teenage suicide 207, 215, 220

false negatives 237
false positives 237
families
alcohol 129
birth, working with 55–6
losing touch with 77–8
family group conferences 53–4
family placements 40–51
knowledge base 42–5
process 45–9
see also adoption and fostering; lesbian and gay carers
family systems theory 43
fears
drug use 119–20
residential homes 88–9
file systems (open) 168
fire 111
Food Safety Act (1990) 110, 111
fostering see adoption and fostering
framing 16–19, 24–6
friends, paedophiles 75
fulfilment 87

gains 17, 25
gas 111
gays see lesbians and gays
gender
domestic violence 277–8
suicide risks 209–10

harm
children's homes 68–9
indicators of 308–9
reduction 236, 240–1
see also self harm; serious harm
hazard, defined 82
hazards 112
health
alcohol 128
care, children's homes 77
homelessness 146
Health and Safety at Work Act (1974) 110
heuristical biases 22–4
hindsight effect 104
HIV, prisoners 258–9
holidays 112
Homeless Mentally Ill Initiative (HMII) 141, 143, 146, 147, 148
homelessness, mental health 141–58
accident and emergency services 155–7
categories of 141–4
confidentiality 149
housing and resources 145
networking and liaison 145–6
prevention of 147
risk assessments 148–9, 149–52
risks of 146–7
risks to others 153–5

service provision 144–5
suicide and self harm 153
homicide inquiries see community care
hospital closures 176
housing
alcohol 129
mentally ill 145
psychiatric patients 176
Housing Act 1985 147
human resources, community care 177
hygiene 111

identity 43
imprisonment 258–9
independence 11, 87
independent inquiries, homicide 183
individuality 11
information
homelessness 149
learning difficulties 116
prison suicides 190–1
victim contact 257, 292–4, 296
Inquest 230
intent, suicide 214–16
inter-generational attachment 58
interventions
domestic violence 273–81, 281–2
family placements 49
learning difficulties 109–10
probation officers 303–4
introductions 48, 60–1

jealousy, domestic violence 279

Jekyll and Hyde 280
Jo's story, alcohol abuse
    138–9
judgement 15–26

knowledge base, family
    placements 42–5

law of small numbers 21
learning difficulties,
    people with 103–17
    citizenship,
        obligations and
        safeguards 105–6
    environment 110–14
    interventions 109–10
    negative incidents 116
    records 114–16
    risk assessments 106–9
    risk management
        104–5
Leeds Inter Agency
    Project 269
legislation
    community care 10,
        11–12
    learning difficulties
        117
    mental health services
        161
Lesbian and Gay
    Bereavement Project
    230
lesbian and gay carers
    27–39
    debate 28
    notions of risk 29–34
    risk assessment 35–6
liaison, mental health
    teams 145–6
lifting 111–12
linking
    adoption and
        fostering 60
    cost/benefit analysis
        47–8

location, homelessness
    145
loss
    feelings of, children
        42–3
    suicide risks 212–13
losses 17, 25

management, probation
    officers 244–5, 301–11
Manual Handling
    Operatives
    Regulations (1992)
    111
market, drugs 120–1
mediation, victim
    contact 296–7
medication
    administration of 112,
        170
    non–compliance 177
mental health
    community care
        policy 175–8
    see also homelessness;
        residential care
Mental Health Act 1983
    142, 150, 154, 160,
    161, 165, 178, 217
Mental Health (Patients
    in the Community)
    Act (1995) 161, 165,
    178
Mick's story, alcohol
    abuse 132–3
middle managers,
    probation service
    301–11
Minibus (Conditions of
    Fitness, Equipment
    and Use)
    Regulations (1977)
    113
Mitchell, Jason 184–5
multi-agency responses,
    domestic violence
    281–2

multidisciplinary teams
    homelessness 145
    mental health 167–8

NAFSIYAT 231
networking, mental
    health teams 145
Neutral Reference Point
    (NRP) 24–6
new penology 234
new risk penalty 256,
    262
Newby, Jonathan 183–4
NHS and Community
    Care Act (1990) 10,
    142, 147
non-compliance,
    medication 177
non-disclosure, victim
    information 296
non-interventions,
    learning difficulties
    109–10
normalisation 103, 105
nursing homes,
    registered 160

open file systems 168
openness 58–9

paedophiles, children's
    homes 70–2, 75
Papyrus 231
parole 233–54
    probation officers
        244–5
    risk assessments,
        probation service
        239–44
    risks and potential
        dangerousness
        235–9
penal policy, public risk
    260–2

permanence,
    preparation for 55–9
perpetrators, domestic
    violence 270, 274–81
personality traits,
    domestic violence
    279
physical abuse,
    children's homes
    72–4
physical assaults,
    domestic violence
    269
planned risks 107–9
planning, short-term
    care 52–4
Police and Criminal
    Evidence Act (1984)
    154
policies
    agencies 11–12
    community care,
        mental health
        175–8
    elderly, residential
        care 89–90, 99
    mental health services
        161
post placement 48–9,
    63–4
post release supervision
    259–60
post sentence lifer case
    299
poverty of expectation
    77
practice experience 44–5
pre-release lifer case
    299–300
pre-sentence reports
    (PSRs) 260, 267
predictability 179
predictions
    recruitment of carers
        45–7
    testing out 48
    violence 242–3
preventability 179

principles, risk
    decisions 12
prison suicide 188–204
    characteristics 188
    recorded information
        190–1
    research 192–4
    risk identification
        189–90
    risks 198–9, 199–202
    self injury 191
    statistics 190
    stress 223
    typology of 194–8
prisoners' rights 255–66
    Actuarial Society
        262–4
    imprisonment and
        individual risk
        258–9
    penal policy and
        public risk 260–2
    post-release
        supervision 259–60
    risk assessments 254–8
prisons, subculture
    258–9
privacy 11, 87
probation officers
    coaching 306–7
    decision making 307–8
    management and
        training 244–5, 283
    managerial
        intervention 303–4
    parole risk assessment
        239–44
    skills 303
probation service
    domestic violence
        267–87
    middle managers
        301–11
    parole 239–44
    post-release
        supervision 259–60
    victim contact 288–300

professional
    boundaries,
        maintenance of 221
professional
    requirements 309–10
prostitution 75–6
psychiatric risk
    assessments 153–4,
    174, 178–80
public
    community settings,
        mentally ill 164
    penal policy 260–2
    protection 259–60,
        302–9

quality, risk
    management 104–5

race, domestic violence
    277–8
reactive assessments
    107–9
recidivism, parole
    239–40, 241
records
    alcohol abuse 139–40
    case management
        304–5
    prison suicide 190–1
    risk assessments
        114–16
recruitment, carers 45–7
registered mental
    nursing homes 160
registered residential
    care homes 160
rehabilitation 169
relationships, domestic
    violence 269
reparation 115–16
representativeness bias
    20–1
research
    adoption and
        fostering 57–8

disruption 61–3
family placements
    43–4, 49, 50
gay and lesbian carers
    28, 30–1, 32–4, 36
prison suicide 192–4
residential care,
    mentally ill 159–73
facilities 159–61, 162
legislation and policy
    161
risk assessments 164–6
risk management
    166–8
risks 163–4
taking risks 169–71
see also elderly,
    residential care
residents
children's homes,
    abuse by 74–5
elderly, specific
    problems 95–100
mentally ill 163, 166
responsibilities,
    agencies 12–13
responsivity 242
Restorative Justice 297
restraint
children's homes 72,
    73
residential homes 97–8
reviews
alcohol abuse 139–40
family placements 49
risk decisions 96
rights
of citizenship 11, 87
prisoners 255–66
victims 289–90
risk, defined 82
risk society 255, 264
risks
alcohol abuse 128–9
children's homes 68–9
elderly, residential
    care 89

from homeless
    mentally ill 153–5
gay and lesbian carers
    29–34
of homelessness 146–7
mental health services
    163–4
Road Vehicles
    (Construction and
    Use) Regulations
    (1986) 112–13
Rough Sleepers
    Initiative (RSI) 143

safe caring 59
Samaritans 231
security information
    reports (SIRs) 258
selection, mental health
    services
residents 166
staff 166–7
self control, alcohol
    135–6
self harm
adolescents 209
deliberate 225–6
depression 211
homeless population
    153
self injury, prison
    suicide 191
self-esteem, domestic
    violence 280
sentencing, America 262
separation 42–3, 52, 64
serious harm 301–2
service networks,
    mental health
    services 168
service provision,
    homelessness 144–5
service standards 289
Sex Offender Treatment
    Programme 257, 261

sexual
abuse 70–2, 75
assaults 269
exploitation 75–6
offenders 50, 258
sexuality, lesbian and
    gay carers 33
short-term care 52–4
single homeless,
    mentally ill 143–4
situational triggers
domestic violence
    280–1
suicide 223
Smith, Anthony 185
social learning 43
social life, alcohol 128
social pressure, alcohol
    135
social role valorisation
    103, 105
social workers
approved (ASWs) 154,
    155, 177, 180
support for 99–100,
    140
teenage suicides
    219–22
training 15
socio-economic status,
    domestic violence
    278–9
South East London
    Probation Service
    250–4
staff, mental health
    services
risk management
    166–7
risks to 163–4
standards, residential
    homes 87–8
statutes 117
stress
prison suicide 223
teenage suicide 221

substance misuse
  domestic violence 276
  homelessness 147
  see also alcohol; drugs
suicide
  homeless population 153
  see also prison suicide; teenage suicide
supervision
  alcohol abuse 140
  care workers 99
  post release 259–60
support
  alcohol abuse 140
  networks 61
  residential care workers 99–100
  services 110–13, 221
supported hostels 161
Survivors Speak Out 231

teenage suicide 205–32
  adolescents 206–11
  checklist 224
  cultures 211–12
  precipitating factors 212–13
  repeated attempts 213–14
  risk assessments 214–17
  risk management 217–19
  risks to workers 219–22
theoretical models, placements 42–3
through care see probation service
training
  probation officers 244–5, 283, 306–7
  residential care workers 99–100
  social workers 15

victim contact work 294
treatability 242
Trust for the Study of Adolescence 231
typology, prison suicide 194–8

unaskable questions 293–4
unregistered care homes 161

values, risk decisions 12, 87
vehicles 112–13
victim contact 288–300
  information 292–4
  managing 294–6
  mediation 296–7
  resourcing 291–2
Victim Support 292, 295
victims, proximity, domestic violence 276–7
Victim's Charter 289–90
violence
  mentally ill 180–2
  prediction 242–3
  see also domestic violence
vulnerability
  learning difficulties 103
  prisoners 258–9
  social workers 100
  teenage suicides 209–11, 223
  see also elderly, residential care

wandering, residential care 97–8
water 111

weapons, domestic violence 276
West Minster Joint Homelessness Team (JHT) 141–2, 150
Who Cares? Trust 232
women
  black domestic violence 269–70, 271, 277–8
  perpetrators, domestic violence 278
work, alcohol 128

Young Minds 232
youth, perceptions of 118
Youth Access 232

Zito Trust 174–6, 177, 185–6

Author Index

Abbott, P. and Wallace, C. 29

Alaszewski, A. and Manthorpe, J. 159

Alberg, C., Hatfield, B. and Huxley, P. 185, 211, 216

Allan, K. 96, 97

Andrews, J.A. and Lewinsohn, P.M. 211

Andrews, D.A. 242

Andrews, D.A. and Bonta, J. 242

Andrews, D.A. and Bonta, J. and Hoge, R.D. 242

Armstrong, L. and Reymbaut, E. 96

Arthur, R. 237, 238

Association of Chief Officers of Probation 259, 267, 290, 296, 297

Association of Directors of Social Services 81

Atkinson, J.M. 190

Au, S. and Bau, H. 280

BAAF (British Agencies for Adoption and Fostering) 31

Bachrach, L. 143

Backett, S. 189

Bailey, J.M., Bobrow, D., Wolfe, M. and Mickach, S. 31

Barret, R.L. and Robinson, B.E. 31

Barrett, M. and McIntosh, M. 29

Barth, R. and Berry, M. 40, 43, 44, 47, 49

Bazerman, M.H. 16, 21

BBC *Heart of the Matter* 27

BBC North West News 28

Beattie, K. 274, 275, 277

Beck, A.T. 199, 264

Beck, A.T., Weissman, A., Lester, D. and Trexler, L. 165

Beck, U. 255

Beckett, C. and Groothues, C. 57

Bernheim, J.C. 189

Berridge, D. and Cleaver, H. 40

Berry, P. 29

Bhatti-Sinclair, K. 270, 271, 278

Bhugra, D. 142

Biddle, D. and Wincote, T. 239

Biles, D. 189

Blom-Cooper, L., Hally, H. and Murphy, E. 182

Blom-Cooper, L., Grounds, A., Guinan, P., Parker, A. and Taylor, M. 184

Bornat, J. 96

Boushel, M. 48

Bozett, F.W. 31, 36

Brearley, C.P. 9, 16, 81, 82, 92, 235

Briere, J. 270

Brockington, I.F., Hall, P., Levings, J. and Murphy, C. 163

Brodzinsky, D. and Schechter, M. 63

Brooks, A.D. 240, 242

Brown, H.C. 33, 34, 35, 36

Bryan, B., Dadzie, S. and Scafe, S. 270

Burgess, E.W. 233, 237, 239

Butler Committee, Home Office and Department of Health and Social Security 236, 301

Cameron, D. 278

Carlen, P. 269

Carlisle, Rt. Hon Lord of Bucklow 233, 234, 235, 240

Carroll, J.S. 233, 237

Carroll, J.S. and Payne, J.W. 237

Carson, D. 97, 104, 108, 164, 170, 244, 303, 308, 309

Casey, M. 257

Children's Legal Centre 271

Christie, N. 234

Clark, D.A., Fisher, M.J. and McDougall, C. 238

Cleveland Inquiry 12, 22

Cohen 263

Coid, J. 180

Coleman, J. 208

Coleman, J., Lyon, J., and Piper, R. 205, 209, 210, 211, 212, 213, 214, 216, 218, 222, 223

Coleman, J. and Hendry, L. 206

Community Care 27

Cooper, H.H.A. 191

Copas, J., Marshall, P. and Tarling, R. 239, 240

Copas, J., Ditchfield, J. and Marshall, P. 237, 239

Copas, J.B. and Tarling, R. 237

Correctional Services of Canada 189
Counsel and Care 94, 98
Cowburn, M. and Modi, P. 263
Craig, Baylis, Klein, Manning and Reader 143, 146, 147, 148, 154
Craig *et al.* 148, 153
Creamer, A. and Williams, B. 262
Creighton, S. and King, V. 256, 257
Crown Prosecution Service 267

Davies, N., Lingham, R., Prior, C. and Sims, A. 163, 176, 184
Davies, H., O'Sullivan, E., Sharman, D. and Wallace, C. 273
Dean, M. 70
Department of Health 11, 27, 28, 43, 44, 47, 52, 53, 67, 68, 69, 72, 73, 74, 77, 87, 88, 98, 146, 159, 161, 163, 168, 175, 178, 180, 182
Department of Health and Social Services 163, 167
Department of Health and the Special Hospital Service Authority 163
Department of Health/Welsh Office 27, 28, 165
Dexter, P. 201
Diekstra, R.F.W. 191
Dobash, R.E., Dobash, R.P. and Cavanagh, K. 274

Dobash, R.E., Dobash, R.P., Cavanagh, K. and Lewis, R. 273
Dobash, R.E. and Dobash, R.P. 268, 269, 270, 275, 277
Domestic Violence Intervention 273
Dooley, E. 189, 190, 195
Dorrell, S. 66, 79
Douglas, C. 57, 61
Douglas, J. 190
Douglas, M. 256
Dyer, C. 262

Eaton, M. 269
Edwards, Susan S.M. 270
Eiser, J.R. and Plight, J. van der 21
Elsmore, K. 147
Eronen, M., Tihonen, J. and Hakola, P. 180
Estroff, S.E. and Zimmer, C. 163

Fahlberg, V. 41, 42, 57
Farrington, D.P. and Tarling, R. 237
Feeley, M. and Simon, J. 234, 255
Feld, B.C. 202
Ferris, D. 29
Fielding, N. and Fowles, T. 256
Fitzgerald, J. 63
Flaherty, M.G. 189
Floud, J. and Young, W. 264
Flynn, E. 233, 234
Fratter, J., Rowe, J., Sapsford, D. and Thoburn, J. 49, 61
Fratter, J. 58
Fry, E. 47, 49

Garland, D. 261, 262
Gibson, F. 96
Giddens, A. 255
Glaser, D. 233, 234, 237
Gloucestershire Social Services Department 80
Goldberg, D.P., Bridges, K., Cooper, W., Hyde, C., Sterling, C. and Wyatt, R. 160
Goldney, R.D. and Burvil, P.W. 191
Golombok, S., Spencer, A. and Rutter, M. 30
Golombok, S. and Tasker, F. 29, 30, 32
Gottfredson, S.D. and Gottfredson, D.M. 237, 238, 239
Gould, N. 163
Gover, R.M. 189
Green, G.D. and Bozett, F.W. 30
Grenier, P. 147, 153
Griffiths, A.W. 189
Gunn, J. 180, 181
Gunn, J., Maden, T. and Swinton, M. 163
Guttman, D. 94

Hague, J. and Malos, E. 269, 275, 277, 278, 281, 283
Hall, P., Brockington, I.F., Levings, J. and Murphy, C. 163
Hammerlin, Y. and Bodal, K. 189
Hankoff, L.D. 189
Harper, J. 55
Harris, P. 238
Harwin, N. 270, 271
Hatty, S. and Walker, J. 189
Hawton, K., Fagg, J. and Simkin, S. 205

Hayes, L. 189
Hearn, J. 267, 269, 270
Heidensohn, F. 268, 269
Her Majesty's
   Inspectorate of
   Prisons 258
Her Majesty's
   Inspectorate of
   Probation 234, 256,
   259, 260, 267, 291,
   302, 306, 310
Her Majesty's Prison
   Service 257
Hester, M., Kelly, L. and
   Radford, J. 29, 269
Hester, M. and Radford,
   L. 270, 271, 275, 276,
   277, 279
Hicks, S. 27, 28, 32, 33,
   34, 36
Hill, K. 209
Hirsch, A. and
   Ashworth, A. 237
HMCIP 194, 202
Hodgkins, S. 180
Holden, U. and
   Chapman, A. 96
Home Office 10, 11, 193,
   235, 241, 267, 268,
   270, 281, 289, 292,
   301, 303
House of Commons
   Health Committee
   159
Howe, D. 58
Howe, Lady 66
Hudson, B.A. 256, 262,
   263
Hughes, B. 58
Hughes, G. 54

Independent, The 178
Ingram, R.L. 269, 280

Jee, M. and Reason, L.
   221

Johnston, P.H. 289, 292
Jones, A. 277

Kahneman, D. and
   Tversky, A. 16, 17,
   20, 21, 237
Kanuik, J. 42
Katz, L. 54
Kelby and White 146
Kelly, E., Wingfield, R.,
   Burton, S. and
   Regan, L. 75
Kelly, L. 276
Kemshall, H. 11, 16,
   159, 235, 239, 244,
   245, 259, 263, 267,
   270, 274, 275, 283, 295
Kemshall, H., Parton,
   N., Walsh, M. and
   Waterson, J. 235
Kemshall, H. and
   Pritchard, J. 84, 150
Kennedy, D.B. 189
Kennedy, H. 269
Kerfoot, M. 210, 213
Kerfoot, M.,
   Harrington, R. and
   Dyer, E. 219
Kerfoot, M. and
   McHugh, B. 213
Kingsbury, S. 210

Labour Party 270
Lambert, E.W., Cartor,
   R. and Walker, G.L.
   241
Lambert, L. and
   Streather, J. 40
Lash, S. and Wynne, B.
   256
Law, K.M. 238
Law Commission 81
Lawson, J. 12, 90
Leff, J. 163

Lelliot, P., Audini, B.,
   Knapp, M. and
   Chisholm, D. 159
Levy, A. and Kahan, B.
   69, 78
Levy, A. 66
Liebling, A. 188, 190,
   191, 192, 194, 199,
   201, 202, 210, 258
Liebling, A. and
   Krarup, H. 188, 192,
   194, 195, 197, 202
Limandri, B.J. and
   Sheriden, D.J. 241,
   274, 275
Lindqvist, P. and
   Allebeck, P. 180
Lingham, R., Candy, J.
   and Bray, J. 179
Link, B., Andrews, H.
   and Cullen, F. 180
Littlechild, B. 163
Lodge-Patch, I. 143
Logan, J., Kershaw, S.,
   Karban, K., Mills, S.,
   Trotter, J. and
   Sinclair, M. 34
Luce-Dickinson, J. 10
Lyon, J. and Coleman, J.
   211, 219

MacFadyen, S. 43
McGuire, J. 244
McGurk, B.J. and
   McDougal, C. 202
Madge, N. 209, 212
Main, M. and Goldwyn,
   R. 58
Mama, A. 270, 277, 278
Mannheim, H. and
   Wilkins, L.T. 237
Marchant, C. 28, 269
Mark, P. 274
Marsh, P. and Crowe,
   G. 54
Marshall, M. 143
Martin 34

Marttunen, M.J., Aro, H.M. and Lonqvist, J.K. 213
Massachusetts Special Commission 189
Maynard, M. and Purvis, J. 29
Maynard, M. 271
Megargee, E. 236, 242, 274
Merseyside Probation Service 273
Mezey, Dr. G. 276
Modestin, J. and Ammann, R. 180
Monahan, J. 236, 241, 274, 275
Monahan, J. and Hood, G. 236
Monahan, J. and Steadman, H.J. 177, 180, 236
Morley, R. and Mullender, A. 270, 271, 275
Morris, A., Wilkinson, C., Tisi, A., Woodrow, J. and Rockley, A. 258
Morton, F. 267
Mulvey, E.P. and Lidz, C.W. 242
Murphy, C.J. 96

National Association for the Care and Resettlement of Offenders (NACRO) 277
National Foster Care Association 41, 45, 59
National Health Service Management Executive 159, 161
NCH Action for Children 270, 271

NHS Health Advisory Service 165
NHS Health Advisory Service Review 209, 211, 218, 224, 226
Nisbett, R., Borigda, E., Crandall, R. and Reed, H. 237
Norman, A.J. 90
North West London Mental Health Trust 154
Novaco, R.W. 165
Nuffield, J. 233
Nuttall, C.P. 233, 235

Observer, The 177, 178
Office of Corrections Resource Centre 189
Office of Population Censuses and Surveys 209
O'Hara, J. and Hoggan, P. 40
O'Hara, M. 271, 272
Ohlin, L.E. and Duncan, O.D. 237
O'Mahoney, P. 188
Orlowski, R.J. 189

Pahl, J. 268
Parton, N. 235, 256, 264
Patel, K. and Strachan, R. 22
Patterson, C.J. 30
Penal Affairs Consortium 235
Pence, E. and Paymar, M. 268, 269, 273, 274, 275, 276, 278, 279, 280, 281
Perrott, S. 274
Perry, T. 274
Phillips, M. 189
Phillips, J. 258

Plant, M. and Plant, M. 206
Platt, S. 278
Pleace, N. and Quilgars, D. 144, 146
Pollack, S. 29
Polvi, N. and Pease, K. 235
Poupard, S. and Jordan, M. 68
Priest, R. 143
Prins, H. 293
Probation Service Division 235

Radar, J. 97
Radar, J., Doan, J. and Schwab, M. 97
Ralli, R. 259
Randall, G. and Brown, S. 145
Reece, H. 28
Residential Forum 169
Revolving Doors Agency 153
Rich, A. 29
Richardson, D. 29
Ricketts, W. 28, 29
Ricketts, W. and Achtenberg, R. 28
Rights of Women Lesbian Custody Group 29
Ritchie, J., Dick, D. and Lingham, R. 148, 153, 175, 181
Ross, L. and Waterson, J. 13
Rowe, J., Hundleby, M. and Garnett, L. 40
Rowe, J. and Lambert, L. 52
Rowett, C. 164
Royal College of Nursing 163

Royal College of
Psychiatrists 142,
153, 177, 178
Royal Society 235
Russo, J. Edward and
Schoemaker, Paul
J.H. 16
Rutter, M. 206
Ryan, T. 13, 159, 163,
166, 169
Ryan, W. 238
Ryburn, M. and
Atherton, C. 54

Saffron, L. 30
Samaritans 210
Sampson, A. 257, 261
Sapsford, R.J. 233
Saunders, A. 271
Scott, J. 142, 163
Scott, P. 236, 241, 242
Scott-Denoon, K. 189
Scottish Council on
Crime 301
Scourfield, J. 273, 274
Sedgwick, E.K. 29
Seiffge-Krenke, I. 208
Sellick, C. and Thoburn,
J. 61
Shah, S. 237
Shaw, R. 243, 261
Sheppard, D. 164, 167,
175, 182
Shneidman, E. 188
Simon, J. 262
Single Homeless in
London (SHIL) 143
Skeates, J. and Jabri, D.
28, 29
Sleightholm, D. 267, 268
Smalley, H. 189
Smallman, C. 264
Smart, C. 269
Smellie, E. and Crow, I.
277
Smith, G. 49

Smith, L.F. 267, 268,
269, 281
Smith, S. 63
Social Services
Inspectorate,
Department of
Health 12, 87, 97
Sparks, J.R. 191, 201
Sparks, R. 256, 261
Spielman, A. 189
Stark, E. and Flitcraft,
A. 270
Steadman, H.J. 165
Steadman, H.J.,
Monahan, J.,
Appelbaum, P.S.,
Grisso, T., Mulvey,
E.P., Roth, L.H.,
Robbins, P.C. and
Klassen, D. 243
Steering Committee of
the Confidential
Inquiry into
Homicides and
Suicides by Mentally
Ill People 164
Stelman, A. 267, 268,
269, 270, 276, 281
Stern, V. 277
Stevenson 10
Stevenson, O. 13
Stordeur, R.A. and
Stille, R. 268, 269,
270, 271, 274, 275,
276, 279, 280, 281
Sumner, C. 259
Swanson, J., Holzer, C.,
Gunju, V. and Jono,
R. 180

Tallant, C. and
Strachan, R. 17
Tasker, F.L. and
Golombok, S. 30
Taylor, J.M. 262
Taylor, S. 190
Thaller, R. 16, 20

Thoburn, J., Murdoch,
A. and O'Brien, A. 57
Thoburn, J. and Sellick,
C. 44
Times, The 177
Timms, P.W. and Fry,
A.H. 163
Tissier, G. 163
Toch, H. 191
Topp, D.O. 189
Tuck, M. 270, 274

Utting, W. 66, 79

Victim Support 269,
281, 292, 295

Wagner, Lady 66
Walker, N. 236, 243
Walmsley, R., Howard,
L. and White, S. 188,
199
Ward, H. 41
Ward, D. 233
Warner, N. 66, 67, 68,
73, 74, 76, 77, 79
Wasik, M. and Taylor,
R.D. 10, 233, 236, 240
Watts, D. and Morgan,
G. 211
Webster, C.D., Harris,
G.T., Rice, M.E.,
Cormier, C. and
Quinsey, V. 242
Wedge, P. and Mantle,
G. 53
Weist, J. 242
Wessely, S., Castle, D.,
Douglas, A.J. and
Taylor, P.J. 180
West Yorkshire
Probation Service
292, 293, 294, 296
Whitehouse, A. 32
Whiteley, J.S. 143

Whittington, R. 163
Who Cares? 76
Wilkinson, S. and
    Kitzinger, C. 29
Williams, B. 257, 258,
    259
Wolfensberger, W. 103,
    105
Wolfsenberger, W. and
    Thomas, S. 110
Women's Aid
    Federation 268, 270,
    277, 278, 281
Wood, J. 185
Wright, M. 297
Wykes, T. 160
Wykes, T. and
    Whittington, R. 163

Young, J. 119

Zamble, E. and
    Porporino, F.J. 188,
    193, 238